Transformations of Work

Bulletin of Comparative Labour Relations

VOLUME 105

Founding Editor

The series started in 1970 under the dynamic editorship of Professor Roger Blanpain (Belgium), former President of the International Industrial Relations Association. Professor Blanpain, Professor Emeritus of Labour Law, Universities of Leuven and Tilburg, was also General Editor of the International Encyclopedia of Laws (with more than 1,600 collaborators worldwide) and President of the Association of Educative and Scientific Authors Authors. He passed away in October 2016.

General Editor

In 2015 Frank Hendrickx, Professor of labour law at the Faculty of Law of the University of Leuven (Belgium) joined as a co-Editor. Frank Hendrickx has published numerous articles and books and regularly advises governments, international institutions and private organisations in the area of labour law as well as in sports law. He is the Editor-in-Chief of the European Labour Law Journal and General Editor of the International Encyclopaedia of Laws.

Introduction

The Bulletins constitute a unique source of information and thought-provoking discussion, laying the groundwork for studies of employment relations in the 21st century, involving among much else the effects of globalization, new technologies, migration, and the greying of the population.

Contents/Subjects

Amongst other subjects the Bulletins frequently include the proceedings of international or regional conferences; reports from comparative projects devoted to salient issues in industrial relations, human resources management, and/or labour law; and specific issues underlying the multicultural aspects of our industrial societies.

Objective

The Bulletins offer a platform of expression and discussion on labour relations to scholars and practitioners worldwide, often featuring special guest editors.

The titles published in this series are listed at the end of this volume.

BULLETIN OF COMPARATIVE LABOUR RELATIONS – 105

Transformations of Work

Challenges for the Institutions and Social Actors

Edited by

Giuseppe Casale

Tiziano Treu

Contributors

Takashi Araki
Janice R. Bellace
Jesús Cruz Villalón
Kübra Doğan Yenisey
Maria Katia Garcia Landaburu
Fausta Guarriello
Thomas A. Kochan
Sylvaine Laulom
Franz Marhold
Adalberto Perulli
Humberto Villasmil Prieto

General Editor

Frank Hendrickx

Founding Editor

Roger Blanpain

Wolters Kluwer

Published by:
Kluwer Law International B.V.
PO Box 316
2400 AH Alphen aan den Rijn
The Netherlands
E-mail: international-sales@wolterskluwer.com
Website: lrus.wolterskluwer.com

Sold and distributed in North, Central and South America by:
Wolters Kluwer Legal & Regulatory U.S.
7201 McKinney Circle
Frederick, MD 21704
United States of America
Email: customer.service@wolterskluwer.com

Sold and distributed in all other countries by:
Air Business Subscriptions
Rockwood House
Haywards Heath
West Sussex
RH16 3DH
United Kingdom
Email: international-customerservice@wolterskluwer.com

Printed on acid-free paper.

ISBN 978-94-035-0891-7

e-Book: ISBN 978-94-035-0894-8
web-PDF: ISBN 978-94-035-0901-3

Printed in the United Kingdom.

Notes on Contributors

Takashi Araki, University of Tokyo
Janice R. Bellace, Wharton School, University of Pennsylvania
Giuseppe Casale, Deputy Director ITCILO, Director TSD, Secretary General, ISLSSL
Jesús Cruz Villalón, University of Seville
Kübra Doğan Yenisey, Istanbul Bilgi University
Maria Katia Garcia Landaburu, Catholic University of Peru
Fausta Guarriello, University of Chieti and Pescara
Thomas A. Kochan, MIT Boston
Sylvaine Laulom, University of Lyon 2
Franz Marhold, Institute for Austrian and European Labour Law and Social Security Law
Adalberto Perulli, Cà Foscari University of Venice
Tiziano Treu, President of ISLSSL and President of CNEL (Rome)
Humberto Villasmil Prieto, ILO and President ILO Section of ISLSSL

Summary of Contents

Table of Contents

CHAPTER 1

Introduction

Giuseppe Casale

The rapid changes affecting the world of work are at the centre of this volume, which contains the general reports presented by leading scholars of labour law and social security at the XXII ISLSSL World Congress held in Turin (Italy) on 4–7 September 2018.

In particular, the reports make a constant reference on how to shape an equitable and inclusive new world of work. A common denominator is the constant reaffirmation of the efforts that many countries and regions in the world are trying to put in place for promoting innovative social and economic policies, including skills policies, strengthening social protection and formalizing labour markets with a view to shaping a more equitable and inclusive society.

The challenges ahead demand global solutions, and in this regard, the authors of the reports have stressed that multilateralism remains a key force that is uniquely suited to resolve many of the new world of work most challenging problems.

This volume is a source of inspiration for all those who strive to ensure that everyone benefits from the opportunities that will be created in the coming future. It also recognizes the critical role that social protection plays in achieving this and highlights the need to put people and work at the centre of national strategies for sustainable development.[1]

The authors of the general reports have covered the following seven research themes, which were selected for the XXII ISLSSL World Congress.

§1.01 INFORMAL WORKERS

Most of the world's workers are in the informal sector. In many emerging economies, over 75% of the labour force is composed of informal businesses and workers.

1. *See* the 2030 Agenda for Sustainable Development.

Consequently, labour law studies should focus more specifically on the informal sector. Under this theme, the researchers focussed on:

- to deepen our understanding of the multifaceted aspects of informal and irregular work as they exist in different nationals and territorial contexts;
- to evaluate the different policy approaches and best practices in labour law and social security adopted by public institutions and by social actors, having regard to the various aspects of informal work and taking into account the regulations most frequently disregarded in the various situations;
- to investigate the possible techniques and policy measures (incentives, disincentives, private and public controls, development programs etc.) useful for promoting the opportunities of informal work to emerge and to be stably accepted in the formal economy;
- to discuss whether and to what extent labour unions and employers, by ensuring collective agreements application, also within SMEs, may help to fight irregular work, and promote the access of informal workers to the essential protections and benefits of professional training, of labour law and of social security.

§1.02 MIGRANT WORKERS

Many factors have given new and dramatic dimensions to people migrations: economic globalization, divergent conditions of work and life among different areas of the world, political and civil conflicts in many regions, which force entire groups to expatriate. The pressure of various forms of migrations is hitting in different degree many national states and communities.

Some progress has been made in the definition of the legal status of migrants, setting forth the general obligations to respect basic human rights. Nevertheless, more intense attention has to be paid also considering the expansion of this trend, to factors as the high rate of unemployment, the risk of exploitation, trafficking and social segregation, the lack of adequate social protection which makes migrant workers more vulnerable than others employees.

Such vulnerability and distortion determine, among other effects, human labour trafficking. This has attracted a renewed interest due to changing trends in migration flows and the globalization of labour. In this area, the researchers gave priority to some aspects of migratory trends, in particular of workers and also on:

- How to find new measures, national and international, to regulate the flow of migrant workers across national and continental borders in a socially sustainable way.
- How to combine controls and security checks necessary to guarantee social acceptance of migrants with measures to promote their integration in the civil communities and in the labour markets.
- Which specific provisions are effective to protect migrant workers against labour exploitation and to favour their employability in the formal economy?

§1.03 GLOBAL TRADE AND LABOUR

International trade has been promoted and regulated in recent years through various regional and international agreements.

The analysis of the agreements of various dimensions (bilateral, regional) focused on their impact not only on economic growth but also on employment and on working conditions and workers' rights. In this respect, the researchers investigated:

- Possible contents of social clauses, and the technologies that they adopt in order to guarantee international labour standards to the individuals and groups affected by trade agreements.
- The role of the law and social actors in implementing and enforcing social clauses.
- The increasing legal relations between foreign direct investments, multilateral trade agreements, domestic labour law regimes.
- International trade agreement effects, in the name of free trade on national measures addressing inequality such as minimum wages, prevailing wage requirements, unemployment benefits, affirmative action for historically excluded groups and other social protections.
- The compliance of recent international trade agreements with the ILO standards.
- A specific attention to ISDS clauses.

§1.04 ORGANIZATION, PRODUCTIVITY, AND WELL-BEING AT WORK

In the last years, the role played by trade unions and collective bargaining at national level has decreased in importance, while, as a consequence of decentralization processes, a central role is played by collective bargaining at enterprise and at plant level.

Enterprise collective bargaining is regarded as a possible way of fostering workplace flexibility/productivity, efficiency and workers' well-being. In addition, individual negotiation appears to be a possible tool to regulate working conditions, to increase the individual worker's productivity and, at the same time, his/her satisfaction about wages and other benefits.

Under this theme, the researchers focussed on:

- The role of collective and individual negotiation in the regulation of wages and working conditions.
- The role of enterprise-level collective bargaining in fostering workplace flexibility/productivity and workers' well-being.
- The role of enterprise collective bargaining in the regulatory competition.
- The role of corporate social responsibility.
- National reforms concerning enterprise collective bargaining in a comparative perspective.

- Best practices of high involvement and teamwork systems, and of innovative use of technology in work organization (e.g., remote and smart working) in respect to their impact on firms' performance and on employee's well-being.
- Role of management initiatives and of collective agreements in promoting new forms of welfare, such as supplementary pension funds, supplementary health insurance, flexible benefits of various contents.

§1.05 TRANSNATIONAL COLLECTIVE AGREEMENTS

With the internationalization of the economy and increasing competitive pressures, collective bargaining is developing in new directions. The growing number of transnational companies has introduced new actors and different strategies for collective action, on both the workers' and the employers' side: transnational collective bargaining is a response to this challenge.

The transnational dimension acquired by collective bargaining addresses new questions to be investigated by labour law research:

- New and old social actors involved. Is unionism suited for a transnational action?
- New and old issues negotiated at transnational levels: distinguish firm level and sectoral collective agreements.
- The link between the agreements signed by transnational firms and the governance of these firms.
- The role of national governments.
- The role of international organizations.
- The legal and practical effects on labour relations, national and local: distinguish enterprise level and sectoral collective agreements.
- Relations between enterprise-level agreements and corporate social responsibility.

§1.06 NEW FORMS OF SOCIAL SECURITY

The social security systems of most countries, developed and developing, are facing new and pressing problems.

Suitable social security models need to address the challenge of widespread precariousness in work as well as the low wages often provided for precarious workers. While often benefits are conferred according to the length and the status of employment relationship, new types of employment based on a low and fragmented income are spreading and are increasing the number of working poor for which the State must provide means of support. A wider scenario of social exclusion is present in less developed countries, but also in some areas of Europe.

Under this theme, the researchers have analysed:

- The challenges to sustainability of the national social security system.
- The possible response to these challenges by public institutions and social actors, at national and international level.
- The role and domains of private and collective forms of supplementary social security and welfare benefits.
- The possibility to extend social security schemes to non-standard employees.
- The ways to strengthen social security systems through minimum income or other inclusion measures and how to activate the beneficiaries.

§1.07 THE ROLE OF THE STATE AND INDUSTRIAL RELATIONS

The globalization of markets is changing the traditional power relations among countries and among their institutions. To what extent it is altering the role and power of the national states is an open question. The question is of particular importance with respect to industrial relations because the national states have played in most countries a major role in the foundation and development of collective labour relations and institutions.

The researchers have analysed in particular the impact of globalization on the national regulations of the various aspects of industrial relations: rights and representativeness of the social actors, collective bargaining structure and effects, strike action and other adversarial activities. For example, the following aspects have been examined:

- the old and new forms of state intervention in industrial relations: legislation, soft law guidelines, mediation and conciliation, promotion of social pacts;
- national reactions to global trade agreements: social clauses and other measures to prevent social dumping, promotion of fair trade practices, support to transnational collective bargaining, conditions to foreign investments and to labour mobility;
- cooperation among national states and institutions to monitor the effects of interstate commerce and to guarantee the enforcement of transnational agreements.

In a way, the authors emphasize the need for the different regions of the world to promote economic and social policies in a coherent manner in order to secure a fair, inclusive and sustainable world of work. Decent work, inclusiveness, gender equality and the protection of fundamental principles and rights at work are necessary along with the promotion of social dialogue between governments and the social partners.

From the reading of the reports, it comes out that while global economic growth and employment outlook continue to improve, labour markets still face diverse challenges including persistent unemployment in certain countries and regions. At the same time, there are significant changes driven by digitalization and automation, globalization, demographic transitions, migration, and a shift in individual and societal expectations about work and welfare. These changes lead to the requirement of new skills, new forms of work, a need for innovative institutional frameworks as well as new employment and social policies.

From a comparative point of view, labour law and social security systems need to be readapted with a view to maximizing opportunities and enabling workers and employers to benefit from them. In this regard, the authors of the papers examine in each of the seven themes the emerging trends in the labour market governance, legal frameworks, institutions, and policy approaches.

Improving the employment situation of young people remains a priority as well as addressing income inequalities that is central to achieving better jobs, more inclusive societies, and stronger economic development.

Creating opportunities and managing risks require coordinated and coherent actions, both at the national and international level. In this regard, the authors in this volume address the current challenges to labour law and social security systems bearing in mind the need to further develop multidimensional responses and to put people, work and livelihoods at the core of the economic and social strategies.

One strong element, which is examined in this volume, is that the future of work is likely to see changes to jobs and tasks, which will inevitably bring about deep and rapid shifts in the skills requirements. Thus, broad access to quality skills training to address mismatches and skills gaps become a priority for the majority of the national systems. Reskilling and upskilling strategies need to be put in place with a view to increasing the employability of the workforce. However, this is not enough, for building sound skill policies also requires a serious State's approach and effective social dialogue. Social dialogue with employers, workers, governments, but also an open dialogue with education and training institutions is necessary if the countries want to promote and improve policy design and implementation in this specific area.[2] The challenges for the national systems of labour law and social security have to do with the adaptation of labour institutions and existing labour legislation to cover all workers. Indeed, labour relations and labour institutions continue to evolve. Certain forms of employment, such as part-time work, temporary employment, and third-party agency work, among many others, present opportunities for job creation, including self-employment, labour mobility, access to labour market, and the inclusion of vulnerable and under-represented groups. At the same time, some forms of work may pose a number of new challenges for job and life quality, skill training, social protection, income distribution, and industrial relations. In this regard, the role of the State is essential for reducing the possible abuses and misuses.

In addition to many other challenges, there are those arising from work obtained or delivered through digital platforms. Although the share of this type of employment remains low, it is after all growing very fast. In this regard and considering the international nature of the phenomenon, there should be better policy responses at national and international level.[3]

2. *See* the Declaration of the Ministries of Labour of the G20 in Argentina, September 2018.
3. *See* J. Berg, M. Furrer, E. Harmon, U. Rani, M. Six Silberman, Digital Labour Platforms and the Future of Work. Towards Decent Work in the Online World, ILO, Geneva, 2018.

This goes hand-in-hand with the commitment to advance in the transition to formality as a means toward improving living conditions, productivity, growth, and sound policies to reduce absolute poverty. In this context, the main challenge for the labour law systems is how to ensure that new forms of employment are in the formal economy. The promotion of formalization in all forms of employment, including digital platforms, should be activated through the reduction of the decent work gaps present in the new labour market.

The volume addresses one crucial issue that is to say strong, equitable, and well-functioning social protection systems play a crucial role in fostering employment, reducing labour market insecurity and promoting social justice and inclusive growth. Currently, social protection systems are facing serious challenges regarding their sustainability and universal coverage as defined in national law. In that sense, it is key that social security systems should strengthen their financial sustainability while providing scope for innovation. The financial aspects of the reforms of the social security systems are essential for a brighter future of the next generations.

In this regard, this volume emphasizes the importance to promote active access to adequate social protection for workers in all forms of employment and work arrangements and the need to foster non-discrimination and fair treatment regardless of the individual employment status.

From the reading of the various reports, we find that gender gaps in labour force participation are still substantial but there are promising initiatives that will accelerate progress towards gender equality. In this regard, efforts should be made to increase the participation of women in the digital economy, including a more equitable distribution of care responsibilities between men and women.

As the reader will notice, the above-mentioned seven themes have identified key elements, which will inspire future research in comparative labour law and social security, such as developing skills for an inclusive future of work, promoting formalization, developing comprehensive social protection systems, increasing labour market integration for migrants, gender equality, sound industrial relations, a renewed role for the State, and a better governance of globalization.

In further arguing on the above issues, it should be noted that whatever the future of work looks like, it will present opportunities for employment growth. There is a need to make sure that these newly created jobs are quality jobs. The new forms of work associated to the new forms of employment provide opportunities but also challenges. It can result, if these phenomena are not well guided, in a higher number of workers exposed to the risk of informality. As we know, the informal economy refers to those activities that are not covered or are insufficiently covered by formal arrangements, either in law or in practice. Nowadays, informal work poses serious challenges to decent work and inequality.[4]

These phenomena are coupled by the emergence of the platform economy, which offers job opportunities that often take place in the form of activities or services performed online and across borders. In this regard, one major challenge is to ensure

4. *See* G. Arrigo, G. Casale, International Labour Law Handbook from A to Z, Giappichelli, Torino, 2017.

that workers in all forms of employment enjoy adequate levels of protection. Improving the compliance with labour law, addressing the scope of the legal coverage, and the level of adequate legal protection are core elements for a coherent labour legislation framework to be applied in the different national systems. The following issues can be looked at: clarifying the classification of workers' employment status and relative employment rights; raising awareness among employers and workers of the rights, obligations and responsibilities regarding different forms of work; promoting fair treatment in working conditions, access to social protection and training opportunities for all workers, regardless of the type of the employment relationship; expanding social dialogue through innovative means and promoting collective bargaining.[5]

Against this background, the informal economy is expanding. Indeed, the informal economy is a complex and multidimensional phenomenon that affects a wide range of sectors and occupations. It should be noted that in a good number of countries workers in some of the new and different forms of employment are at risk of being in informal work. The challenges of labour formalization are evident in a good number of countries. In this regard, there should be a better application of the ILO Transition from the Informal to the Formal Economy Recommendation, 2015 (No. 204) with a view to promoting labour formalization. For example, some of the recommendations to be introduced in the national systems should include taking appropriate measures, including a combination of preventive measures, law enforcement and effective sanctions, addressing tax evasion and avoidance of social contributions, labour laws and regulations; providing incentives linked to facilitating the effective and timely transition from the informal to the formal economy including improved access to business advisory services, finance, infrastructure, markets, technology, education and skills programmes, social security and property rights; adapting and strengthening the labour inspectorates; fostering compliance with labour legislation and regulations in force; promoting social dialogue and sound industrial relations.[6]

When dealing with the specific phenomenon of the features of digital platforms, whenever possible there should be a recall to the application of international labour standards. In so doing, the digital platforms could reduce the governance gap in the digital economy. For example, there should be transparency regarding working conditions and levels of earnings related to digital platforms; support improvement of earnings and working conditions for platform workers; consider the portability and social security benefits in line with national practices and legislation; tackle all forms of discrimination; clarifying workers' employment status and associated rights in the platform economy; promote social dialogue and where appropriate cross-border social dialogue.[7]

Migrant workers are too often considered a part of the modern slavery. The ratification and implementation of relevant international instruments by countries are necessary. It should be recognized that this phenomenon could only be guided if there is a comprehensive and integrated approach at international and regional level. In this regard, the part of due diligence and transparency in global supply chains is essential.

5. *See* J. Berg et al., *supra*.
6. *See* G. Arrigo, G. Casale, *supra*.
7. *See* J. Berg et al., *supra*.

Business should be encouraged to implement strong social compliance systems that would encourage a better integration of the migrant workers in the various labour market systems. In this context, the UN Guiding Principles on Business and Human Rights, the ILO Tripartite Declaration of principles concerning Multinational Enterprises and Social Policy, and the 2016 ILO resolution concerning decent work in global supply chains represent a coherent international policy framework to tackle the phenomenon of migration.

The reports collected in this volume stress another serious challenge that has to do with social security systems due to their sustainability, universal coverage, adequate level of protection, and the portability of social security entitlements. In this volume, such challenges are examined and some targeted actions have been presented. Among others, mention should be made of the following areas:

(a) promote access to social protection which ensures that workers in all forms of employment benefit from adequate levels of protection;
(b) in light of the increasing labour mobility and recognizing the need to protect workers' rights there should be an effective portability of social security entitlements between different statutes and within and between countries, according to national law and practice;
(c) improve effective mechanism to promote and monitor compliance with legal frameworks, through a clear definition of rights and responsibilities of workers and employers in the area of social protection;
(d) develop awareness-raising campaigns and enhance public communication of social protection rights and obligations.

The labour market integration of migrants and gender equality is a current challenge for labour law and social security systems. In some of the reports presented in this volume, there are specific references to various policy options that can be introduced in the various systems. For example, there should be nationally defined employment goals for the labour market participation of migrants and gender targets; promote practices that combat discrimination in the workplace, including hiring and promotion decisions; incentivize and support private sector investment in accessibility to help disadvantage workers retain their jobs or access to employment.

Effective use of inclusive legislation and social security schemes could boost the creation of quality jobs and the implementation of appropriate and effective anti-discrimination policies.

From the above-mentioned arguments, labour law plays the part of a labour market institution, able to make the market work more efficiently from an economic and social point of view. Labour law and social security law need to perform new tasks. One task could be the optimization of job opportunities, and this applies to all forms of employment (subordinate, freelance, part-time, third sector jobs, social care) that the market does not value appropriately. Another task is to improve the quality of human capital, providing support for continuous professional development as jobs and workers become more and more mobile.[8]

Transition from one job to another can be effectively assisted if the national policies are designed for anticipating changes and enterprises crisis. This can be done only if workers and employers are involved in the design of these policies since the very beginning. Develop and upgrade skill and upskilling training policies is becoming necessary for too many countries nowadays.

In this context, labour law and industrial relations become essential instruments contributing to enterprise development and market efficiency, with a view to further developing economic growth. Although industrial relations are affected more directly than individual labour law by the changing economic environment, the shift of collective bargaining to enterprise level is forcing the social partners, and first of all the workers' organizations, to face up to new labour and economic problems without the full support of national legal and contractual arrangements, often in competition with the initiatives from innovative management.

Therefore, the search for new solutions to these new changes is emerging with substantial difference among themselves. For example, in the European countries, despite the common EU regulatory mechanisms, the countries have started to adopt nationalist approaches.

However, at closer look the increasingly transnational dimension of labour and business matters calls for even more in-depth analysis of the interdependence among the national systems with a view to better understanding the implications for the new generation of workers and enterprises.

For sure, the national labour law and social security systems are faced with the difficulty that the crisis in labour regulations and arrangements is aggravated by the fact that there is an historical asymmetry between the increasing mobility of capital, and a very limited mobility of labour. In this regard, the absence of a real transnational regulation of working conditions, the tendencies towards completion, and divergence among national systems will continue to persist. A more coherent international economic and social governance is needed, if we do not want to assist to an increase of inequality between countries and within countries.

In conclusion, although operating in difficult times, labour law and social security law should never miss their main function that is to say to regulate in a fair manner the working and living conditions of all working people in the world.

8. *See* the Declaration of the G20 Ministers of Labour, Argentina, 2018.

CHAPTER 2

Transformations of Work: Challenges to National Systems of Labour Law and Social Security

Tiziano Treu

§2.01 RESEARCH ON LABOUR LAW FRONTIER TOPICS

At the 2015 World Congress in Cape Town, our international company launched seven research groups on topics we believed to be particularly important for the future of work and for the challenges they represent for our disciplines.[1]

The choice of topics was made taking into account our discussions in recent years. We do not claim that the list of topics is exhaustive, but we believe they cover some of the crucial issues facing not only us jurists but all students of social science, and this is confirmed by the work done by the groups themselves.

The objective of this research, and indeed of our tradition, is to draw on the experience and knowledge of national systems acquired by the different associations and offer comparative and interdisciplinary analyses to the international community of academics and operators.

We are convinced that only in-depth research, as objective as possible, on the various aspects of these issues can shed light on a future that appears more than ever uncertain, and much in need of critical thinking. In this way we can avoid the ideological controversies and simplistic solutions that are unfortunately common in our field, exposed as it is to social tensions and influenced by conflicting interests. Analytical and participatory research work is also the basis for putting forward, with all

1. The principal contributions to the Congress are published in *Labour Law and Social Progress, Bulletin of Comparative Labor Relations*, 92, ed. D'Arcy du Toit, W. Kluwer, 2016.

the necessary caveats, suggestions and proposals to national and international policy-makers.

We are convinced – and I am personally – that despite the radical changes in the world of work and business brought about by globalization and the new digital technologies, the impact of these factors is by no means predetermined. It can be influenced by the decisions of institutions and public and private actors operating in various areas. Our analyses provide meaningful examples of such influence and therefore of the space opening up to institutional and social action and to our studies.[2]

I would emphasize here, as I have done at other times, the importance of the comparative approach. Although for a hundred years our discipline has been constructed on national bases, it is now being transformed by the increasing interdependence not only of businesses and financial institutions in various countries but also of entire national, legal and social systems.

The multilevel character of current regulation is a further urgent reason for renewing our national surveys and analyses, and above all our comparative work. The theory, still held by many, that different systems cannot be compared is invalidated in actual fact, as well as discredited by the weak international authorities. Rather, the closeness, and often the osmosis, between provisions in different systems changes the very nature of the comparison. It is no longer (only) a matter of observing the various legal and social models with an attentive and 'distant' eye, but of fathoming the close interrelations and influences between these models and/or sectors of them as they appear day by day in the economic and social life of all countries.

Comparative analysis of the various national systems and the solutions they have devised is not only an essential tool for acquiring theoretical knowledge but also the basis for resolving the problems with which company, trade-union and institutional operators have to wrestle. These problems, which determine economic and social decisions, are more and more often transnational, despite the current nationalistic reactions we are seeing, even in the labour law policies of various countries.[3]

Comparative analysis, if it is to go beyond the mere descriptive juxtaposition of national institutions, is difficult for academics and policymakers, who until now have concentrated on national problems and are persuaded of the specific character of their solutions. Our Association, with its research and seminars, can provide fuel for innovation in these studies and good examples of comparative practice in the field of labour law and industrial relations.

The complexity of the challenges and experiences inherent in the various systems does not allow for easy solutions or quick answers.

General analyses of major economic and social trends may also be inadequate if not misleading. In-depth and detailed analyses are needed if we are to grasp the

2. The wide range of reactions on the part of the various European systems to changes in the economic and social context is examined in my paper *Employment for a Sustainable Society: What Is to Be Done?*, Keynote Speech to the ILERA World Congress, 23–27 July 2018, Seoul.
3. *See* similar remarks in R. Gumbrell-McCormick, R. Hyman, *Trade Unions in Western Europe: Hard Times, Hard Choices*, OUP, 2016, p. 6; S. Lehndorff, H. Dribbush, T. Schulten (eds), *Rough Waters: European Trade Unions in a Time of Crisis*, ETUI, 2017, pp. 14 ff.

complex reality of labour law and labour relations and understand the answers to common challenges devised by different national systems.

Specific analyses of this type are important in a period of rapid and uncertain transition in which partial innovations in some environments, which are not taken into account by (over)-general analyses, may be of interest in indicating current tendencies.[4]

The research topics explored by our groups are indicative of the changes – some would say the crisis – affecting our discipline. Indeed, the analyses raise questions about fundamental aspects of the regulatory structures handed down from the past. The challenge concerns above all the role of the State in regulating labour relations and the labour market. This role must now be performed in settings that go beyond national boundaries, by entities lacking traditional state powers and acting under general and, in the broad sense, public legal instruments, ranging from transnational collective contracts to the social clauses in commercial agreements.

In addition, the international scene is characterized by epoch-making phenomena, such as mass migration, which present huge problems for the regulation of working conditions, seriously testing the effectiveness of the relevant laws and even presenting a threat to human life. Other aspects of security and the reception and integration of migrants are covered by fragile and inadequate interstate agreements, as we have seen with the dramatic events taking place in Europe, with particular reference to refugees and illegal immigrants. The report of the research group presented by Kubra Dogan Yenisey deals with the complex problems posed by these migrations, pointing out the lack of binding international regulations and the decisive role of nation states, which until now has been expressed in contradictory and often conflicting solutions. The report also shows how migration has made the conflict between the rights of migrants and those of local workers a central issue in labour law. The resolution of this conflict is a difficult task for labour lawyers, but essential if we are to fulfil our mission in promoting the equality of all working people. It needs to be tackled not on a national basis but with solutions agreed among the various national systems.

§2.02 A CRISIS OF LEGAL CATEGORIES

The issues of the quality of labour relations and corporate productivity have assumed unprecedented and potentially disruptive dimensions in our field, as a result of the processes of decentralization that have affected industrial relations and production and social systems generally.

4. ILO, *Transitioning from the Informal to the Formal Economy*, International Labour Conference, 2014, *Recommendation*, 2015 (no. 204). The ILO's conclusions take into account the policies adopted in various countries to encourage this transition and affirm that the promotion of decent work in the informal economy requires an integrated approach, based on the ratification of fundamental rights at work, the creation of better employment and income-earning opportunities, the extension of social protection and more engagement in social dialogue.

These are tendencies that accentuate aspects of the 'incorporation' of both collective and individual labour relations, with far-reaching implications for frontier issues such welfare and the connection between work and productivity. On the other hand, the same tendencies also open up new possibilities for trade union activity and for innovative management in the use of technologies in corporate organization and in the regulation of digital employment.

But the issue that is central to our thinking, which affects many specific aspects, such as the last mentioned, is the very concept of work and the legal categories in which it is framed for the purposes of regulation.

Cutting across all subjects, this issue emerges from the discussions of the other groups and from almost all our conferences.

Our discipline is now concerned above all with the many forms of employment that differ from those prevalent in the twentieth century on which our subject was constructed, i.e., subordinate employment (especially in a corporate setting). But the expression 'informal employment' also refers to those activities that are developing in the various sectors of the informal economy. This second aspect is covered by our first research group, as reported by H. Villasmil. The first aspect is analysed in the report by T. Araki and S. Laloum.

As the ILO reminds us, in emerging countries and societies the informal economy and informal employment account for more than 75% of business activity and workers in employment. But I would point out straight away that informal sectors and informal jobs as also present in so-called advanced economies.[5] This coexistence of ancient and modern is one of the deepest cleavages in our economic and social systems, raising the question of the effectiveness of our employment and social security systems. Indeed, as European trade unions have stressed with great concern, the most recent forms of 'crowd working' may lead to the uncontrolled spread of informal employment.[6]

Our comparative analyses paint a picture of persistent uncertainty[7] and consistent diversity in the solutions adopted by different countries. The impact of the new digital technologies on the organization of work and businesses is the extreme manifestation of this uncertainty.

This is true where the quantity of work is concerned. Forecasts that most traditional jobs will disappear in the near future are probably exaggerated. But the impact is bound to grow. Throughout the world, there has been an explosion of gig economy jobs on digital platforms, the extreme example of 'anytime anywhere' working. In California, which is often in the forefront of new trends, 400,000 Uber drivers have mobilized and taken legal action against the corporate platform. And it is

5. ILO, *Transitioning from the Informal to the Formal Economy*, International Labour Conference, 2014, *Recommendation*, 2015 (no. 204). The ILO's conclusions take into account the policies adopted in various countries to encourage this transition and affirm that the promotion of decent work in the informal economy requires an integrated approach, based on the ratification of fundamental rights at work, the creation of better employment and income-earning opportunities, the extension of social protection and more engagement in social dialogue.
6. ETUC, *Resolution on Digitalisation: 'Towards Fair Digital Work'*, 8-9 June 2016, www.ETUC.org.
7. M. Weiss, *Challenges for Labour Law and Industrial Relations*, paper presented to the ILERA World Congress, 23-27 July 2018, Seoul.

estimated that there are already more than 14 million online workers active in the USA.[8]

In any case, the effects of digital innovations on employment are bound to grow, especially in repetitive traditional jobs.[9]

It is significant that, in Europe, the threat from the digital revolution has reopened the debate not only on flexible working hours, but also on their reduction. The recently renegotiated German metalworkers' agreement entitles them to reduce (for two years) their weekly working hours to twenty-eight (with a partial reduction in salary), as well as to return to a normal week of thirty-five working hours. In return, the employers have been allowed to exercise greater flexibility in organizing working time. And part-time working (not always voluntary) is on the increase, emerging as a widespread system of work-sharing, often within the family.[10]

As well as the overall scale of employment, the forms and quality of labour will be affected by unprecedented change, especially where repetitive jobs are concerned, leading to a polarization of employment positions. The change is so profound that it is showing up the inadequacy not only of the traditional rules but also of the very categories on which labour law is founded, beginning with subordinate employment.[11] This is not a matter of doubts expressed by theoretical jurists, but of uncertainties that are beginning to affect lawmakers, the social partners and even the rulings of the law courts.[12]

---

8. Cfr. my article *Rimedi, tutele e fattispecie: riflessioni a partire dai lavori della Gig Economy*, LD, 2017, pp. 367 ff.
9. There are now many analyses on this subject. *See* in particular S. Scarpetta, *The Future of Work*, INAPP–ANPAL–CNEL Conference, 9 November 2017, www.CNEL.it; M. Arntz, T. Gregory, U. Zierahn, *The Risk of Automation for Jobs in OECD Countries*, OECD Social, *Employment and Migration*, WP, no. 189, 2016; Eurofound, *Automation, Digitalization and Platforms: Implications for Work and Employment*, 2018; OECD, *The Future of Work*, Policy forum, January 2016; European Economic and Social Committee, 2017, *Impact of Digitalization and the On-Demand Economy on the Labour Market and the Consequences for Employment and Industrial Relations*, www.cesc.Europa.eu; World Bank, World Development Report 2018, *The Changing Nature of Work*, in which many policy proposals are also presented; IMF, *Technology and the Future of Work*, Group of Twenty, 2018.
10. In Holland, part-time work now accounts for almost half of all employment (47%), but it is on the increase in all European and most OECD countries. *See* Eurofound, *Part Time Work in Europe 2004*; *Working Time*, July 2018; OEDC data, *Part Time Employment Rate*, 2017.
11. *See* B. Hepple, B. Veneziani, *The Transformation of Labour Law in Europe, a Comparative Study of 15 Countries*, Hart Publishing, 2009; E. Ales, O. Deiuert, J. Kenver (eds) 2009, *Core and Contingent Work in the European Union, a Comparative Analysis*, Hart Publishing, 2017; *New Forms of Employment*, Eurofound 2015, Luxembourg.
12. This type of work has attracted a great deal of legal analysis. *See*, for example, M.A. Cherry, *A Taxonomy of Virtual Work*, in Georgia Law Review, 2011, vol. 45, p. 951; C. Degryse, *Digitalization of the Economy and Its Impact on Labour Markets*, Working Papers, 2016, 2; V. De Stefano, *The Rise of the Just in Time Workforce: On Demand Work. Crowdwork and Labor Protection in the gig Economy*, ILO Working Papers, *Conditions of Working Series*, no. 71, 2016 b; J. Prassl, M. Risak, *Uber, Taskrabbit and Co.: Platforms as Employers? Rethinking the Legal Analysis of Crowdwork*, in CLLPJ, 2016, vol. 37, p. 619; G. Davidov, *The Status of Uber Drivers: a Purposive Approach*, in Spanish Labor Law and Employment Relations Journal, to be published; Eurofound Working *Anytime, Anywhere. The Effects on the World of Work* (www.eurofound.Europa.eu/publications/report/2017/working-anytime-anywhere-the-effects-on–the-world-of-work), 2017.

The research group analysis presented by T. Araki illustrates and comments on the various solutions being put forward by the various national legal systems in dealing with the new platform-based forms of employment.

§2.03 GIG ECONOMY JOBS

European judges, like their Common Law counterparts, are divided between those who try to include gig economy workers in the category of subordinate employees and accord them the associated rights and those who, on the contrary, emphasize their independent status. But all of them acknowledge the novelty of such cases, due to the fact that they often combine aspects of freelance and subordinate status. Understandably, some judges, especially those applying the Common Law, avoid judging their cases within either of the two traditional categories and concentrate on the workers' needs for protection (accidents, minimum wage standards and so on). The cases of Uber and Foodora point to a more general trend. There will probably be a degree of autonomy in the more advanced forms of subordinate employment and a degree of dependency in the freelance jobs spawned by the internet.[13]

I have been convinced for a long time that, to get a handle on this trend and provide an adequate response, we need to pay more attention to the need to protect workers in these new jobs (without forgetting the old ones) than to traditional categories.

We have also begun to do some research on this subject. The aim is to find a common basis of rules which meets the fundamental needs of working people, drawing inspiration from the decent work standards set by the International Labour Organization, and to supplement this common basis with specific rules adapted to the different employment and business situations.

The fact is that in many legal systems the formerly compact regulation of labour law has already become diversified as a result of both legal initiatives and collective labour agreements in order to take into account the diversity and variability of the different forms of employment, and this has led not only to variations within individual types of employment relationship, thus destroying their unity, but also to osmosis between the different types.[14]

Given the varied nature of these jobs, there is little point in seeking 'quick fixes', and this is confirmed by our comparative studies. Nor is introducing many different types of employment contract a valid solution, as has been tried in a number of countries, including Italy.

Many European judges have interpreted the once-rigid notion of subordinated employment in a more elastic way so as to adapt it to many of these jobs, which, though not formally included in an enterprise's structures, manifest aspects of dependency, albeit combined with margins of autonomy.

13. Cf. my analysis, *Rimedi, tutele, fattispecie*, cit.
14. This is the conclusion of the T. Araki, S. Laloum report to the Turin Congress. For evidence of this osmosis in the Italian setting, *see* T. Treu, *Rimedi, tutele, fattispecie*, cit., pp. 388 ff.

National legislators have adopted similarly diverse attitudes. Some have created intermediate categories of employment contracts under various names: parasubordinated jobs (Italy), financially dependent employment (Spain), relations similar to subordinated employment (Germany) workers (United Kingdom). To these are applied some, but not all, of the traditional protections afforded to subordinate employees: in particular, minimum wages, safety standards, social security, and accident insurance. But the creation of these new categories has not clarified the borderlines between them; on the contrary, it has sometimes made them more difficult to identify. The proof is that such regulations have turned out to be difficult to implement.[15]

§2.04 FROM LEGAL QUALIFICATION TO THE MODULATION OF PROTECTIONS

More appropriate, as I see it, is the solution adopted by the French lawmakers (Law no. 1088, Article 6, of 8 August 2016), who have come up with general response focusing on a number of essential rights and protections, without claiming to provide legal definitions of digital employment, while abandoning the all-or-nothing logic inherent in the rigid traditional categories.[16]

Another possible route, to some extent taken by the Italian legislature, is to leave it to collective bargaining to redefine and clarify the borders between different forms of employment, while adapting their regulation to the specific requirements of individual types of work and business (Leg. Decree 81/2015, Article 2 (2)).

There are similar difficulties in identifying frameworks for the various occupations, because digital technologies are changing the relationship between intelligent machines and the workers who operate them, with the consequence that the content of traditional jobs is radically changed and the very concept of a contractual framework is rendered obsolete.[17] These changes confirm my, and others', conviction that the strengthening of workers' occupational identity and skills, with targeted investment in training, is the most positive strategy for facing up to the challenges of technological innovation and promoting equality of opportunity in the digital era.[18]

§2.05 CRITERIA FOR REGULATING PROTECTIONS

The subordinate employment category still corresponds to a large number of jobs in different sectors of the economy and cannot simply be declared out of date from an exaggerated love of all things new. But treating it as an exclusive descriptive filter

15. The different types of response to these new regulatory problems are well documented in the report of T. Araki and S. Laloum. *See also* M. Weiss, *La platform economy e le principali sfide per il diritto del lavoro*, DRI, 2018, pp. 718 ff.
16. A. Jammaud, *Uber, Deliveroo: requalification des contrats ou denunciation d'une fraude à la loi*, Semaine Sociale Lamy, *178*, 4 September 2017, pp. 4 ff.
17. M. Faioli, *Mansioni e macchine intelligenti*, soon to be published by Giappichelli, 2018.
18. Many of the research projects referred to in notes 8 and 9 converge on this point. The IMF research, in particular, emphasizes the importance of education, observing that '*spending on education may be a particularly effective policy tool*', cit., p. 20.

would obscure the various forms of working activity that are rapidly increasing in modern economies, as well as the need to regulate and protect them.

The legal materials provided by our comparison confirm what has already been said: that the varying forms of employment have provoked different regulatory and social responses from the different legal systems, often far removed from traditional ones.

In this respect, the ruling of the European Commission regarding the most controversial forms of digital employment is significant. While mentioning the possible use of subordinate employment criteria for settling so-called platform workers' cases and disputes, the Commission merely invites Member States to ensure that workers benefit from 'fair working conditions' and 'adequate and sustainable social protection', identified by considering 'the different needs and the innovative nature of collaborative business models'.[19]

Evidently, this is an open ruling which suggests that research should be focused more on the regulatory needs of the jobs concerned than of the traditional descriptive categories. And it indicates that two main factors need to be considered: on the one hand, people's need to enjoy fair working conditions and adequate protection, and on the other, the innovative character of these business models. The reference to their cooperative character seems to allude to certain aspects of the 'sharing economy', which in any case are far from being present in all the cases subject to discussion and dispute.

This opens up a field of research for jurists and policymakers with a view to identifying criteria for regulating such new arrangements, over and above the need for fairness and social justice. These criteria are necessary to avoid a situation in which, having cut loose from the traditional descriptive categories, we merely register the existence of moveable boundaries between different cases and scatter protective measures at random without any theoretical basis.

As we have seen, the mobility and variability of individual cases mean that rigid legal interventions are ineffective. Flexible regulation as established in collective labour agreements may be more practical, provided that they truly represent the needs of these new types of jobs.

In any case, the guidelines for regulation must be inspired by the general principles of the legal system, as sanctioned by national constitutions and European and international charters of rights.

§2.06 DEVELOPMENT OF BASIC STANDARDS

Of particular importance in dealing with these new working arrangements, which represent a frontier zone in labour law, is the development of basic standards corresponding to the concept of decent work championed by the International Labour Organization.

19. European Economic and Social Committee (2017), *Impact of Digitalization*, cit.

The ILO's basic standards are of different kinds. Some are concerned with rights relating to freedom of association and trade union autonomy, recognized in many countries but still often disputed. Many social rights need to be specified as regulations implementing legislation or collective agreements which determine their content, primarily the right to fair pay for work done. This has assumed central importance in all countries because of competitive pressures on businesses and on the cost of labour, resulting in the traditionally unknown phenomenon of the 'working poor'.

More recently, new rights, both individual and social, have assumed growing importance, such as the right to ongoing training, and, following the spread of new digital technologies, the right to privacy in the workplace (as well as elsewhere) and the right of workers operating online to disconnect from the web under certain conditions. It has also become necessary to recognize or reinforce another right which is not purely defensive (like the right to disconnect) but more proactive: the right of workers to have a 'voice', as individuals and through their organizations. This is essential for giving expression to the new needs of workers, as well as their proposals, and for ensuring that their voices are not drowned out by the frenzy of competition and the workings of intelligent machines.

Basic rights are becoming more important at present because of the diversification of labour into forms that often do not correspond to traditional legal categories. As already recognized in theory, this makes it even more urgent to identify a hard core of rules and protections applicable to all working activities, whatever their legal status. The need is for a common core expressing the universal principles of the dignity of human labour. Their concrete translation into the various legal systems is an essential policy objective if we are to provide a unifying basis for the fragmented jobs of the future and free them from the danger of deregulation or regulatory anomie (lack of social or ethical standards).[20]

In reality, an effort to adapt and select protections is also required for many jobs performed within or alongside subordinate employment settings, but which are distinguished by new characteristics that make many of the traditional rules inapplicable. Think, for instance, of the forms of 'smart working' already widespread in many businesses, which not only accentuate the autonomous features of the work being done but also remove them from the traditional constraints of time and place.

The changed geography of work calls for a plurality of innovative solutions in the regulation of labour relations and in other areas of our discipline, from labour market management to social security. The complexity of the new working arrangements requires differentiated or 'tailor-made' labour law on several levels, based on common rules and adapted to the specific needs of the various forms of activity.[21]

20. Cfr. my surveys in *Labour Law and Social Policy; An Agenda for International Research*, presented following the XXI ISLSSL World Congress in Cape Town, 2015, now in WP M. D'Antona, INT, 128/2016.
21. M. Weiss, *The Challenges*, cit.; and T. Araki and S. Laloum's report to the Turin Congress, cit.

§2.07 REGULATION OF THE ECONOMY AND INFORMAL EMPLOYMENT

The prospect of basic standards may also be significant in tackling the widespread phenomenon of informal economy jobs that are legally non-compliant or borderline. Such jobs are also largely outside the scope of collective labour agreements. Experience in various countries confirms the difficulty involved in formalizing the informal economy and the ineffectiveness of both incentives and repressive measures in achieving this end.

Attempts made in some countries, including Italy, to harmonize informal working conditions with those prevailing in the regular labour market by adopting a variety of contractual incentives have been unsuccessful.

If this objective is to be achieved, an integrated policy-based approach is required, as advocated by the ILO, with interventions that go beyond employment-related measures and rules. These interventions must tackle the economic and social context in which the informal economy develops, not only backward areas but also modern sectors affected by the new technologies, such as logistics.[22]

These interventions should aim to foster both economic and institutional/social development, supporting legality, the formation of capital and the strengthening of social networks. Specific initiatives have been recommended by the ILO to remove the obstacles in the way of the formalization and growth of the activities in question. We might mention in particular the simplification of bureaucratic procedures for setting up and running a business, and for the management of workers, as well as measures to facilitate access to the instruments needed for this purpose: financial services, information and consultancy on business and employment opportunities, advice on how to compete for public contracts, and support for managerial training.

In areas directly connected with employment, it is vitally important to improve inspection services, which are almost everywhere underdeveloped, training staff to rise to the challenge of preventing and monitoring illegal activity. It is in any case recognized that this type of intervention is of itself insufficient and needs to be supplemented with a set of preventive measures and incentives to encourage legality.

A more direct intervention is needed in respect of the informal or irregular employment common in decentralized production processes (contracting and subcontracting chains), which is widespread even in advanced sectors of the economy. Many legal systems have introduced forms of more of less extensive co-responsibility incumbent on the lead firms in such decentralized arrangements, with penalties for non-compliance with labour and social security standards on the part of contractors and subcontractors.[23]

Interventions to regularize informal employment arrangements also need to be adapted to the economic and social context. They may require a gradual approach to

22. *See* the *ILO Recommendation 2015*, cit.
23. The recent French law, referred to above, has also extended this responsibility to cover violations committed in countries other than France.

the process and different levels of harmonization and should aim for the enforcement of basic standards, rather than an unrealistic alignment with wages in established sectors of the economy. Acceptance of a certain degree of regulatory differentiation may be necessary to achieve effective results, with the possibility of making improvements over time.

The changes in employment that have upset the traditional categories of labour law have had a no less direct impact on social security arrangements.

The reasons for and implications of this change in social security provision have been studied by a specific research group. They were presented by our colleague Prof. Marhold at the European Congress held in Prague in September 2017 and are presented once again here in Turin.

§2.08 CHANGES IN SOCIAL SECURITY: FINANCIAL SUSTAINABILITY AND SOCIAL FAIRNESS

I will simply mention some aspects of this change which are more directly connected with the transformations we have previously analysed in the rules governing employment relationships.

In the field of social security, too, legislators in many countries have introduced reforms of the traditional systems in response to the new circumstances. These circumstances are, first of all, the reduction in the financial resources available for spending on social security, which was already a factor prior to the crisis and has been aggravated by it;[24] second, the growing volatility affecting employment, which has reduced the tax base on which many social security provisions depend, from pensions to income support for the unemployed; and, finally, the radical demographic changes associated with lengthening life expectancy, often combined with falling birth rates.

National reforms have responded to these challenges with differing strategies and results, but with the chief aim of ensuring the financial sustainability of the principal benefits and of the social security system as a whole.[25]

The results have been less satisfactory in ensuring the social sustainability and fairness of social protection measures. In many cases, as shown by official European and OECD surveys, financial sustainability has been achieved to the detriment of fairness for current beneficiaries and even more so for those who will benefit in the future.[26]

24. Even though, in most European countries, the overall share of spending on social security has not suffered significant reductions.
25. *See*, for pensions in particular, J. Visser, *Neither Convergence Nor Frozen Paths: Bounded Learning, International Diffusion of Reforms, and the Open Method of Coordination*, in M. Heidenreich, I. Zeitein, *Changing European Employment and Welfare Regimes*, Routledge, pp. 37 ff. The title is significant because the author indicates that the EU has experienced a higher intensity of reforms than other OECD countries.
26. European Commission, *Pension Adequacy Report*, vol. I, 2018, pp. 17 ff.; *World Social Protection Report*, 2017–2019, pp. 157 ff.

The dramatic consequences are inequality and poverty, which have increased particularly among the younger generations, to the point of undermining the intergenerational pact that has so far sustained our welfare systems.[27]

Complex strategies are required to ensure both the financial sustainability and the fairness of social security provisions. Above all, economic interventions are needed to foster growth and enhance the quality of employment, so as to support the social security institutions that depend on these factors. The connection between employment and social security may be more or less direct, depending on the structures of the various provisions, but in any case it is vital.

§2.09 BEYOND INSURANCE SCHEMES

At the same time, traditional social security schemes, in particular those that are insurance-based, need to be reformed. Like the traditional rules governing labour relations, these schemes were established on the assumption of a stable labour market and stable jobs. Today they need to be recalibrated to reflect changes in employment, above all the fragmentation and frequent interruptions and transitions in people's employment records. Keeping the old schemes unchanged is bound to jeopardize the fairness of social protection for all non-standard jobs, and this is already happening.

The necessary changes, already initiated in some countries, are many and various, and often have parallels with those we have already indicated for the rules governing labour relations.[28]

The first line of approach, in some European countries, has been to set aside the category-based arrangements of many social protection provisions and adopt a universalist philosophy, extending some basic provisions to all forms of work, including non-standard ones.

Another measure, first introduced some time ago but gradually spreading, has been to take into account for pension purposes periods when a person has not been able to work for personal reasons (sickness, accidents, parental leave and so on) or due to economic circumstances (unemployment).

Similar measures have been adopted in some countries to support the tax base of part-time workers. This type of employment has been neglected in the past, and not only where social security is concerned, because it was regarded as marginal. But its rapid spread in modern economies has made it necessary to review its status, to ensure that part-timers, too, are fairly treated in terms of remuneration and social protection.

A further and more radical correction of traditional schemes has been to uncouple to a large extent social security benefits from work performed by the beneficiary.

---

27. Consequently, the total age dependency ratio, the proportion of the non-active population in relation to the total population, has increased so drastically, especially in European countries and Japan, as to radically change the traditional balances where welfare is concerned. In Europe, the total age dependency ratio was already high in 2010 (46.6%) but is likely to rise to 64.7% by 2030 (OECD data).
28. Cfr. *Pension Adequacy Report*, European Commission, cit., pp. 27 ff.; F. Marhold's report to the Turin Congress; my report on *Sustainable social security* for the European Social Security Association, Venice, 11–12 October 2018.

Some countries now provide pension benefits that depend only on a person's citizenship status, or that are commensurate with the number of years worked but do not depend on the amount of contributions paid in.[29]

The common factor in all these measures is that they set aside the commutative principle of insurance-based schemes and bring in the principle of solidarity, thus introducing into the system redistributive elements intended to ensure not only greater financial sustainability but also greater fairness in social security provision.

These corrections to social security schemes to ensure fairness, especially for non-typical workers and irregular career trajectories, are intended to slow the tendency discernible in many countries for all or many of the forms of social protection to shift into the area of welfare.[30]

The distinction between the social security and welfare systems is still important, though the boundaries have become blurred. The distinction is sanctioned by some national constitutions, including the Italian one, which distinguishes between, on the one hand, the right to maintenance and social assistance of citizens who are unfit to work and lacking the means of livelihood, and, on the other, the right of workers to financial support in the event of accidents, sickness, invalidity, old age and redundancy.

The difference is important in terms of the level of benefits provided: welfare benefits are generally less generous and have not been increased in recent years.[31] And the same is true of the circumstances in which benefits are payable. Welfare benefits are conditional on means testing, which in some countries has become so rigorous as to reduce access to benefits or dissuade beneficiaries from applying for them.[32]

§2.10 MINIMUM WAGE AND COMBATTING POVERTY

The inability of existing income support systems to respond to the needs of people in difficulty, and the spread of various forms of poverty, has led almost all European countries to introduce some form of minimum wage. Though differing widely, these measures to combat poverty have maintained the approach common to other forms of assistance and welfare of requiring the beneficiaries, more or less bindingly, to engage in work, training or other socially useful activities.

---

29. *See* examples in the texts referred to in the previous note; also OECD, *Pensions at a Glance*, 2017, p. 86.
30. All the international documentation on this subject also points out the need to integrate basic public pensions with supplementary pension schemes, which take various forms and are in some cases obligatory. Cfr. OECD, *Pensions at a Glance*, 2017, cit., pp. 87 ff. At the same time, the sustainability of the pension system, and of public welfare in general, requires upstream interventions to support the levels and quality of employment and, more specifically in the case of pensions, 'active ageing' initiatives in response to the raising of the pensionable age, together with measures to support the employability of older workers. Cf. *L'importanza di essere vecchi. Politiche attive per la terza età*, ed. T. Treu, Mulino, Arel, 2012; Eurofound, *Employment Trends and Policies for Older Workers in the Recession*, Report, Dublin, 2012.
31. F. Berton, M. Richiardi, S. Sacchi, *The Political Economy of Work Security*, cit., p. 16.
32. A. Atkinson, *Inequality*, Harvard University Press, 2015, pp. 229 ff.

Proposals to introduce a generalized and unconditional citizen's (or basic) income have been widely discussed. Limited experiments have been conducted, with unclear results, but have not yet been adopted on a large scale.[33]

An apparently insuperable obstacle is the cost of such schemes, especially if, as Prof. Marhold's report illustrates, they are viewed in conjunction with the other welfare measures currently forming part of the system. The adoption of a minimum income in addition to the existing provisions would involve an increase in social spending that would be difficult to sustain. On the other hand, its introduction in place of the other measures might well increase, rather than decrease, social inequalities because the well-off are more capable than the poor of accessing the various social protection benefits.

The analysis conducted up to this point confirms the complexity of the connections between the various social security benefits and the dynamics of the labour market, and points up the need for a better understanding of these connections if we are to establish effective forms of coordination between the policy measures adopted in both areas.[34]

Because of the increasing fragmentation of people's working careers, labour policies need to include new measures to guarantee continuity of employment despite frequent changes of job. The welfare system should also be stimulated to support changes of employment with more effective instruments than at present: in particular social shock absorbers designed to encourage the relocation of the unemployed for work purposes and access to the labour marker for the jobless, paid leave to make periods of inactivity for personal reasons more fruitful (not only for parenting, sickness or accidents but also for retraining), and, more generally, services for those receiving tax credits to help them achieve a better work-life balance and improve their occupational and geographical mobility. The resulting inclusion of welfare benefit in employment policy would help in combatting poverty/fragility and in promoting decent work.

§2.11 LABOUR POLICIES AND WELFARE POLICIES

As an example of the closeness of the two areas and the need to coordinate strategies, I would simply mention the spread in almost all countries of some form of legal minimum wage.[35] This is a provision that combines the function of paying a wage for work done with the social function of ensuring a level of income that meets the needs of workers and therefore prevents and combats poverty. It is apparent that this function converges with that of the social security provisions we have been examining, again no longer inspired only by commutative principles but by principles of solidarity.

33. For a review of the various proposals and measures, *see* A. Atkinson, *Inequality*, cit., pp. 230 ff. Regarding the Italian minimum wage, *see Il reddito di inclusione sociale*, ed. C. Gori, Mulino, 2016.
34. F. Berton, M. Richiardi, S. Sacchi, *The Political Economy of Work Security and Flexibility*, cit., p. 16.
35. Cf. Eurofound, *Statutory Minimum Wages in the EU*, 2018.

The convergence of these different strategies is also evident in the minimum-wage-provision function. The objective of combatting poverty now concerns large numbers of workers who cannot make ends meet, either because they are on low wages or because that have come to the end of their entitlement to the unemployment benefits provided by workers' insurance schemes.

As we have said, workers' insurance-based protection schemes are still distinct from general welfare measures, but the dividing line is beginning to blur. Some insurance-based protection schemes are relaxing the connection with workers' employment records and, at the same time, welfare provisions such as the minimum wage are gathering in large groups of workers at risk of poverty. It has been noted that the various forms of minimum wage have increasingly taken on the function of supporting people in poorly paid employment, in addition to combatting poverty. This new task leads us to consider the design and application of the minimum wage, not only on account of its effects on poverty but also for the impact it may have on the dynamics of the labour market.

We need to consider that the guaranteed wage levels in most European countries (with a few exceptions) are not sufficient to take the beneficiaries out of poverty, but only reduce its intensity, and this deficiency also persists in the case of poor workers, as shown by the German mini-jobs experiment.

To such an extent that, to remedy the deficiency, the German government decided to introduce a national minimum salary, i.e. a specific measure that has an impact not on welfare, like the minimum wage, but directly on the content of the employment relationship. This decision confirms that the two instruments of social protection and market regulation are operating in different spheres, but need to be coordinated in the way they function, as well as in the levels of benefits paid out.

This intersection of functions and their growing importance raises a more general issue, which we can only mention briefly here. In order to evaluate the various policy options, there needs to be some in-depth analysis of the spread and new manifestations of poorly paid work in modern labour markets.

Comparative analyses of legal minimum wage provisions have shown that fears that they may have a negative influence on the dynamics of employment are unfounded.

Similar analyses are needed to find out whether and how income support measures affect changes in poorly paid jobs, how we can avert the risk that they will tend to perpetuate the spread of such jobs and how they can be useful, in combination with active development policies, in helping people out of the poverty trap.

The closely related nature of these provisions is also working in a different way, in the sense that some social security provisions aim to encourage beneficiaries to be active in the labour market, as well as performing their traditional compensatory function.

The fact is that the traditional functions of welfare provisions are also open to further enrichments, in some degree already achieved, whereby such provisions are deployed as forms of social investment, intended not only to defend certain levels of income, but also to promote people's capacities and human development.[36]

§2.12 THE ROLE OF THE NATION STATE IN GLOBALIZATION

We have several times noted that the issues of regulation and policy covered by our analysis have attracted different solutions in different countries, and this diversity confirms the importance of the choices made by national institutions and actors in responding to the global changes taking place.

In recent years, we have also seen growing state interventionism in many sectors of labour law and social security, and even in industrial relations, an area which has always been particularly resistant to outside interference.

Only some of these legislative interventions have followed common trajectories. On the whole, they have accentuated regulatory and policy divergences, even in relatively homogeneous areas long committed to convergence such as the European Union (EU), to the point of taking on an unprecedented nationalistic character, even in the social sphere.[37]

The comparative analyses presented by Prof. Cruz confirm that the role of the State as an actor in regulation and policy continues to be decisive and without competition (partly) because globalization has not produced public organizations endowed with regulatory powers akin to those of national governments.

But the same analyses show that this role has been weakened for a number of convergent reasons. On the one hand, competition between countries and the transfer of many essential decisions affecting community life to settings much broader than those in which state institutions operate have reduced the scope for independent decision-making on the part of national governments. The factors behind the current changes brook no frontiers and operate with an unprecedented intensity in increasing the interdependence of the various national systems.

In addition, technological and social changes have affected the efficacy of the regulatory and policy instruments with which national governments have operated, primarily legislation and partly collective bargaining. It is clear that the weakening of the authority of nation states also represents a crisis for traditional regulatory instruments and legal categories. Not only are traditional legislative sources losing their prestige in favour of 'soft' regulations or general principles, but the new transnational sources referred to above are developing along uncertain lines that reflect the weaknesses and/or disagreements between the actors concerned.

One of the most discussed manifestations of this crisis is the transformation of legislative sources, with the emergence of various forms of 'soft' law. It is no

36. Cf. M. Ferrera, *From the Welfare State to the Social Investment State*, in Riv. Int. Sc. Sociali, 2009, 3-4, pp. 513 ff.; *Investire nel sociale. La difficile innovazione del welfare italiano*, ed. M. Ascoli, C. Ranci, G.B. Sgritta, Mulino, 2015, especially pp. 7 ff.
37. Cf. R. Pedersini, *European Industrial Relations Between Old and New Trends*, in Stato e Mercato, 2014, pp. 345 ff; and the European Reflection Paper *On the social dimension of Europe* (COM 2013), pp. 206–207.

coincidence that these new regulatory forms have been used very widely in the regulation of various kinds of supranational relationship (and not only in relation to labour matters), where the regulatory authority of nation states cannot be exercised. In the EU system, soft-law techniques have been adopted as being best suited to laying down guidelines for the regulation of emergent new forms of employment on the cutting edge of the labour market.[38]

The regulatory crisis has also affected collective labour agreements, especially at national level, which have traditionally reproduced the regulatory techniques of national legislation. In the meantime, forms of intervention are taking root in negotiations at company level that are midway between 'micro' regulation and the often bilateral management of labour relations in the day-to-day administration of employment contracts.

The consequence, as observed by many people, is that a plurality of both forms and levels of regulation – national, international and, on our continent, European – has begun to operate in our field. In addition, we have seen the development of regional and local regulatory sources, also affecting labour issues, encouraged by the decentralization of the economy and corporate relations.[39]

While it is true that the origin and consequences of labour regulation are manifested at national level, it is by no means certain that, in the future, such regulation and state action will be able to cope with the challenges presented by international markets.

At the same time, the projection of regulations beyond national frontiers is limited in its effectiveness by the fact that the instruments defining and implementing the rules still depend on national authorities and powers.

---

38. But their significance and real impact have always been subject to contrasting assessments. *See* the various articles brought together in M. Barbera (ed.), *Nuove forme di regolazione: il metodo aperto di coordinamento delle politiche sociali*, Milano, Giuffrè, 2006; B. Caruso, *Il diritto del lavoro fra hard e soft law: nuove funzioni e nuove tecniche normative*, in WP CSDLE 'Massimo D'Antona', INT., 39/2005; S. Sciarra, *Is Flexicurity a European Policy?*, in G. Bronzini et al. (ed.), *Le scommesse dell'Europa. Diritti, istituzioni, politiche*, Roma, Ediesse, 2009, pp. 293 ff.
39. The diversity of the environments in which these new sources are active, and their diverse nature, is transforming from within the traditional institutions handed down from the twentieth century. The change is already visible in the products of industry-related, and above all company-related, transnational collective bargaining. The content of these agreements – especially those stipulated between multinationals and EWCs – are more circumscribed than the often all-embracing content of traditional industry-related collective bargaining and are mostly specialized in relation to the topics of priority interest for the contracting companies. Moreover, the main emphasis is on the 'obligatory' part and on relations between the various group entities, rather than on the regulation of individual employment relationships, which for the most part are left to the local human resources departments in the countries concerned. The distance compared with the bargaining conducted within the individual companies is even more marked where the efficiency mechanisms of transnational agreements are concerned. These cannot be based on (direct) legal instruments, given the diversity of the rules in force in the various countries where the multinationals operate, and therefore the influence is expressed more than ever on the level of efficiency, guaranteed by the rules and decisions of the companies themselves. Similarly distinctive, as we shall see, are the contents and efficiency mechanisms of the social clauses of trade agreements.

To conclude on this point, I would point out that there is a contradiction or tension in the present relationship between globalization and state initiative, the full implications of which are not generally understood.

As unbiased authors also point out, State action is important, indeed vital, in tackling the negative effects that uncontrolled globalization can have on living conditions and even on people's sense of identity. Not doing enough to protect citizens and workers, especially those who have been defined as the 'losers from globalization' has fuelled protests and reactions of a populist and nationalistic character in many countries, with enormous effects on political life.

This gives rise to a new and critical problem: defining what measures are acceptable in mitigating the negative effects of globalization, and at what point such measures cross the borderline with protectionism and forms of economic and social nationalism that are contrary to the principles of universality and cooperation between countries as enshrined in international charters, beginning with those of the ILO. These principles point the way not to mere defence of one's national assets, even less to pulling up the drawbridge, but rather to greater international commitment on the part of nation states to strengthening the weak international apparatus for regulating social relations.

§2.13 INSTRUMENTS FOR INTERNATIONAL LABOUR REGULATION: SOCIAL CLAUSES IN TRADE AGREEMENTS

Our comparative analyses show how various vectors and techniques for regulating supranational labour relations have been tried and tested.

The social clauses in international trade agreements are widely used, directly involving the regulatory and administrative role of the State. Modifying a well-known formula, one might say that such clauses have the consensual form of a contract, but have an interstate substance that is accentuated in the implementation phase. Their implementation is in fact based on relations between public bureaucracies. It is free of legal interventions and, when verification by third parties is required, recourse it had to arbitration procedures, which are embedded in the public procedure but maintain a private, often party-based, essence.

As the reports of Profs. Perulli and Bellace illustrate, clauses of this kind are included in a growing number of international agreements and have developed in terms of content, expressing increasingly stringent commitments by the parties concerned, particularly regarding compliance with the ILO's core labour standards.[40] But, as J. Bellace observes, the link between the social clauses and the ILO conventions on fundamental rights is still unclear in many cases and needs to be reinforced. Procedures for the implementation of these commitments are also expressed in complex formulae.

40. Cfr. also T. Treu, *Globalizzazione e diritti umani: le clausole sociali dei trattati commerciali e negli scambi internazionali fra imprese*, Stato e Mercato, 2017, pp. 7 ff.; T. Treu, *Globalization and Human Rights. Social Clauses in Trade Agreements and in International Exchanges among Companies*, in A. Perulli, T. Treu (eds), *Sustainable Development. Global Trade and Social Rights*, W. Kluwer, 2018, pp. 99 ff.

Most recently, the agreements between the EU and Canada (CETA) and between the EU and Japan (EPA) have included significant procedural innovations, providing for panels of experts and the involvement of civil society to provide comments and opinions on the implementation of the clauses concerned, and even setting up impartial specialized tribunals to settle disputes with private investors in respect of the Treaty, thus avoiding the disadvantages reported by many in the so-called ISDS system.[41]

But such procedures continue to be the weakest part of these instruments because their enforcement depends essentially on the initiative of the governments stipulating the agreements (and in actual fact on their bureaucrats), and in practice they are applied with varying degrees of effectiveness.

In addition, public opinion in many countries continues to view trade agreements with suspicion because there is often a lack of transparency in the way they are concluded, and because of doubts as to whether the social clauses protect against the risk of such agreements opening the way for a 'race to the bottom' where social and environmental standards are concerned.

At the same time, the very existence and usefulness of present forms of multilateral negotiation of the rules of international trade are now being challenged by the renascent protectionism championed by many countries, first and foremost the United States.

In reality, as the Perulli report notes, the justification for social clauses cannot be solely economic. They need to be seen in a wider context, as instruments promoting sustainable development and human rights.

§2.14 CONTINUED: CODES OF CONDUCT AND TRANSNATIONAL COLLECTIVE AGREEMENTS

Other vehicles for the international regulation of labour relations are driven by the social partners. Some, such as codes of conduct, are unilateral initiatives on the part of multinational enterprises; others, for instance various kinds of collective labour agreement, are bilateral in character.

Codes of conduct have gained traction and been enriched to the point of including principles similar to those contained in international charters of human rights.[42] But they continue to lack binding legal efficacy and their impact depends on companies' internal monitoring procedures, and therefore on their determination to comply with them. More effective than these procedures has been the pressure of public opinion and

41. Cfr. M. Faioli, *The Quest for a New Generation of Labour Chapter in the TTIP*, Economia & Lavoro, 2015, pp. 101 ff., especially pp. 111 ff.; in general, L. Compa, *Labor Rights and Labor Standards in Transatlantic Trade and Investment Negotiations. A US Perspective*, Economia & Lavoro, 2015, pp. 87 ff.
42. Cfr. in general, N. Rogovsky, *Socially Sensitive Enterprise Restructuring*, ILO, Geneva, 2005; A. Perulli (ed.), *La responsabilità sociale dell'impresa. Idee e prassi*, Mulino, Bologna, 2013; and very recently, D. Gottardi, *CSR la scelta unilaterale datoriale a oggetto di negoziazione collettiva: la responsabilità sociale contrattualizzata*, in F. Guarriello, C. Stanzani (eds), *Sindacato e contrattazione nelle multinazionali*, F. Angeli, 2018, pp. 59 ff.

the civil organizations of the countries involved, whose criticisms can damage companies' reputations.

Different and potentially more significant prospects arise from the development of various forms of transnational collective agreement. F. Guarriello's report shows positive developments in both the content and the procedures implementing such agreements.

Some multinationals, particularly those based in Europe, maybe influenced by the social and institutional context, have consulted trade union organizations in preparing their codes of conduct and have concluded a growing number of collective agreements with these organizations or, more often, with European Works Councils (EWCs).[43]

The rapid increase in these agreements has been encouraged by the trend towards the decentralization of industrial relations to company level. But they are limited in their effectiveness because collective labour agreements do not have a common legal status in Europe. At the same time, international trade union organizations which sign collective agreements, for instance with employers, have not received powers from their national associations to represent them with binding effect, though there has been some movement in this direction.

Here again, the role of the State may be decisive in compensating for the weakness of these agreements with innovative regulatory and promotional instruments.

In any case, these international agreements, like other international sources, are effective only within national legal systems. In the absence of the common legal status of a supranational source, states can only ascribe legal force to these agreements in accordance with the regulations that apply to national collective agreements. They can do so by adopting regulatory and support measures that take account of the features of the supranational agreements, which often include provisions that are different and more specialized than those of national agreements.

Many legal systems, and not only European ones, ascribe to collective agreements stipulated by the most representative social partners effects that go beyond the sphere of the partners themselves (*erga omnes*). Ascribing to agreements stipulated by supranational organizations legal effects that apply to member national associations and their members would be a different kind of extension, but justifiable if deemed useful for the regulation of relations concerning the sphere of representation of the stipulating parties, albeit operating in different national contexts.

An intervention of this kind would give the supranational rules greater effectiveness than could be achieved by international organizations exercising their (weak) powers of influence over the national associations that form their membership.

43. Cfr. in general, European Commission, *Industrial Relations in Europe*, 2014, pp. 117 ff.; M. Peruzzi, *L'autonomia del dialogo sociale europeo*, Mulino, 2011; S. Sciarra, *Transnational and European Way Forward for Collective Bargaining*, in WP CSDLE 'M. D'Antona', INT., 73/2009, pp. 20 ff.; U. Rehfeldt, *La posta in gioco. La contrattazione collettiva aziendale transnazionale*, in M. Carrieri, T. Treu, *Verso nuove relazioni industriali*, Mulino, 2015, pp. 159 ff.; G. Casale, *Collective Bargaining at the Transnational Level*, in A. Perulli, T. Treu, *Enterprise and Social Rights*, cit., pp. 161 ff.

The collective agreements concluded by multinationals with trade unions or works councils can have a direct impact on the regulation of labour relations through the implementing decisions taken by such enterprises, as they take into account the obligations they have assumed in exercising their management powers.

§2.15 INSTRUMENTS FOR MAKING TRANSNATIONAL COLLECTIVE AGREEMENTS MORE EFFECTIVE

National legal systems can support the negotiation of transnational agreements by recognizing the binding nature of these agreements for the stipulating parties, in particular the contractual obligations assumed by the multinational enterprises concerned. The effects of such recognition, and the enforcement of the contractual obligations, will depend on the specific national regulations and can be arranged in different ways. These modalities need to be explored through legal analysis, a project still to be undertaken.

Moreover, national support can be organized in advance of negotiations, in ways already adopted in some legal systems, i.e., by attributing negotiating and participatory powers to the workers' representatives in these enterprises, as provided for by German co-management regulations.[44]

Regulations of this kind would strengthen the capacity of these representatives to co-determine working conditions in the various units of the multinational enterprises and would support the transnational scaling-up of virtuous labour relations of the kind widely tried in the history of industrial relations and currently practised under some recent agreements between multinationals and EWCs.

There have been few practical tests of the possibility of legal verification of the effects of these transnational agreements because the parties tend to settle disputes relating to the application of the agreements via internal arbitration procedures. National tribunals are reluctant to rule on questions that have arisen in other jurisdictions because this would imply recognition of the extraterritorial efficacy of labour legislation.

The collective bargaining undertaken in groups of enterprises may be fertile ground for experimenting with innovative solutions in this area. Group agreements can influence the behaviour of the various group units, even if located in different countries, taking advantage of constraints internal to the group, in particular if managed by the group's dominant enterprise.[45]

Such constraints may also be supported on the external legal level by taking advantage of the tendency already present to some extent in many legal systems to

44. Cfr. For the latest developments in such regulation, M. Weiss, *Workers' Participation in the Enterprise in Germany*, in A. Perulli, T. Treu (eds), *Enterprise and Social Rights*, cit., pp. 293 ff.
45. Cfr. S. Leader, *Enterprise Network and Enterprise Groups. Trends and National /International Experience*, in A. Perulli, T. Treu, *Enterprise and Social Rights*, cit., pp. 121 ff; V. Speziale, *Groups of Companies and Employment Contracts*, in A. Perulli, T. Treu, *Enterprise and Social Rights*, cit., pp. 147 ff; M. Barbera, *Trasformazioni della figura del datore di lavoro e flessibilizzazione delle regole del diritto*, in GDLRI, 2010, pp. 203 ff.; L. Corazza, O. Razzolini, *Who Is an Employer?*, in M. Finkin, G. Mundlak (eds), *Comparative Labor Law*, Edward Elgar, 2015.

ascribe unitary legal status to a group of enterprises, and in particular to attribute responsibility for the behaviour of the group companies to the dominant enterprise. The most explicit example of this is the French law adopted in 2017, mentioned by F. Guarriello in his report, which requires a parent company (and also a main contractor) to supervise the activities of its peripheral units, subcontractors and suppliers, and to establish the liability of these companies for damages caused by violations of human rights and environmental standards, even if committed abroad.

Interestingly, one of the few cases of the transnational efficacy of collective agreements concerns a group-related dispute initiated by a Korean trade union in contesting the dismissal of an employee in violation of a collective group agreement. The action was taken against the American parent company of the Korean enterprise. The judge, ruling in New York, admitted his competence by recognizing the violation of the collective agreement, and undue interference with the local management by the parent company, though he did not feel able to confirm the responsibility of the parent company because of a procedural obstacle.[46]

If a ruling of this kind were confirmed, the unitary status of the group, already recognized in various aspects of case law in national legal systems, including Italy, would be extended 'across frontiers'. This would be a very important innovation because it would confirm that transnational group agreements could be used as a source of regulation of labour relations, outside the limits and without the involvement of national legal systems.

To conclude this point, experience indicates that, in the absence of a supranational authority, the development of more effective social rules in global economic relations must rely on a large number of different implementing strategies and instruments. These can be activated either by public institutions, national governments or international institutions as they apply their own legal arrangements, treaties, conventions and regulations, or alternatively by corporate organizations, in the form of codes of conduct, guidelines and collective agreements. The weakness of existing international bodies with competence in social matters limits their capacity to contribute to the social regulation of globalization. It is therefore important to use the existing instruments as best we can to promote by consensus the convergence and international application of at least the fundamental social principles and standards.[47]

§2.16 THE IMPACT OF DECENTRALIZATION ON THE NATURE AND CONTENT OF COLLECTIVE BARGAINING

The group researching 'Organization, productivity and wellbeing at work', coordinated by T. Araki and S. Laloum, has confirmed that the current changes in the world of work

46. Cf. further elements T. Treu, *Globalizzazione e diritti umani*, cit., pp. 35 ff.; L. Compa, *Pursing International Labor Rights in US Courts. New Uses for Old Tools*, in Ind. Relations 2002, vol. 57, I, pp. 48 ff.
47. The defence of fundamental rights acquired in some countries is essential, but not enough; indeed, as we have already seen, there is a risk of it attracting accusations of protectionism on the part of less developed countries. Cf. my thoughts on this in *Globalizzazione e diritti umani*, cit., pp. 45 ff.

and business have exerted strong pressures to decentralize collective bargaining, even in European countries which have traditionally had arrangements for nationwide category-based, or at least 'multi-employer', collective bargaining.[48] The European system has always been different from the systems of Anglo-Saxon and many Asian countries, where the main or exclusive level for bargaining has traditionally been the individual company.[49]

The trend towards the decentralization of production and contractual negotiation has general implications, indicating the (renewed or acquired) centrality of enterprises in the national and global economy. Especially since this decentralization is not only 'spatial' and technical, but is also becoming normative, also giving the enterprise or company a central role in the 'system of market regulation'.[50]

The group's research report shows how national legislators who have intervened in this field have encouraged the process of contractual decentralization, albeit on differing terms and with different impacts on the system.[51]

Some (e.g., the Spanish) have introduced radical changes, to the point of overturning the traditional hierarchy of the system, ascribing primary importance to company collective agreements and giving them general powers to amend agreements reached at a higher level. Others, as in France, have adopted more nuanced positions, ascribing priority to decentralized company agreements in regulating some matters not reserved for national agreements, but at the same time establishing an obligation on employers to bargain collectively in respect of the majority of working conditions.

The ability of the parties' central organizations to control decentralized processes also differs considerably. In some countries, such as Germany and Italy, it has been significant, at least in strong economic sectors and in medium-to-large enterprises, and has proved able to limit the scope of damaging company derogations.

But in every case this trend has resulted in a substantial alteration of the system and of the nature of the agreements concerned. National agreements have tended to become framework contracts, concentrating on regulating wage levels and minimum standards.

The role of central bargaining in coordinating the fundamental employment regulations in the various sectors, in particular in relation to wages, nevertheless remains important because a coordinated contractual system, as the OECD points out, results in fewer imbalances in remuneration and better employment conditions,

48. For a recent comparative survey of collective bargaining, *see The Role of Collective Bargaining in Labor Law Regimes*, U. Liukkunen, Report to the 20th Congress of the International Academy of Comparative Law.
49. On trends and problems relating to collective bargaining in Japan, cf. T. Araki, *Japan's Decentralized Industrial Relations, Internal Flexicurity and Challenges Japan Faces*, in A. Perulli, T. Treu, *Enterprise and Social Rights*, cit., pp. 173 ff.
50. A. Bavaro, *L'aziendalizzazione nell'ordine giuridico-politico del lavoro*, Lavoro & Diritto, 2013, pp. 213 ff.
51. Cfr. for the various positions, F. Guarriello, *Legge e contrattazione collettiva in Europa, verso nuovi equilibri*, DLRI, 2017, pp. 97 ff; T. Treu, *La contrattazione collettiva in Europa*, DRI, 2018, pp. 371 ff; and more recently, F. Guarriello, C. Stanzani (eds), *Sindacato e contrattazione nelle multinazionali*, cit.

especially for more vulnerable groups.[52] And, as the report presented by T. Araky shows, it responds better to the need to reconcile flexibility and secure regulation, and reduces the risk that decentralization will lead to the decollectivization of labour relations.

Decentralized bargaining tends to be more managerial than normative in the true sense, and in any case firm-specific, i.e., reflecting the priorities and needs of the individual company.

Local conditions and the quality of industrial relations are key in determining the significance of this development in decentralized bargaining and assessing whether it leads to better regulation of employment contracts. Is it more effective in reconciling the interest of the parties because it is close to the needs of each as expressed in local circumstances? Or do company agreements concluded in conditions of unequal power relationships tend to favour company rationality as opposed to the interests of workers. In Japan, where bargaining has traditionally taken place at company level, they have developed the practice of *shunto*, whereby demands are periodically made at national level to compensate for the results of in-company bargaining.

In the more advanced companies, collective bargaining and trade union activity generally are often in competition with innovative management in defining working and welfare conditions and creating a rational atmosphere that engages the loyalty of employees.[53]

§2.17 PAYMENT BY RESULTS AND CORPORATE WELFARE

Two particularly significant areas in this respect are bonus schemes and various forms of company welfare.

Forms of payment by results are part of the history of industrial relations, from traditional piecework, which we find reproduced in the new working practices of the gig economy, to the many variants of bonus payments, linked to sometimes very sophisticated indicators of productivity and company profitability, and various forms of profit-sharing and employee share ownership.

These forms of remuneration have always given rise to controversy because while on the one hand they may stimulate workers' motivation and contribute to flexible cost management, on the other they transfer part of the risk involved in running the company to the workers themselves.[54]

52. The importance of organizing the process of decentralization is recognized by many students of industrial relations. *See* C. Crouch, F. Traxler (eds), *Organized Industrial Relations, in Europe, What Future?*, Ashgate, 1995; and most recently, OECD, *Employment Outlook 2018*.
53. The importance of innovative managerial practices capable of promoting another way is emphasized by T. Kochan, *Challenges and Opportunities Facing ILERA and Our Field*, paper presented at the ILERA World Congress, Seoul, July 2018, to be published.
54. Cfr. in general, T. Treu, *Le forme retributive incentivanti*, in RIDL, 2010, no. 4, pp. 637 ff.; P. Campanella, *Decentramento contrattuale e incentivi retributivi nel quadro delle politiche di sviluppo alla produttività del lavoro*, in WP M. D'Antona, IT, 185/2013; M. Gandiglio, *Partecipazione agli utili; azionariato dei dipendenti e salario di produttività: dialoghi con le aziende sulla partecipazione finanziaria*, in M. Carrieri, T. Treu (eds), *Verso nuove relazioni industriali*, cit., pp. 113 ff.

In actual fact, the significance and impact of these incentives depend on various factors: the types of indicators chosen, the magnitude of the variable as compared with the fixed amount of remuneration and the degree of influence and participation of the workers concerned in the defining and administering the various incentive schemes.[55]

The trend towards contractual decentralization emphasizes their importance because it is within companies themselves and that these systems of remuneration are mostly devised and developed. And the quality of relations between the parties involved is therefore the key factor in determining the outcomes.

Research confirms this. Indeed, it indicates that the effectiveness of incentive systems in achieving the stated objective of promoting company productivity cannot be assessed simply by observing the design and internal dynamics of the bonuses, but must take into account the overall context of relations between the parties, i.e. the degree of participation of all those concerned in managing the schemes.

Forms of welfare that supplement public provision also go back a long way in many systems, but they have acquired different content and fresh importance in recent years because of the inadequacies of public social security provision, and due to the spread of new and more individual needs among workers.[56]

In many countries, including those with consolidated public welfare systems, forms of company benefits, whether unilaterally accorded or negotiated, have become an important component of the social protection system. The result is that this system is now based on two or more pillars in addition to public provision: collective welfare and private insurance arrangements. These two pillars have mobilized growing amounts of private social spending in order to meet needs that in many cases would otherwise remain unmet.

Research shows that supplementary welfare benefits can contribute not only to the welfare of workers and to company productivity, but also, if well distributed and targeted, to the overall efficiency of the system, in particular in promoting a mixed service economy. It generally emerges that these positive effects depend on benefits being geared to priority social needs not met by the public system and, in addition, on

55. Cfr. in general, M. Carrieri, P. Nerozzi, Introduction, *Partecipazione e democrazia nelle imprese: un'altra via è possibile*, in M. Carrieri, P. Nerozzi, T. Treu (eds), *La partecipazione incisiva*, Mulino, 2015, pp. 7 ff; L. Zoppoli, R. Santagata, *Il coinvolgimento dei lavoratori nella gestione delle imprese e l'azionariato di base collettiva*, ivi, pp. 299 ff.; L. Pero, A. Ponzellini, *Il nuovo lavoro industriale tra innovazione organizzativa e partecipazione diretta*, ivi, pp. 45 ff.; and for a specific case, P. Pini (ed.), *Innovazione, relazioni industriali e risultati di impresa*, Milano, F. Angeli, 2008.

56. Cfr. in general, S. Malandrini, *Contrattazione di prossimità e welfare aziendale*, RIDL, 2013; T. Treu (ed.), *Welfare aziendale 2.0*, IPSOA, Walter Kluwer 2016; and F. Maino, G. Mallone, *Welfare aziendale contrattuale e territoriale. Trasformazioni in atto e prospettive di sviluppo*, ivi, pp. 73 ff.; *Terzo rapporto sul secondo welfare*, ed. by M. Ferrera, F. Maino, 2017; E. Pavolini, U. Ascoli, M.L. Mirabile, *Il welfare delle aziende in Italia*, Mulino, Bologna, 2013, pp. 13 ff.; A. Tursi, *Il welfare aziendale. Profili 'costituzionali'*, Riv. Politiche Sociali, 2012; B. Caruso, *The bright side of the moon. Politiche del lavoro personalizzate e promozione del welfare occupazionale*, in RIDL, 2016, pp. 177 ff.; ID, *Recenti sviluppi normativi e contrattuali del welfare aziendale (nuove strategie di gestione del lavoro o neoconsumismo?)*, in RIDL, 2018, gone to press.

their being distributed in a balanced way throughout the system, and in particular in small enterprises.

Careful selection of priorities for this kind of welfare and balanced distribution of the resources necessary to sustain it are necessary conditions if such provisions are to supplement the system of protections in a balanced way and not increase inequalities.

Achieving these conditions depends on their management by the social partners, together with policy decisions made under the various legal systems. In many countries, the development of company welfare benefits has been supported by the legislator with different kinds of tax incentives. In some cases, as in Italy, it is a condition that the benefits must be negotiated between the parties or managed through participatory procedures, in which case the incentives are increased. These forms of welfare do in fact lend themselves to cooperative management and have proved to be particularly appreciated if the beneficiaries are informed and involved in the way they work (Finance laws for 2016 and 2017; Law 208/2015, Article 1 (189 ff); Law 205/2017; and Leg. Decree 80/2015, Article 25).

The innovations introduced in the two areas mentioned above have implications not only for the concept of an enterprise, but also for the content of the employment relationship.

The traditional exchange arrangement, fixed remuneration for stable work, has been changing as a result of new developments in the ever-more-variable forms of employment and in the ways in which they are remunerated. The departure from the traditional exchange arrangement is particularly marked when the parameters of these forms of remuneration do not depend directly on the quality and quantity of the work performed, but on external factors connected with the company's economic and/or financial progress, as in the case of participation in company profits, possibly effected through the distribution of shares and stock options.

Contractual welfare measures inject a further variant into the relationship because these do not translate into monetary payments but into benefits in the form of services. Unlike bonuses, these measures are not direct incentives. They nevertheless benefit the worker, but rather in meeting personal or collective needs relating to the welfare of the individual and his or her family. We might say that they enrich the content of the relationship through an exchange of a social, rather than a market-related, goods.

This innovation corresponds to a general and long-standing development in the concept of remuneration, as opposed to straightforward pay, as experienced in other reciprocal relationships.

The growth of welfare is a further manifestation of the social enrichment taking place in the changing pattern of labour relations because it associates welfare with the worker's personal and family needs, which can also be met within the company and the employment relationship itself. This development reflects changes in the character not only of individual employment relationships but also of labour relations generally, guiding them towards forms that are in the broad sense participatory.

§2.18 MATTERS FOR FURTHER RESEARCH

The observations made in this paper lead us to reflect on new problems we shall have to face. They point to areas that will require further exploration because clearly the present circumstances regarding employment and its regulation present more uncertainties than definite tendencies. The components of the new employment mosaic have only partially fallen into place, which means that all the new developments analysed in our research are problematic.

The objectives and functions of labour law are more fully developed than those concerned with the protection of workers, which are not easy to fit into a pattern. Our discipline, with its different protagonists and ever more levels of regulation, is required to satisfy tangible and intangible needs more complex than those of the workers of the industrial era.

Workers' needs for protection are still essential, but the needs themselves are changing in response to new circumstances arising both from different kinds of employment, whether subordinate, freelance or mixed, and from the contexts in which they are performed. Moreover, present-day production systems are far removed from the Fordian enterprise model, which has been disrupted by digital technologies and restricted in its decision-making by global competition.

If they are to be effective, the objectives and techniques of protection need to be changed, taking into account the sheer variety of digital employment and the functional requirements of global business. The reconciliation of different interests, which has always been the task of labour law, implies innovative choices, themselves having to be developed in conditions of uncertainty.

For this reason, our discipline is called to differentiate its interventions and develop a common core of employment standards that can be applied to all jobs. In this wider area of application, it needs to come to terms with human rights.[57]

In addition, the increasing mobility and variability of both employment and the organization of production means that our discipline must equip itself with new legal and managerial tools to regulate transitions between different jobs, which are an increasingly common aspect of people's careers.

In this respect, labour law plays the part of a labour-market institution, being able to make the market work more efficiently from an economic and social point of view. In this respect, too, our discipline will have to perform new tasks. One is to optimize job opportunities, and this applies to all jobs, from subordinate, freelance and third-sector jobs to service jobs and those of social importance, which the market penalizes because it fails to value them. Another of its tasks will be to improve the quality of human capital, providing support for continuous professional development as jobs and workers become more mobile.

In international best practice, support for the transition between one job and another is not only for the unemployed, but is also available in the course of

57. Some of these thoughts have already been sketched out in my book *Il diritto del lavoro: realtà e possibilità*, ADL, 2000, especially pp. 520 ff.

employment, in anticipation of changes and corporate crises, involving enterprises themselves in policies to develop and upgrade their workers' skills and competencies.

Thus, the regulation of labour relations is integrated with the tasks of promoting jobs on the labour market and ensuring employment continuity and opportunity.

In this vision, which is barely outlined in the various practices, labour law can become an instrument contributing to enterprise and market efficiency, as well as economic development.[58]

With this goal in mind, incentive payments/bonuses and supplementary welfare, mentioned above, are of special significance, especially in a context of participatory labour relations. With the spread of such phenomena, the task of our discipline, which has always been required to balance the opposing (or at least differing) interests and values of labour and business, needs to be conducted with one main objective: to pursue the interests of both with a view to common development in achieving both quality and the fair distribution of rewards.

Market volatility and uncertainty have put welfare and social security policies back centre stage, and point up the need for closer links with employment policy. Both are called to meet the security needs of all workers, subordinate and self-employed, in work and unemployed. These needs are different and more diffuse than the risks covered by traditional social insurance; they require forms of coverage adapted to market instability and able to provide active security in unstable economic circumstances.

Industrial relations are also affected more directly than individual labour law by changed economic conditions and changes in the relative strengths of the parties. As we have seen, the shift in the centre of gravity of collective bargaining to enterprise level is obliging the parties, and primarily the trade unions, to face up to new labour and business problems without the defences of national, legal and contractual regulation, often in competition with the initiatives of innovative management. Regulated coordination involving both in-company and national bargaining is important in lending stability to the system and avoiding the dangers of 'decollectivization'.

The ambitious objectives adopted by the protagonists of our discipline are being pursued under differing conditions within the various national contexts, and often in production sectors that are more or less exposed to the shocks of competition.

The search for new solutions is being conducted, as we have seen, not only with more or less urgency but also with differing approaches. There are differences even between neighbouring countries in Europe, despite the fact that they have established common regulatory mechanisms, but these have not withstood growing populism and often state-sponsored nationalism.

The diversity of regulatory systems coexists with opposing global trends towards standardization, which some people think could lead to convergence in the deregulation of traditional labour law arrangements.[59]

---

58. P. Davies, *Lavoro subordinato e lavoro autonomo,* in DRI, 2000, pp. 208 ff.
59. Cfr. the well-known thesis: L. Baccaro, C. Howell, 2011, *A Common Neoliberal Trajectory. The Transformation of Industrial Relations in Advanced Capitalism,* Politics and Society, no. 3,

The increasingly transnational dimension of labour and business matters calls for research and initiatives to gain a deeper understanding of the implications of growing interdependence among national systems.

The regulation of these matters has relied on a network of instruments that have been agreed over time, but which are still fragile because they lack support from national governments.

While all sectors of national legal systems are facing difficulties because of their territorial anchorage, the crisis in labour regulation is aggravated by the structural asymmetry between the increasing mobility of enterprises and the limited mobility of labour.

In the absence of effective transnational regulation of working conditions, the trends towards competition and divarication among national systems are bound to increase. These trends are reinforced by growing inequalities in economic and social circumstances between and within countries.

There are no predetermined outcomes where labour regulation is concerned, as our analysis makes clear. Nation states, which played a decisive role in the last century in constructing legal and social systems capable of improving people's working and living conditions, are now called to apply themselves to the establishment and spread of supranational rules and institutions that can promote the same objectives of welfare and social progress for all the world's citizens.

Accepting the present disparities in the global employment situation by concentrating national powers on the defence of the status quo would only magnify the imbalances and injustices and would betray the mission of our discipline, which is to fairly regulate the working and living conditions of all working people.

pp. 521-563, and most recently L. Baccaro, C. Howell, *The Trajectories of Neoliberal Transformation*, Cambridge University Press, 2018.

CHAPTER 3

Learning from Our Past: What Would Our Most Respected Forefathers and Mothers Want Us to Do in Our Time of Crisis?*

Thomas A. Kochan

It can be tempting to see our current political moment as unique. The 2016 U.S. presidential election and the actions that have followed laid bare how deeply divided our nation is by income, region, and political ideology. Trust in government and the key institutions in civil society—business, labor, education—have fallen to some of the lowest levels observed in years. Political discourse has devolved, and our labor and employment policies are woefully out of date and ill-prepared to address changes in work. Meanwhile, longstanding political gridlock in Washington continues to block any efforts to update them.

Indeed, America is not alone. Too many nations in Europe are similarly torn between extreme political groups. The rise of intolerance for immigrants and the turn to neo-fascist political candidates has risen to dangerous levels while authoritarian leadership practices are proliferating.

In many respects, these conditions are quite similar to the 1930s and so perhaps it is time for each of us to look back and ask: What can we learn from our experiences in that difficult era.

* This paper was prepared for presentation at the World Congress of the International Society for Labour and Social Security Law in Turin, Italy, September 4, 2018. It is drawn from remarks made at the Frances Perkins Center Annual Garden Party, Newcastle Maine on August 19, 2018. An abridged version is published in *The Boston Review* online edition, August 30, 2018. http://bostonreview.net/.

§3.01 ON THE SHOULDERS OF GIANTS: THE LEGACY OF FRANCES PERKINS

Fortunately, in the U.S. we have a role model to turn to for inspiration and guidance: Frances Perkins, the country's most innovative, influential, and accomplished Secretary of Labor (and first ever female member of a President's Cabinet).[1] She observed many similar troubling economic and political trends in America in the years before she took office at the request of President Franklin D Roosevelt in 1932.

As in the 1920s, the U.S. economy has been booming for the past five years with rising stock prices, strong profits, and robust employment growth. Yet now, as then, the majority of U.S. workers and families are not sharing in the prosperity—wages continue to lag growth in profits and productivity while income inequality has returned to the high levels of 1928.[2] Like the farmers who lost their land to the Dust Bowl and the industrial workers whose jobs evaporated in the aftermath of the stock market crash, today's economic forces have ravished workers, families, and communities that have been hardest hit by globalization and trade.[3]

Indeed, the United States today faces a similar dearth of courageous and intelligent action that Perkins rose up to fill. "Most of man's problems upon this planet, in the long history of the race," she wrote, "have been met and solved either partially or as a whole by experiment based on common sense and carried out with courage."[4] If we look to Perkins today, and if we learn from all that she accomplished on behalf of U.S. workers, we just might be ready to similarly rise to the occasion when the next window of opportunity to do so opens.

If that window of opportunity feels distant at the moment, it is crucial to note that Perkins's history-making relationship with President Roosevelt started long before he was elected; it was grounded in their shared experiences in New York. So, too we now need to begin the task of finding and working with candidates running for president and Congress who are ready to stand up for workers, families, and communities most in need of a new voice—candidates who, once elected, can be trusted to follow through.

Perkins recognized that her vision could not be fully realized without the support of the president and without having a seat at the table of economic policy making. She famously warned President Roosevelt not to nominate her for Secretary of Labor unless he was prepared to work with her to translate her labor protections into national policy.[5] He heartily accepted her challenge, and no Secretary of Labor since has been

1. For two good biographies of Frances Perkins, *see* George Martin, *Madame Secretary: Frances Perkins*. New York: Houghton Mifflin, 1976; Kirsten Downey, *The Woman Behind the New Deal*. New York: Doubleday, 2008.
2. Thomas Piketty and Emmanual Saez, "Income Inequality in the United States, 1918–1998." *Quarterly Journal of Economics*. 2003, 118, 1, 1–41.
3. David H. Autor, David Dorn, Gordon H. Hanson, and Kaveh Majlesi "Importing Political Polarization: The Electoral Effects of Rising Trade Exposure." MIT Department of Economics, Working Paper, December 2017.
4. Quote cited in https://www.brainyquote.com/authors/frances_perkins. Downloaded October 9, 2018.
5. Frances Perkins, *The Roosevelt I Knew*. New York: Viking Press, 1946, 152.

as influential in economic policy making nor has had the access and ear of the president like she did. This allowed her to win many internecine battles with the men in the Cabinet who saw her as an unwelcome rival.

And there were battles. When Perkins took office union membership was down to 11% of the workforce. Many economists and other experts said labor's day was over—the economy had changed and unions were no longer relevant. Fast forward to today and we see the same trend. Union membership has been in steady decline for years and is again down to 11%.

Once again, some believe labor's day is over—the economy has changed they say and labor leaders are woefully out of date with the changing workforce and changing nature of work. Perkins would, I believe, agree with part of this argument—the economy and workforce have changed and labor unions have been slow to adapt. Yet she would also recognize and applaud the fact that labor is opening up to new ideas and approaches and that a new generation of worker advocates—inside and alongside the labor movement—are using the tools of modern communications to give workers a voice.[6]

As Industrial Commissioner in New York—in the years before she went to Washington—Perkins helped foster such innovative thinking. She reached out to fellow Progressives in states such as Wisconsin and Massachusetts in order to experiment with and test new policy ideas for unemployment insurance, minimum wages, overtime, and safety and health. These state-level policies, as her periodic advisor Justice Louis Brandeis said, served as "laboratories for democracy."[7]

Today, we see similar experimentation with states increasing minimum wages, enacting paid sick and family leave policies, and testing new approaches to retirement insurance.[8] Once again we are well situated to translate these state-level innovations into national policy.

§3.02 FRAMING THE CHALLENGE: NEED FOR A NEW SOCIAL CONTRACT

Any national progress, however, has to start by framing the challenges and opportunities we face in ways that resonate with those who are frustrated and angry about being ignored and left behind as they bear the brunt of changes beyond their control. In my own writing, I have framed the task ahead as the need to build a new social contract or compact between U.S. workers and leaders in business, labor, education, and government—a compact that allows people to pursue their aspirations and

6. "Labor Union Research for the Labor Relations Community: Social Media for Labor Unions." Rutgers University Libraries, 2017. https://libguides.rutgers.edu/c.php?g=336780&p=2267265. Downloaded October 8, 2018.
7. Michael S. Greves, "Laboratories for Democracy: Anatomy of a Metaphor." American Enterprise Institute, March 31, 2001. http://www.aei.org/publication/laboratories-of-democracy/. Downloaded October 8, 2018.
8. Thomas A, Kochan, "Building Institutions to Strengthen Worker Voice." The Aspen Institute, August, 2018. https://www.aspeninstitute.org/blog-posts/building-the-institutions-needed-to-strengthen-worker-voice/. Downloaded October 8, 2018.

expectations for work while also holding each other accountable for structuring employment relationships that achieve a more productive and inclusive economy, broadly shared prosperity, and a just society.

Whether this metaphor or some other one helps communicate the broad idea, it must be successful in rebuilding trust in our key governmental, business, and civil society institutions and it must provide hope for those who have been left behind by globalization, technological change, and narrow and short-term focus of business on shareholder interests. And it needs to be backed up with specific actions capable of delivering on its promise. We need new employment policies that are as ambitious and broad-based as those Perkins envisioned as she and her colleagues invented the New Deal legislation that served U.S. economy and society well for five decades.

Those New Deal policies are now woefully out of date and some, like our basic labor law are badly broken. We need to take a comprehensive approach to develop a new set of employment policies capable of building a social contract suited to today and tomorrow's economy. Let me outline some basic building blocks for what I believe is needed.[9]

First, a modern employment policy has to be grounded in labor standards built for the modern labor force. The vast majority of Americans support increasing minimum wages and providing paid family and sick leave—just as states across the country are now doing. We need to learn from those innovations and make these bedrock principles of national policy so all who work earn a living wage and all who work can afford to start a family and care for family members when needed. The time has come to end the embarrassment of being the only industrialized country that does not ensure paid leave is available to all who work.

§3.03 CLOSING THE WINNERS-LOSERS GAP FROM GLOBALIZATION

There is a long overdue and dire need to focus directly on closing the existing gaps between the winners and losers from globalization.[10] The most direct and effective strategy for doing so is to invest in community economic development and innovation in the communities that have been hit hardest by job losses that build on their local competitive advantages at a scale equivalent to the infrastructure and job creation investments of the New Deal. American who travels overseas, or international visitors to the U.S., recognize just how far behind the U.S.'s physical and digital infrastructure already is—and it will continue to lag behind if adequate investments are not forthcoming. This is perhaps the one area of near consensus across business, labor, and party lines—a consensus that needs to move from words to actions.

---

9. A more complete outline of a comprehensive labor and employment policy is provided in Thomas Kochan and Lee Dyer, *Shaping the Future of Work*. Cambridge: MIT Press, 2017.
10. David H. Auto, David Dorn, and Gordon H. Hanson, "The China Syndrome: Local Labor Market Effects of Import Competition in the U.S." *American Economic Review*, 2013, 103, 2121-2168.

§3.04 PROACTIVE STRATEGIES FOR THE DIGITAL ECONOMY

We must ensure we do not make the same mistakes of not attending to those left behind from globalization as we experience how digital technologies will transform work of the future. This will require three initiatives.[11]

We need forward-looking policies that ensure everyone shares in the potential of the digital revolution. This starts by ensuring the workforce of today and tomorrow have the skills and ongoing training—what many call lifelong learning—needed to participate effectively in the digital economy. Perhaps the best way to ensure that all workers will have access to lifelong learning is to use tax policy to build lifetime training accounts and jointly funded and administered union management training programs so workers can take the time needed for training and continuous education.

Training alone, however, will not ensure that workers will share in the benefits of new technologies. Workers also need to have a voice in defining the problems these technologies address and in the early stage design decisions that will affect their jobs. We have learned this lesson from prior waves of automation, particularly from the auto industry in the 1980s. While companies like General Motors tried to automate their way back to being an industry leader and failed because they did not engage the workforce and integrate technology and work system strategies, Toyota came out the winner in auto markets around the world by effectively integrating innovations in technology and work systems and giving workers a voice in continuous improvement strategies—what the Japanese famously called "workers giving wisdom to these machines." Today, we need to build on this lesson and make sure that workers and their representatives have a voice in the earliest stages of the planning and design decisions that shape how digital technologies will transform, augment, and improve work and industry competitiveness.

Some people will lose their jobs to automation. America currently ranks near the bottom of advanced industrial countries in the percent of GDP (0.01%) invested in labor market adjustment policies, a rate far lower than Germany and Scandinavian countries. Yet the U.S. has a potentially rich set of educational institutions, labor organizations and labor advocacy groups, and other labor market intermediaries that could serve as instruments for aiding in lifelong learning and assisting those adversely affected by the changing economy.

Those nations that address all three of the challenges posed by the digital economy—providing lifelong learning to prepare workers to participate in the digital economy, ensuring workers have effective voices in shaping the early-stage decisions on technology and work systems, and providing suitable and equitable transition and income support policies—will be the winners in the coming wave of automation, and their workers will both accept technological change and share more fully in its benefits.

---

11. For a more detailed outline of these three points *see* Thomas Kochan and Lee Dyer, "Robots Won't Steal Our Jobs If We Put Workers at the Center of the AI Revolution." *The Conversation*. August 30, 2017. https://theconversation.com/robots-wont-steal-our-jobs-if-we-put-workers-at-center-of-ai-revolution-82474. Downloaded October 8, 2018.

§3.05 REBUILDING WORKER VOICE AND BARGAINING POWER: A "CLEAN SLATE" LABOR POLICY

Today, like in the 1930s, many proclaim labor's day if over—unions have been slow to adjust to changes in the economy and labor force and are no longer relevant institutions in our labor markets. Yet as our research at MIT is discovering, more workers than ever before want to join a union. In a national survey we conducted, about half of the nonunion workforce—the equivalent of 58 million workers—have told us they would join a union if given the opportunity to do so,[12] and the courageous teachers in states such as West Virginia, Oklahoma, and Arizona are speaking out more publicly for their right to fair pay.

I have no doubt that Frances Perkins would be hearing these calls from the workforce—and she would be acting. The forms of worker voice and representation these workers want and need go far beyond those envisioned in the 1935 labor law. That law is now so out of date and failing so miserably that a new "clean slate" approach, as colleagues at the Harvard Labor and Work Life Program have labeled it, [13] is needed. This does not mean we start in a vacuum, however. Just as the 1935 law built on innovations in collective bargaining that had been tested in the clothing industry, so too the best companies and the best union-management relationships in the U.S. today can serve as models for how to implement collaborative design processes that both generate improvements in productivity and new ways of working with advancing technologies. We can build, for instance, on successes like the one that has served one of our major health-care providers, Kaiser Permanente, and its workers and patients so well for the past twenty years. [14]

We can also go beyond the current boundaries of collective bargaining and allow new emerging models of worker voice and representation to grow and be tested. Across the country we are witnessing a wave of innovation in new forms of worker advocacy ranging from the fight for a USD 15 an hour minimum wage to use of artificial intelligence and machine learning tools to advise workers of their rights, to organizations that help workers file petitions to change employer practices and so on. We should learn from these experiments, evaluate them, and then build those that show the most promise for rebuilding worker voice and bargaining power into a new national labor policy. And perhaps we should pay special heed to the lessons of the biggest and boldest labor mobilization in the U.S. of this century: the broad-based coalition of workers, managers, and customers at a the Market Basket grocery company who, in the summer of 2014, stood up to save the good company they helped build from being

12. Thomas A. Kochan, Duanyi Yang, William T. Kimball, and Erin L. Kelly, "Worker Voice in America: Is There a Gap Between What Workers Expect and What They Experience?" *ILR Review*, 2019, 72, 1, 1-36.
13. "Clean Slate." Labor and Work Life Program, Harvard Law School. https://lwp.law.harvard.edu/programs/clean-slate. Downloaded October 8, 2018.
14. Thomas Kochan, Adrienne Eaton, Robert McKersie, and Paul Adler, *Healing Together: The Kaiser Permanente Labor Management Partnership*. Ithaca, NY: Cornell/ILR Press, 2009.

taken over by greedy shareowners.[15] Their courageous actions sent a message heard across the country: U.S. workers and customers value successful companies that produce good profits, good jobs, good customer service, and are good citizens in their communities. These employees and customers ignored the constraints of labor law and in doing so successfully illustrated what is possible if we let people exercise their voices in new ways.

§3.06 INTEGRATED SYSTEMS OF WORKPLACE JUSTICE

A new "clean slate" law could account for much of this, but any new set of labor laws will only be as good as the tools and avenues available to enforce them. Given the current makeup of the Supreme Court—and, indeed, the entire federal judiciary—some new approaches will be needed to ensure workplace justice is served. A new integrated system of justice has to be grounded on fair, effective conflict resolution systems at the workplace that are available to all who work regardless of their employment status.[16] These systems can draw on and embody the tried and true principles of due process developed over the years in labor arbitration and on the best practices of organizations that provide multiple options for addressing workplace issues such as ombuds advice, peer counseling and review, affinity group networks, and mediation.

Workplace systems, in turn, need to be backed up by effective enforcement strategies in the government agencies responsible for overseeing them. A very positive set of steps was taken by the Department of Labor during the latter years of the Obama Administration in updating overtime provisions and using modern innovative strategies for enforcing basic wage and hour laws. Today those innovative efforts have not only been abandoned, other actions have been taken to weaken safety and health, labor relations, pension protections, access to class action lawsuits, and countless other workplace rules.[17] To reverse these actions and to protect the American workforce against what will be a very hostile federal judiciary, I believe we need to learn from our partners in Europe and institute specialized labor courts staffed with knowledgeable, experienced, and trusted judges.[18] Workplace justice is too important to leave in the hands of the current and likely future judges dominating the federal

15. Daniel Korschum and Grant Welker, *We Are Market Basket.* Philadelphia: Temple University Press, 2015.
16. *See* Mary Rowe, "Guidelines for Designing Integrated Conflict Management Systems within Organizations." Committee Report for the Society of Professionals in Dispute Resolution, 2001. Available at: https://www.mediate.com/articles/spidrtrack1.cfm. Downloaded October 10, 2018.
17. Amela Semuels, "The Future of the Department of Labor under Trump." https://www.theatlantic.com/business/archive/2017/03/the-department-of-labor-under-trump/518307/. Downloaded October 10, 2018.
18. For a classic article analyzing the relevance of European labor courts to the United States, *see* Benjamin Aaron, "Labor Courts: Western European Models and their Significance for the United States." 16 *UCLA Law Review*, 1969, 847–882.

judicial system or in the hands of sham arbitration systems lacking due process protections that many firms have implemented.[19]

§3.07 TIME FOR OUR OWN WISDOM, COURAGE, AND ACTION

These, I believe, are just some of the basic building blocks of a new forward-looking labor and employment policy that would live up to the legacy of Frances Perkins. Many of the conditions we face today are similar to those she recognized as needing decisive action and, with wisdom and courage, she took up the mantle of challenging the powerful forces favoring the status quo. Inspired by her, we must do the same today.

Perhaps each of our countries has leaders like her from which equivalent wisdom and courage can be drawn. It is time for all of us to step up to the challenges of our time in ways that reflect the deep and long-standing values of our field of study, practice and public policy.

19. Alexander J.S. Colvin, "The Growing Use of Mandatory Arbitration." Economic Policy Institute, April 6, 2018. https://www.epi.org/publication/the-growing-use-of-mandatory-arbitration-access-to-the-courts-is-now-barred-for-more-than-60-million-american-workers/. Downloaded October 10, 2018.

CHAPTER 4

New Forms of Labour: New Solidarities?

Franz Marhold

§4.01 INTRODUCTION

When talking about new forms of social security it is understandable that we ask ourselves what the starting points and the ideas and ideologies of the existing concepts of social securities are in order to identify where and whether there is need of new forms of social security. New forms generally spoken may be reflected in different aspects of our social security systems.

First of all we could think about the scope of applicability of our social security regulations. Second we could think about new risks with which we could deal with social security instruments and whether it is still appropriate to organize social security protection along the definition of risks. Furthermore we could ask ourselves whether the benefits that our social security systems grant are still appropriate to cope with new challenges for our social security institutions. It is quite obvious that in the framework of this conference, it is impossible to present an in-depth research of all the possible questions linked to new forms of social security. In the contributions of the discussions we will see that there are far more aspects to be dealt with than I have just mentioned. The 4.0 societies may and will provoke the development of new perspectives on the traditional conceptions of social security and will dramatically show how the existing systems will come to their limits. I will profit of this rare chance to discuss basic questions of social security before the background of the dramatic changes that we might face in our economic systems.

§4.02 SOLIDARITY

The first topic that I want to deal with and which seems to me very relevant is the question of solidarity and solidarity who for whom. Our traditional concepts of social security both Bismarckian or Beveridge systems link social security protection with the belonging to a certain group be it employees, be it self-employed in commerce or in agriculture (so in Bismarckian systems) or to a given community be it city, region, province or state (Beveridge approach).[1]

The connection between the integration in a given social group and the social protection is reflected by the contribution which one member of the group makes to the whole society and the expectation of being protected by that given society from certain risks because of the fact that he has contributed to the protection system at first. In that sense there is no difference between social security systems based on taxes or on contributions. The reason for protection is the contribution to a system of common risk sharing which in the case of the manifestation of a social risk protects its members. Of course there are important technical legal differences between tax finance systems or systems based on contributions. However in the prospect of solidarity, solidarity only exists amongst the members of a given group, be it taxpayers or payers of contributions. Only the boundaries of risk sharing are narrower in Bismarckian systems because the belonging to the group is defined by the similar execution of an economic activity, whereas in a Beverage system it is the group of all citizens.

But is that really solidarity? Of course it is when thinking about the sharing of common risk by a group of workers or citizens who do not receive benefits as a mathematically defined result of their contribution to the system regarding their social situation.[2] The principle is still the same: Mutual protection of the taxpayers, contributors or residents. Such a system with all its historical and present merits and advantages has difficulties to cope with new challenges arising from the social needs of people, who did not contribute and have not been covered by a social programme which demands whatever kind of previous participation. That is why we can hear phrases in public discussions postulating that benefits may only be awarded to those who contributed in the first place. This is clear and even consequent in a logic of common risk sharing. Those who did not contribute to the risk sharing system should not profit from it. When the risk sharers are defined as citizens or residents one has at least to belong to the residing population.

It is the logic of our traditional systems which exclude non-residents, non-taxpayers, non-contributors from social protection.[3] Saying this, it is quite obvious what I am talking about is the limits of the capabilities of our social security systems to deal with the social situations of migrants and refugees, but as well with forms of non-standard employment or other non-economically active persons.

The jurisdiction of the Court of Justice of the European Union (CJEU), especially in the often discussed cases of *Brey*,[4] *Dano*[5] and *Alimanovic*,[6] made it visible that in the case of non-economic active migrants we are still in search for the necessary link

1. Cf. *Eichenhofer*, Sozialrecht der Europäischen Union[6] (2015) Rz 72.
2. Cf. *Pfeil*, Österreichisches Sozialrecht[10] (2014), 13.
3. Cf. *Kapuy*, Zugehörigkeit in der sozialen Sicherheit: Ändern sich die Zugehörigkeitskonzepte in Europa?, DRdA 2016, 396.
4. EuGH 19.9.2013, C-140/12, EU:C:2013:565.
5. EuGH 11.11.2014, C-333/13, EU:C:2014:2358.
6. EuGH 15.9.2015, C-67/14, EU:C:2015:597.

between the adherence to a community and the right to social protection. Free movement regulations chose time limits in order to constitute the relationship between belonging and receiving. It also sets limits to the financial capabilities of the states of residence to grant benefits to the non-economic active new participants. What we can see is that even in an integrated economic and political system as the European Union it is difficult to manage the social protection of people who do not belong to the group of risk sharers. Most of the discussions, be it in scientific literature or be it in politics, tour around this genuine link,[7] a link which we try and have to define because the existing concepts of solidarity focus on the protection of the group members and not on people coming from outside. However, it is not only the non-economic active migrants and the refugees who are affected by this concept. It is also the young people who are unable to get access to the protection schemes for labour market reasons. But how - in social security dimensions rather than mere political actions - can we deal with these situations? Can we find new forms of social security which can contribute to an improvement of that situation?

§4.03 LIMITS TO EQUAL TREATMENT

The idea of common risk sharing of course leads to equal treatment. People who join themselves together or are forced by law to join a group have to be treated equally of course; otherwise, the compulsory social security systems would not have any political and juridical legitimacy. If I belong or if I am forced to belong to a social security system, I at least may expect that I am treated in the same way as all the others risk sharers. The principle of equal treatment therefore is a result of the homogeneity of the risk sharing group. Therefore it is already questionable, whether it is appropriate to extend the principle of equal treatment to persons who - at least initially - did not belong to the group of risk sharers.

[A] Self-Employed Persons

In that respect, Austria has gradually extended the scope of its social security system to cover persons finding themselves in so-called non-standard employment relationships as well as self-employed persons.[8] While the first term includes everyone who is personally and economically dependent in a contractual relationship and receives a remuneration, the second term addresses independent contractors who are either in possession of a trading licence and are thus mandatory members of the Chamber of

7. Cf. *Rebhahn*, Bedürftigkeitsabhängige Sozialleistungen - Bedingungen, Pauschalierungen, Differenzierungen, DRdA 2017, 431 (436); Cf. *Kapuy*, Zugehörigkeit in der sozialen Sicherheit: Ändern sich die Zugehörigkeitskonzepte in Europa?, DRdA 2016, 396; Cf. *Schreiber*, Die Bedeutung des Aufenthaltsrechts für die sozialrechtliche Gleichbehandlung von Unionsbürgerinnen und Unionsbürgern, ZAR 2015, 46.
8. *Marhold*, Social Protection of Contingent Work: Austria and the Full Coverage Social Insurance System in *Ales/Deinert/Kenner* (eds), Core and Contingent Work in the European Union (2017) 233.

Commerce or generate a certain income.[9] As a result, there were legislative changes in 1997 to include those professions, which are not obliged to obtain a trading licence (such as for instance lawyers, veterinarians or architects) in the statutory insurance system. However, there is a possibility to opt-out of statutory insurance, provided another compulsory self-insurance system exists, which has equivalent benefits as does the statutory system.[10] Other legislative measures included self-employed persons into the statutory system of severance pay (2008), which is considered as a second pillar in the old-age insurance system[11] and gave self-employed the possibility to voluntarily join the Austrian unemployment insurance (2009). When it comes to the social protection of self-employed, Austria is ranked first according to a comparative study which analyzed the level of social protection for self-employed in eighteen European states.[12]

At European level, there is a certain tendency for upward convergence in this context. For example, in March 2018, as part of the implementation of principle twelve of the European Pillar of Social Rights, the European Commission has adopted a proposal for a Council Recommendation on access to social protection for workers and the self-employed.[13] The Recommendation does not stipulate binding results, but merely provides guidelines for national-level reforms.[14] In terms of content, the European Commission is aiming at closing formal coverage gaps and providing for an adequate effective coverage, especially when it comes to non-standard forms of employment. In order to better reflect the nature of self-employed work with regard to unemployment risk, it was decided to adopt a more refined approach, leaving the extension of coverage for unemployment benefits on a voluntary basis (point 9).

[B] Non-standard Work

Besides independent contractors, one of the most challenging questions of our time is to how to deal with persons, not falling under the term employee nor self-employed in terms of social security, especially when thinking of 'new' phenomena as platform-based or crowd and 'click' work.[15] Those persons who may be considered as an intermediate category are usually legally and personally independent while performing

9. *Auer-Mayer*, Die Grenze zwischen selbständiger und unselbständiger Tätigkeit aus sozialversicherungsrechtlicher Sicht, ZAS 2015, 4, for a more specific distinction.
10. *Marhold*, Social Protection of Contingent Work: Austria and the Full coverage Social Insurance System in *Ales/Deinert/Kenner* (eds), Core and Contingent work in the European Union (2017) 234.
11. *Gleitsmann/Kircher*, Soziale Errungenschaften für Selbständige aus rechtspolitischer Sicht, in *Aschauer/Kohlbacher* (eds), Jahrbuch Sozialversicherungsrecht 2017, 95.
12. *Traub/Finkler*, Soziale Absicherung von Selbständigen im internationalen Vergleich, Scientific study by order of the Austrian Economic Chamber and the Social Insurance Authority for Business, https://news.wko.at/news/oesterreich/Soziale_Absicherung__von_Selbstaendigen_im_internationalen_V.pdf (accessed 25 June 2018).
13. Proposal for a Council Recommendation on access to social protection for workers and the self-employed, COM(2018) 132 final.
14. CF *Maier/Wolfgarten/Wölfle*, Zugang zum Sozialschutz, ZESAR 2018, 259 ff.
15. CF *Eichenhofer*, Sozialer Schutz in der sich wandelnden Arbeitswelt, in *Aschauer/Brameshuber* (eds), Jahrbuch Sozialversicherungsrecht 2017, 75 (81).

their work, although they are economically dependent on one or a few clients.[16] In 1996, there has been an attempt in Austria to include persons who fulfilled a contract of service in the scope of the general social security act. This has been criticized a lot in literature, and the Austrian Constitutional Court declared that the criterion if a person is in regular employment or not is too vague, since the preconditions would be met as long as a person had concluded more than three agreements with a client over the last six months or the activity lasted more than two months.[17] Following the decision of the constitutional court, the respective section was adopted and has a very narrow scope of application ever since. Those so-called new self-employed (freelancers according to section 4 paragraph 4 of the Austrian general social security act) who receive remuneration above the level of marginal work, perform their work in person, do not possess significant own working equipment and are not compulsorily insured by other regulations are integrated into the statutory insurance scheme. To illustrate one of the problems coming from that provision: persons who mainly perform intellectual activities, such as consultation services i.e. professional experts do most likely not need a lot of working equipment in a material sense. In such cases, the distinction provided for by law does not work. Furthermore, as already explained above, entrepreneurs who have to obtain a trade licence are excluded as well.[18] In fact, these provisions brought about a lot of legal uncertainty since the application of the social security scheme is decided on a case-by-case basis and therefore contributions have to be paid retrospectively in the event of incorrect allocation to one of the systems. That is why the Austrian government tried to overcome this uncertainty by introducing a binding system on the assignment of persons to one of the social security acts.[19] However, the design of the system increases bureaucracy and therefore does not bring the outcome one might have hoped for.

When it comes to marginal employment, meaning that the remuneration or the number of working hours does not reach a certain threshold, one has to be aware that the CJEU did not object to the exclusion of such minor employment relationships given its justification by legitimate aims of social policy,[20] while Austria introduced a lump-sum contribution to be paid by employers who employ more than one person in a marginal work contract and the duty for the employee to get insurance as soon as his remuneration exceeds the threshold of marginal employment. Even though these examples display the Austrian system, they may serve as general examples of the challenges of our social security institutions in contribution-based systems.[21]

Another issue may be illustrated when it comes to crowd workers or platform-based work, since their status in social security depends on their respective status in

16. Cf. *Marhold/Friedrich*, Österreichisches Arbeitsrecht[3] (2016) 53.
17. Section 4 para. 5 ASVG, suspended after the decision of the Constitutional Court.
18. Cf. *Marhold*, Social Protection of Contingent Work: Austria and the Full Coverage Social Insurance System, in *Ales/Deinert/Kenner* (eds), Core and Contingent Work in the European Union 2017, 242 et seq.
19. Sozialversicherungs-Zuordnungsgesetz (SV-ZG), BGBl I 2017/125.
20. CJEU, C-317/39, *Nolte v Hannover*, EU:C:1995:438; CJEU, C-444/93, *Megner v Innungskrankenkasse*, EU:C:1995:442.
21. Cf. *Eichenhofer*, Sozialer Schutz in der sich wandelnden Arbeitswelt, in *Aschauer/Brameshuber* (eds), Jahrbuch Sozialversicherungsrecht 2017, 75 (81).

labour law.[22] We might have to think broader in terms of social security, especially given the fact that the systems tend to gradually shift from making distinctions with regards to different professions and underlying contracts to an income-related approach.[23] That brings us to the next group, which let us face the limits of our social security systems in the past years.

[C] Recognized Refugees

I do not want to go into details in that connection, but it is obvious that there is a certain tension between the limited social protection of non-economically active European citizens and recognized refugees.[24] Whereas the first group may be excluded from social security systems, the second one has to be treated equally. One more time the question of the genuine link is at hand. Generally spoken, in most of the cases the principle of equal treatment is not even appropriate regarding the benefits given. In many cases, especially refugees and asylum seekers rely on benefits in kind because they are unable at least for the first weeks or months to organize their living out of financial benefits. As the principle of equal treatment obliges the Member States to grant the same benefits as provided for by national law, these are to a large extent financial benefits which are of less use for recognized refugees and asylum seekers. Furthermore, the principle of equal treatment could have been introduced easier while the numbers of refugees and asylum seekers were rather small compared to what we have seen in the year 2015. This raises another question of solidarity who for whom; will the European citizens accept that because of the principle of equal treatment migrating European citizens suffer disadvantages compared to the situation of refugees and asylum seekers? There are many taboos in that discussion but I think from a social security perspective we cannot avoid dealing with these problems in order to maintain cohesion in the population. But let us turn to another topic of solidarity who for whom.

IV Solidarity of the economically active with the economically non-active persons and the idea of an unconditional basic income.

A new social security benefit appears on the horizon: the unconditional basic income. The idea is to grant a certain amount of money to people residing in one country regardless whether they are or intent to be economically active. Whereas traditional social security benefits are granted to substitute the loss of income due to illness, disabilities, old age or dependence for care (for example), the unconditional basic income tries to disconnect social security from the risks of the labour market and grant social security benefits regardless whether the beneficiary works or is willing to work.

22. *Risak*, Crowdwork – Erste rechtliche Annäherungen an eine 'neue' Arbeitsform, ZAS 2015, 18.
23. *Marhold*, Social Protection of Contingent Work: Austria and the Full Coverage Social Insurance System in *Ales/Deinert/Kenner* (eds), Core and Contingent work in the European Union 254; *Tomandl*, Rechtsprobleme einer umfassenden Sozialversicherung, ZAS 1998, 9 (12).
24. Cf. *Eichenhofer*, Armutswanderung und Europäisches Sozialrecht in *Aschauer/Kohlbacher* (eds), Jahrbuch Sozialversicherungsrecht 2015, 55.

There are different concepts of unconditional basic income.[25] The fundamental question to be answered is whether it is granted in addition to other social benefits or to replace other social benefits. This simple difference is dramatic. *Monika Köppl-Turynam*, an economist, working for the thinktank 'Agenda Austria' estimated that a non-conditional basic income of EUR 800 - per month granted in addition to other social benefits would - in the case of Austria - result in a state quota of 70% of the National GDP.[26] For the time being, the percentage of public expenditures on the economic performance is 20% lower. In other words, this quota would rise by twenty points. We do not know whether these considerations led to the defeat of a people's initiative for the introduction of an unconditional basic income in Switzerland. Nevertheless, it is very probable that an unconditional basic income would overstress the capacity and the willingness of the economically active population to share that burden. As from January 2017, Finland was testing this model. A number of 2000 randomly selected unemployed people between the age of 25 and 58 received a monthly payment of EUR 560 - without adding any additional conditions to it. The main objectives were to reduce bureaucracy within the social security system, to provide a safety net especially in order to address insecurities arising associated with the gig economy and to establish if motivation to find a job in - or decreases among the recipients of - the basic income.[27] Although *Marjukka Turunen*, Director of Change Management at Kela (Finland's Social Security Institution), states that after one year the experiment was running smoothly and it was already possible to yield results by cutting bureaucracy,[28] Finnish government decided not to prolong the testing period and end the trial after the first two-year pilot. Instead, legislation has been introduced to create social security benefits for unemployed people based on stricter conditions, i.e., taking training or working at least eighteen hours in three months. Another expert, *Olli Kangas*, who was involved in designing the basic income experiment, claims that two years is a period too short to draw proper conclusions, and in his mind, the scope of the project should have been broadened by including a number of employed persons instead. By all means, the results from the two-year pilot unfortunately will not be available until the end of next year, so we will have to wait. In addition, a group of people working at the OECD's Economics Department published a paper, which states that a universal credit system, like the one being introduced in the UK, would work better than a basic income in Finland. Universal credit replaces several benefit

25. Cf. *Reuter*, Das bedingungslose Grundeinkommen als liberaler Entwurf: Das bedingungslose Grundeinkommen als liberaler Entwurf: philosophische Argumente für mehr Gerechtigkeit (2016).
26. Cf. *Köppl-Turynam*, https://www.agenda-austria.at/statement-zum-thema-bedingungsloses-grundeinkommen/ (accessed 23 August 2018); Der Standard, https://derstandard.at/2000063385423/Zehn-Dinge-die-man-ueber-das-Grundeinkommen-wissen-sollte (accessed 23 August 2018).
27. Cf. *Peter*, No Plans to Expand Finland Basic Income Trial, https://www.bbc.com/news/world-europe-43866700 (accessed 22 June 2018); *Der Standard*, Ernüchterung in Finnland: Regierung stoppt Grundeinkommen, https://derstandard.at/2000078525937/Ernuechterung-in-Finnland-Regierung-stoppt-Grundeinkommen? (accessed 22 June 2018).
28. *Turunen*, Basic Income: An Answer to Social Security Problems?, OECD Yearbook 2017, http://www.oecd.org/social/basic-income-an-answer-to-social-security-problems.htm (accessed 22 June 2018).

payments with a monthly sum.[29] As another recent example, in 2016, Switzerland held a national referendum on the introduction of a basic income and the proposal was severely rejected by Swiss' voters.[30] Besides, if I have understood the recent Italian labour market reforms correctly, we can also identify a contribution of social security measures in favour of more flexibility in the labour market (reddito di cittadinanza) while extending the scope social protection to atypical workers at the same time.[31] The reforms in Italy do not abolish conditionality as such, on the contrary, it is built on the unemployed person's willingness to work (not more than two out of three job offers may be denied).

However, the idea of an unconditional basic income is not very new. In 1955 already, *Erich Fromm*[32] argued in favour of an unconditional basic income in his book on the Sane Society. Supposed that human beings suffering from inactivity are not lazy by nature, an unconditional basic income would not – according to *Fromm* – endanger the economic system. There are, however, other questions to be addressed in connection with an unconditional basic income. Would it result in a withdrawal of women from the labour market because staying at home is paid?[33] Will equality increase if an unconditional basic income replaces all the other social security financial benefits? If it did, the gap between rich and poor would be likely to grow because economically disadvantaged groups of people may profit more from social benefits. That in turn would be replaced by the unconditional basic income. Moreover it is questionable, how an unconditional basic income effects consumers and consumption patterns and which part of the population would in fact refrain from working if such an incentive as an unconditional basic income exists. There is no empirical evidence to confirm or refute any of these assumptions. We may calculate the costs of an unconditional basic income, but we do have huge difficulties to estimate its consequences. Furthermore, an unconditional basic income would be contrary to the concept of social security to activate the people by contributing and finally reintegrate them into the labour market.

What we can say is that the arguments for introducing an unconditional basic income mostly rely on unproven and unprovable assumptions. Therefore, *Philip Kovce*, an economist and philosopher working at the Philosophicum Basel in Switzerland,

29. *Pareliussen/Hwang/Viitamäki*, Basic Income or a Single Tapering Rule? Incentives, Inclusiveness and Affordability Compared for the Case of Finland, Economic Department working papers No. 1464, ECO/WKP(2018)12, http://www.oecd.org/officialdocuments/publicdisplaydocumentpdf/?cote=ECO/WKP(2018)12&docLanguage=En (accessed 22 June 2018).
30. *Peter*, No plans to expand Finland basic income trial, https://www.bbc.com/news/world-europe-43866700 (accessed 22 June 2018); *Der Standard*, Ernüchterung in Finnland: Regierung stoppt Grundeinkommen, https://derstandard.at/2000078525937/Ernuechterung-in-Finnland-Regierung-stoppt-Grundeinkommen? (accessed 22 June 2018).
31. *Del Conte*, Re-structuring the Standard Employment Relationship: Italy and the Increasing Protection Contract in System in *Ales/Deinert/Kenner* (eds), Core and Contingent work in the European Union 111; https://www.eurofound.europa.eu/observatories/eurwork/articles/industrial-relations-law-and-regulation/italy-reforms-to-system-of-unemployment-benefits (accessed 26 June 2018).
32. *Fromm*, The Sane Society (1955).
33. CF *Derndorfer* in Der Standard, Zehn Dinge, die man über das Grundeinkommen wissen sollte, https://derstandard.at/2000063385423/Zehn-Dinge-die-man-ueber-das-Grundeinkommen-wissen-sollte (accessed 24 August 2018).

strongly opposes to the idea of experimentally testing the unconditional basic income. His most important argument is that basic income cannot be tested such as democracy, human rights, and the rule of law cannot be tested in an experiment[34] This introduces a human rights aspect in the discussion around the unconditional basic income. However, we have to be aware that certain aspects of an unconditional basic income are strongly supported by a neoliberal approach to social security. If the unconditional basic income replaces all the social security benefits that we know and leaves it to the beneficiary to organize his social protection out of the unconditional basic income, it would certainly reduce bureaucracy. Nevertheless, it would as well reduce the standard of social protection in our societies.

To me it seems impossible that traditional social risks could be counterbalanced by ways of an unconditional basic income. This is at least true in my opinion, with regards to the dimensions of a basic income that we keep discussing recently (between EUR 800 and EUR 1,000 in rather wealthy economies); 22% of the Swiss voters have been in favour of an unconditional basic income. We will see whether this percentage rises if unemployment due to technological changes will rise as well. Whatever the prophecies are, we can be sure that there will be a long transition period in which traditional work patterns will still be dominant and we have to be very cautious not to destroy work-related social security by assumption-based theories on the end of work. Was not that a famous title of a widespread book in the late eighties?

§4.04 SOLIDARITY OF BENEFICIARIES TOWARDS THE COMMUNITY

I want to highlight another aspect of the interaction of solidarity between communities and beneficiaries. Within the framework of new forms of social security a new tendency can be recognized, the solidarity of the beneficiaries with the community. In recent years, we could observe a tendency in social security legislation to raise the standards, beneficiaries have to meet in order to fulfil the preconditions of social rights. It is due to the aging population and fiscal constraints that pension systems across Europe experience a shift towards longer working periods and later retirement. Furthermore, less and less workers are recognized as working in arduous and hazardous jobs and therefore would be entitled to an early retirement. A recent study of the European social policy network, drafted by *David Natali, Slavina Spasova,* and *Bart Vanhercke,* analyzed pre-retirement systems in thirty-five European countries and found out that many early retirement routes have been closed or more strictly conditioned.[35] We can observe the same situation in unemployment benefits and invalidity pensions. The conditions for these rights have become more and more strict,

34. *Kovce* in Der Standard, Grundeinkommen ist eine Investition in die Zukunft, https://derstandard.at/2000063376726/Grundeinkommen-ist-eine-Investition-in-die-Zukunft (accessed 23 August 2018); Cf. *Häni/Kovce,* Was fehlt, wenn alles da ist? Warum das bedingungslose Grundeinkommen die richtigen Fragen stellt (2015).

35. *Natali/Spasova/Vanhercke,* Retirement Regimes for Workers in Arduous or Hazardous Jobs in Europe, European Social Policy Network (ESPN), 2016, https://publications.europa.eu/en/publication-detail/-/publication/e23e8180-9ac9-11e6-868c-01aa75ed71a1/language-en (accessed at 23 August 2018).

and the beneficiaries have longer waiting periods for the different entitlements. Besides, beneficiaries are expected to accept lower qualified jobs more easily or jobs that can still be carried out in accordance to their health conditions despite a disability. All these conditions are getting more and more severe and strict. The keyword to legitimate the measures to increase conditionality very often is responsibility. The potential beneficiaries are held responsible for reducing the burden which is laid on the community. In turn, this tendency could also be understood as a way of solidarity from the beneficiaries to the community. The beneficiary should at first try to remain in the labor market, whereas the community is obliged to give the beneficiary adequate assistance to do so instead of having an early labour market exit at the expense of the community.

If you think back to the seventies and eighties of the last century where in many Member States social security schemes were the tool to reduce pressure on the labour market, the concepts nowadays have dramatically and completely changed. Social security benefits are still and again used as a labour market instrument, not in order to finance the (early) exit of the labour market, but to contribute to activating the people to at least partly remain in the labour market. Therefore, the distinction between social security benefits and labour market instruments vanishes to some extent. In many states, we can identify social security provisions – especially in retirement schemes and in unemployment schemes – where one cannot say precisely, where labour market policy ends and social security schemes begin. That is true as well for part-time retirement regulations or the shift from disability pensions to rehabilitation programmes financed by healthcare insurance. The general idea behind these programmes is exactly to activate and use the beneficiaries' remaining capacity to work. I can give you a number of other examples in the field of unemployment, where we cannot distinguish anymore, what social security is and what labour market policy. If you subsidize professional training in the framework of an existing and valid employment relationship with financial means deriving from unemployment insurance, in order to avoid unemployment can you tell me what that is, labour market policy or unemployment prevention? In the end it does not matter but we are supposed to be aware of the increasing links between social security and labour market, which – as I have already mentioned – are not new at all but have a very different direction. Social security does not – to a growing extend – finance unemployment by pre-retirement programmes or generous unemployment benefits but contributes to activation of the beneficiaries with the aim of keeping them in the labour market.

Contrary to what we have seen at the end of the last century, workers are not 'sourced-out' to social security systems anymore but social security systems rather try to activate or to reactivate employees who are at risk of exiting the labour market early. To combine that kind of model with the previously discussed unconditional basic income is a completely different approach, which I think is much more promising than investing in unconditional basic income schemes. Social security more and more is becoming an instrument of active labour market policy and we have not talked yet about combined salaries.

To sum up, talking about new forms of social security makes it worthwhile to look at the ancient principles of social security, therefore I thank you for your company while revisiting solidarity.

CHAPTER 5

World Report on Informal Workers

Humberto Villasmil Prieto

§5.01 HISTORY AND REASON OF A TERM: THE PATH FOLLOWED IN ORDER TO ADOPT THE RECOMMENDATION NO. 204 (ILO) ON THE TRANSITION FROM INFORMAL ECONOMY TO FORMAL ECONOMY 2015

[A] First Devisings

The concept of *informal sector*[1] was coined for the first time in 1972 and since then, a wide-ranging debate on its significance and dynamics has been raised. This concept underlies, at least, two approaches that have different policy implications. On the one hand, the one followed by the International Labour Office (ILO) and other organizations of the United Nations system which consider the informal sector as a consequence of the structural deficit of the development and labor surplus of the countries.

In this sense, several works of the ILO and ECLAC made during the 80s and 90s of the last century and especially those of the *Regional Employment Program for Latin America and the Caribbean* (PREALC) would show how the term was tackled since then and the theoretical developments that arose later.

This approach understands that the dynamic of economic growth has been insufficient to hold the growing workforce productively, and it must be inserted into segments of low productivity such as independent or microenterprises workers, many of which work in subsistence conditions and certainly with a minimum of protection. This point of view favored public policies to promote modernization, productivity and a more balanced growth at the sectoral and regional levels, although other views on informality have certainly been influential.

1. OIT (1972). *Employment incomes and equality*: A strategy for increasing productive employment in Kenya. http://www.ilo.org/public/libdoc/ilo/1972/72B09_608_engl.pdf.

In fact, another line of thought estimated that informality was a consequence of an over intervention of the State, with rigid rules and regulations that made more difficult to formalize activities and businesses, especially those that operate on a small scale. It refers to the multiple rates, taxes and administrative rules of various public institutions that, apparently, make formalization more expensive. Consequently, this approach will place emphasis on state deregulation and on the simplification of corresponding norms and procedures.

The World Bank, on their behalf, presented informality as an escape strategy or a manifestation of exclusion that confronts an important sector of the productive units or the labor force with the costs of formality.[2]

On the one hand, informality is seen as a manifestation of the exclusion of many production units on the benefits granted by the State to the formal economy, which complicates a group of workers' jump to the formality or prevents many small and microenterprises (SMEs) formalize themselves due to the high costs of formalization. On the other, informality is presented as a voluntary escape decision that economic agents follow as a consequence of implicit costs/benefit analyses which show that the benefits obtained from formality do not compensate their costs. Those economic agents (self-employed workers, microenterprises, among others) find higher (or equivalent) benefits in informality in terms of income, some flexibility in work (remunerations, working hours and rest, among others), and probably levels of protection (in health) and social welfare similar or superior to those obtained in a formal job and at a lower cost.

This approach of the World Bank emphasized on the role that labor regulations play in order to introduce *rigidities* in the market, explicitly referring to institutions such as minimum wages or collective labor agreements that put pressure on labor costs and induce the companies to be informal.

A broad view of the informality has been gathered at the international conferences of labor statisticians (CIET) of the ILO, decisive events that enable to appreciate the historical evolution of the concept.

In the report of the Director-General of the ILO of the 1991 International Labour Conference, the informal sector—as it was called before informality—was defined as follows:

> (...) the very small units of production and distribution of goods and services placed in urban areas of developing countries; these units almost always belong to independent producers and independent workers who sometimes employ family members or some employees or apprentices.
>
> These units have very little or no capital at all; they use rudimentary techniques and scarcely skilled workforce, so their productivity is reduced; those working in them tend to get very low, irregular income and their employment is extremely unstable.[3]

---

2. Perry, Guillermo E (et al.) (2007). Informality: exit and exclusion. Washington, World Bank. http://documents.worldbank.org/curated/en/326611468163756420/pdf/400080Informal101OFFICIAL0USE0ONLY1. pdf.
3. ILO (1991): "The dilemma of the informal sector" In: Report of the Director-General (Part I). International Labour Conference (78th session). Geneva, Switzerland.

Otherwise, *Resolution II, concerning statistics of employment in the informal sector,* adopted by the fifteenth International Conference of Labour Statisticians (January 1993) states in number 5(1):

> The informal sector may be broadly characterized as consisting of units engaged in the production of goods or services with the primary objective of generating employment and incomes to the persons concerned. These units typically operate at a low level of organization, with little or no division between labour and capital as factors of production and on a small scale. Labour relations—where they exist—are based mostly on casual employment, kinship or personal and social relations rather than contractual arrangements with formal guarantees.

As it is shown, at the beginning of the 90s of the last century, the ICLS still understood informality as part of a sector.

In another way, and less than ten years later, the *resolution concerning decent work and the informal economy* adopted by the General Conference of the International Labour Organization, meeting in its 90th Session, 2002:

> Although there is no universally accurate or accepted description or definition, there is a broad understanding that the term "informal economy" accommodates considerable diversity in terms of workers, enterprises and entrepreneurs with identifiable characteristics. They experience specific disadvantages and problems that vary in intensity across national, rural, and urban contexts. The term "informal economy" is preferable to "informal sector" because the workers and enterprises in question do not fall within any one sector of economic activity, but cut across many sectors. However, the term "informal economy" tends to downplay the linkages, grey areas and interdependencies between formal and informal activities. The term "informal economy" refers to all economic activities by workers and economic units that are—in law or in practice—not covered or insufficiently covered by formal arrangements. Their activities are not included in the law, which means that they are operating outside the formal reach of the law; or they are not covered in practice, which means that—although they are operating within the formal reach of the law, the law is not applied or not enforced; or the law discourages compliance because it is inappropriate, burdensome, or imposes excessive costs. The ILO's work needs to take into account the conceptual difficulties arising from this considerable diversity.[4]

The resolution, as it is clear, moved from the notion of *the informal sector* to a broader one of *informal economy*, recognizing not only the deficit of productivity and quality of work in the informal sector but also *an area of unprotected employment and therefore, informal, in the formal sector of the economy.* This will be precisely the point of connection for the appropriation of the category by the labor law.

The ILO was always aware that there was a problem of limiting the definition which still persists in some way and furthermore, and this is very relevant for what comes next, it emphasized the unprotected informal employment.[5]

---

4. The italics and bolds are ours.
5. For the resolutions adopted by the ICLS, *see* https://www.ilo.org/global/statistics-and-databases/standards-and-guidelines/resolutions-adopted-by-international-conferences-of-labour-statisticians/lang--en/index.htm.

The *Seventeenth International Conference of Labour Statisticians (*ICLS*)* of *2003* adopted "the following guidelines, which complement the resolution concerning statistics of employment in the informal sector of the 15th ICLS, and encourages countries to test the conceptual framework on which they are based."

It can be read in this document:

(1) *The concept of informal sector* refers to production units as observation units, while the concept of informal employment refers to jobs as observation units. Employment is defined in the sense of paragraph 9 of the resolution concerning statistics of the economically active population, employment, unemployment and underemployment adopted by the 13th ICLS.

(2) *Informal sector enterprises and employment in the informal sector* are defined according to the resolution concerning statistics of employment in the informal sector adopted by the 15th ICLS. For the purpose of statistics on informal employment, paragraph 19 of the resolution concerning statistics of employment in the informal sector adopted by the 15th ICLS should be applied to exclude households employing paid domestic workers from informal sector enterprises, and to treat them separately as part of a category named "households."

(3) (1) *Informal employment* comprises the total number of informal jobs as defined in subparagraphs (2) to (5) below, whether carried out in formal sector enterprises, informal sector enterprises, or households, during a given reference period.

(2) As shown in the attached matrix, informal employment includes the following types of jobs:

(i) *own-account workers* employed in their own informal sector enterprises (cell 3);

(ii) *employers employed in their own informal sector enterprises (cell 4);*

(iii) *contributing family workers*, irrespective of whether they work in formal or informal sector enterprises (cells 1 and 5);

(iv) *members of informal producers' cooperatives (cell 8);*

(v) *employees holding informal jobs* (as defined in subparagraph (5) below) in formal sector enterprises, informal sector enterprises, or as paid domestic workers employed by households (cells 2, 6 and 10);

(vi) *own-account workers engaged in the production of goods exclusively for own final use by their household* (cell 9), if considered employed according to paragraph 9(6) of the resolution concerning statistics of the economically active population, employment, unemployment and underemployment adopted by the 13th ICLS.

In any case, what is quite evident is that the category *informal work*, previously called *informal economy,—the informal sector before*—is diverse and perhaps multivocal notions which complicate the fact that the labor law appropriates the term.[6]

The subject raises enormous interest worldwide. A recent study published by the ILO (*Women and Men in the Informal Economy: A Statistical Picture, International Labour Office, Geneva, 2018)* concludes that two billion people—more than the 61% of the active population—practice the informal economy, despite the fact that the transition to the formal economy is a necessary condition in order to make decent work a reality for everyone.

The report indicates that in Africa 85% of jobs are informal; 68.2% in Asia; 68.6% in the Arab States; 40% in the Americas and 25.1% in Europe and Central Asia. Among the authors of the report, it is worth mentioning Florence Bonnet and Vicky Leung who clarify that not all informal workers are poor, so that poverty would be in itself, neither cause nor necessary consequence of the informality. In any case, they conclude that poor people face higher informal employment rates and that, at the same time, poverty rates are higher among workers in the informal economy.[7]

However, these authors insist that "(...) informality implies a lack of social protection, rights at work and decent work conditions and it means low productivity and lack of access to credit for companies."[8]

Certainly, terminological movements to finally arrive at informality with the Recommendation No. 204 indicate a sequence in the same International Labour Standards which should initially be located from Convention 150 of 1978 on labor administration which refers to the unstructured sector. The same terminology was maintained with the Recommendation No. 169 of 1984, but in this case to say "(that) the members should adopt measures to allow the progressive transfer of workers from the unstructured sector, where it exists, to the structural sector" (General principles of employment policy, No. 9)

This reference is especially interesting since the idea of a necessary transfer, at that time from the unstructured to the structured sector, nowadays from informality to formality begins to be evident in international labor standards. This trend line, as it will be evident, not only remained but also became established in the same title of a modern recommendation, which was Recommendation No. 204 of 2015.

However, in the following decade the notion of the informal sector is abandoned. Recommendation No. 193 of 2002, on the Promotion of Cooperatives, mentions "marginal or survival activities (sometimes referred to as 'informal economy')."

6. "Mapping the informal economy so as to comprehend its size, composition and evolution is an extremely difficult and inevitably imprecise exercise. International comparability is not possible. This is because different definitions have been used, statistical information is collected on an ad hoc rather than a regular basis and reliability of data is inconsistent." ILO (2002). Decent work and the informal economy. International Labour Conference, 90th Session. Report VI. Sixth item on the agenda. Geneva. p. 10. https://www.ilo.org/wcmsp5/groups/public/---ed_norm/---relconf/---reloff/documents/meetingdocument/wcms_078849.pdf.
7. ILO (2018). Women and men in the informal economy: A statistical picture. Third edition. Geneva. https://www.ilo.org/wcmsp5/groups/public/---dgreports/---dcomm/documents/publication/wcms_626831.pdf.
8. *Ibidem.*

Recommendation No. 195 of 2004 on Human Resources Development also includes mention of the informal economy and so does Convention 187 on the Promotional Framework for Occupational Safety and Health in 2006. That same year the Employment Relationship Recommendation No. 198 was adopted, which includes workers in the informal economy among the most vulnerable groups, regarding "uncertainty about the existence of an employment relationship."

Later, two recommendations, from the year 2010 and 2012, can be indicated as clear precedents of the meaning and content of Recommendation No. 204, beginning with Recommendation No. 200 of 2010 on HIV/AIDS, which recalls in its preamble "(...) the importance of reducing the informal economy through decent work and sustainable development (...)." On the other, Recommendation No. 202 of 2012 on Social Protection Floors prefers to support "the transition from informal employment to formal employment."

In 2015, Recommendation No. 204 was adopted dedicating a specific section to this matter. Finally, Recommendation No. 205 on Employment and Decent Work for Peace and Resilience, 2017 (205), maintained the informal economy terminology including in title III (Strategic Approaches) the obligation of members to adopt a global and multidirectional approach "the transition from the informal economy to the formal economy", which, after Recommendation No. 204, seems to be a consistent policy design.

[B] The Approach to Informal Work from the ILO'S Supervisory Bodies

The regular or special ILO's supervisory bodies approached informal work and informal workers in two areas that will be tackled separately.

[1] The General Surveys of the CEACR

The answer to the question about how the control bodies of the ILO approached the issue of informal work would verify that the labor law in general and the control bodies of the ILO in this specific case have only recently come to the consideration of informal work and informal workers. Until 2010, the General Surveys of the Committee of Experts did not deal with the issue of the informal economy and informal work in detail.

The first three General Surveys of the Committee of Experts on the Application of Conventions and Recommendations (CEACR), beginning with that of 1985 (Labour Inspection), the 1986 (Equal Pay) and the 1987 (Safety in the Work Environment), do not make any reference to informal work, not even to any category that preceded it.

In the General Survey of 1988 (Equality in Employment and Occupation) there is a mention to the "unstructured sector." The reference became relevant due to a report of the Suriname government that had pointed out the lack of statistical data on the condition of women in the rural and urban unstructured sector as a difficulty to ratify the Convention No. 111. The mention of this sector came from a Government and not from a consideration of the CEACR, despite the fact that Convention 150 and Recommendation no.169 had already been adopted.

The General Survey of 1989 (Old Age Protection by Social Security) does not make any reference to the informal sector and neither does that of 1990 (Merchant Shipping Working Rules). But in the General Survey of 1991 (Human Resources Development) the mention to the *"unstructured sector"* reappears. The topic—unstructured sector—was discussed in a special section related with the modalities of worker training, especially the traditional learning. The difficulty in the application of the Human Resources Development Convention, 1975 (No. 142) in that sector was admitted.

In the 1992 General Survey (Minimum Wages) there is already an explicit mention to *the formal sector* of the economy. It is recognized that in several countries, workers in the formal sector to whom the minimum wage is applicable make up a minority. The need of effective protection for domestic, rural and informal workers becomes one of the criteria for setting the minimum wage. The category "informal sector" starts to emerge in the general studies of the CEACR but still in a non-systematic and not entirely precise way.

In the General Survey of 1993 (Workers with Family Responsibilities) *"unstructured sector"* category is mentioned again. Indeed, in this study, it is noted that statistics on women's employment tend to underestimate, among other variables, their participation in that sector.

But the 1994 Survey (Freedom of Association and Collective Bargaining) does make an explicit mention of *the informal sector* to indicate that, among the categories of workers excluded from the right to unionize, are usually those in this sector. This is an important subject since the way in which the control bodies dealt with the issue of informal work was through the fundamental conventions and therefore, their application was universal and included workers in the informal sector.

The General Survey of 1995 (Protection against Unfair Dismissal) made no mention of the informal sector but—and this confirms a trend—the General Survey of 1996 did (Equality in Employment and Occupation). It was done in the context of discrimination by sex, and it refers to informal employment as a factor of vulnerability for women. The topic will be mentioned again since the treatment of the informal sector from the control bodies occurred, it is good to reiterate it, in a more systematic way since the application of the fundamental conventions.[9]

The General Survey of 1997 (Labour Administration) mentions *the unstructured sector* once again, indicating that, according to the Labour Administration Convention, 1978 (No 150), everything related with employment promotion policies and the extension of the functions of labor administration had to be incorporated.

In the General Survey of 1998 (Professional Rehabilitation and Employment of Disabled Persons), *the unstructured sector* was also mentioned in order to explain the difficulty in obtaining detailed information regarding persons with disabilities living or working in rural areas or remote communities.

9. ILO Declaration on Fundamental Principles and Rights at Work and its Follow-up. International Labour Conference, 86th Session. Geneva, 1998.

The General Survey of 1999 (Migrant Workers) expressly refers to *the informal market* and it does regarding two conventions which, although not specific fundamental conventions (the Migration for Employment Convention (Revised), 1949 (No. 97) and the Migrant Workers (Supplementary Provisions) Convention, 1975 (No. 143) both have an obvious connection with fundamental conventions, as migrant workers are a particularly vulnerable category in terms of protection of the right to nondiscrimination and equality. This Survey highlights that certain categories of migrant workers, including those in the informal market, do not enjoy the protection of Conventions 97 and 143.

The General Survey of the Year 2000 (Tripartite Consultation), a very important survey since it was *a governance priority convention*[10] such as the Tripartite Consultation (International Labor Standards) Convention, 1976 (No. 144), makes reference to the legal agents of workers in the rural and informal sectors as representatives of people widely interested in the application of the convention. This concept is not necessarily identical to the representation recognized to the most emblematic workers' organizations, and it is worth noting.

The 2001 General Survey (Night Work of Women in Industry), the 2002 (Port Work) and the 2003 (Protection of Salaries) do not make any reference to the informal sector, nor to the unstructured sector or to another previous category understood today as informal workers.

However, the General Survey of 2004 (Promoting Employment) dealt with the employment policy related with *the transition from the informal to the formal economy* and, additionally, with the challenges that *the informal sector* implies for decent work: safety at work, child labor, participation in workers' organizations, among others. This survey is an obvious precedent—not exclusive—of the Recommendation on the transition from the informal economy to the formal economy, 2015 (No. 204) in public policies adapted to this objective. Due to its relevance, this matter will be reconsidered later.

The General Survey of 2005 (Working Time) mentions informality once again. It dealt with working hours, and it mentions young men and women who work in precarious conditions, often in *the informal economy.* The idea that the informal economy is less protected began to consolidate or, in other words, what marks the transition from informality to formality is a line that goes from lack of legal protection to protection, the thread of Recommendation No. 204 to understand how that transition would be verified.

In the 2006 General Survey (Labour Inspection), a reference is made to the informal sector to recognize that inspection functions in the informal and agricultural sectors seem to be very difficult. The element of deprotection appears increasingly clear and became, as it has already been mentioned, key in the adoption of Recommendation No. 204.

In the General Survey of 2007 (Eradicating Forced Labor) no mention is made of the informal sector, which seems surprising, since it is a study on fundamental

10. ILO Declaration on Social Justice for a Fair Globalization adopted by the International Labour Conference at its Ninety-seventh Session, Geneva, June 10, 2008.

conventions such as the Forced Labor Convention, 1930 (No. 29) and the Convention on the Abolition of Forced Labour, 1957 (No. 105) and it is even more striking if one considers that forced labor is among the most notorious manifestations of unprotected and therefore informal work.

In the 2008 Survey (Labour Clauses in Public Contracts) a mention is made of *informal workers* (and this background is important because now the reference, rather than to informal economy is to informal workers). This mention explains the risk that the beneficiary of a tender with public authorities employs informal workers who would lack legal protection. A second trend line is being consolidated: informality as a synonym of lack of protection and, moreover, a subjective vision of the informal sector that wants to emphasize the approximation of informal workers.

The 2009 Survey (Safety and Health at Work) reiterates the mention in order to display the problem that national laws do not usually extend the protection in matters of safety and health at work to *the informal sectors*. Once again, the criterion of protection/lack of protection delimits the boundary between formal and informal work.

From 2010, the CEACR General Surveys address *the informal economy* in much greater detail which coincides with a momentum in which International Labour Standards (ILSs) do so in a more consistent manner. The Survey of that year (Employment Instruments) deals with the informal economy within the areas of employment policies, training and job instruction, small and medium enterprises and policies specifically aimed at the informal sector.

The General Survey of 2011 (Social Security Instruments) assumes that *the informal economy* has changed the concept of the social security. It deals with the challenges that the informal economy raises regarding coverage, with regard to the possibility of ratification of the Social Security (Minimum Standards) Convention, 1952 (No. 102).

The 2012 General Survey (Fundamental Conventions) mentions *the informal sector* to show the right to establish workers' organizations, child labor and everything related to *the informal economy*. This trend line is important as it entails the approximation of supervisory bodies to the informal economy, hand in hand with the control of application of fundamental conventions.

The 2013 General Survey (Labor Relations in Public Administration and Collective Bargaining) makes no mention of the informal sector and informal workers.

However, the general surveys that go from 2014 to 2018 do mention them. The 2014 one (Minimum Wage Fixing Instruments) deals with the relationship of *the informal sector* with the mechanisms for setting minimum wages; the possibility of extending the protection of the minimum wage to the informal sector and the difficulty in obtaining data about income from the sector.

The 2015 Survey (Right of Association (Agriculture) and Rural Workers' Organizations Instruments) reiterates the mention of *the informal sector* to say that there are challenges inherent to the informal economy in the rural and agricultural sectors, especially regarding the right of association and protection against discrimination and, on the other, highlights the role of cooperatives as a possible way of transition towards formalization. It is important to mention this survey because it reveals how the supervisory bodies ended up tackling and approaching informality, particularly from the perspective of fundamental rights, considering that the right of association in agriculture is an essential content or part of the hard core of freedom of association.

The Survey of 2016 (Instruments Concerning Migrant Workers) makes a mention of the *informal economy* by highlighting the trend of migrant workers to serve in it and the situation of vulnerability in which they find themselves. The idea of the lack of protection seems already consolidated as a delimiting criterion of informality from the perspective of labor law.

The General Survey of 2017 (Instruments concerning Occupational Safety and Health) recognizes that *the informal economy* is not usually covered by national standards for safety and health at work and it is not often subject to supervision by the relevant inspections. The idea that the inspection function normally bumps into the scope of informality had been reiterated in previous surveys.

Finally, the most recent survey (Instruments on Working Time) of 2018 treats the informal economy on regard to workers who either are excluded from protection time of decent work or lack mechanisms to control working time.

All mentioned above justifies to bring up some preliminary conclusions:

(a) It is only since 2010 that the CEACR's general surveys address the issue of the informal economy and informal workers in more detail.

(b) From 1985 to 2010 mentions of the informal economy and informal workers were infrequent—most of the time the surveys did not address the issue—and when they did, they referred to *the unstructured sector* of the economy, terminology that Recommendation No. 204 discarded.

(c) From the first general surveys to Recommendation No. 204 (2015), there is a clear terminological change that, at least, would highlight four moments: (1) the *unstructured sector,* (2) the *informal sector,* (3) the *informal economy* and finally, (4) *informality,* bearing in mind that some general surveys referred specifically to the "informal market." It seems evident that the concept was moving in a more holistic and, therefore, inclusive sense.

(d) The supervisory bodies concerned about informality and informal workers from the fundamental conventions and, as they involve the protection of human rights, its subjective scope tends to be universal.

(e) For this reason, and despite the fact that they do not make explicit or literal reference to workers in the informal economy, "it is widely accepted that the eight fundamental conventions be applied to the informal economy."[11,12]

11. "Extending the scope of application of labour laws to the informal economy. Digest of comments of the ILO's supervisory bodies related to the informal economy." ILO First edition 2010, p. 84, from here on cited as "Digest."

12. The Freedom of Association and Protection of the Right to Organise Convention, 1948 (No. 87) states in its Article 2:

> Workers and employers, without distinction whatsoever, shall have the right (...).

The Right to Organise and Collective Bargaining Convention, 1949 (No. 98) states in Article 1:

(f) The same trend reappears with the priority conventions that tend to recognize a subjective and spatial scope of application which does not exclude any category of workers.[13]

Workers shall enjoy adequate protection against acts of anti-union discrimination in respect of their employment.

The Forced Labour Convention, 1930 (No. 29) states in its Article 2:

For the purposes of this Convention the term forced or compulsory labour shall mean *all work or service which is exacted from any person* under the menace of any penalty and for which the said person has not offered himself voluntarily.

The Abolition of Forced Labour Convention, 1957 (No. 105) states in its Article 2:

Each Member of the International Labour Organisation which ratifies this Convention undertakes to take effective measures to secure the immediate and complete abolition of *forced or compulsory labour* (...).

The Minimum Age Convention, 1973 (No. 138) states in its Article 2:

no one under that age shall be admitted to employment or work in any occupation.

The Worst Forms of Child Labour Convention, 1999 (No. 182) states in its Article 3:

the term the "worst forms of child labour" comprises: (d) *work* which, by its nature or the circumstances in which it is carried out, is likely to harm the health, safety or morals of children.

The Equal Remuneration Convention, 1951 (No. 100) states in its Article 1:

For the purpose of this Convention—(a) the term remuneration includes the ordinary, basic or minimum wage or salary and any additional emoluments whatsoever payable directly or indirectly, whether in cash or in kind, by the employer to the worker *and arising out of the worker's employment*; (b) the term equal remuneration for men and women workers for *work of equal value* refers to rates of remuneration established without discrimination based on sex.

The Discrimination (Employment and Occupation) Convention, 1958 (No. 111) states:

". For the purpose of this Convention the term discrimination includes—(a) any distinction, exclusion or preference made on the basis of race, colour, sex, religion, political opinion, national extraction or social origin, which has the effect of nullifying or impairing equality of opportunity or treatment in *employment or occupation*; (...) For the purpose of this Convention the terms employment and occupation include access to vocational training, access to employment and to particular occupations, and terms and conditions of employment." All bolded letters are ours.

13. The Labour Inspection Convention, 1947 (No.81) states in Article 2:

The system of labour inspection in industrial workplaces *shall apply to all workplaces* in respect of which legal provisions (...) are enforceable by labour inspectors.

[2] The Extension of the Scope of Application of the Labor Legislation to the Informal Economy from the Comments of the Supervisory Bodies of the ILO: CEACR and Commission for the Application of Standards of the International Labour Conference (CAS)

As indicated in the Digest, which is an edition of the year 2010, it was from the International Labour Conference in 2002 that the supervisory bodies dealt more systematically with the informal work: "it was during 2002 International Labour Conference that a conceptual framework of employment in the informal sector was presented in the context of the discussion on decent work and the informal economy. Highlights of this framework included the following:

- The term 'informal economy' was proposed in lieu of the 'informal sector' to accommodate 'all economic activities that are—in law or practice—not covered or insufficiently covered by formal arrangements' (...).
- The informal economy includes wage workers and own-account workers, contributing family members and those moving from one situation to another.
- It includes some of those who are engaged in new flexible work arrangements and who find themselves at the periphery of the core enterprise or at the lowest end of the production chain."[14]

The comments of the ILO's supervisory bodies related to the informal economy, as is well known, can be made through observations or direct requests from the CEACR or conclusions of the CAS.

The observations and direct requests of the CEACR regarding the informal economy have been made, and it is possible to qualify them depending on the conventions concerned.

The Labour Inspection (Agriculture) Convention, 1969 (No. 129) states in its Article 4:

> The system of labour inspection in agriculture *shall apply to agricultural undertakings in which work employees or apprentices, however they may be remunerated and whatever the type, form or duration of their contract.*

The Tripartite Consultation (International Labour Standards) Convention, 1976 (No. 144) states in its Article 2:

> The nature and form of the procedures provided for in paragraph 1 of this Article shall be determined in each country in accordance with national practice, after consultation with the representative organisations (...)", while Article 3 states "The representatives of employers and workers for the purposes of the procedures provided for in this Convention shall be freely chosen by their representative organisations (...).

The Employment Policy Convention, 1964 (No. 122) Article 3 states:

> In the application of this Convention, representatives of the persons affected by the measures to be taken, and in particular *representatives of employers and workers, shall be consulted* concerning employment policies (...).

14. *Ibid.*, Digest, p. 13. What follows under this section summarizes the text with the author's free criteria.

[a] *Observations and Direct Requests of the CEACR Related to the Fundamental Conventions*

[i] Freedom of Association and Collective Bargaining

With regard to freedom of association and collective bargaining, direct observations and requests from the CEACR emphasize that workers in the informal economy must not be excluded from freedom of association and collective bargaining conventions. Some observations to illustrate this matter would be:

- *An observation regarding the C87 (Bangladesh, 2008)* says: "workers without distinction whatsoever, including casual and informal sector workers in the shipbreaking industry, shall have the right to establish and join organizations of their own choosing."[15]
- *An observation of the CEACR on the C87 (General observation of 2009)* said: "The Committee, in reaffirming that Convention No. 87 is applicable to all workers and employers without distinction whatsoever, is heartened by innovative approaches taken by governments, workers' and employers' organizations over recent years to organize those in the informal economy, but observes that these are few and far between and that the full benefits of the Convention rarely reach the informal economy."[16]

[ii] Child Labor

The CEACR has reiterated on multiple occasions that the conventions related to child labor, specifically on the worst forms of child labor and the minimum age for admission to employment must be applied to all types of employment, regardless whether it is formal or informal, paid or unpaid. Even so, the greatest difficulty in the application of these norms in the informal sector is recognized, although, as it will be seen later, the references to the unstructured sector reappear in a consistent manner. Some observations illustrate the mentioned above:

- *Individual observation C138 Ukraine (2010):* "The supervision of the use of child labour in the informal sector of the economy remained an outstanding issue. This concerns, above all, the right of access to workplaces in the informal sector."[17]
- *Direct request C138 Bahamas (2008):* "The Committee recalls that the Convention applies to all branches of economic activity and that it covers all types of employment or work, whether under a labour relationship or contract of employment or not, and whether it is remunerated or not (...) Moreover, the

15. *Ibid.*, Digest, p. 15.
16. *Ibid.*
17. *Ibid.*, Digest, p. 20.

majority of children work in the informal sector, which is not generally inspected by the Inspectorate."[18]

- *Direct request C138 Cote d'Ivoire (2009):* "(...) the minimum age for admission to employment or work applies only to an employment relationship and that consequently no minimum age for admission to employment or work is laid down for children who perform an economic activity outside this employment context, particularly in the informal sector or on a self-employed basis. It reminds the Government that the Convention applies to all branches of economic activity and that it covers all types of employment or work whether or not it is performed on the basis of an employment relationship and whether or not it is paid."[19]
- *Direct request C138 Papua New Guinea (2009):* "The Committee further noted the Government's information that Parliament adopted in 2004 the Informal Sector Control and Management Act, which allows for people to engage in informal businesses for their living. The Ministry of Community Development with the Consultative Implementation and Monitoring Council are mandated to coordinate and monitor the implementation of this Act and consequently oversee the situation with child labour in the informal sector throughout the country."[20]

[iii] Equality of Opportunity and Treatment

In terms of equal opportunities and treatment, informality appears as a manifestation of discrimination and unequal remuneration that affects women in particular. But also, and in a more general sense, discrimination against workers in the informal economy is mentioned in a specific case.

In fact, in a *Direct request C111 Cote d'Ivoire (2010):*

> The Committee draws the Government's attention to the fact that granting equality of rights and duties to nationals is not sufficient to fulfil its obligations under the Convention. The Government has a duty to take proactive measures to ensure effective protection against discrimination on all the grounds set forth in the Convention (...) Noting also that the Labour Code only applies to persons with an employment contract, the Committee asks the Government to provide information on how it affords protection against discrimination to workers without an employment contract such as self- employed workers and workers in the informal economy.[21]

18. *Ibid.*, Digest, p. 22.
19. *Ibid.*, Digest, p. 25.
20. *Ibid.*, Digest, p. 27.
21. *Ibid.*, Digest, p. 32.

[b] *Observations and Direct Requests from the CEACR Related to the Priority Conventions*

The issue of informality mainly appears in relation to employment policy conventions (Employment Policy Convention, 1964 (No. 122), dealing with the following topics:

- Participation and/or consultation of the informal sectors in the elaboration of public employment policies that affect them.
- Relationship between the informal sector and poverty.
- How to promote decent work in that sector.

Some types of observations (one general and one particular) would illustrate as mentioned below:

- *General Observation C122 (2006):* "In reviewing the application of Convention No. 122, the Committee has examined the information contained in Governments reports concerning employment and unemployment trends overall, and for groups historically disadvantaged in the labour market, such as young people, women, minorities, indigenous peoples and workers in the informal economy (...) In some cases, the Committee noted the concerns voiced by the observations of the social partners concerning their insufficient involvement in the design and evaluation of employment policies. The Committee recalls that the Convention provides that the measures to be taken in relation to employment policy should take fully into account the experience and views of the social partners with a view to securing their full cooperation in formulating and implementing employment policies, including the opinions of those working in the rural sector and the informal economy."[22]
- *Individual Observation C122 Perú (2008):* "In general, poverty and employment in informal enterprises have a definite link, i.e. the greater the percentage of persons occupied in informal enterprises in an area, the greater the degree of poverty of its inhabitants. The Committee is aware that the informal economy constitutes a challenge for the creation of productive employment in the country [and] hopes that the Government's policies will stimulate the growth of formal micro- enterprises and that incentives will spur the formalization of informal enterprises (...)The Committee notes with interest the activities undertaken by the National Council for Labour and Promotion of Employment (CNTPE) and the progress made by setting up a body to revise and debate draft policies or legislation with respect to employment and vocational training. The Committee asks the Government to supply information on the activities of the CNTPE and repeats its interest in examining information on the measures adopted for consulting the representatives of the informal economy with regard to the policies to be adopted in order to improve their prospects of obtaining decent work."[23]

---

22. *Ibid.*, Digest, p. 33.
23. *Ibid.*, Digest, pp. 34–35.

[c] *Observations and Direct Requests from the CEACR Related to Technical Conventions*

This section exemplifies what is related to occupational safety and health (and the lack of extension of national standards to workers in the informal sector), and the conventions on human resources, specifically with regard to training policies for workers in the informal sector. Some typical cases would be useful to highlight:

- *CEACR: Individual observation on the Occupational Safety and Health Convention, 1981 (No. 155) Brazil (ratification: 1992) Published: 2006 (fragments).*

  "Articles 1 and 2 of the Convention. Application of the Convention to all branches of economic activity and to all workers in the covered branches. The Committee notes with interest the information provided regarding efforts by the Government to extend occupational safety and health protection to all Brazilian workers, inter-alia, through legislation conferring the right to such protection also to workers in the informal economy of the country. The Committee welcomes this initiative, which holds an interesting promise of an increased scope of application of this Convention, and requests the Government to keep it informed not only of the progress achieved, but also of the manner in which this initiative is translated into practice."[24]
- *Individual observation on the Human Resources Development Convention, 1975 (No. 142) United Republic of Tanzania (ratification: 1983) Published: 2010 (fragments).*

  "The Government indicates that the vocational training policy takes into account the training needs of all groups of workers; however, it refers to difficulties in balancing training provision, especially in the informal sector and between rural and urban areas. The Government also indicates that a skills training programme has been implemented by the Ministry of Labour, Employment and Youth Development, in collaboration with local government authorities, in 111 rural districts. The Committee notes that, among the specific objectives of the National Employment Policy, there is the promotion of equal access to employment opportunities for vulnerable groups, such as women, youth and persons with disabilities, as well as the enhancement of skills and competencies of workers in the informal sector, especially in rural areas."[25]

[d] *Model Cases Related to Informal Economy That Came to Light in the CAS*

- *Child labour:* In the reports on child labor in Ukraine, Gabon and Zambia, it was observed that most child labor takes place in the informal economy which

24. *Ibid.*, Digest, p. 38.
25. *Ibid.*, Digest, p. 39.

is a very important factor, since it hinders the work that could be carried out by the labor inspection to prevent and detect cases of child labor.[26]

- *Discrimination*: This is the case of the wage gap between men and women in Mauritania, stressing that "It was very important not to limit activities in this area to the formal economy. In fact, a large proportion of women worked in the informal sector and an appropriate policy was necessary in this field, first in order to ensure respect for equality in the informal sector and, more importantly, for the transition of women into the formal economy, which offered more protection and social guarantees for the application of labour standards."[27]
- *Employment policy*: A report on employment policy in Thailand highlights actions taken to improve the conditions of migrant workers and access to training, education and employment of vulnerable workers such as women, workers with disabilities and workers of the rural sector and in the informal economy.

[e] Model Cases That Came to Light in the CFA

- *Case 2221*[28] (Argentina and the Trade Union of Newspapers and Magazines of Federal Capital and Buenos Aires) The Freedom of Association Committee states: "The criterion for determining the persons covered by that right, therefore, is not based on the existence of an employment relationship, which is often non-existent, for example in the case of agricultural workers, self-employed workers in general or those who practice liberal professions, who should nevertheless enjoy the right to organize."
- *Case 2259*[29] (Guatemala and Independent Trade Union Workers of the Central Campus of the San Carlos University of Guatemala). This case is relevant because the union in question is a union of workers in the informal economy that brings a conflict to the Committee on Freedom of Association (CFA).
- *Case 2551*[30] (El Salvador and the Central Latin American Workers' Federation). Case brought by Latin American Central of Workers for the arrest of union leaders, including the president of the Salvadoran National Association of Sellers and Small Merchants, which is recognized as a trade union organization for workers in the informal economy.

26. *Ibid.*, Digest, pp. 42–52.
27. *Ibid.*, Digest, p. 53.
28. Case No. 2221, 332nd report approved by the ILO Governing Body at its November 2003 session, paras. 214–227.
29. Case No. 2259, 334th report, approved by the Governing Body at its June 2004 session, paras. 541, 556, 574 and 580(h).
30. Case No. 2551, 348th report, approved by the Governing Body at its November 2007 session, paras. 564–584.

§5.02 INFORMALITY FROM THE NOTION OF ATYPICAL WORK RELATIONSHIPS: A PRECURSOR DEBATE IN LATIN AMERICAN LABOR LAW

In the 11th World Congress on Labour Law and Social Security held in Caracas in 1985, Professor Efrén Córdova Cordobés was in charge of a general report titled: "New forms and aspects of atypical work relationships."[31]

That was a precursor and still a mandatory text that was written by one of the greatest Cuban and Latin American jurists of any time. In this report, Dr. Córdova highlighted the importance of the issue of atypical work relationships, indicating that:

> Although the labor legislation of almost all countries has always included a classification of employment contracts and many codes accepted the existence of special relationships that deviated from the basic employment pattern, the magnitude and intensity of the deviations that are now observed, constitute an unprecedented phenomenon in the history of labor law. It also draws attention, the marginal or clandestine nature of many of these deviations. This explains why some authors consider that the new atypical forms represent a threat to the maintenance of the tutelary principles that have guided the evolution of labor law.[32]

At the same time, Dr. Cordova emphasized in his report that the absence of adequate regulation means that atypical work is in a vulnerable and unstable situation and those who perform it are exposed to being treated unequally compared to the workers in typical employment relationships.

In his words:

> (...) In light of the above, the importance that the proposed topic has come to acquire, is not only about the emergence of special relationships and that the proliferation reaches respectable proportions. What worries the scholars is that such relations arise outside the channel that had contained the general and special relations of work until now without configuring the classic forms of contracting of common law. It is feared in these conditions that they may generate a new labour order, different and contrary to the principles which have governed the labor relationship up to now, or that the absence of regulation of this new phenomenon generates anomic and irregular situations that could undermine the effectiveness of labour law. There is also concern about the fragile, provisional and precarious nature of the new atypical modalities and the consequences that would result for the worker. More than a simple observation of the variety of manifestations of work as a social phenomenon, it is a matter of discussing whether the array of these new relationships entails a danger or constitutes a challenge to the principles carefully established after a century and a half of experience with wage labour.[33]

---

31. Córdova Cordobés, Efrén. "New Forms and Aspects of Atypical Work Relationships". Eleventh International Congress of Labor Law and Social Security. Volume I. General presentations. September 17–20, 1985, Caracas, Venezuela. p. 245. All the following translations of this text are ours.
32. *Ibid.*, p. 247.
33. *Ibid.*

However, the greatest contribution of that rapporteur is that Dr. Córdova proposes an essay of a typology. First, he tries to delimit how atypical work in these conditions could be defined and resolves the issue stating that there are three generic postulations needed to attempt a terminological approach to the typical contract and from that—and in contrast—to propose an approach to atypical work: first, a full-time employment within the limits of the maximum working day; second, a contractual bond of indefinite duration and, finally, work for a single employer within the employer's premises.

These elements, indicated Dr. Córdova:

> (...) served as the basis for the elaboration of the normative framework that today constitutes the tutelary regime applicable to normal or typical work. They also configured the complex of circumstances that allowed the development of the phenomena of worker concentration and interaction of groups that made the play of collective labour relations possible.[34]

But he even proposes a definition of atypical work, saying that:

> (...) includes new forms of productive activity, which deviate from the classic dependent wage-earning model or from one of its three generic characteristics -as indicated-, as well as preexisting variants of this model, which are now used in a more intense way or respond to purposes different from those previously anticipated.[35]

The work contract, then, represented a paradigm that was raised on subordination and tried to attract any modality of work for others.

Based on this logic, Dr. Cordova tried a typology in a precursor way, concluding that what is known as atypical activity actually consists of three large groups of different activities, namely: (1) the atypical contract itself, (2) self-employment and (3) clandestine work.

In that Congress and in relation to this subject, several national reports were presented, coming from the German Democratic Republic, the Federal Republic of Germany, Argentina, Australia, Austria, Belgium, Bolivia, Colombia, Chile, USA, Finland and France.

I would like to emphasize that four of these reports came from the Argentine Republic and one of them was signed by Dr. Máximo Daniel Monzón. When reading it, thirty-three years later, it is possible to understand what Latin American *ius laboralismo* thought at that time about atypical work employment and justify that those reflections remain valid as essential intellectual referents to understand how the debate on informality in labor law started by the hand of these great masters:

> The possible behaviors escape any typological description or cataloging, since they form open series, variables in each historical- cultural situation, non-determinable quantitatively and non-finite qualitatively, within the deontic scheme of what is due, what is forbidden and what is allowed (depending on whether the positive law requires its execution or its omission or authorizes both its execution and its

34. *Ibid.*
35. *Ibid.*, p. 249.

> omission); in this non-limiting plane, the existential reality (which the doctrine sometimes covers with the linguistic proposal "needs of the traffic") creates and imposes certain binding forms that are not foreseen in legislative regulation; these are the "atypical contracts" or the "atypical work relationships" which, in turn, enter into the system of positive law through decisions of the judges who rest (although they do not say so) in the "postulate of prohibition" (what is [not][36] legally prohibited is legally allowed) or through creations of the legislator.
>
> But the science of law (the cognitive system of the prescriptive or normative system) in its application to labor law (the doctrine of labor law), for reasons of clarity, uses the words "typical-atypical" to designate certain differentiated contractual relationships to appear or not, in the catalogue or "official list" contained in the legislated law.[37]

As it is evident, the debate about atypical or precarious labor relations made an early appearance in Latin American law. The concern was justified by the emergence of sectors unprotected by labor law and public labor administration: precarious employment and therefore unprotected and unstable, where the incidence of unionization was very low and where there was no coverage of collective bargaining. Since the mid-80s of the last century the idea began to arise, even in political discourse, that if the trend did not stop in time, employees would become a privileged sector in the ocean of poor, peasants and informals.[38]

Precariousness and atypical relations were then related to poverty. Today we know that not all informal workers are below the poverty index. But the initial reflection revolved around the typical or normal forms in salaried employment, which, as indicated by the general rapporteur before the 1985 World Congress, was understood as full-time salaried employment, performed in a specific place, where a worker was linked to a single employer and where there was protection of labor legislation and collective bargaining.

Precarious work, Pedro Galin said in the text cited above, "is characterized by its deviation from any of these characteristics."[39] But something else was debated then in the Latin American context: temporary work included within the atypical forms of contracting and other forms of subcontracting. It was years before the attempted adoption of the Subcontracting Convention and Recommendation in 1998, which were finally not adopted and twenty-one years from Employment Relationship Recommendation No. 198 (2006). The loans of workers between companies, part-time work, seasonal work, the uninterrupted succession of fixed-term employment relationships, new forms of work at home and even clandestine work were also discussed. The reflection revolved around precarious salaried work, which should be distinguished

36. Perhaps due to a mistake, the adverb "not" does not appear in the original text, so it is added under our responsibility.
37. Monzón, Máximo Daniel (1985). New Forms and Aspects of Atypical Work Relationships. p. 154. The translation is ours.
38. Galin, Pedro (1986). Wage Earners, Precarization and Working Conditions. In Revista Nueva Sociedad n° 85 September–October 1986, pp. 30–38. http://nuso.org/media/articles/downloads/1424_1.pdf. All the following translations of this text are ours.
39. *Ibid.*, p. 32.

from the so-called urban informal sector that refers to forms of work with low productivity and income, but in which both employers and independent and salaried employees are included.[40]

Galin concludes, in a work that was referential in this sense, saying that "the phenomenon of precarious work or contemporary advance, differs from previous forms because it has the explicit purpose of 'reducing or eliminating the protections that labor law grants to those that are carried out according to the traditional pattern'."[41] Quoting it, echoes the text of the general rapporteur of Dr. Cordova at the World Congress of Labor and Social Security Law of Caracas in 1985.

To sum up, the subject knew precedents that were, at first, seen from a spatial point of view; the IUS (Informal Urban Sector) category came to say that informality was located in a predetermined sector and that, consequently, it was an urban phenomenon. Today neither one thing nor the other would be admissible. Even Recommendation No. 204 abandoned the "informal sector" category to end up coining a more holistic, comprehensive term "informal economy" (and even "informality").

Second, the journey in search of a delimitation of a category finds the notion of precarious work not far from the notion of atypical work. This indicates a distancing from the paradigm on which the Latin American labor law had been raised: on the one hand, subordination and alienation (ajenidad) as areas of specific knowledge of labor law and, on the other, the idea that a unitary labor contract would be able to capture or attract all forms of work for others.

Third, it should be noted that in predecessor works in Latin America, such as that by Pedro Galin at the beginning of the 1980s, there was already a reference and an explicit reflection on the subject of informality.

In a specific mention about employment studies, said the text quoted above, that:

> 50% of precarious workers in Buenos Aires (excluding domestic service) work in companies with more than 5 workers and 46% of Lima workers in companies with more than 10, which excludes them from the so-called informal sector, usually located in micro-enterprises, with low productivity. In both cities it was distributed in all branches of activity.[42]

In the first reflection on informality there was, as it was said before, an objective or material approach that understood that it was found not only in the urban sector but also in that of microenterprises and low-productivity companies. Of course, these are dimensions and delimitations of the concept that have already been overcome. For this reason, it is explained how the terminological change moved from "unstructured sector", "informal sector", "informal economy" to "informality / formality."

A final mention to Galin's work would be pertinent: "Precarization, consequently, would not 'cut' by activities, qualifications or sizes but within companies, segmenting employment in each productive unit."[43] This is a crucial reflection, independently of the fact that, at that moment, informality was understood as an urban

40. *Ibid.*, p. 33.
41. *Ibid.*
42. *Ibid.*, p. 37.
43. *Ibid.*, p. 38.

phenomenon and referred exclusively to a certain type of company. Hence, Galin does not cut the concept by activities, qualifications or sizes, but within the companies. This represents the indisputable contribution of that reflection. But it adds more value the idea that employment ends up being segmented in each productive unit. Because this is the problem that effectively transpires in this postmodernity: *the dualization of the labor market* and the tendency to reduce, sometimes aggressively, the segment of protected work.

What happened since Córdova reflected on atypical work relationships and since in the mid-70s of the last century Italian labour law developed the doctrine of para-subordination[44] was that the crisis of subordination also became that of a legal system built on that cornerstone, such as labor law.

Professor Umberto Romagnoli said: *there is no subordination but subordinations*[45]; an increasingly complex web in charge of reordering work is challenging a legal system that, like the *Nuevo Derecho* (Alfredo Palacios's initiatory book[46]), was raised taking the industrial or secondary sector of the economy into account and is now experiencing an overflowing growth of the service sector, which has resented it in its foundations.

In addition, the capture of those expelled from this scheme of protections and guarantees would be given by three means: (1) legislation, (2) jurisprudence and, of course, (3) public policies. First, with legislative reforms as labor law is, precisely, "labour law, period," (*derecho del trabajo, y punto*) as Professor Oscar Ermida Uriarte said in an unsurpassable way. Second, with a jurisprudence that recognizes indicators of employment—especially to the most expansive ones in their inclusion effect—starting, for example, with Recommendation No. 198 on the Employment Relationship, of 2006.[47] And finally, with the formalization of informality in the logic of Recommendation No. 204 of the ILO that marks the transition from informality to formality which goes hand in hand with protection. In other words, the transversal axis of the formalization is to recover the lost protection or to achieve the protection that never existed before.

Nothing which has been said here is new. The new law or *the tertium genus*, as Georges Gurvitch[48] said, is nowadays interpellated. Some years ago, professors Robert Castel and Adrián Goldin wondered whether we were facing a redeployment or a refoundation of labor law. That dilemma, posed as an intellectual debate, remains, in my opinion, in full force.

---

44. On *parasubordination*, *see* Perulli, Adalberto (2002). Study on Economically Dependent Work/Para-Subordinate (Quasi-subordinate) Work.
45. Romagnoli, Umberto (1992). Deregulation and Sources of Labor Law (p. 7). Madrid: Ed. Complutense. Cuaderno de Relaciones Laborales, No.1. "(...) there is no subordination; there are subordinations; there is no prototype of a subordinate work contract, but a variable typology of intermediate negotiating figures, to which the application, unconscious to the limit of the fiction, of the highest protective standard, cannot be followed, but rather the selection of the most congruent discipline (...)."
46. Palacios, Alfredo (1928). The New Law. 2nd ed., with new author's notes. Buenos Aires: El Ateneo.
47. Employment Relationship Recommendation 2006 (no. 198), No.13.
48. Gurvitch, Georges (1932). L'idée du droit social; notion et système du droit social. Histoire doctrinale depuis le 17. siècle jusqu'à la fin du 19. siècle. Paris: Librairie de Recueil Sirey.

§5.03 THE WORLD COMMISSION ON THE FUTURE OF LABOR (INITIAL REPORT) AND OTHER RECENT ILO STUDIES LINKED TO THE TOPIC

The validity of the approach to informal work from the point of view of atypical work is ratified by the initial report for the World Commission on the Future of Work, published by the ILO in Geneva in 2017,[49] in which, although it is indicated that the atypical work modalities have varied, the relationship of these with the informality is maintained.

The report recognizes that: "Informal employment persists as a main feature of the labour market in many emerging and developing countries. The world has seen steady progress in the transition from informality to formality, but at an unacceptably slow pace."

However, it insists that the transition to the formal economy is "the key to correcting decent work deficits in emerging and developing countries." But with regard to the difficulties faced by companies and workers in the informal economy, the first thing that stands out in the report is the polysemic nature of the concept:

> A striking feature of informality is its sheer diversity. Informal work includes, for example, subsistence farming and survivalist waste picking; it also includes informal work in the formal sector, such as informal wage labour or home-based work.

However, what characterizes informal work according to the report is that it goes beyond the framework of labor legislation and social security. In its terms, "without the protection of laws and regulations covering minimum wages, hours of work, social protection, collective bargaining, OSH, among others, informal workers are deprived of the benefits of economic development."

The companies are also interested in the subject. Companies in the informal sector usually have deficits with regard to property regimes or cannot access to public services, they have difficulties with credit that would help them grow and, finally, they have problems entering the formal sector and to be able to cope with high levels of competency.

That same report pays attention to the so-called diversification of labor relations and begins by stating that:

> The "standard employment relationship", i.e. full-time work understood to be indefinite employment in a subordinate employment relationship, while still the most common form of salaried employment in developed countries, has nonetheless lost ground over the past few decades, in both developed and developing countries, to NSE (...)[50].

49. ILO (2017). Inception Report for the Global Commission on the Future of Work. Geneva. pp. 29–35. Available at https://www.ilo.org/wcmsp5/groups/public/---dgreports/---cabinet/documents/publication/wcms_591502.pdf.
50. *Ibid.*, pp. 38–40.

The report adds that it is about the impact on new organizational forms of work in the face of the challenges of globalization but "also to respond to gaps and regulatory changes and attend the demands for greater flexibility of workers."

The report continues considering the atypical employment, which it recognizes as:

> (...) a grouping of employment arrangements that deviates from standard employment and includes temporary employment, part- time work, temporary agency work and other multiparty employment relationships, disguised employment relationships and dependent self-employment.

As shown, the reflection on the atypical employment maintains absolute validity and it is, of course, the most important point to obtain the appropriation of the informality by labor law. The problem remains the same; what it is different and contemporary are the ways in which this atypicality manifests itself: it has to do with the appearance of work on demand, or with zero-hours contracts (without a guaranteed number of hours), or the so-called gig economy or the sporadic work economy.[51]

The report highlights the impact of these new forms of work management. In the last quarter of 2016, there were 905,000 people working with zero-hours contracts in the United Kingdom, which means no more and no less than 2.8% of all employees. But the economy of sporadic labor or platform economy represents a small proportion of the labor force: in the United States, it is around 0.5% according to different estimates, but there is no doubt that the sector is growing aggressively.

This sporadic work economy would include two types of work: (1) "collaborative work" and (2) "work on demand through applications." The particularity of "collaborative work" is that it is done remotely on online platforms, which indicates a cybernetic dimension or the cyberspace of new forms of work.

"Work on demand through applications", particularly influential in the transport, cleaning, or courier services sectors, uses applications that, administered by companies, impose certain quality standards on workers. All of this is obvious and, as the report recognizes, it will impose legal problems, of which the most relevant is the classification of these workers as independent contractors or, even, as self-employed workers, which means that—according to the case—would be out of the employment relationship.

There is no shortage of classifications that refer to the term "dependent contractors" or "independent workers", which cover some traits of the traditional relationship but which are definitely nuanced. The notion of a dependent contractor reveals the trace of subordination, while that of an independent worker, the nuance of that same subordination, or the already classic para-subordination; that is, the way in which the reordering of work has diluted the concept of subordination but without being able to dispense of it completely.

Of course the impacts of atypical employment for workers, according to the report, have to do with the security of employment, with income and with risks of wage penalties that are not befitting of typical jobs, with a schedule that touches other

51. *Ibid.*, p. 39.

variables that they end up very weakened, such as rest time or the balance of professional, private and family life; naturally, the impact has to do with health and safety at work, as they are considerably risky jobs, not only because of the lack of training but also because of supervisory problems, taking into account that the incidence of *the inspective function* in the area is weak.

The report highlights that labor accident rates are higher among workers in atypical employment. As regards social security and its coverage, it usually does not apply to workers linked by atypical work relationships, especially because they do not meet the minimum requirements related to the duration of employment, working time or income. Also, as regards training, workers involved in an atypical relationship are less likely to receive on-the-job training.

In addition, and very importantly, the almost absence of union organizations in the sector tends to negate the right to freedom of association and collective bargaining.

Thus, the terms of the discussion about informal workers—that is, the link to atypical work and the lack of protection—have not changed even three decades later, as can be seen in three ILO's studies of a more holistic nature published between 2016 and 2017, which focus more systematically on the issue of informality; however, they still show that there is no definitive terminological demarcation.

In 2016, the study "Non-standard employment around the world: Understanding challenges, shaping prospects"[52] was published, in which, although informal employment itself was not tackled, many of its observations are applied to what we would understand today by informal employment as one of its components is atypical work. This reference to atypical work is made with regard to occasional employment, which the study points to as a characteristic feature of informal salaried employment in low-income developing countries. As it is evident, the reference to the atypical employment after that general report of Dr. Efrén Córdova Cordobés of 1985 is maintained.

Another study from the same year 2016 was published under the title "Women at Work: Trends 2016."[53] In the executive summary and regarding the quality of women's jobs, it is stated that women continue to be overrepresented as auxiliary family workers and as self-employed workers, understanding both as informal work modalities. The study highlights that even when women have wage and salaried jobs, this is not consistent with contributions to social protection, which would mean that many of these salaried jobs are equally informal, understanding that informality is related to the lack of access to protection and social security. Once again, the defining feature of informality is highlighted, making it emerge from lack of protection.

Finally, in 2017 the study "Addressing governance challenges in a changing labor migration landscape" was published. In different parts of the study, reference is made to the informal economy. While it does not address informal employment per se, it does present the participation of migrant workers in the informal economy as a factor that hinders protection and decent work.

52. ILO (2016). Non-standard Employment Around the World: Understanding Challenges, Shaping Prospects [Overview]. Geneva.
53. ILO (2016). Women at Work: Trends 2016 [Summary]. Geneva.

The much larger supply of less-skilled workers in relation to available jobs abroad means that they tend to be recruited under temporary migration schemes, often after paying fees to labor recruiters, and into sectors characterized by nonstandard forms of employment and greater informality and where decent work deficits are most prevalent.[54]

As shown, the atypical forms of employment and informality are sometimes overlapping concepts and, on the other, the lack of protection as what finally defines the workers' stage in the informal sector. Certainly, "Moreover, where bilateral and multilateral social security conventions exist, they mostly cover formal workers, leaving migrant workers in the informal economy unprotected."[55]

It seems evident that the study understands that migrants, as a particularly vulnerable group, are a determining component of the informal sector. On the other, the study highlights that, "Globally, there are examples where national labour laws exclude certain sectors from coverage, such as agriculture and domestic work, with a disproportionate impact on the large numbers of migrant workers in those sectors (many of whom are working in the informal economy)."[56]

In addition, it emphasizes: "Among the fundamental components of the relevant policies for labor migration, they highlight (...) the transition of migrant workers from the informal to the formal economy."[57] This is the logic of the Recommendation No. 204: the shift from informality to formality. But at the same time, it is clear that migrant workers, as being especially vulnerable and unprotected collectives, are part of the informal sector.

A final mention of the study is worth highlighting.

> At the same time, abusive practices also characterize a segment of this industry, which includes informal intermediaries, unauthorized subagents, and others operating in the informal economy and outside of the legal and regulatory framework.[58]

It is discussed about informal intermediaries operating in the informal economy, that is to say, there is an approach to the informality issue from a subjective perspective (the intermediaries) and an objective one (the informal economy scope). In both cases, this action takes place outside the legal and regulatory frameworks, which reiterates the lack of protection as a defining criterion to move from informality and what should be undertaken if you want the transition of those workers to the field of formal employment. On several occasions, the study references the special vulnerability and lack of protection of migrant workers, domestic workers, construction and agriculture workers. These are groups associated with informality, as they are often unprotected.

54. ILO (2017). Addressing governance challenges in a changing labour migration landscape. International Labour Conference, 106th Session. Report IV. Fourth item on the agenda. Geneva. p. 17.
55. *Ibid.*, p. 24.
56. *Ibid.*, p. 24.
57. *Ibid.*, p. 37.
58. *Ibid.*, p. 60.

As recent studies published at the same time as Recommendation No 204 show, the informal economy is not directly tackled but there is a clear reference to the informal employment in relation to the recognition of groups that are especially vulnerable and tend to be unprotected as migrant workers.[59]

§5.04 THE CHALLENGE THAT INFORMALITY REPRESENTS FOR LABOR LAW

Professor Luigi Mengoni said that "work as a legal category does not exist. What exists are people who work." This seems quite obvious but, on the contrary, summarizes an existential challenge for labor law.

The labor law, at the beginning, intended to regulate *work for others (ajenidad)*, mainly in the secondary sector of the economy: the industry or manufacturing sector. The truth is that it would take many decades until the categories linked to the informal economy emerged. This is a tendentially broad and expansive term that reveals the idea of a system or an economic circuit.

Gone are the initial terms of *the informal urban sector* or *the informal sector* itself. However, if more than work what really exists are men and women who work, the personal dimension linking the worker and the person receiving this benefit is confirmed, a specificity that the labor law did not always attend in a convenient manner. Perhaps an approach to labor law is necessary from the personal dimension of the legal link that explains it—the working relationship—and that it is called to regulate.

Informality is an existential challenge for the labor law, since in this growing and sometimes aggressively expansive area, is where the effective validity of labor legislation is at stake.

The working relationships of postmodernism or post-Fordism are marking some trends that are crucial and hopefully not definitive:

59. The Report of the Director-General before the 19th American Regional Meeting, Panama, October 2–5, 2018, says: "Preparing the future of work we want in the Americas through social dialogue":

> 58. Informal employment affects certain groups more than others. For example, women, young people, workers with lower levels of educational attainment, workers with lower incomes and some other categories of workers. In the case of women, the informality rate in 2015 was higher for them than for men (46.5 per cent compared with 43.3 per cent), in part due to the high rate of informal employment in households (74 per cent), in the own-account category (81.6 per cent), in some subsectors such as commerce, restaurants and hotels (60 per cent) and community, social and personal services (39 per cent) which have a high concentration of female employment.
>
> About 80 per cent of total formal employment is concentrated in occupational categories such as own-account workers, employees of companies with up to 10 workers and workers in the household sector.
>
> There is a close relationship between informality and inequality, both of which represent different dimensions of the same phenomenon: exclusion.

(a) The first is the progressive reduction of the scope of work effectively protected. This trend moves in the direction of a clamp that gradually reduces the effective application space of labor law.

(b) On the other hand and from a theoretical point of view, *a dualization of the labor market* by the segmentation or informalization of work is evident, and, on a material level, a *sustained expulsion of workers* from the field of protection is progressively verified, since, although they actually provide services for third parties, they do not do so under the effective coverage (protection) of the labor legislation.

(c) Professor Antonio Ojeda Avilés distinguished two clearly differentiated moments in the evolution of labor law: a centripetal or inclusion period and a centrifugal period of exclusion of those who previously experienced the protection of a guarantee-based statute by offering a work for others.[60]

"The lines of expansion of the labour law,' the sevillian professor teaches', go in the following directions (which we come to erect in more and more substantial branches of labor regulations by contemplating this or that aspect, starting from the common part):

(1) The company in crisis.
(2) The dual company.
(3) Autonomous and semiautonomous workers group.
(4) The worker as a person.
(5) The worker as a commercial subject.
(6) Public employment."[61]

(d) At the same time, a reprivatization of public law is perceived alongside a momentum that is gradually justifying a labor law by segments or by scales. This is explained by a discourse that preaches the need for labor regulation that caters to specific sectors of work or areas of activity: SMEs, youth work, economically dependent self-employment, informal work, among others.

(e) In this scenario, the famous principle of territorial application and *erga omnes* of the labour law would capitulate and would arise in its place a *modular labour law* that risks that the trip is not towards the threshold of more protection but exactly the opposite. For all these reasons, the future rival of labour law might not be civil law but commercial law.

(f) Furthermore, and this is the most relevant at *Recommendation on the transition from the informal economy to the formal economy,* 2015 (no. 204) from the perspective of labour law, it is clear that lack of protection is the common thread between informality and formality, or what is the same, that the worker who provides services for others will move from one to another depending on whether the work offered is protected.

(g) This is the core of *the paradigm of decent work* that, having emerged in the memory of the Director General of the ILO before the International Labour

60. Ojeda Avilés, Antonio (2009). The "Externalization" of Labour Law. In International Labour Review, Volume 148, Issue 1-2, pp. 47-67. The translation is ours.
61. *Ibid.*, p. 55.

Conference in 1999,[62] would end up being part of one of the statements, few indeed, that the organization adopted throughout its almost century-old history: *The ILO declaration on social justice for an equitable globalization of June 10, 2008.*[63]

(h) Now, what is the condition that determines the effective protection of this work that means the scope of knowledge and regulation of labor law? In other words, what will make the transition between informality and formality possible from the perspective of labour law? Undoubtedly, *the work relationship* that represents *the act-condition* and places work for others under a protective and guarantee statute represented by labour legislation.[64] This is, in my opinion, the epicenter of a strictly legal and labour law approach to Recommendation No. 204, an approach that is necessarily partial given the thematic complexity of the instrument.

§5.05 THE NOTION OF THE INFORMAL ECONOMY IN ILO RECOMMENDATION NO. 204

This notion determines the scope of application of Recommendation No. 204 and shows how a terminology started with the urban informal sector, moved to informal sector and ended in the informal economy.

> For the purposes of this Recommendation, the term "informal economy": refers to all economic activities by workers and economic units that are—in law or in practice—*not covered or insufficiently covered by formal arrangements.*

It is a definition more descriptive than ontological but also tautological.

The purpose of the recommendation is to promote public policies to facilitate the transition of workers and economic units from the informal economy to the formal economy and promote the creation, preservation and sustainability of businesses and decent jobs in the formal economy. Besides, it is also very important, to prevent informalization of jobs in the formal economy, which means that the jobs that were formalized could return to informality.

---

62. "The primary goal of the ILO today is to promote opportunities for women and men to obtain decent and productive work, in conditions of freedom, equity, security and human dignity." https://www.ilo.org/public/english/standards/relm/ilc/ilc87/rep-i.htm.
63. "I. Scope and principles. The Conference recognizes and declares that: A. In the context of accelerating change, the commitments and efforts of Members and the Organization to implement the ILO's constitutional mandate, including through international labour standards, and to place full and productive employment and decent work at the center of economic and social policies, should be based on the four equally important strategic objectives of the ILO, through which the Decent Work Agenda is expressed (...)" https://www.ilo.org/wcmsp5/groups/public/---dgreports/--- cabinet/documents/genericdocument/wcms_371208.pdf.
64. This idea appears in: "Crítique of the labor law" by Alain Supiot: "The labor contract thus acquires the virtue of giving the worker a true 'status'. To use the expression of Georges Scelle, the contract plays a role of 'act-condition' that determines the application of a systematic set of rules, regardless of the will of the parties to the contract." Supiot, A. (1996). Critique of Labor Law. Spain: Ministry of Labor and Social Affairs. p. 47. The translation is ours.

However, what determines the transition from the informal economy to the formal one is protection and/or coverage: this is where the legal and more specifically labor dimension of Recommendation No. 204 resides.

The scope of *the economic units of the informal economy* in Recommendation No. 204 is defined as follows:

"For the purposes of this Recommendation, '*economic units*' in the informal economy include:

(a) Units that employ hired labour.
(b) Units that are owned by individuals working on their own account (...).
(c) Cooperatives and social and solidarity economy units."

It is a definition of an objective and/or spatial nature that reveals three types of legal relations essential for labor law:

(1) *The employment relationship for a third party or subordinate* mentioned in literal a).
(2) *The unsubordinated autonomous work* mentioned in literal b).
(3) *The triangular, intermediated or outsourced work relationship* mentioned in literal c).

This reveals three key categories to understand the informal economy from the perspective of labor law:

(1) The subordinate employment relationship.
(2) *Autonomous, non-subordinate work*—which logically suggests the existence of a work halfway between autonomy and subordination, that is, *self-employed workers* (that can sometimes represent *false self-employed workers*) and *subordinated workers*.
(3) *The triangular, intermediated or outsourced relationship*, which is typical of the associated work cooperatives or other experiences of the social and solidarity economy.

This shows a crucial piece of information for the proposed approach: in the informal economy there are different legal relationships that involve the provision of services; formal jobs that live in the informal economy or also informal jobs that come from the formal economy and that somehow integrate it, which reveals a fact of unquestionable practical importance: the way in which the informal economy integrates itself into the formal economy. That is, formal economy jobs that are relocated to the informal economy.

At last, *the subjective scope of application of Recommendation No. 204* "applies to all workers and economic units—including enterprises, entrepreneurs and households—in the informal economy, in particular:

(a) *Those in the informal economy who own and operate economic units, including:*
   (i) own-account workers;
   (ii) employers; and
   (iii) members of cooperatives and of social and solidarity economy units;
(b) *Contributing family workers,* irrespective of whether they work in economic units in the formal or informal economy.
(c) *Employees holding informal jobs in or for formal enterprises,* or in or for economic units in the informal economy, including but not limited to those in subcontracting and in supply chains, or as paid domestic workers employed by households; and
(d) *Workers in unrecognized or unregulated employment relationships,*" which obviously alludes to disguised employment relationships as described by the Employment Relationship Recommendation, 2006 (No. 198).

§5.06 THE STATE OF THE ART: INFORMALITY IN CONTEMPORARY LATIN AMERICAN LABOR LAW

[A] General and Approach Criteria

The national reports for the drafting of this rapporteur allow to confirm certain trends that seem consolidated, with regard to the approximation of informal work and informal workers from the perspective of labor law.

National reports were received from Argentina,[65] Bolivia,[66] Chile,[67] Costa Rica,[68] Mexico,[69] Panama,[70] Peru,[71] Uruguay[72] and Venezuela.[73]

In each of these reports, it is confirmed that there is no legal definition of informal work and that the regulation of informal work is not included explicitly and systematically in labor legislation.

With this, two constants that mark trends can be anticipated:

The labor legislation does not still have the category of informal work and informal workers; therefore, there is no specific regulation of the informal sector. In any case, national reports do not fail to mention criteria that could define informal work. These criteria move in three areas:

65. Aquino, Marcelo G.; Carugo, Agustín H.; Khedavan, Eugenia (2018). The Informal Work in the Argentinian Labour Law. The translation of this and all other national reports is ours.
66. Campero Villalba, Iván (2018). National Report. Bolivia.
67. Chile (2018). Survey on Labour Informality. Chile.
68. Costa Rica (2018). National Report of Costa Rica. Informal work.
69. Natividad Sánchez, Tomás (2018). National Report of Mexico.
70. Centella G., Margarita; Santamaría, Zulphy; Ayala, Carlos (2018). Informal Working Report. Panama.
71. Perú (2018). Questionnaire about Informal Workers in Peru.
72. Nicoliello, Ariel; Riva, Ana; Castro, Natalia (2018). Uruguay: National Report on Informal Work.
73. Jaime Kellerhoff, Daniel (et al.) (2018). "Chapter Venezuela". Report for the World Congress of Labor and Social Security Law, Turin, Italy. Sponsored by the SIDTSS.

(1) The worker's participation in social security systems.
(2) The formal employment relationship is followed in some way within a legal framework.
(3) The employment relationship that involves informal workers is not registered.

The report from Argentina indicates that informal workers do not have coverage in social security systems and are not included under specific registers.

For its part, the Bolivian report indicates that informal workers are considered similar to self-employed or independent workers which opens another perspective that comes to ratify the overlap of informal work with other categories or typologies that are close but not exactly similar.

The Chilean report says that the informal sector includes workers without a contract of employment.[74]

In Costa Rica, the mention has to do with the non-coverage of social security and that the employment relationship is not subject to national labor legislation.

The Mexican report highlights, on the one hand, the noninclusion of informal workers in social security systems, but at the same time the exclusion of formal work systems, which is usually associated with socioeconomic problems and the failure to comply with basic labor obligations.[75] A criterion is highlighted here that in the long run will be important:

> in the informal sector, the basic labour obligations are usually not fulfilled, which means that this work is not done under conditions of protection.

In Panama, informal work occurs "outside of current legal protections, including social security and labor standards.[76]" The Peruvian report highlights the lack of coverage of the sector by social security and tax systems. In the Uruguayan national report, "the expression *informal work or employment* refers to the non-registration of workers in social security."[77] In the case of Venezuela, "informal work is the one that is outside the framework of legality."[78]

Although the reports indicate that there is no exact definition of informal employment in the law and that there is no specific regulation of informality in the labor legislation, there would be criteria that define informal work linked to social security, legal framework and registry, among others. These others would mean the assimilation of informal work with autonomous or independent work (Bolivia) or work without a contract (Chile) or that of basic labor obligations (Mexico).

74. Chile (2018). Questionnaire Labour Informality in Chile. p. 1.
75. Natividad Sánchez, Tomás (2018). National Report Mexico. p. 1.
76. Centella G., Margarita; Santamaría, Zulphy; Ayala, Carlos (2018). Informal Work Report. Panama. p. 1.
77. Nicoliello, Ariel; Riva, Ana; Castro, Natalia (2018). Uruguay: National Report on Informal Work. p. 1.
78. Jaime Kellerhoff, Daniel (et al.) (2018). "Chapter Venezuela." Report for the World Congress of Labor and Social Security Law, Turin, Italy. Sponsored by the SIDTSS. p. 2.

[B] The Regulation of Informal Work

The consequence of this overlap and the evident fact that there is neither a specific *corpus iuris* on informal work nor with a particular definition of work or informal workers[79] is that the national legislation clearly demonstrates the different legislations that, in some way, would regulate informal work. Thus, when asked about the national legislation that is applied to informal workers, the Argentinian report responds by indicating that they appear in the agrarian labor regime or in the special regime of the construction industry, but at the same time, in the personal of private homes and also, self-employed workers who are governed by service contracts.[80] There is then evidence of a diversity of types within the category of informal workers.

This is reiterated in the Chilean report, which highlights the reference to work or informal workers in the status of workers subcontracted and supplied and also in that of workers in private homes.

In Costa Rica, the legislation applicable to the sector and to informal workers has to do with the rules for strengthening small and medium enterprises.[81] In Mexico, according to the national report and in line with the Costa Rican report, the link to informal work is given by the law of social and solidarity economy that is applicable to "ejidos", communities, cooperatives, workers' organizations, among others.

In Peru (this has to do with a precedent that was previously indicated) the special labour regime of micro and small enterprises results a legislation applicable to informal work and to informal workers.[82]

In Uruguay, the monotax law and social security laws, as well as the special statutes for domestic services and rural workers, would extend their coverage to informal workers.[83]

In Venezuela, the law of cooperative associations and the organic law of the communal economic system mention informal work and informal workers.

The Bolivian report[84] says that work and informal workers would pay particular attention to the mechanisms of punishment for simulation and labor fraud.

The Panamanian report makes no mention of this particular topic.

This could suggest two added trends: the first one, that the lack of definition and the lack of legislative delimitation on work and informal workers will raise not strictly labor regulations—which may be close if they are understood as more comprehensive categories like the social right: agrarian work, work of the construction, small and

79. For this reason, the Pan-Hispanic Dictionary of Legal Spanish of very recent appearance, edited by the Royal Spanish Academy of Language, the General Council of the Judicial Power of Spain and the Ibero-American Judicial Summit (2017), does not yet record the term "informal worker." It records the self-employed and the economically dependent (Vid. p. 1977), which is explained by a direct influence of Spanish legislation.
80. Aquino, Marcelo G.; Carugo, Agustín H.; Khedavan, Eugenia (2018). Informal Work in the Argentinian Labour Law. p. 17.
81. Costa Rica (2018). National Report of Costa Rica: Informal Work. p. 5.
82. Perú (2018). Questionnaire about Informal Workers in Peru. p. 6.
83. Nicoliello, Ariel; Riva, Ana; Castro, Natalia (2018). Uruguay: National Report on Informal Work. pp. 4-5.
84. Campero Villalba, Iván (2018). National Report of Bolivia. p. 12.

medium industry, workers of private houses, laws of monotax or extensions of the social security and even laws of cooperative associations.

But at the same time, the old precedent is reiterated in that the informal sector had a very specific scope of manifestation in the sector of micro- and small enterprises, where a sort of modular labor statute arose that would justify a further comment later.

[C] The Revival of the Paradigm of Subordination

In any case, what does seem to be an evident trend is that there is a legislative protection of the informal worker, as long as it is understood as a worker who provides services under a subordination regime, which is not new, as all Ibero-American labor codes are called upon to regulate subordinate work or work for others (ajenidad).

The national reports of Argentina, Chile, Costa Rica, Mexico, Panama, Peru and Uruguay ratify that protection, but there are exceptions of enormous relevance. The Bolivian report emphasizes that there is no protection to informal subordinate work, since it is understood as necessarily autonomous. This fact marks a distance from the paradigm of work given under conditions of subordination, moving the notion of informality to the category of autonomous workers, where either there is no subordination or this is qualified in a very particular way.

In the case of the Venezuelan report, it is emphasized that there is no particular protection of informal subordinate work.[85]

From all said above, it can be drawn that most of the nations studied consider protection for the worker who does not have a contract, registration or access to social security, as far as they provide services under a relationship of subordination, which in fact should be declared by a labor court or by an administrative authority.

To the question of whether there was a protection of the autonomous informal worker in the national legislation or practice, the reports of Argentina, Bolivia, Chile, Costa Rica, Mexico, Panama, Peru, Uruguay and Venezuela, that is, all the reports received answered that there was not.

However, to the question of whether there would be a protection of the autonomous but economically dependent informal workers, all the national studies received conclude that there is no specific protection or regulation, except in the case of what is highlighted by the Argentinian report which shows that the subject is precisely under discussion by the doctrine and jurisprudence.

In the reports of Bolivia, Chile, Costa Rica, Mexico, Panama, Peru, Uruguay and Venezuela, there is no provision or practice of protection for economically dependent informal self-employed workers.

There are two tendencies: on the one hand, the mention of the protection of the subordinate informal worker and, on the other, the lack of protection of the autonomous informal worker and the virtual absence of protection to the autonomous informal worker economically dependent, which means that subordination remains,

85. Jaime Kellerhoff, Daniel (et al.) (2018). "Chapter Venezuela." Report for the World Congress of Labor and Social Security Law, Turin, Italy. Sponsored by the SIDTSS. p. 2.

clearly, the element that continues to characterize the employment relationship and what somehow still marks the difficulty of an appropriation of the category informal sector and informal workers by labor law .

[D] Freedom of Association in Informal Work

But one more trend can be established with regard to the approximation of labor law as a whole to the phenomenon of informality and has to do with the manifestations of freedom of association. It is true that the national reports in general indicate the establishment of trade union organizations of informal workers.

The Argentinian report indicates that, in general, there are no specific trade union organizations of informal workers, as they can join workers' centers but not exclusively as informal organizations.[86]

The Bolivian report does not mention experiences of union organization of informal workers. Neither does Chile's report. In the case of the Mexican report, only one instance reported as an experience of union organization of informal workers[87] is mentioned. The same happens in the Peruvian national report. In general, there are experiences of union organizing in informal sectors as highlighted in the report of Costa Rica,[88] Panama,[89] Uruguay[90] and Venezuela.

However, the consequence of this not too widespread union organization of the sector still does not reach a significant coverage in relation to collective bargaining. As a general rule, the Argentinian report indicates that informal workers are not covered by collective bargaining, although there are very relevant exceptions for groups of specific workers, such as agricultural workers and domestic workers, who bargain in tripartite committees.[91] The Bolivian, Chilean, Costa Rican, Mexican, Panamanian and Peruvian reports do not highlight experiences of collective bargaining in the sector.

The Uruguayan report, for its part, mentions an only instance reported.[92] And there is a mention of collective bargaining experiences in the sector in Venezuela's national report.[93]

The trend that emerges from the two variables linked to freedom of association seems obvious. In general, a weak, if not inexistent, implantation of the trade union organizations of informal workers brings as a second tendency a very unusual or

86. Aquino, Marcelo G.; Carugo, Agustín H.; Khedavan, Eugenia (2018). Informal Work in the Argentinian Labour Law. p. 45.
87. Natividad Sánchez, Tomás (2018). National Report, Mexico. p. 22.
88. Costa Rica (2018). National Report of Costa Rica: Informal Work. p. 17.
89. Centella G., Margarita; Santamaría, Zulphy; Ayala, Carlos (2018). Informal Work Review. Panamá. p. 22.
90. Nicoliello, Ariel; Riva, Ana; Castro, Natalia (2018). Uruguay: National Report on Informal Work. p. 19.
91. Aquino, Marcelo G.; Carugo, Agustín H.; Khedavan, Eugenia (2018). The Informal Work in the Argentinian Labour Law. p. 44.
92. Nicoliello, Ariel; Riva, Ana; Castro, Natalia (2018). Uruguay: National Report on Informal Work. p. 19.
93. Jaime Kellerhoff, Daniel (et al.) (2018). "Chapter Venezuela." Report for the World Congress of Labor and Social Security Law, Turin, Italy. Sponsored by the SIDTSS. p. 2.

limited coverage of collective bargaining in the sector. For this reason, if it is understood that social dialogue is a corollary of freedom of association—the ILO has always understood that the first requirement for the exercise of an effective social dialogue is freedom of association—the experience of social dialogue in the scope of informal work and informal workers is quite uneven and clearly weak.

However, the Argentine report indicates that there are councils or bodies of social dialogue that include informal workers.[94] The same is said in the reports of Costa Rica,[95] Panama[96] and Uruguay. But, in those received from Bolivia, Chile, Mexico, Peru and Venezuela[97] it is explicitly indicated that there are no councils or bodies of social dialogue involving informal workers, which seems to confirm not only an open weakness in the essential contents of freedom union (union implantation and collective bargaining) but also a glaring weakness of social dialogue and its promotion.

[E] New Form of Work Organization

However, as regards the relationship between informal work and new forms of work management, national reports provide very rich information about the so-called triangular relations.

The Argentinian national report indicates that the joint and several liability of the beneficiary company in the fulfillment of labor obligations and also of workers' registration is recognized. The Argentinian regime[98] sanctions the fraudulent intermediation (when the user grants ordinary tasks and not eventual to the supplied worker). In this case the user is considered as an employer and therefore responsible for the registration; the registration achieved by the intermediary does not satisfy legal requirements and thus, it is considered informal.

The Bolivian report highlights the sanction to simulation or labor contract fraud when it occurs through subcontracting or outsourcing.[99]

In Chile subcontracting is fully accepted for any item, and there is, however, joint and several liability of the user company for the contractor's labor obligation, with possible subsidiary liability if the power of control is exercised. The user is directly responsible for safety in the workplace.[100]

In the report of Costa Rica, it is indicated that if the contractor does not have autonomous capital, the user company is jointly and severally liable for its obligations.[101] Intermediary contractors in agriculture and construction often do not have

94. Aquino, Marcelo G.; Carugo, Agustín H.; Khedavan, Eugenia (2018). Informal Work in the Argentinian Labour Law. p. 47.
95. Costa Rica (2018). National Report of Costa Rica: Informal Work. p. 18.
96. Centella G., Margarita; Santamaría, Zulphy; Ayala, Carlos (2018). Informal Work Report. Panamá. p. 22.
97. Jaime Kellerhoff, Daniel (et al.) (2018). "Chapter Venezuela." Report for the World Congress of Labor and Social Security Law, Turin, Italy. Sponsored by the SIDTSS. p. 18.
98. Aquino, Marcelo G.; Carugo, Agustín H.; Khedavan, Eugenia (2018). The Informal Work in the Argentinian Labour Law. pp. 37–39.
99. Campero Villalba, Iván (2018). National Report Bolivia. p. 12.
100. Chile (2018). Questionnaire on Informal Work in Chile. p. 2.
101. Costa Rica (2018). National Report of Costa Rica: Informal Work. p. 9.

their own capital, so it is estimated that the employer is the user company, but these cases are not known or quantified due to the lack of an effective inspection.[102] In addition, in the matter of cooperatives fraud cases are recognized as non-associated employees are employed.

The Mexican report mentions a proposal for a decree to promote decent work that includes the regulation of subcontracting, in order to avoid evasion or avoidance of labor obligations.[103] The social sector of the economy includes shared land, communities, workers' organizations, cooperatives, among others.

The Panama report indicates that contractors and subcontractors are considered employers. The joint and several liability of the user company for the compliance of labor obligations is recognized, provided that the work be a task related to the company.[104] When contractors perform work exclusively or principally for another user, it is considered as an employer.

In the report of Peru, it is highlighted that informal work in triangular relationships "occurs when the requirements established in the legal system to make the use of these triangular relationship possible, are not fulfilled,"[105], once again, informality is defined as breach of the labor legislation, or what is the same, from the lack of protection.

In Uruguay, the joint and several liability of the user company has the aim of guaranteeing the fulfillment of labour obligations. The law includes subcontracting, intermediation and supply figures,[106] and in fact, there is informal work in these modalities. The non-registered worker does not have the protection of registered subcontracted workers.[107]

The report from Venezuela[108] indicates that contractors that execute works or services with their own elements are not considered intermediaries or outsourcers. The user companies are jointly and severally liable when the services involved are inherent or related. Outsourcing, understood as simulation or labor fraud with the purpose of ignoring or hindering the application of labor law, is also highlighted in the report. This outsourcing includes the subcontracting of permanent works, contracting by intermediary, simulation or fraud by civil or commercial contracting.

From what is indicated with regard to the relations between informal work and new forms of work organization and particularly of triangular or outsourced relationships, what stands out is the possibility that the mechanism, lawful in principle, can serve as an elusion modality of labor obligations and therefore suppose a type of unprotected work. The simulation and contractual fraud contribute to increase the

102. *Ibid.*, p. 12.
103. Natividad Sánchez, Tomás (2018). National Report Mexico. p. 11.
104. Centella G., Margarita; Santamaría, Zulphy; Ayala, Carlos (2018). Informal Work Report. Panamá. pp. 11–12.
105. Perú (2018). Questionnaire about Informal Workers in Peru. p. 10.
106. Nicoliello, Ariel; Riva, Ana; Castro, Natalia (2018). Uruguay: National Report on Informal Work. p. 9.
107. *Ibid.*, p. 18.
108. Jaime Kellerhoff, Daniel [et.al.] (2018). "Chapter Venezuela." Report for the World Congress of Labor and Social Security Law, Turin, Italy. Sponsored by the SIDTSS. pp. 10–12.

scope of the unprotected work segment, setting trend towards the dualization of the labor market.

[F] Public Policies

The answers received in the National Reports to the question of how the States have tried to reduce informal work in public policies are indeed distinct and particularly suggestive.

In the case of Argentina, the policy of incorporating workers into social benefit programs for formal companies,[109] training policies and the provisional reduction of social security contributions is highlighted in order to encourage incorporation into the formality of the sector and of the workers.[110]

In the case of Bolivia,[111] the national report draws attention to the policy of extending social security benefits, especially in relation to vulnerable groups.

In Chile, the national report highlights the policy of flexibilization aimed at microenterprises,[112] while in Costa Rica, the national report mentions an agreement for the implementation of Recommendation No. 204,[113] along with a law to strengthen the small and medium company.[114]

In the case of Mexico, the national report emphasizes the voluntary adhesion of independent workers to social security[115] and also policies to disseminate benefits of labor formality.[116]

In Panama, emphasis was placed on training and qualification policies for workers.[117] In Peru a special labor regime for micro- and small enterprises was highlighted.[118]

In Uruguay, the national report shows campaigns aimed at domestic and rural workers; the extension of the monotax; the creation of national health insurance and the promotion of unionization and collective bargaining in the sector.[119]

The report from Venezuela makes no mention about this topic.

The tendencies deduced from the response to the questionnaires of the national reports particularly highlight the public policies aimed at increasing the coverage of social security, on the other hand, the flexibilization of working conditions in the field of micro-enterprises, training and qualification of workers and in the case of Uruguay,

109. Aquino, Marcelo G.; Carugo, Agustín H.; Khedavan, Eugenia (2018). Informal Work in the Argentinian Labour Law. p. 7.
110. *Ibid.*, pp. 9–12.
111. Campero Villalba, Iván (2018). National Report Bolivia. p. 13.
112. Chile (2018). Questionnaire Informal Work in Chile. p. 2.
113. Costa Rica (2018). National Report of Costa Rica: Informal Work. p. 18.
114. *Ibid.*, p. 6.
115. Natividad Sánchez, Tomás (2018). National Report Mexico. p. 9.
116. *Ibid.*, p. 12.
117. Centella G., Margarita; Santamaría, Zulphy; Ayala, Carlos (2018). Informal Work Report Panamá. p. 8.
118. Perú (2018). Questionnaire about Informal Workers in Peru. p. 3.
119. Nicoliello, Ariel; Riva, Ana; Castro, Natalia (2018). Uruguay: National Report on Informal Work. p. 2.

campaigns for domestic and rural workers, with the extension of monotax, health insurance, but especially and this must be highlighted, the promotion of unionization and collective bargaining.

[G] Gender Dimension

In the field of public policies and initiatives related to the treatment of the informal sector, the questionnaire asked about informality and the gender dimension. The responses indicate that there is no sustained and consistent treatment of informality and gender. This was seen in the national report of Argentina, Chile, Costa Rica, of Peru, neither of Uruguay nor of Venezuela. In three national reports, an explicit reference is made between the issues of informality and gender equity.

The Bolivian report mentions that, on average, women participate more in the service sector, working on their own, have a greater deficit of quality work, receive lower income and enter the labor market with "lower levels of human capital" and experience, which is a reflection of the inequalities in the labour market in general, including the scope of informal work and informal workers.[120]

In the national report of Mexico, it is highlighted that, among the measures designed to mitigate the effects of informality, life insurance was created for vulnerable households in conditions of poverty headed by women.[121] This is the most interesting mention of the answers of the national questionnaires regarding the issue of informality and gender.

Finally, in the case of Panama, informality is predominantly male in all areas, with the exception of work at homes.[122]

The wide space of informality of work at homes must be taken into account, since they are jobs with a high rate of feminization. At the same time, a deficit of gender equity occurs particularly in the service sector where there is a high rate of self-employed women and where the decent work deficit is even more noticeable, especially in terms of lower incomes.

[H] Work Inspection

The report from Argentina highlights that the Labour and Social Security Inspectorate has, among its objectives, to control the compliance of labour and social security standards and contribute to the elimination of non-registered employment.[123] However, the national report recognizes that it has not been effective enough in detecting labor informality.[124]

120. Campero Villalba, Iván (2018). National Report Bolivia. p. 5.
121. Natividad Sánchez, Tomás (2018). National Report México. p. 12.
122. Centella G., Margarita; Santamaría, Zulphy; Ayala, Carlos (2018). Informal Work Report. Panamá. pp. 3 y 7.
123. Aquino, Marcelo G.; Carugo, Agustín H.; Khedavan, Eugenia (2018). Informal Work in the Argentinian Labour Law. p. 12.
124. *Ibid.*, p. 40.

The Bolivian report has no mention of labor inspection and its incidence in informality, neither does those from Panama, Uruguay and Venezuela.

In the report of Chile, it is highlighted that informal workers can come into the protection of the law through the courts of justice and through the inspection and complaints to labor inspection.[125]

The national report of Costa Rica highlights that there is an absence of effective inspection with the intention of detecting contracting by intermediaries.[126]

In the report from Mexico, it is recognized that the role of labor inspection in the detection of evasive practices of the labor standard would be especially important.[127]

Finally, Peru's report highlights that, among the functions of labor inspection, one is to provide information and guidance to workers and companies in the informal economy.[128] It also recognizes the lack of labor control in the use of informal work, especially in the area of outsourcing.

A trend that seems to be evident is the weakness of the inspection and control function in the informality sphere; the difficulties of labor inspection in the detection of evasive practices of labor legislation and the weakness of inspection in terms of new forms of work management, especially in what corresponds to the outsourcing of functions. A particular constant of this tendency would have to do with the weakness of labor inspection in the field of family work.

[I] Informality and Family Work

A final mention should be made in relation to the national questionnaires, which has to do with the treatment of auxiliary family workers. The report from Argentina indicates that the work of children for their parents is not considered a labor link. The work between spouses can be considered as a labor link if it is not a common endeavor.[129] Among other relatives, there may be a labor link depending on whether the work is typical of family life.

The Bolivian report highlights the high incidence of unpaid family work in the agricultural sector and rural communities.[130]

In the Chilean report, the emphasis is placed on work in family microenterprises, which is estimated by the third party who performs the task (and not on behalf of the relative who runs the microenterprise).[131]

The Costa Rican report highlights that they are defined as "unpaid helpers", subject to labor legislation, as far as subordination is proven.[132]

125. Chile (2018). Questionnaire Informal Work Chile. p. 2.
126. Costa Rica (2018). National Report of Costa Rica: Trabajo Informal. p. 13.
127. Natividad Sánchez, Tomás (2018). National Report México. p. 19.
128. Perú (2018). Questionnaire about Informal Workers in Peru. p. 4.
129. Aquino, Marcelo G.; Carugo, Agustín H.; Khedavan, Eugenia (2018). Informal Work in the Argentinian Labour Law. p. 30.
130. Campero Villalba, Iván (2018). National Report Bolivia. p. 10.
131. Chile (2018). Questionnaire Informal Work in Chile. p. 3.
132. Costa Rica (2018). National Report Costa Rica: Informal Work. p. 11.

Mexico's report says that there is no definition of auxiliary family workers and that they are finally considered employees.[133]

In the report of Panama, it is mentioned that what characterizes the auxiliary family workers is that they are workers who provide services in companies or places belonging to the family group and who do not have the condition of employees. However, jurisprudence has estimated that there is a labor link as long as subordination is proven and the service provided is not a function of family coexistence.

In the report of Peru, the law establishes that between consanguineous relatives and spouses there is no labor link unless otherwise agreed; therefore, they are considered excluded from the application of labor legislation.[134]

The Uruguayan report mentions that these auxiliary family workers are not regulated and the general rules of work should be applied to them if there is subordination.[135] The report from Venezuela points out that only homeworkers are regulated.[136]

As a tendency deduced from the answers received and that have been tried to summarize, the solutions move in a pendulum that goes from the nonrecognition of a labor link, as long as it involves auxiliary family workers, up to the recognition of a bond when there is a subordinate work relationship. Several answers indicate that unpaid helpers or auxiliary family workers will be subject to labor regulation to the extent that subordination is proven. It is clear that subordination is still the most important, relevant element to recognize if we are in the scope of a work relationship, still informal but a labor relationship which also involves the treatment of auxiliary family workers.

§5.07 CONCLUSIONS

Informality, at least from the perspective of labor law, *remains a polysemic category and is still not sufficiently limited.* There were antecedents about this matter that were oriented in an initially spatial way: *the urban informal sector* category said that *informality* was located in a predetermined sector and, consequently, it was an urban phenomenon. Today neither one thing nor the other would be admissible. In the first reflection on informality, there was an objective or material approach that said that it resided not only in the urban sector but particularly in that of microenterprises and low-productivity companies. From that point of view, the informal sector had a very specific and reiterated manifestation scope, a sort of modular labor statute. Of course, these are dimensions and delimitations of the concept that have now been overcome.

133. Natividad Sánchez, Tomás (2018). National Report Mexico. p. 18.
134. Perú (2018). Survey on Informal Workers in Peru. p. 10.
135. Nicoliello, Ariel; Riva, Ana; Castro, Natalia (2018). Uruguay: National Report on Informal Work. p. 9.
136. Jaime Kellerhoff, Daniel (et al.) (2018)."Chapter Venezuela". Report for the World Congress of Labor and Social Security Law, Turin, Italy. Sponsored by the SIDTSS. p. 12.

For this reason it is explained how the terminological change moved among "unstructured sector", "informal sector", "informal economy" to "informality/formality" and why Recommendation No 204 abandoned the category of "informal sector."

Only since 2010, that is, relatively recently, the CEACR's general surveys deal with the issue of the informal economy and informal workers in more detail. From 1985 to 2010 mentions of the informal economy and informal workers were infrequent—most of the time the surveys did not pay attention to the issue—and when they did, they referred to the unstructured sector of the economy.

From the first general surveys to Recommendation No. 204 (2015), there is a terminological change with four clear moments: (1) *the unstructured sector,* (2) *the informal sector,* (3) *the informal economy and finally,* (4) *informality,* without ignoring that some general surveys referred to the "informal market."

The arrival of the supervisory bodies of the ILO to the issue of informality and informal workers was, above all, *based on fundamental conventions.* They involve the protection of human rights; therefore, its scope of subjective application tends to be universal. For this reason, and despite the fact that they do not make explicit or literal reference to workers in the informal economy, it is widely accepted that the eight fundamental conventions are applied to the informal economy. This same tendency is also reiterated with the priority or governance conventions that tend to recognize a subjective and spatial scope of application without excluding any category.

Looking for a delimitation of the category, one finds *the notion of precarious work near the atypical work,* which is far away from the paradigm on which the Latin American labor law was raised: on the one hand, the subordination and the alienation (ajenidad) and, on the other, the idea that a unitary labor contract and therefore typical was going to be able to capture or attract all forms of work for others. This shows a crucial piece of information for the proposed approach: in the informal economy there are different legal relationships that involve the provision of services, but also—and this is particularly important—formal jobs that live in the informal economy or also informal jobs that come from the formal economy and that somehow integrate it. This reveals a fact of unquestionable practical importance: the way in which the informal economy ends up integrating itself into the formal economy. Here we talk about the formal economy jobs that are relocated to the informal one.

Subordination continues to be what still characterizes the employment relationship and what complicates that the labor law appropriates the informal sector category and informal workers. The reexamination of subordination taking into account the informal sector is still a pending issue. This is confirmed in the national reports received, which reveal that the informal worker receives protection as long as they are in a subordinated relationship, and the absence of protection of the informal worker in general when he/she is self-employed. Something similar is observed especially in the field of auxiliary family workers.

Labor laws still do not specifically take over the category of informal work and informal workers; therefore, there is no specific regulation of the informal sector. In any case, the national reports received mention *criteria that could define informal work in three areas:*

(1) Participation of workers in social security systems.
(2) The formal employment relationship is followed within a legal framework.
(3) The employment relationship that involves informal workers is not registered.

There is evidence of *a diversity of types within the category of informal workers* which arise from the evident fact that there is no specific "corpus iuris" on informal work, nor is there a particular definition of work or informal workers. For this reason, the national reports clearly show the different legislations—not necessarily labor—that in some way would regulate informal work.

The exercise *of freedom of association* in all its manifestations and particularly in what it does to collective bargaining, together *with the experience of social dialogue is absolutely unequal and manifestly weak* in informal work.

With regard to the relations between informal work and new forms of work management and particularly of triangular or outsourced relationships, it is highlighted that the mechanism, lawful in principle, might serve as a form of evasion of labor obligations and therefore it might suppose a type of unprotected work. The simulation and fraud given in the field of so-called covert employment relationships certainly contribute to increase the scope of the unprotected work segment, marking the trend towards the dualization of the labor market.

The answers to the questionnaires of the national reports particularly highlight *public policies* aimed to increase social security coverage; flexibilization of working conditions in the field of microenterprises; training and worker formation policies; campaigns for domestic and rural workers, with extension of monotax and health insurance; but particularly and this must be emphasized, the promotion of unionization and collective bargaining.

There is large informality in the area of work at homes, which are jobs with a high rate of feminization. *A deficit of gender equity* occurs in the services sector where there exists a prevalence of women who work on their own and where the decent work deficit is even more noticeable.

Finally, there is evidence of the weakness of the inspection and audit in the detection of evasive practices in labor legislation. This causes new forms of work management, especially as regards the outsourcing of functions and in the scope of family work, to be vulnerable or unprotected sectors and, therefore, informal.

CHAPTER 6

The Perspective of Social Clauses in International Trade

Adalberto Perulli

§6.01 INTRODUCTION

In my paper I analysed in a rather systematic way the linkage between international trade and labour rights, with particular reference to the theme of social clause as a tool capable of connecting different regulatory regimes, namely that of the international labour law and the international economy law. Such regulatory regimes have deep common roots that date back to the inception of international labour law: the first draft of the British delegation in the commission for international labour law, appointed after the first World War by the Peace Conference, declared that one of the main objectives of International labour conventions should be to eliminate unfair competition based on oppressive working conditions and that States signing conventions should reject commodities produced under unfair competition conditions. This is to say that the linkage deals with a recurrent theme in the history of labour law, which has its roots as right of regulation of the competition among States and among enterprises, in an epoch in which the national economies were compared out of a regulatory frame of the international commerce and the United Nation Society had not been founded yet. The links of labour law with this component of the liberal economy – the commerce and the philosophy of the free trade – have marked the history of the twentieth century, with alternate stories and different perspectives. If with the foundation of the ILO the respect of the social rights on the part of nations was already conceived as a condition for the advancements of the other States desirous to progress in the social regulation, the perspective of an institutional connection between regulation of the commerce and respect of the social rights will find a consecration in the Havana Charter, in which it is foreseen expressly that the States adherent to the new Trade International Organization must respect equitable conditions of labour.

The failure of the negotiations of the Havana Charter and the conclusion of the GATT will mark a decisive setback of social conditionality as a requirement for international trade regulation. Negotiations for the foundation of the WTO will be marked by the resurgence of this issue, but it will nevertheless find the sharp contradiction of developing countries, the jealous guardians of its elements of competitiveness in a 'Ricardian' logic of safeguarding the comparative advantages of nations. However, the failure of the insertion of a social clause in the WTO does not mark the end of the idea and the practice of social conditionality in the treaties of international trade, and this for reasons linked to the philosophy that informs the social reparation of free trade by two great powers of the global economy, (1) the US and (2) the EU. Both these actors have, for different reasons, made the respect for social rights a constant element of external relations, with generalized preference systems (albeit very different) or in the ambit of bilateral treaties. This stage of relaunching the historical link between international trade and social rights has been followed by the progressive realization of the social clause in the field of macro-regional treaties (NAFTA, CETA, MERCOSUR) and finally in the framework of the so-called mega-treaties, such as TTP, TTIP, CETA, EPA, with a progressive enhancement of the Sustainable Development model as a regulatory framework that can stabilize and institutionalize the link between social rights and free trade.

Today, we are experiencing a slowdown, if not a real crisis of these models of regional integration, caused by the resurgence of economic nationalisms. Therefore, new questions are going to arise. What is the future of global trade in the light of US and Brexit neo-protectionism? What tools can be used to convey a new consensus and cohesion phase in the international community where development policies, international business transactions and social and environmental sustainability coexist harmoniously? And what responsibilities, in this confused and fluid scenario, must take the economic actors, first of all, the multinational companies that move investment and productive locations globally?

Of course, answering these questions is hard matter. However, I think that social clauses could be relaunched and find space and unexpected revival. The difficulties in negotiating commercial mega-treaties could be resolved in a new impetus for bilateral treaties, which China is practicing with great determination, assuming for the first time commitments, albeit still very temperate, in the field of the protection of social rights and environmental issues. The role of the World Bank and of institutional investors could be result amplified in this context, by developing a financing project and an international cooperation where stabilization clauses prohibiting States from amending the existing regulatory framework at the time of funding will eventually contain derogations for social and environmental rights. And the multinational enterprise, whose social and economic power surpasses that of individual national States, could find a new planetary legitimacy if it adopted and carry out with seriousness and commitment, throughout the production chain, the guidelines contained in the new ILO tripartite declaration. Thus, to a destabilizing de-globalization guided by populisms, it could oppose a new, more socially oriented globalization.

§6.02 INTERNATIONAL TRADE AND SOCIAL RIGHTS: THE JUSTIFICATIONS FOR THE LINKAGE

It is commonly known that the current context of globalization has been for several decades characterized by the expansion of both bilateral and multilateral commercial exchanges. The first direction has its evidence in the increase of commercial relations among countries, and it has led to the stipulation of a large number of FTAs; in the second direction there has been an initial (1990s and 2000s) impulse to economic regionalism, that is to say the constitution of free trade areas, customs unions and common markets that imply forms of economic integration, which go beyond the trade sector, since they refer to issues like services and investments, that have been followed (from 2010 to today) by a tendency to the negotiation of mega-treaties that have involved several economic areas, like in the case of TTIP, CPTPP, and so on. This model of free trade has largely dominated the global scenario from the foundation of WTO to today. However, in the last years, we can see an inversion of this trend: multilateral negotiations to bring down barriers to trade have largely stalled and economic and social protectionism, linked to an upswing in initiative of National States in the global arena, is making a comeback.[1] Even countries that have traditionally championed an open global economy, like Us and UK, are now looking into ways to put a brake on imports, limit immigration and favour domestic production. These developments have all contributed to the recent marked slowdown in the growth of global trade, to the point that some experts have predicted a future characterized by processes of 'de-globalization' and of upswing of national States' sovereignty on economic processes and on monetary and trade policies.

However, in this evolving complex geopolitical scenario, whose balances are hard to predict, several bilateral and multilateral Free Trade Agreements (further on, FTAs) are on the table of negotiations or have been recently stipulated. This confirms the will of national States and of economic powers to go for the liberalization of exchanges and the integration of markets.

In the field of this free trade perspective, we have progressively witnessed a model of regulative 'linkage' – or inter-normativity – within the economic dimension of trade exchanges that arises social and environmental concerns. Actually, we are dealing with a regulative logic that dates back to the past: to the failed attempt – with the Havana Charter – to link the ITO to the ILO, with the perspective to obligate States to the compliance with fair labour standards.[2]

This model of regulation based on the linkage between commercial and social spheres can, matter-of-factly, be distinguished in two sub-models. The first, that has its roots in the unilateral commercial policy of the USA and is then developed in a multilateral perspective – most of all with the NAFTA – is linked to the idea of 'fair

1. The WTO, OECD and UN Conference on Trade and Development report showed that since 2008 over 1,500 new trade restrictions have been recorded in G20 economies. Only a quarter of these had been rolled back by May 2016.
2. The United Nations Conference on Trade and Employment, held in Havana, Cuba, in 1947 adopted the Havana Charter for an International Trade Organization which was meant to establish a multilateral trade organization.

trade' and sees in the respect of social rights a principle of respect of basic conditions for a trade without any distortion under the profile of competition (level playing field). Such a model is characterized by an instrumental perspective directly linked to trade and thus dependent to the regulation of exchanges (in the USA internal legislation, the practises of non-compliance with social rights on the part of commercial partners are included in the 'unfair' commercial praxis; in the NAALC, the social clause works with sanctionatory mechanisms only if the behaviour of States is 'affecting trade'). The first model is very ambiguous under the profile of the identification of social rights, generally defined as 'internationally recognized' social rights, without any reference to the ILO conventions and therefore without a precise setting of supranational standards, but actually very often explicitly linked to the compliance with the 'internal' standards of each State.

The second sub-model is to be placed within a wider axiological perspective, that is not only and not as much as directly linked to the 'fair' regulation of trade exchanges' system but also it is more characterized by the promotion of fundamental human rights and values: thus intended to the promotion and diffusion on a global scale of certain values of social justice, and such a model has its main feature in being based on mechanisms of dialogue and cooperation. In this model, where the EU's GSP probably represents the most advanced achievement, the references to the ILO's standards are much more clear, both with reference to the 1998 ILO Declaration on Fundamental Principles and Rights at Work, and to the fundamental Conventions (core labour standards), with a logic intended to the promotion of a supranational system of social standards. This sub-model has in the latest years been redefined thanks to the more and more recurring reference in the field of commercial negotiations to the paradigm of sustainable development (*see infra*). One of the main promoters of this strategy is the EU, which wants to keep a trade policy which contributes to the integrated policymaking of the 2030 Agenda for Sustainable Development by focusing not only on economic aspects but also furthering social and environmental objectives and contributes to the European Agenda on Migration and the European Agenda on Security.[3] As a matter of fact, the planetary triumph of capitalistic economy and the insertion of national economies within a global market arise again the issue of the social dimension of liberalization within international trade in the world scenario.

Even though they are inspired by different logics, the two sub-models coexist, complete each other and can contribute, even if with different levels of consistency and efficiency, to the idea of commercial exchanges' governance not only in a perspective of free trade but also of protection of fundamental social rights, in view of phenomena of social dumping, regulatory competition and law shopping that constitute at the same time the causes and the effects of a globalization without any rule.

On the background, there is the *linkage* between liberalization of exchanges and labour law, which cannot but overwhelmingly come up again in the light of the process of globalization, which entails a growing interdependency among economies, favoured

3. Brussels, 13 September 2017 COM(2017) 492 final Communication from the Commission to the European Parliament, the Council, the European Economic and Social Committee and the Committee of the Regions A Balanced and Progressive Trade Policy to Harness Globalisation.

by a strong expansion of the movements of capital and transnational companies within international exchanges.

Moreover, this linkage between the processes of liberalization of exchanges and labour regulation constitutes a foundational element of international labour law, contemporaneously in the construction of the ILO's normative policy and in the relation between the latter and the economic-oriented international organizations. In particular, as far normative policies are concerned, the function of labour law has been clearly evident since its inception: it consisted in contrasting the opportunism of States that would push – or actually were pushing – to postpone the protection of workers' rights with respects to the economic or competitive interest of their enterprises. As we have already pointed out, the recurring dialectic connecting the norms of labour law to international exchanges is presented in the formulation of the Havana Charter, forefather of the forthcoming (however, never constituted) International Trade Organization (ITO), whereby not only was it provided the obligation to comply with equal labour conditions but also, even the necessity of an institutional bridge between the ILO and the ITO, in the direction of a profitable integration between liberalization and social *standards* (*see* below).

Hence, we face the perspective to insert a social clause in international trade treaties that may institutionalize a formal linkage between openness of the market, economic and social progress, improvement of labour conditions and abolition of the most intolerable forms of exploitation. The social clause is at the centre of the debate on globalization and nowadays constitutes a very controversial matter because, if on one hand it may be considered one of the most efficient instruments in order to sustain and promote the interactions between international trade and social rights, on the other hand, it shows many criticalities for its structure and concept. Such criticalities may be found even in the most advanced chapters intended to sustainable development: in terms of ability to create effective processes of harmonization of social standards (on the contrary, this is often explicitly excluded), in terms of effectiveness of the assumed commitments, with problems both in terms of monitoring, and, most of all, in terms of procedures of controversies resolution and of sanctionatory system, therefore risking of being a merely exhortative instrument for social justice 'on paper'. We will deal further on with these profiles (paragraph 7). Now we must examine the rational 'justifications' for the integration of the social clause in International trade Treaties.

In this respect, there are two sets of justifications which can be reconducted to a rational justification as regards scope and value.

[A] First Justification (Scope)

The first justification (scope) stresses the economic interest of trade, a typically mercantilistic interest, and the instruments of regulation in order to overcome market failures, and the limits of rationality of an unregulated market. This operative and instrumental justification of regulation looks into the harmonious development of the market and is based on the idea of fair trade. The protection of the fundamental social norms guaranteed in the framework of international trade is justified when the sense of violation of those standards by the exporting States is likely to damage the economy of those countries which respect the standard of the supranational 'level playing field.' Adam Smith himself stated the principle of reciprocity in trade relationship. Although it has been considered as 'unilaterally aggressive', the USA praxis, codified in the section 301 of the 1974 Trade and Tariff Act, allows to get to the notion of fair trade, connoting it in a social perspective: as a matter of fact, having in mind that regulation, the trade policies of foreign Countries founded on the systematic violation of workers' internationally recognized labour rights, represent an unreasonable, unfair and inequitable trade practice. *It is a trade practice that is considered unreasonable, not the violation of social rights* per se. It is well known that also in the European construction, the social harmonization has been conceived since its inception as functional to avoid forms of dumping and competition distortions founded on normative disparities, judged as inconvenient with regards to the functioning of the internal market. This justification is therefore based on a certain idea of a regulated market, an ordo-liberal vision in which the adoption of a minimum of internationally recognized social norms is a prerequisite for trade, which can facilitate the liberalization of interstate trade by guaranteeing equality of basic legal conditions for any economic operator.[4]

The reciprocal loyalty in the trade relations therefore implies the respect of fundamental social rights. It is important to observe that this conception of loyalty/equity within international trade exchanges is spreading into areas so far considered as immune to this logic, that, on the contrary, have been representative of a basically opposite pattern: like in the case of China, which has, even though in a limited way, started to insert work-related clauses in some FTAs (*see infra*).

In this perspective, the introduction of social clauses in international trade Treaties has full validity. Such clauses will be able to internalize the externalities produced by the liberalization of exchanges and to absorb the non-trade issues in the governance of the world trade, on a multilateral and bilateral basis. Thus, the notion of fair trade can be considered as a means to complete the game of free trade, guaranteeing to the State and economic actors that none of the global players will take advantage of the unfair benefits that result from the non-application of the national or international social norms. Social standards therefore penetrate in the regulative sphere of trade law as an instrument of implementation of a principle of fair competition at the international level, aimed at limiting the phenomena of social dumping.

4. It is important to observe that this conception of loyalty/equity within international trade exchanges is today spreading into areas so far considered as immune to this logic, like in the case of China, which has, even if in a very limited way, started to insert work-related clauses in some FTAs. Since 2008 China has taken a new approach in international trade and some FTA such as with New Zealand and Australia include special chapter on movement of person, and in FTA with Peru and Switzerland there are special provision on labour cooperation.

[B] Second Justification (Value)

The second type of justification (value) privileges the axiological dimension of fundamental social rights.[5] In this perspective the demand to link social goals and trade agreements is instrumental in 'arming' social rights by making them accessible to the sanctioning system provided for in commercial matters against countries violating fundamental social rights; from this point of view the social clause is a device assisted by sanctions that accompanies the other softer measures based on cooperation and moral suasion.

The demand to link trade agreements with social agenda objectives recalls the use of general trade sanction towards violating Countries, as the suspension or prohibition of market access for those products which violate the fundamental social rights.

An alternative solution, which anyway uses international trade as a lever to guarantee the respect of social rights, could be to consider ILO Conventions as *erga omnes* obligations, that, if violated, can lead to the use of economic sanctions by States that respect and apply them effectively. This opinion has been supported by an authoritative doctrine,[6] but unfortunately could not be accepted because it was unfounded in terms of general international law: in fact the ILO conventions are not mandatory obligations *erga omnes* and they are not *ius cogens*; according to Hobbes, these are 'covenants without sword', contrary to humanitarian treaties. In fact ILO conventions operate in a reciprocal regime, and subjectively limit their scope to the contracting States. Consequently, the use of commercial sanctions outside the provision of a social clause would result in the violation of international trade law and would expose the sanctioning State to receive sanctions from the WTO in turn. In conclusion according to the current state of international law, the only way to go beyond the mere logic of 'moral suasion' is the social clause, which allows a decisive step forward to the promotion of fundamental social rights.

This axiological perspective is strongly relaunched by the paradigm of Sustainable Development. Development is often understood as a synonym for economic development or economic growth. Sustainable development builds and modifies the international approach to development which needs to be understood more broadly. The international community development in the past half-century includes at least four related concepts: peace and security, economic development, social development and national governance that secures peace and development. Each concept is reflected in major multilateral treaties that provide a common framework for relations among nations as well as a shared set of national purposes. In particular, I would stress

5. *See* M.J. Trebilcock, *The Fair Trade Debate: Protection of Labour Standards and International Economic Law*, in S. Griller (ed.), *International Economic Governance and Non-Economic Concerns: New Challenges for the International Legal Order*, Springer, New York, 2003, p. 299.
6. Failure to respect fundamental social rights, in particular the ILO Conventions, should give rise to the right of those who respect them to open their markets only to those States that have ratified the same Conventions: *see* A. Supiot, *Quelle Justice Sociale Internationale Au XXI Siécle?*, Conférence d'ouverture du XXIème Congrès ISLSSL, Le Cap, 15-18 September 2015.

the idea that social and economic developments are closely related, not only conceptually but also in the practices of social and economic relationships. Countries that have emphasized education, health and related aspects of social development tend to have the best economic performance. Therefore, the link between economic and social sphere is not an unnatural invention and it is not related to utopia or ideology. It is not for nothing that a fundamental Treaty on human rights, *The International Covenant on Economic, Social and Cultural Rights,* contains in itself the idea of integration between economic and social sphere.

Labour law, especially if projected in the international and supranational dimension, may therefore be considered as a *right of Sustainability*: the respect of fundamental social rights and, more generally, the conditions of effectiveness of labour laws are part of the prerequisites of a globally sustainable competition. Whereby we should face their lack, the economic development without integration would lead to the deterioration of the quality of life in the short term and the consumption of capital in the long term.[7] As Dani Rodrick pointed out, today's challenge is to make the openness of markets sustainable and compatible with wider social aims, and this might be achieved even through a revisitation of the safeguard measures of WTO, in order to allow the countries to react to the violation of social rights, especially if those praxis are carried out by non-democratic countries.[8]

We may discuss whether this setting should indicate more a cosmopolite vision, centred on the generalization of 'universal' principles and values,[9] that is to say whether this process should most of all preserve the national self-determination against hyper-globalization. In any case, the legitimacy of the World trade's socially conditioned regulation on the basis of double rationality (instrumental and axiologically oriented) on which it is founded finds growing evidence both in case studies, which confirm its economic efficiency (*see* next chapter), and in the more and more spread and politically meaningful matters on the compliance with global norms of protection of human rights.

---

7. Cf. M. Giaoutzi, P. Nijkamp, *Decision Support Model for Sustainable Development*, Aldershot, Avebury, 1993.
8. R. Rodrik, *The Globalization Paradox. Democracy and the Future of the World Economy*, New York - London, W.W. Norton & Company, 2011.
9. U. Beck, *Cosmopolitan Vision*, Cambridge, MA Polity Press, 2006.

Figure 6.1 Justification in Evolution

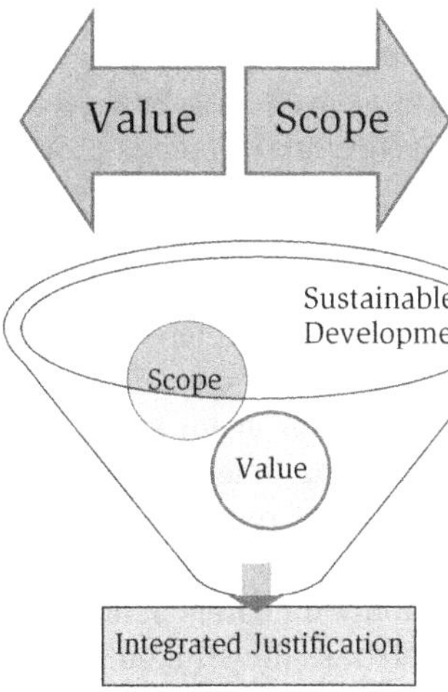

[C] An "Integrated" Justification

Today, according to this scenario, the two above-mentioned justifications have evolved, and in particular the idea of fair trade results as more interrelated with the axiological dimension of social rights. Both theoretical reflection and the individuation of a much more comprehensive normative paradigm of development have contributed to this evolution.

In this path, an important contribution in the reformulation of Sustainability was given by Amartia Sen. Overcoming the thesis of economists such as Brundtland and Solow, Sen has definitively explained that development must be conceived as a broadening of *capabilities* of human beings and in this perspective the social choice assumes a fundamental role in development. In this way values influence economic action making it sustainable. A good example of the recognition of the importance of international human rights in the international regulation of trade can be found in the CETA Preamble, that provides for the implementation of the whole agreement in a way consistent with the enforcement of labour and environmental laws (*see* paragraph 5.2.).

§6.03 ECONOMIC AND SOCIAL RATIONALITIES: THE POSITIVE EFFECTS OF RESPECT FOR SOCIAL RIGHTS

The positive relationship between economic and social rationalities, in the field of international trade, is confirmed by empirical evidence. The positive effects of social clauses both in terms of economic efficiency and protection of fundamental social rights represent a mostly confirmed result in the scientific literature of economic matrix. Analysing the data relative to the linkage between social rights and development of trade exchanges in India in the period 2005–2014, we can see that the growth of salaries does not reduce exportations, but it facilitates internal spending and promotes exportations, contradicting the traditional objections on the negative effects induced by social conditionality, as well as proving wrong the competition issue legitimating social dumping.[10] Even China, which is promoting a strong FTAs policy, has developed an openness in the sectors of cooperation on labour and employment, without anyway recurring to international standards (like in China-Switzerland FTA) or providing for the protection of domestic labour force (like in China-Costa, China-Singapore, China-New Zealand FTAs). The references contained in the trade agreements have stimulated the protections of social rights, as showed by the total cancellation of practises of re-education against ILO Convention n. 105. Effective measures in matter of discrimination assumed by the Chinese Government show its potentialities to implement social clauses relative to condition of labour at a domestic level, with particular reference to principles of equal retribution, equality of treatment between man and woman in retribution matters and non-discrimination (think about the efforts made in order to overcome the 'Hukou' system, despite the number of migrant farmers that keep on being discriminated in the access to labour).[11] Other researches have recently surveyed, on the basis of the Global Preferential Trade Agreements Database (GPTAD), the quantitative effects of social clauses in countries with medium-low GDP.[12] The confrontation between systems that have adopted the social clause and those who have not shows a strong and positive impact on conditionality on the ratification of the ILO conventions, especially the fundamental ones, with an average of + 27%. Better Factories Cambodia is as well an excellent example of the benefits derived from a proper implementation of labour standards. Originally known as the ILO Garment Sector Project, it subsequently has changed the name in Better Factories Cambodia to better reflect the ILO's aim of continuous improvements in working conditions.[13]

Since its establishment in 2001, the programme evolved also with the help of the trade agreement between Cambodia and the United States,[14] and exports increased over the years, with exception to the biennium 2008–2009 when trade performance decreased due to the financial crisis. This positive impact at a macroeconomic level explains the beneficial outcomes also at a microeconomic level. Brown, Dehejia and Robertson evidence the relationship between the factory-level compliance and factory survival.[15] The analysis confirms that factories that increase compliance with labour

10. *See* H. Chen, *Social Clause in Trade Agreements and China's Experience*, in Beijing Law Review, 2015, 6, p. 1 s.
11. H. Chen, *supra* p. 7.
12. R. Baziller, A.T. Rana, *Social Clauses in Free-trade Agreements: An Efficient Tool to Improve Labour Standard?*, 4th Conference on the Regulating Decent Work Network, 9 July 2015.
13. Hall, 'The ILO's Better Factories Cambodia Program: A Viable Blueprint for Promoting International Labour Rights?', 2010.
14. ILO, Better Factories Cambodia. http://www.ilo.org/asia/projects/WCMS_099340/lang--en/index.htm.
15. Brown, Dehejia, and Robertson, 'Laws, Costs, Norms, and Learning: Improving Working Conditions in Developing Countries,' IZA Discussion Paper No. 10025, June 2016.

standards are more likely to survive compared to factories that do not. Indeed, the probability of survival grew as firms conformed with the wage standards. Productivity and profitability increase as well when working conditions are improved.

At this point, the discourse evolves according to the different levels and subjects of such internormative regulation. First of all, it is necessary to consider the economic forms of trade organized at global level, which include multiple or multidimensional juridical areas, meeting and overlapping. Each of these areas should be analysed in accordance with the measure to which it can or does guarantee the operative realization of a link between trade liberalization and respect of social norms, each in its own way.

In this regards, four pertinent levels or areas can be distinguished:

(1) The global level, governed by the criteria of decision-making centralization and a multilateral framework (WTO); at this level, the aggregate and regulative processes typical of social rights are generally absent, or else very weak and fragmented.
(2) Regional level, governed by multilateral and diversified criteria, which depend on the intensity of forms of integration. They follow the model of the EU or of the NAFTA or other forms of regional integration such as MERCOSUR or ASEAN, and vary as to whether there are supranational organs with normative and/or judiciary power having a direct effect on the Member States.
(3) The level of bilateral agreements between States, in which the social clause is very present.
(4) Levels unilaterally governed by States or economic aggregations of States; labour issues are often present at this level as the social condition for trade liberalization.

The following analysis aims to provide a reconstructive synthesis of these levels in which, with some differences deriving from the different geopolitical and institutional profiles of the regulatory framework, the social clause is present in the weaving of international trade relations.

§6.04 THE MULTILATERAL GLOBAL DIMENSION: THE GATT/WTO SYSTEM: THE ORIGINS

On 30 October 1947, the General agreement on tariffs and trade (GATT) was signed, with the aim to liberalize the international economic exchanges, progressively abolishing barriers and customs tariffs. The project of constitution of the International Trade Organization, started in those years with the editing of the Havana Charter, was, on the contrary, interrupted due to the opposition of the USA. In that document, the States committed to economic and social cooperation entrusting to what should have been the newly constituted ITO the task to promote economic growth and, at the same time, the elimination of *sub-standard* labour conditions, especially in *export-oriented* enterprises, more induced to apply unfavourable employment conditions for reasons of international competition.

Above all, in the Havana Charter, in Article 7, we find the first example of social clause: 'the Members recognize that measures relating to employment must take fully into account the rights of workers under inter-governmental declarations, conventions and agreements; they recognize that all Countries have a common interest in the achievement and maintenance of fair labour standards. The Members recognize that unfair labour conditions, particularly in production for export, create difficulties in international trade, and, accordingly, each Member shall take whatever action may be appropriate and feasible to eliminate such conditions. Members which are also members of the International Labour Organization shall cooperate with that organization, and in all matters related to labour norms that will be presented to the ITO, the latter shall consult and cooperate with the International Labour Organization'.

The missed ratification of the Havana Charter on the part of the Congress of the USA interrupted the construction of a stable normative and institutional order, where to collocate the issue of the social clause. Therefore, the GATT was founded on the ashes of the Havana Charter and had limited goals and competences, since it did not include any mechanism referring to protection and fundamental social rights issues, nor recognizing any value to the action of the ILO. From that moment on, there was a phase of negotiations in trade matters, outside of a predefined institutional framework; this was interrupted in 1944 when, in the occasion of the eighth cycle of multilateral negotiations held within the GATT, the World Trade Organization's institutional agreement was signed among 124 Countries. The agreement incorporated in a single text the totality of negotiations in trade matters according to the GATT system so far occurred, and it included agreements relative also to other sectors previously not provided for (GATS). The agreement did not contain any explicit reference to fundamental social rights even though, on the matter, most of all France and the European Commission, supporting the USA's requests, had proposed to introduce within trade agreements some provisions intended to internationalize the social costs produced by the decisions in matter of international trade. Moreover, the agreement did not deal with the cooperation between the WTO and the ILO, that is to say it did not acknowledge to the ILO neither the possibility of participation to the negotiations nor the possibility to participate to yearly Rounds, where Member States meet.

[A] The Debate on the Social Clause

With social clause we intend peculiar norms having as an object the internationally recognized rights that States (in their activity of production and application of law) and, consequently enterprises (in their role of employers) must comply with, in order to be able to benefit from determined effects of international trade liberalization, that is to avoid incurring in actual economic sanctions.

The idea, long nurtured both within law studies and intergovernmental praxis, refers to the debate concerning the possibility to insert a social clause in the field of the system GATT/WTO, in order to fulfil the integration of social rights in the space designated to regulate international exchanges. As it is known, this perspective presents evident criticalities, but just as many potentialities.

First of all, we are facing the difficulty to define what social *standards* should be, that is to say what are the minimum rules to comply with in order for the clause to find its full achievement, in the framework of fair trade's rules. This definition needs an agreement that is way more difficult to obtain, compared to the one relative to the adoption of labour multilateral conventions in the field of the ILO. However, as it has been proved when we examined the 'international labour code' elabourated by the ILO, a careful analysis of the sources of international law allows to explain a hard core of 'unconditioned' social rights, that is to say they may not be inflected by reason of the different economic and cultural situations. These rights have already been contemplated by the ILO's Conventions, by the Universal Declaration of Human Rights and by the 1966 UN Treaties on political and civil rights and economic and social rights; they have been recognized as 'fundamental' by the Declaration of Copenhagen on social development and eventually consecrated by the historical Declaration adopted by the 1998 International Conference of Labour in Geneva. We are dealing with freedom of association and right to collective bargaining; with the prohibition of forced and mandatory labour; with the protection of minor labour; with the prohibition of discrimination. This set of *core labour standards* must therefore be considered of universal application, so much so that the ILO requires the compliance with it to Member States merely by reason of their belonging to the Organization. As we have already said, we are dealing with workers' rights that essentially behave like internationally recognized human rights, having most likely an *opinio iuris* on the basis of which the international community results as bound to comply with them. For example, to the usage of minor labour in cases that, by their nature or circumstances where they take place, put at risk the physical and moral health of minors is a praxis to be included in the notion of 'cruel, inhuman and degrading treatments' (Articles 1 and 56 of UN Charter) whose prohibition is undoubtedly referable to (and sanctionable according to) *jus cogens. This is to say that the social clause has a codification function of already operating principles in the field of general international law: the trade treaties that bear it inside should, consequently, be interpreted as a confirmation, broadening and specification of already existing common norms.*

However, the reason for the difficulties encountered by the social clause at global multilateral level is explained most of all according to a political-structural factor, regarding the conception of the international division of labour supported by the WTO, strongly connected to the classical theory - dating back to David Ricardo - of comparative advantages. In the ministry Declaration of Singapore, the parties declare '*to refuse the usage of labour norms with protectionist aims and agree that the comparative advantages of Countries, in particular developing Countries with low salaries, must not in any case be put into discussion*'. The principle of comparative advantages is founded on the idea of integration of national economies in the international division of labour according to competences and according to the richness in natural resources, manpower and capital. The WTO has therefore inherited - and so far jealously conserved - a conception of loyalty within exchanges unable to remedy the trade distortions determined by the diversity of national legislations, especially regarding the management of labour.

At the same time, it is true that the interpretations that recognize in the social clause a risk of aggressive unilateralism intended to impose protectionist conditions to poor countries' trade appear as less and less convincing. The objections regarding the lack within the WTO of a tripartite structure allowing the participation of governments and social parties in the definition and in the application of social *standards* are not shareable; moreover, the background theoretical objections on the utility of exploiting market logics in the modernization of international social-economic relations are equally non-satisfying. It is actually hard to understand why the forced convergence is easily imposed when it comes to obligating jurisdictions unwilling to accept non-appreciated trade rules, while coercion is not allowed when it comes to protect the workers' fundamental rights. The ILO itself (*see* above) has solemnly stated within the 'Declaration on social Justice and a fair globalization', adopted in Geneva on 10 June 2008, that '*the violation of labour principles and fundamental rights can neither be invoked nor utilized as legitimate comparative advantages*', thus definitively repudiating the lawfulness of the practises of *social dumping* founded on the theory of comparative advantages.

The idea of social clause, as a juridical mechanism that goes with the liberalization of international exchanges subordinating the fruition of the connected tariffs benefits to the compliance with the respect of some social fundamental principles, therefore constitutes a perspective to be pursued in the field of the international community. It should overcome the traditional intrinsic limits of international labour law, thanks to a more elevated level of effectiveness guaranteed by trade sanctions to be inflicted to the countries non-complying with the most elementary rules of protection of fundamental human rights. The identification of basic social rights (*id est* 'fundamental' or 'internationally recognized') through the recognition of the norms elabourated by international organizations (ILO and UN, first) has allowed to put forward the reconstructive hypothesis that considers social clauses not as instruments of disguised protectionism (as reported by a lot of developing Countries that oppose to its adoption), but as an operational improvement of universally recognized human rights, already sanctioned in the field of general international law and, perhaps by *ius cogens* itself. The crucial point of this clause does not consist in eliminating the competitive advantages - on a compared basis - of developing and transitional economies, but in creating within the system of free exchange the necessary requisites in order that the minimum conditions of social and Union equality are respected.

[B] The Compatibility of Social Clause in the GATT/WTO System

Despite the basically unsuccessful outcomes of the debate on the social clause, the pressure of industrialized countries and the critiques by the organizations of consumers, of workers' Unions and by other NGOs interested in the 'social' failures of *trade liberalization* represent a guarantee for the relaunch of the social clause within the WTO. While waiting for a development in this sense, it is necessary to verify the compatibility of a social clause with the principles in force in the field of GATT/WTO, checking the possible actionability of restrictive trade measures, adopted by single States with an 'anti-social dumping' function. Regarding this matter, we have a series of extremely interesting provisions, whose analysis leads to problematic possible outcomes.

The first problematic aspect regards the fact that the concept of social *dumping* cannot be technically referred to the notion of *dumping* on prices, complying with art. VI of the GATT. In principle, there is no relationship between the technical definition of *dumping* offered by the GATT and social *dumping* (the same is valid for the so-called environmental *dumping*). First of all, the reason for this lies both in the historical and textual interpretation: in the phase of negotiation of the GATT, the parties effectively agreed on the existence of four types of dumping, relative to (1) prices, (2) services, (3) exchanges and to (4) 'social' issues (the latter recognized by negotiators as '*very difficult to define*'). However, they opted for a more restricted definition, that is to say limited to the dumping on prices, considering the forms of *non-price dumping* as additional compared to the parameters posed by *anti-dumping* norms and avoiding to include workers and their Union representatives among the subjects willing to (and for this reason qualified, according to the *standing* rules) propose the action intended to activate the *anti-dumping* procedures. International trade law does not recognize the differential cost among producers as a potential cause of *dumping*: in a market economy system the reduction of the price of a product is, as a matter of fact, included in the classic goals of free competition. On the contrary, international trade law asserts that the producer may sell the same product at different prices in the domestic market (i.e., to say, the one of the exporting Country) and in the foreign exportation market. Therefore, if the price of the commodity in both markets reflects the costs of production, we do not have *dumping*. We have to reaffirm that *social dumping* is not based on a discrimination between the price of sale on the domestic market of the producer and the price of sale on the importing market because also in the domestic market the price may be just as much low: we infer that such practise does not constitute *dumping* complying with the General Agreement.

Closer to the praxis of social *dumping* is the notion of public subsidization to exportations, characterized by the fact that the lower price compared to the normal one derives from a help directly or indirectly granted by States to enterprises; in view of such praxis, the GATT, in addition to allow the injured States to react with the imposition of compensative customs duties (Article VI), disciplines the phenomenon by limiting or prohibiting the concession of subsidizations. Therefore, one may wonder whether the State allowing national enterprises to violate social norms does not end up in granting them a subsidization; we are dealing with a suggestive interpretative hypothesis, provided also in the case of environmental *dumping*, which, however, clashes with textual-oriented obstacles, because in this hypothesis we do not have the requisites of the subsidization outlined by the relative agreement edited during the *Uruguay Round*, that is to say a *financial contribution* of the authority and the specificity of the subsidization.

Further, the mechanism of the social clause can be commensurated to the so-called safeguard clause, conventional provisions that provide for, in view of particular situations, the faculty to temporarily infringe to the norms of a treaty of interstate economic cooperation, adopting measures of protection such increase of customs tariffs, quantitative restrictions, that is to say subsidizations to domestic enterprises. For example, all the Countries adhering to GATT/WTO can temporarily limit their importations whereby the national production is likely to be disturbed by low-price importations (Article XIX). A perspective that sees the safeguard clause operating as an instrument to react with protection measures against unfair trade practices due to the non-compliance with social *standards* cannot therefore be excluded.

For this reason, the only norm within the GATT's *corpus* that may be linkable to a social clause is anyway constituted by the art. XX, relative to a regime of dispensations called general exceptions, intended to establish a domestic jurisdiction in favour of single States, which are authorized to give priority to certain interests of national policy, with regards to trade liberalization. In particular, the norm allows the parties to adopt restrictive measures of exchanges that are justified by, in addition to considerations relative to protection of moral, life and health of people, animal and plants, to the defence of environment and of natural resources, to the protection of artistic heritage and of the consumer, by reasons linked to the trading of commodities produced in prisons (Article XX, lett. 'e'). On the basis of these provisions, the States may therefore adopt restrictive measures of international trade in order to protect their markets from the importations of commodities produced with low-cost manpower. We are dealing with a norm that has never to date been invoked in order to justify such restrictions; however, it is theoretically very much relevant, since it authorizes the States to adopt protectionist measures based on the assessment of the *production processes* of a foreign commodity. The main path should therefore lead to the reformulation of art. XX, inserting new exceptions relative to the missing compliance with certain fundamental social rights; however indeed, an extensive interpretation of 'the measures necessary to the protection of health and life of people' could at least include the prohibition of minor labour and some minimum norms of security within labour, allowing the States that suffer from social *dumping* to adopt restrictive measures of importations.

Eventually, art. XXIII of the GATT deserves our attention, as explained by the *Dispute Settlement Rules*. The norm, relative to the 'protection of concessions and advantages', provides for the case in which a contracting part considers that an advantage deriving from the Agreement is 'cancelled or compromised', or that the realization of one of the aims of the Agreement is compromised, due to other parties' behaviours contrary to the Agreement, that is to say that 'there is another situation' that may cancel or compromise such advantages. Within these hypotheses, one party may ask to start an inquiry, which may lead to the suspension of concessions or other obligations deriving from the general Agreement. An official document of the USA emanated in the 1950s declared that '*trade problems stemming from unfair labour standards were already actionable under Article XXIII*'[16]; and the same opinion was

16. *US Commission on Foreign Economic Policy: Staff Papers*, 1954, p. 437.

supported by the Trade Union Congress (TUC), that invoked the recourse to art. XXIII in order to impose trade sanctions to countries violating international standards in matter of labour. This perspective can be appropriately updated. As a matter of fact, in the strictly juridical field, the reference to the existence of 'another situation' that may 'cancel or compromise' the advantage deriving from the GATT appears so undetermined that it constitutes a sort of 'general clause' wherein a social clause may exist; however, there is no evidence that art. XXIII was ever invoked to fulfil such aim.

[C] The Perspectives of Social Clauses in FTAs

On the one hand, we observed the predominance of a market model centred on social *dumping* and on the competition between social systems and juridical orders; however, on the other hand, the most recent developments, within GATT/WTO and more in general in the international dimension, seem to conceal a different idea, grounded on *fair* trade, respectful of rules, principles of equality, solidarity and fairness on exchanges; a trade that is founded on the paradigm of equity and not, on the contrary, on the competitive devaluation of social regimes which could contribute to a sustainable development, as promoted by the recent UN Agenda 2030.

According to the first and more restrictive hypothesis, fair trade alludes to an organization of international trade exchanges that may ensure an equal sharing of flows. The 'right' quantity of exportations and importations for each country would then be the one guaranteeing the equilibrium of the bilateral trade balance with each partner. The issue about equality can also be utilized to claim an equal treatment of economic actors, according to which governments should grant to their national enterprises the same advantages of their foreign competitors. In this acceptation of equality, we can find the idea of a balanced ground among *players*, achievable both through the elimination of unfair advantages of foreign enterprises and through compensational mechanisms. Also in this perspective, the idea of fair trade breaks up one of the cornerstones of social *dumping*, that is to say the principle of comparative advantages as a foundation of international trade policies. As a matter of fact, social dumping, that consists in less strict labour *standards* within exporting fields, is a possible cause of distortion of trade flows, that may be caused by a 'failure' of the government in the *enforcement* of *labour rights*: basically it is definable as an 'unfair subsidy' that legitimates the activation of the procedure to impose compensational duties, according to an interpretative line suggested in the cases of environmental dumping, where the tolerance of some countries with respect to environmental degradation (particularly typical of developing countries) would result in a sort of subsidization for national industry.

Considering all this, the idea of fair trade relaunches the above-mentioned thesis according to which social dumping may be included within subsidizations granted by the State, as an attribution of an advantage to enterprises that falls on the lower cost of the product. However, in this perspective, the usage of art. XVI of the GATT in social matters – according to a perspective put forward also by the International Metalworkers Federation and analysed by the ILO's International Office of Labour – presumes such an extensive interpretation of the concept of subsidization that it would include in itself the inertia of the State that artificially (and with active will) keeps sub-standards labour conditions.

On the basis of these concepts about the notion of fair trade, the notion itself of dumping stipulated by GATT/WTO may appear as obsolete. In the previous paragraph, we said that the concept we are analysing is offered by Article VI, paragraph 1 of the GATT, which states that dumping 'allows the introduction of products of a Country on another Country's market at a lower price than their normal value', whereby the price lower than the normal value is such if the price of that given product is 'lower than the comparable price adopted in the course of normal trade operations for a similar product, destined to the consumption in the exporting Country'; otherwise, in the absence of such price within the internal market of this given country, if the price of the exported product is 'lower than the more elevated comparable price charged for the exportation of a similar product towards a third Country, in the course of normal trade operations', that is to say, 'lower than the cost of production of this commodity in the origin country, plus a reasonable increase for selling costs and the profit' (the so-called normal value, according to the principle of *fair comparison*: Article 2, paragraph 4 of the 1947 Agreement on Implementation of Article VI of GATT).

Basically, dumping, as a consequence of a private strategy of the producing enterprise, consists in the sale of a commodity in a foreign market at a lesser price compared to its normal value, that is to say a lower price than the one charged in the market of origin or, anyway, a price insufficient to cover production costs. The Member States of GATT/WTO, and the following interpretative and implementation codes, consider such forms of *international price discrimination* as detrimental both for domestic industries and for the opportunities of exportation of third countries that do not practise any type of *dumping*. Therefore, we would be dealing with unfair trade practices carried out by single producers that intend to acquire or maintain foreign market quotas through a strategy of price discrimination, which tend to provoke distortions within international trade and disturbances within the importation market. For this reason, if a commodity launched in the market with dumping by a contracting party causes or menaces to cause an important damage to an industry (in the sense of productive field) of such contracting party, the importing country will have the possibility to neutralize its effect by imposing anti-dumping duties, resulting as equivalent or inferior to the dumping margin, that is to say to the difference between the price of the commodity in the importation market and its 'normal value' (Article VI, paragraph 2).

This adopted interpretation does not keep into account of what the ILO's International Office of Labour stated and, in particular, of what the specific 'Group of labour on the social dimension of international trade liberalization' stated: the compliance with social norms inserted in the Conventions of the ILO could prove that the products destined to the exportation and manufactured complying with those norms have been introduced with a price non-inferior to their normal value; on the contrary, we should presume the existence of social *dumping*. Therefore, we need to define the 'normal' level of social protection in just as much objective terms as of what happens for commodities' 'normal value': a value coinciding with the assumption of production's costs that internalize the compliance with core labour standards.

In this perspective, it is thoroughly legitimate to introduce social clauses in international multilateral trade treaties: the social clauses are intended to the respect of the fundamental Conventions of the ILO, according to lines of reform of the WTO, able to 'internalize the externalities' produced by the liberalization of exchanges and to include non-trade issue in the governance of world trade.

§6.05 THE AMERICAN MULTILATERAL FREE TRADE AGREEMENTS

The virtuous linkage among progressive social policies and international trade regulation finds by now several empirical evidences starting from the NAALC, North American Agreement on Labour Cooperation, the Agreement parallel to NAFTA, the North American Free Trade Agreement among Mexico, US and Canada.

NAALC as we will see in detail has favoured a substantial increase of the level of knowledge of the reciprocal systems of labour law on the part of Unions, Governments, NGOs, managers, academic environment and public opinion.

This linkage has nurtured the development of *cross-border* collaborations between Unions and NGOs; it has produced a *climate changing* among whose consequences we have, for example, the anti-discriminatory law that explicitly prohibits the praxis (emerged during the phase of investigation within the field of the Agreement) to impose pregnancy tests to women during the phase of recruitment (12 June 2003 Act, Federal Official Gazette, 11 June 2003). The ILO itself, which recognizes the repercussions of trade and financial policies on employment and social rights, hopes for the realization of an 'integrated approach' in the promotion of decent labour, getting in touch with international and regional organizations that have mandates on 'connected' issues: '*d'autres organisations internationales et régionales peuvent apporter une contribution importante à la mise en oeuvre de cette approche intégrée. La politique relative aux échanges commerciaux et aux marchés financiers ayant des répercussions sur l'emploi, il incombe à l'Oit d'évaluer ces effets a fin d'atteindre son objectif qui consiste à placer l'emploi au coeur des politiques économiques*'. In the famous Myanmar case that regarded the systematic violation of the ILO Convention n. 29 on the exploitation of forced labour on the part of military people, the ILO has promoted the adoption of economic measures, like restrictions to importations, the sequestration of the regime's pension funds, the interruption of economic subsidizations: these are measures that have been adopted by Member States against the non-complying government. This confirms that if *moral suasion* does not work, globalization can exploit mechanisms of *connecting regimes* in order to reach goals of social justice. An integrated approach on the basis of criteria of conditionality linked to the dimension of global trade is on the other hand more and more credited to the internationalist doctrine in matter of protection of human rights, of which social rights constitute integrating and inseparable part.

[A] The NAFTA and Its Labour Side Agreement (NAALC)

The North American Agreement on Labour Cooperation (NAALC) represents a peculiar case of social clause adopted in the context of the multilateral agreement of free trade among the USA, Canada and Mexico (NAFTA). Signed in 1993, it represents the first instance in which the United States has negotiated an agreement dealing with labour standards to supplement an international trade agreement.

NAALC is the first free exchange agreement that sets up a specific normative instrumentation intended to encourage the labour protection through a procedural mechanism allowing the adaption between trade liberalization and the respect of fundamental social rights. By incorporating aims that differ from the ones of trade liberalization, the NAALC therefore acts as a model for the integration of social values in the supranational processes that regulate economic globalization.

The main objective of the NAALC is to improve working conditions and living standards in the United States, Mexico and Canada, and it promotes more trade and closer economic ties among the three Countries. The preferred approach of the Agreement to reach this objective is through cooperation – exchanges of information, technical assistance, consultations – a concept that is explicitly recognized in the very title of the instrument. The Agreement also provides some oversight mechanisms to ensure that labour laws are being enforced in all three countries. These oversight mechanisms are aimed at promoting a better understanding by the public of labour laws and at enhancing transparency of enforcement. The Agreement does provide the ability to invoke trade sanctions as a last resort for non-enforcement of labour law by a Party.

With the NAALC, we have the reaffirmation, within a context characterized by a weak perspective of integration, limited to the economic matter, of a functionalist logic that is very close to the one characterizing the primitive European Community experience. However, within the NAALC, the techniques and goals of supranational social regulation change. The *labour side agreement* has as its object surveillance and cooperation procedures among partner countries that may lead, whereby the missing compliance with the obligations incurred may entail effective competition damages, and actual economic-financial sanctions. Therefore, this mechanism may be intended as a social clause that, differently from what normally provided for in international trade treaties and in the experience of European integration (as well as in the normative tradition of international labour law), does not contemplate the respect of minimum uniform supranational standards, but the guarantee of effectiveness of single national social standards.

In the logic of the agreement, the grounds of the social clause are substantially economic: they regard at the same time the regulation of competition and the preservation of comparative advantages. As a matter of fact, the condition for the application of a sanction is the proof of a competitive advantage deriving from the missing compliance with the internal labour legislation of a given country. Article 3 of NAALC testifies the intention of the parties, who promote the 'respect and the effective application of their own laws in matter of labour through appropriate actions of government': therefore, there is no aim of harmonization or, even more, of standardization of the levels of protection in social matters, that is left to the national legislator's discretionality. It is true that the agreement individuates some *principles*; however – as we can see in the attachment on *Labour Principles*, which is integrating part of the agreement – they do not represent supranational social standards, but they indicate 'guiding values' and 'areas of labour law interest' where each country established its own level of regulation.

A critical profile regards the different protection ensured to the eleven Labour Principles[17]: the agreement excludes Union rights from the *strongest* level of protection, applying to the violation of the rights of organization, collective bargaining and strike not actual economic sanctions but the mere activation of 'Ministerial Consultations'. Only the violation of some *labour standards* regarding matters relative to security on labour and health, minor labour and minimum wage allows the activation of the complex procedure of *Review* that, through the initial experiment of inter-ministerial consultations, reaches the summoning of an *Arbitrary Panel*, which may conclude with the provision of financial sanctions. The field of operativeness of sanctions is therefore strictly circumscribed: they will be active only in the case where the pact violations, in addition to being persistent, will result as being 'trade-related' and 'covered by mutually recognized labour laws' (NAALC; Article 49, 'Definitions'). In other words, not every violation will result as censorable, but only those which, realizing in the missing reaction in the field of the respective orders to the violation committed by the single economic subjects in order to pursue an undue comparative advantage, appear as relevant for the trade-economic integration pursued by the NAFTA; further, the missing application will have to deal with labour law disciplines that have been acknowledged by contractors, regarding the capacity to implement rights and level of protection.

However, paradoxically, all the procedures of violation so far activated have as object the violation of Union Rights, while the procedure of *Review* has provided important outcomes, thanks in particular to the summoning of public forums of public opinion awareness raising and to the consequent 'media' sanctions, as well as to the transnational collaboration among Union Organizations, within an area where factors

17. The Annex 1 defines 'labour principles' as 'guiding values' that the parties commit to respect and it individuates them in the following thematic fields: (1) freedom of association and right to collective bargaining; (2) right to collective bargaining; (3) right to strike; (4) prohibition of forced labour; (5) protection of child and minor labour; (6) protection of minimum standards of employment (e.g., minimum wages and benefits for extra-hour labour); (7) elimination of discrimination on labour; (8) right to equal salary among men and women working in the same enterprise and having the same task; (9) prevention of professional illnesses and injuries on labour; (10) right to compensation in case of illnesses and injuries on labour; (11) protection of migrant workers. We are dealing with an all-inclusive list, which refers to an editing technique used in other treaties and international agreements (*see*, for example, the twelve principles enounced in the 1989 Community Charter of workers' fundamental social rights), even though, in this case, it results as extremely cautious in the individuation of the aspects characterizing the specific cases individuated in order to interpret and to apply the regulating norm; in particular, there is no mention of the relative Conventions of the ILO, that the Principles therefore respect, but do not refer to. As regards this, it is important to point out that such Principles do not set common minimum standards at all, but only 'wide areas of interest' on which the parties have developed (each its own way) 'laws, regulations, procedures and practises' intended to the 'protection of the interests of the respective labour forces' (*Annex 1*).

non-facilitating the international solidarity among Trade Unions are prevailing. Such collaboration is stimulated by the necessity that a procedure of *submission* relative to a country is introduced within the administrative structure of another country, on the part, therefore, of a foreign organization.

The NAALC model, with all its limits, has been therefore appreciated by the doctrine most of all for having stimulated the creation of transnational links and bonds between Unions and NGOs, within a very problematic context, non-favourable to the accomplishment of forms of international solidarities for workers (*see also* Bellace relation on the matter).

[B] The CAFTA-DR

The CAFTA-DR agreement[18] is the first free trade agreement between the United States and a group of smaller developing economies: Costa Rica, El Salvador, Guatemala, Honduras, Nicaragua, as well as the Dominican Republic. This FTA, signed on 2005, is on the list of free trade agreements where we can find, next to the primary goal of exchanges' liberalization, the issue of workers' rights and of the conditions applied to relations. From the Preamble of the Agreement, we can infer that the parties commit not only to the promotion of integration intended in a purely economic sense but also to create new opportunities for the social and economic development of the respective territories, in order to protect and to strengthen workers' rights and the cooperation in matter of labour among the different institutions involved, in order to create new opportunities of employment and to improve the conditions of life and labour.

Examining in particular the chapter dedicated to labour, it may be useful to point out that the CAFTA-DR Agreement largely lies on the model proposed by the NAALC and by the recent Free Trade Agreements stipulated with Australia, Morocco, Chile and Singapore. In this perspective, it is therefore in line of continuity with the previous experiences, even though we have important signs of the gradual acknowledgement of social rights going with economic rationality.

The agreement may ideally be divided into two parts: while the first deals with the references to the structure of protections acknowledged to workers and to the instruments that are functional to guarantee their effectiveness, the second is intended to add value and promote a participative and collaborative model among the different actors that intervene in the agreement.

After the reference to the ILO's principles stated in the 1998 Declaration, pointing out that the parties commit both to respect the mentioned principles and to apply the internal legislation in order to comply with the international norms on labour, the text goes on by acknowledging to the participant States the duty not to encourage trade practices through the weakening of the structure of protections provided by the internal legislation. Further, the States are prohibited, in the attempt to promote trade exchanges or to encourage investments in their territory, to apply labour conditions that

18. Originally, the agreement encompassed the United States and the Central American countries of Costa Rica, El Salvador, Guatemala, Honduras and Nicaragua, and was called CAFTA. In 2004, the Dominican Republic joined the negotiations, and the agreement was renamed CAFTA-DR.

are inferior to those guaranteed by the principles of international law. Specifically, as stated in the 16.8, when the Agreement refers to 'labour laws', it refers to the norms introduced by the participant Countries and directly co-related to internationally recognized principles such as the right of association, the right of organization and of collective bargaining, the prohibition of utilization of every form of forced labour, the minimum age of access to labour, the prohibition and the elimination of forms of exploitation of minor labour, the right to acceptable conditions of labour and in particular with regards to minimum wage, working hour and health and security in workplaces.

Article 16.2 introduces an actual obligation for the stipulating parties and, in case of non-compliance, the agreement provides for the activation of a procedure that inflicts the non-complying party adequate trade sanctions.

With regards to the instruments introduced in order to implement the provisions on the compliance with the ILO's principles and on the need to strengthen the internal legislation in order to guarantee the improvement of the workers' social and professional status, the agreement provides for a procedure of guarantee and the State's responsibility in order to ensure those who are interested in the possibility to address in an impartial way to the judicial authority in order to claim their rights. The procedure must be equal, free and transparent. The subscribers of the agreement must therefore commit themselves so that the holder of a legally acknowledged interest in the country of belonging may address to the judicial authority to lay claim to his/her reasons.

As regards the second part of the agreement, it reflects the intention to improve the cooperation and the exchange among the participating countries as much as possible, so that to monitor the implementation of the agreement and the possible problematic aspects that may arise in the applicative phase. In this perspective, we can understand both the constitution of a Labour affaire Council (LAC), with tasks of periodic verification of the state of implementation of the agreement, of coordination among the parties stipulating the agreement and the provision of a system (capacity building mechanism) intended to promote and to strengthen the cooperation, to improve labour standards, to favour consultations and moments of meeting among the parties.

Should we have to draw some considerations on the extent of the agreement, we could not avoid saying that the part dedicated to labour is by all means included in the agreement for free exchange; basically, we are not dealing with a simple attachment, but a list of principles that are integrating part of the agreement. The attention towards the issues of labour has for this reason great autonomous importance, even though it must be put into relation with the needs of the market.

Second, the agreement intends to focus every effort on the instruments to guarantee the effectiveness of protections: this is the first time that such an issue emerges within a free exchange agreement, compared to the totality of the agreements so far stipulated. As it results, in fact, from the June 2005 ILO report, in the Countries of Central America and in the Dominican Republic, we cannot say that the provisions that acknowledge and promote the respect of *core labour standards* are absent. The problem arises, instead, concerning the actual application of the norms of protection of workers.

As a matter of fact, the first labour dispute under any free trade agreement (since 1993, no country that has signed an FTA with the US has never been finded or had its trade privileges revoked, even when severe infringements of social rights have occurred) regards the CAFTA-DR.

[C] The MERCOSUR and the Social–Laboural Declaration

The Mercosur (Common Southern Market) has been instituted on 26 March 1991 with an act subscribed by Argentina, Brazil, Paraguay, Uruguay and later (2014) by Venezuela.

Venezuela's new membership was short-lived, however, since by the end of 2016 it had already been suspended by the four founding members of MERCOSUR. The official reason was Venezuela's failure to adjust its domestic legislation to existing MERCOSUR law. However, deep ideological differences and doubts about Venezuela's commitment to democracy and the protection of human rights seem to have been the real driving factors for the suspension. The other South American States have obtained the status of Associate Member (Chile in 1996, Bolivia in 1997, Colombia, Ecuador and Venezuela in 2005, and Peru in 2006) and have concluded free trade agreements with MERCOSUR (Free Trade Areas). Bolivia's accession as a full member was signed in 2015 but still requires ratification at the time of writing (August 2018).

In the intentions of its founders, the Mercosur, as an instrument of economic cooperation among participating States, aspired to realize a system of free trade through the elimination of duties and restrictions to trade exchanges within the involved Countries; however, during the course of time, the original project has been widened to encompass also goals of coordination of macroeconomic policies, the definition of a common trade policy and, most of all, a progressive juridical integration of the national orders of Member States.

What interests us most is most of all the 'Social labour Declaration' elaborated in 1998 after a long and tormented process intended to the affirmation of a social and economic identity of the Mercosur and amended in 2015, by its own supervisory tripartite body – the Social and Labour Commission of the Mercosour – and, as a result, it was approved, as amended, in Brasilia, in June, 2015

The Declaration is a political act, so it lacks direct efficiency but, at the same time, it is to be considered a starting point for the development of a common and shared social policy within the Mercosur's Member States. It undoubtedly represents the outcome of big compromises among the opposed interests that lied within the Mercosur, but we should not underestimate its extent and effects on national labour markets. In the Declaration, there is specific reference to the workers' fundamental rights stated in the 1998 ILO's Declaration and in the most important international Agreement on the matter.[19] Therefore, within the Declaration, we find specific reference to the protection of the principle of non-discrimination (Article 1), the

19. 1948 Universal Declaration of Human Rights, 1966 International Covenant on Political and Civil Rights, 1966 International Covenant on economic, social and cultural rights, 1988 American Convention on human rights and on economic, social, cultural rights.

protection of migrant and transborder workers (Article 4), the prohibition of minor labour (Article 6), the prohibition of forced labour, the protection of health and security in the workplace, the freedom of association and of collective bargaining, the prohibition of discrimination by reason of Union membership and the right to strike. Again, the Declaration states the commitment of the States towards the issues of employment, of professional training, of services of sustain to employment. The 2015 amendment also ratifies the provisions regarding the elimination of forced labour and includes regulation on protection against dismissal, on the prevention and elimination of child labour and the protection of young workers, as well as any individual rights which had not been previously considered, such as provision governing the length of a working day, leave and holidays, and the right to a minimum wage according to the national laws, which wage must be sufficient to meet the worker's needs and those of his/her family.[20]

With reference to the instruments of implementation of the Declaration and of its principles, the parties have provided for the constitution of a specific *Comision Socio Laboral*, with mainly advisory functions, and therefore non-sanctionatory, composed of the representatives of governments, of Union organizations and of employers. Even though facing difficulties, the Commission has carried out an important role in order to implement the Declaration, by supporting the action of governments in the direction of an economic as well as social integration.

[1] EU – Mercosur FTA

The EU is negotiating a trade deal with the four founding Mercosur States – (1) Argentina, (2) Brazil, (3) Paraguay and (4) Uruguay, as part of a broader Association Agreement between the two regions.

Negotiations started on 1999, but they stopped due to the Argentina's crisis on 2001 and were suspended until 2010, to restart after the protectionist policies started by Mr President Trump and they apparently stop to the TTIP negotiations: the EU would like to find new ways to expand its market: The current negotiations cover issues that include tariffs, rules of origin, technical barriers to trade, sanitary and phytosanitary measures, services, government procurement, intellectual property, sustainable development and small- and medium-sized enterprises. The final text of the agreement is expected by the end of 2018, even if the last round of negotiations (the EU and Mercosur negotiating teams met in Montevideo, Uruguay, from 4th to 8th June 2018 for a round of negotiations) was not so fruitful.

The thirty-fourth negotiation round of the Trade Part of the EU-Mercosur Association Agreement took place from 9 to 17 July 2018 in Brussels.

The draft of the agreement text is still not available but we are able to find serious commitment by the EU in terms of the promotion of sustainable development and social rights. As a matter of fact, it is possible to observe from the EU's textual

20. A. Goldin, *The MERCOSUR (Southern Common Market): Argentina, Brazil, Paraguay, Uruguay and Venezuela*, in A. Perulli, T. Treu. (eds), *Sustainable Development, Global Trade and Social Rights, Kluwer International*, 2018, pp. 41 ss.

proposals, in line with the EU 2015 *Trade for All Strategy*, when the EU reasserted its ambition to 'promote an ambitious and innovative sustainable development chapter in all trade and investment agreements', vowing to achieve 'far-reaching commitments on all core labour rights' and to ensure 'high levels of occupational health and safety and decent working conditions in accordance with the ILO Decent Work Agenda', even in the context of the Mercosur negotiations as the EU proposed to include a Sustainable Development Chapter.[21]

In particular, the EU want to enhance the integration of sustainable development in the Parties' trade and investment relationship, notably by establishing principles and actions concerning labour and environmental aspects of sustainable development of specific relevance in a trade and investment context, recognizing the right of each Party to determine its sustainable development policies and priorities, to establish the levels of domestic environmental and labour protection. Moreover, Parties should not weaken the levels of protection afforded in domestic environmental or labour law in order to encourage trade or investment or derogate from them or, again, fail to enforce labour laws in order to encourage trade or investment.

Then, according to the proposed article dedicated to 'Multilateral Labour Standards and Agreements', 'The Parties reaffirm their commitment to promote the development of international trade in a way that is conducive to decent work for all, including for women and young people' and each Party shall respect, promote and effectively implement the internationally recognized core labour standards, 'in accordance with the ILO Constitution and the ILO Declaration on Fundamental Principles and Rights at Work and its Follow-up'.

As for the ILO Core Conventions for example, all Countries have already ratified the ILO Core Conventions, a part from Brazil, which has yet to ratify the ILO Freedom of Association and Protection of the Right to Organise Convention, 1948 (No. 87).

[D] The US Bilateral Free Trade Agreements

If we examine the agreements stipulated by the USA following the experience of the NAFTA and of the NAALC, we can highlight significant progresses in the usage and in the formulation of social clauses. Our reference goes, among the others,[22] to the following agreements: 2004 US-Chile, 2010 US-Jordan, 2009 United States-Peru Free Trade Agreement (PTPA), 2012 US-Korea, that, although being very specific, may be considered as virtuous examples of adaptation among economic and social goals, confirming the actual will of the participating countries to seriously face the issue of the *linkage* between social rights and international trade.

We need to point out the positive innovations of these agreements: they integrate the norms on *fair labour practices* in the Treaty's *corpus* itself, without recurring to

21. http://ec.europa.eu/trade/policy/countries-and-regions/regions/mercosur/.
22. The US has twenty Bilateral Trade Agreements in force today: Israel 1985 (The United States-Israel Free Trade Agreement was the first FTA entered into by the United States), Canada 1989, Singapore 2003, Australia 2004, Morocco 2004, Chile 2004, Bahrain 2006, Oman 2009, Peru 2009, Jordan 2010, Colombia 2012, Korea 2012, Panama 2012.

'parallel' agreements like in the case of the NAALC; the social *standards* of reference are specifically those of the ILO, where there is no longer a generic and ambiguous reference to the internationally recognized rights of workers; labour law therefore becomes the *domestic benchmark* in order to evaluate the efficiency of the internal labour regulation; the violation of social norms is compared to the violation of *fair trade practices* by utilizing the same procedural and sanctionatory mechanisms. The emblematic cases, like the one represented by the bilateral agreement *USA–Cambodia* in the textile sector (this agreement expired in 2004), prove the positive effect of the *linkage* in the development of *labour standards* (i.e., to say in the tendency to avoid the *labour standards'* deterioration) in the sectors covered by the Agreement. The project *Better Factories Cambodia* originally negotiated between the US and Cambodia, provides for a strict connection between the expansion of the Cambodian products in the American market and the improvement of social *standards,* with the presence of the ILO as an actor in monitoring through inspections and strict reports, as well as in the technical assistance to the Cambodian Government. The implementation of this model of hybridization between *hard* techniques (social clause) and *soft* techniques (technical assistance, cooperation) has matter-of-factly achieved a promotion of competitiveness founded on the increase of working conditions, that have determined an increase of productivity able in its turn to compensate the higher costs of manpower, with further benefits in macroeconomic and political stability terms. After the expiration of the trade agreement in 2004, the Cambodian Government, together with unions and employers, requested that the ILO set up a sustainability strategy to turn Better Factories Cambodia into a self-financing local institution. The ILO teamed up with the IFC (International Finance Corporation (IFC), a member of the World Bank Group) to design and implement this strategy.[23]

§6.06 THE EU'S APPROACH TO LABOUR RIGHTS AND SOCIAL STANDARDS IN THE LATEST BILATERAL FTAS: TTIP, CETA AND EPA

In the last two decades, in line with the US FTAs we saw, labour provisions in EU bilateral and multilateral trade agreements have widened and deepened. Over 80% of agreements that came into force since 2013 contain such provisions,[24] in order to commit the parties to not lower their labour standards or derogate from labour law with a view to boosting competitiveness.

Social clauses have not only grown in number as to become a common trait of these trade agreements but have acquired great substantive and procedural complexity.[25]

23. https://betterwork.org/where-we-work/cambodia/.
24. ILO, Studies on Growth with Equity, Assessment of Labour Provisions in Trade and Investment Arrangements, Report July 2016.
25. T. Treu, *Globalization and Human Rights: Social Clauses in Trade Agreements and in International Exchanges among Companies*, in A. Perulli, T. Treu (eds), *Sustainable Development, Global Trade and Social Rights*, Wolters Kluwer, 2018, p. 99.

This instrument intends to correct abusive practice and offer the dual advantage of improving the lot of workers in the exporting countries and protecting the industries of the importing countries against unfair competition. The insertion of a social clause in a trade agreement is actually commonly justified for three different grounds: 1) the necessity of protection of labour right; 2) the prevention of the negative effects of the so well-known race to the bottom of social rights competition in the international market; 3) the long-term stimulation of economy profits: trade agreements boost trade between members of the agreement, irrespective of the existence of labour provisions.[26] As regards this last point, as demonstrated by the ILO, a trade agreement which includes labour provisions actually increases the value of trade by 28% on average, similar to 26% for an agreement without labour provisions.[27] This confirms the essentially economic nature of the social clause, which deals with the regulation of competition and the preservation of the comparative advantages at the same time,[28] as it has been demonstrated that States with better social protection and higher wages would not be affected by the unfair competitions from States with low wages in the long term.

So said, the social clause deserves new attention, considering first, the European trend to conclude more and more multilateral free trade agreements, which clashes with the new protectionist policies from the US (and the UK); and second, as we will see, the tendency to include social clauses in FTAs as part of the Chapters generally dedicated to the Sustainable Development, with a progressive enhancement of the Sustainable Development model as a regulatory framework that can stabilize and institutionalize the link between social rights and free trade,[29] as in the case of TTIP (Transatlantic Trade and Investment Partnership negotiated with the US), CETA (Comprehensive Economic and Trade Agreement) and EPA (EU–Japan Economic Partnership Agreement). While TTIP negotiations are stopped for the moment (*see* below), CETA and EPA are the two last most important FTAs recently negotiated by the European Union with, respectively Canada and Japan, both on the top ten of the list of countries of trade with Europe.[30]

This new US protectionism could be considered as a paradox compared to the recent European boost to the FTAs' negotiations.[31]

First, with Canada (CETA has provisionally entered into force on September 2017, but it will enter info force definitely and fully when all EU Member States

26. H. Chen, *Social Clause in Trade Agreements and China's Experience*, in Beijing Law Review, 2015, 6, 1–8, p. 7.
27. ILO, *Studies on Growth with Equity, Assessment of labour provisions in trade and investment arrangements*, Report July 2016.
28. A. Perulli, *Sustainable Development, Global Trade and Social Rights: An Evolutionary Perspective*, in A. Perulli, T. Treu (eds), *Sustainable Development, Global Trade and Social Rights*, Wolters Kluwer, 2018, p. 2.
29. *See* A. Perulli, *Introduction*, in A. Perulli, T. Treu (eds), *Sustainable Development, Global Trade and Social Rights*, Wolters Kluwer, 2018, p. 2.
30. With regards to trade, Canada is the tenth country in the chart of total trade with EU, eleventh for imports and twelfth for exports, while Japan is the sixth country in the chart of total trade, seventh for imports and sixth for exports (Source: European Commission, Client and Supplier Countries of the EU28 in Merchandise Trade (value %), 2017, excluding intra-EU Trade).
31. European Commission, Overview of FTA and other Trade Negotiations, Updated May 2018.

parliaments have ratified the Agreement) and Japan (EPA, the EU–Japan Economic Partnership Agreement was finalized on December 2017). Europe is then negotiating trade agreements with other countries and regions around the world: if we consider Asia, there are FTAs on the table of negotiations with some ASEAN Member States: Singapore and Malaysia (negotiations were launched in 2010), Vietnam (June 2012), Thailand (March 2013), Indonesia and Philippines (2016) and Myanmar/Burma (last negotiations were in April 2017). Then, as regards Oceania, the EU is negotiating by 2017 with Australia and New Zealand, while for Latin America with MERCOSUR (last round on March 2018), Mexico (the FTA's text will be finalized by the end of 2018) and Chile (last round of negotiations was on January 2018).[32]

Despite the opposite policies from the EU and from the US side, the EU is, together with the US, the biggest proponent of linking trade and labour provisions[33]: the two giants of the opposite side of the Atlantic Ocean, even with different tools and manners, have continued to include labour provisions in trade agreements, to reach a sort of social trade.

As a matter of fact, protectionism does not underlie the stronger social clause in trade agreements. If historically, social clause was considered an instrument put forward by industrialized countries to raise tariff barriers blocking imports with competitive price advantages from developing countries, thereby guaranteeing the market of the domestic companies,[34] is it possible to observe an increasing relevance of labour standards on the States free trade agenda, since the mid-2000s. All agreements, negotiated by both protectionist and by liberalist countries, contains a provision stating explicitly that labour standards shall not be used for protectionist trade purposes, and that the parties should not waive or derogate from their domestic labour law to attract trade or investment.

This is justified also by a new scope and use of FTAs and consequently, of the social clause: FTA, signed to reduce or eliminate trade tariff or other trade blocks to international trades, are now seen as a solution to the crisis and then negotiated and concluded, not only with developing countries but also, on the contrary, between (or among) peer economies, as EU, Canada, US and Japan.[35] The examination of the recent

32. In addition, there are some candidate countries for Free Trade Agreements with the EU (Turkey, Bosnia and Herzegovina, Serbia, Morocco, and Tunisia) and other Trade Negotiations with Armenia, Azerbaijan, Belarus, Kyrgyzstan, Uzbekistan, China (investment), Services (TISA), Green Goods, Trade in Agri-Food and Fisheries Products with EEA/EFTA countries, Association Agreements with Andorra, Monaco and San Marino.
33. L. Van Den Putte, J. Orbie, EU Bilateral Trade Agreements and the Surprising Rise of Labour Provisions, in *International Journal of Comparative Labour Law*, 31, n. 3 (2015), p. 263.
34. Servais, J. (1989), The Social Clause in Trade Agreements: Wishful Thinking or an Instrument of Social Progress, in *International Labour Review*, 128, 423.
35. Protectionism would disrupt production and increase costs and prices for consumers. European exports would become less competitive, putting even more jobs at risk 12. An increase in trade restrictions by 10% is estimated to lead to a 4% loss of national income 13. We would lose access to new products, services, technologies and ideas. By hitting the poorest hardest with price increases, protectionism would have the opposite of its desired effect. According to a recent study of 27 European and 13 other large countries, the real income loss from closing off trade would be 63% for the poorest households and 28% for the richest, because the poor spend a higher share of their income on consumption (P.D. Fajgelbaum and A.K. Khandelwal, 'Measuring the Unequal Gains from Trade', in *Quarterly Journal of Economics*, 2016).

trade policy demonstrated that the inclusion of labour provisions in FTA's is more and more legitimized in terms of human rights and in terms of sustainable development, not to protect countries from social dumping (not only) but to contribute, together, to a fair trade, promoting the integration of social provisions and trade liberalization,[36] planning an axiological oriented global order.[37]

EU's approach to labour rights and social standards in FTAs is relatively recent: in 1995 it adopted an approach involving both a withdrawal mechanism and an incentive mechanism for additional preferences, linking trade preferences and labour standards thanks to the Generalized Scheme of Preferences (GPS[38]), which allows vulnerable developing countries to pay fewer or no duties on exports to the EU, giving them vital access to the EU market and contributing to their growth. Over time, the approach has evolved and the levels of commitments have deepened and widened, although there remain important differences across agreements.

The content of the social provisions relates to social policy and labour rights or engage countries in agreeing not to use social policies as protectionist trade measures. There are generally no enforcement mechanisms since most clauses are best endeavoured in nature but nevertheless provide for an 'implementation' mechanism done through cooperation with its partner countries and generally (but contrary to the GSP +[39]) EU FTAs do not require the partner countries to ratify ILO Conventions, although specific reference is made to the implementation of core labour standards. Besides an obligation to enforce labour laws, these provisions also require countries not to reduce their levels of protection and encourage countries to even raise their levels of protection, subject to a provision that this is not done for protectionist purposes. Labour issues are covered under the rubrics of 'social aspects', 'social matters' or, more recently, to that of 'sustainable development', as for the agreement with Japan.

In terms of implementation, contrary to the US approach, the EU adopts a more nuanced approach, with a preference for dialogue and capacity instead of the previsions of sanctions.

36. A. Perulli, Fundamental Social Rights, Market Regulation and EU External Action, in *International Journal of Comparative Labour Law and Industrial Relation*, 27, 41, 2014.
37. T. Novitz, *Core Labour Standards Conditionalities: A Means by Which to Achieve Sustainable Development?*, in J. Faundez, C. Tan (eds), *International Economic Law, Globalization and Developing Countries*, Edward Elgar, 2010, pp. 234 et seq.
38. The Community GSP scheme was actually introduced on 1 July 1971, applying the principles laid down in the UNCTAD generalized system of preferences, which differ from the standard GATT rules and the most-favoured-nation clause, and were authorized by GATT by means of a formal derogation decision, commonly known as the 'enabling clause', which was first adopted on 25 June 1971 and renewed on 28 November 1979. The Community GSP scheme has, since its introduction, been regularly renewed, with a comprehensive review taking place every ten years. The first such revision was implemented on 1 January 1981, and was followed by a more limited mid-term exercise on 1 January 1986. The ten-year revision scheduled for 1 January 1991 was postponed each year until 1 January 1995, when a new scheme, with a link between social provisions and trade, entered into force.
39. *See* further.

Let us then consider three of the most recent and important bilateral FTAs negotiated by the European Union: (1) the TTIP, (2) the CETA and (3) the EPA and the EU social approach to those treaties.

[A] The Social Clause in the US–EU TTIP

The negotiations between the United States and the European Union, in order to stipulate a Transatlantic Trade and Investment Partnership (TTIP) of total liberalization of trade and investments between the USA and the EU, are currently stopped, due to the change of international trade policies.[40]

The US is the main partner of EU trade, the second country for imports (after China[41]) and the first for exports.[42] For this reason, those countries started, on 2013, negotiations for a TTIP, a *Transatlantic Trade and Investment Partnership,* in order to revise standards, to evaluate compliance and to promote regulatory cooperation in order to maintain high international standards and enhance normative compatibility in the various economic and productive sectors.[43]

Despite the success of the various rounds of negotiation, the change of US Presidency, on the starting of 2017, marks definitely a change of course on American trade policies.

First, with the stop to negotiations of the TTIP[44] (and, more generally, of all the FTAs decided by Obama) and more recently, with the war on duties started by the US against EU: at the starting of June 2018, the Trump administration is putting steel and aluminium tariffs on U.S. allies European Union[45] (as Canada and Mexico), and the EU has imposed countermeasures in response to the US actions, endorsing the decision to impose additional duties on the full list of US products notified to the World Trade Organization (WTO).

Despite the stop to the TTIP, the analysis of the treaty deserves our attention as the TTIP represent a historic step towards the creation of a global market ruled by free

---

40. TTIP's future is uncertain because the last round of negotiations dates back to October 2016 and are currently on hold following the change of US Administration.
41. Negotiations of a comprehensive EU–China investment agreement were formally launched at the EU–China Summit of 21 November 2013 in Beijing. The aim of this agreement is to remove market access barriers to investment and provide a high level of protection to investors and investments in EU and China markets. It will replace the twenty-six existing Bilateral Investment Treaties between twenty-seven individual EU Member States and China by one single comprehensive investment Agreement.

    In 2016 the EU and China negotiators reached clear conclusions on an ambitious and comprehensive scope for the EU–China investment agreement and established a joint negotiating text. The seventeenth round of negotiations took place in Beijing in May 2018.
42. European Commission, Client and Supplier Countries of the EU28 in Merchandise Trade (value %), 2017, excluding intra-EU Trade.
43. A. Perulli, Sustainability, Social Rights and International Trade: The TTIP, in *The International Journal of Comparative Labour Law and Industrial Relations* 31, no. 4 (2015), p. 473.
44. Negotiations are suspended with no chance to continue for the time being.
45. Those entities had been exempted from the 25% tariffs on steel imports and 10% tariffs on aluminium imports.

trade principles. The FTA, once (and if) signed, will give way to a 'normalization' of the regulative standards and promote commercial interchange and investments between the two most important economic areas in the world.

Even if its conclusion is uncertain at the moment, this treaty deserves a reflection as regards the approach and the method used by the two Parties during the negotiations, and in particular by the EU, as it represents a recent and concrete example of the building of a social right chapter in the ambit of a trade and investment treaty.

Under a strictly normative profile, TTIP aims to the revision of the standards and evaluations of compliance, enhancing the regulatory cooperation, in order to reach high international standards and to increase the normative compatibility within the various economic and productive sectors. The impact of this agreement in social and work-related terms might be remarkable for both continents. Under the influence of the liberalization of exchanges, it is believed that the TTIP may create hundreds or thousands of new jobs, increase salaries and stimulate workers' mobility towards expanding productive sectors. In view of these optimistic economic growth perspectives, the TTIP raises a series of social concerns linked to the possible (de)regulative competition on fundamental labour norms that such a liberalization may be able to enact. The increasingly global processes of liberalization of exchanges and investments have produced alarming phenomena of social dumping, so far. They are closely linked to a pronounced increase of social inequalities, as a vast empirical literature shows, estimating the incidence of commercial exchanging, of capital transfer and migratory pressure on the increase of inequalities on salaries and on the emersion of new poverty areas in advanced countries.

Those worries were augmented due to the initial provision of the ISDS (*Investor-To-State Dispute Settlement*) in the Treaty.

Scholars are debating on the effects of the TTIP, asking whether he TTIP, if concluded, will be the liberalistic instrument using commerce as a Troy Horse in order to dismantle the social protection, and to extend the deregulation, or if it will represent an occasion to relaunch the linkage between liberalization of exchanges and social rights, within a value line having its cultural and historical roots in the ILO Constitution.[46]

Regarding this matter, some crucial questions for labour law are arising at all levels of normative production (national, supranational, international), as for each FTA signed: what will be the repercussions of such agreement on the system of national industrial relations of Member States? What will be the impact on European workers' social rights? What will be the measures to be previously adopted to protect European (and national) social standards, in view of the entrepreneurial competition and the manpower of the USA? In order to answer these regulatory challenges, the TTIP negotiators will have to overcome the ambivalences that, most of all on the part of the USA, are traditionally connected to the relation between 'free trade' and 'labour',[47] in

46. Cf. A. Perulli, *Sustainability, Social Rights and International Trade: The TTIP*, in IJCLLIR, 2015, vol. 32, pp. 473–49.
47. For historical reference, *see* Ethan B. Kapstein, *Sharing the Wealth. Workers and the World Economy*, trad it. *Governare la ricchezza. Il lavoro nell'economia globale*, Carocci editore, 2000.

order to conjugate the trade agenda with the new issues of value deriving from the de-nationalization of labour law, in the perspective – promoted by the European counterpart – of sustainable development.

We are dealing with needs that include different but convergent *ratios* that refer both to the planning and the institution of an axiologically oriented international order, able to correct the globalization's undesired social consequences, and to regulate the phenomena of the distortion of competition that obstructs the optimal allocation of resources.

This is why the TTIP should conceive a new model of 'social clause' to be inserted within the TTIP's *corpus*, developing a confrontation among the experiences of commercial integration already present in the global market, not only in the field of similar processes of exchanges liberalization (NAFTA, *Free Trade Agreement*), but also in the field of unilateral Trade policies linked to the promotion of social rights (*see* below about the Generalized System of Preferences (GSP) adopted by the USA and the EU).

[1] The TTIP and Sustainable Development

The TTIP negotiators decided to dedicate a chapter on *Sustainable Development and Trade (TSD Chapter)*, conceived not as an external or accidental element of the agreement, but, on the contrary, to 'involve all the areas of the negotiated agreement'. The aims of sustainable development were declared from the beginning of negotiations, starting from the *Directive of negotiation on transatlantic Partnership for exchanges and investments between EU and USA* (17 June 2013). These Directives stated that the TTIP's preamble must take into account that 'the partnership with USA is based on principles and common values that must be coherent with the principles and the aims of the external action of the Union', and contain also: (1) shared values as human rights, fundamental freedom, democracy and state of law; (2) the responsibility of the parties in favour of sustainable development and the contribution to international trade to sustainable development as regarding its social, environmental and economic aspects, economic development, full, productive and decorous employment, as well as the protection and conservation of environment and natural resources; (3) the right of the parties to undertake the measures intended to realize legitimate objectives of public policy on the basis of the level of health, safety, workers, consumers and environment protection, as well as the promotion of diversity of cultural expressions.

There are some precedents in the adoption of external relationships in the EU, having as an aim sustainable development, as it has been for the CETA (Canada and European Union FTA) and are certainly useful to formulate the TDS chapter within the TTIP. As a matter of fact, the EU has long since adopted a regulation model intended to combine trade liberalization and respect of social rights through the Generalized

System of Preferences (GSP),[48] the preferential and non-mutual treatment granted to developing countries in the field of trade exchanges, notwithstanding the GATT normative[49] (*see* further).

The TTIP analysis is useful for our reflections on the protection of social rights in the ambit of free trade as the main points of the Chapter on Sustainability (which will probably called 'Trade and Sustainable Development Chapter') should be the following:

[a] Provision for a Mechanisms of SIA of TTIP in Social Matters

The Sustainability Impact Assessment (SIA) is a DG trade-specific tool for supporting major trade negotiations which provide the Commission with an in-depth analysis of the potential economic, social, human rights and environmental impacts of ongoing trade negotiations. In the field of the 2020 strategy, the EU has provided for all trade initiatives, the activation of economic, social and environmental impact assessments, with 'specific attention to wide consultations and the involvement of the society in the sustainability impact assessment that will be implemented in the course of the trade negotiations'.[50] This impact assessments can therefore legitimately be included within the social aims of TTIP, largely contributing to rebalance the confrontation between social rights and economic freedoms. The *Counsel Negotiation Directives* are then laid in this perspective, providing for a SIA, aimed to verify the TTIP's impact on a social, economic and environmental basis, during the course of the negotiation to which the society and all the components specified in the agreement will participate (point 33).

The assessment of the TTIP's social consequences should disregard the terms of drawing up of the agreement and represent a permanent mechanism able to supply *ex ante* and *ex post* indications on the effects of the Chapter on Sustainable development, providing *follow-up* sessions able to indicate the measures to be adopted in order to guarantee the expected results.[51] Besides, this monitoring impact assessment activity should combine with additional *review* and *follow-up* mechanisms, to be considered in the agreement. They should include mutual learning and circulation of good procedures, to be adopted on the basis of shared guidelines, in the field of an open

48. F. Pantano, R. Salomone, *Trade and Labour Within the European Union Generalized System of Preferences*, Jean Monnet WPS, New York University School of Law, 2008.
49. *See* T.M. Franck, *Fairness in International Law and Institution*, Oxford, 1995, p. 58; L. Bartels, C. Haberli, Binding Tariff Preferences for Developing Countries under Article II GATT, in *Journal of International Economic Law*.
50. Communication of the Commission to the European Parliament, to the Counsel, to the Social and Economic European Committee and to the Region Committee, 'Trade, Growth and World business. Trade Policy as an essential component of 2020 EU Strategy'. COM(2010) 612 def.
51. Also according to K. Lukas, A. Steinkellner, *Social Standards in Sustainability Chapters of Bilateral Free Trade Agreements*, p. 11, 'A continuous repeated review of the impact of the agreements is also required'.

coordination mechanism, on the basis of the EU (MAC) directives to coordinate the labour policies of Member States.[52]

In March 2017, the European Commission published its position paper on the Sustainability Impact Assessment in support of negotiations of the TTIP,[53] where it is stated that from the perspective of potential impact on social human rights if the projected economic and social results can be obtained with full respect for social and economic human rights TTIP is not expected to have a negative effect on social and economic human rights in the long run - as long as labour and social rights and levels of social protection are upheld or increased. In the short-run labour displacement could put pressure on the human right to an adequate living as workers move from one sector to the other. However, the wage data suggest that most mobility will be a consequence of workers being drawn into growing sectors that offer higher wages, as opposed to being made redundant against their will.

With regards to the ratification of the ILO Core Labour Conventions (the EU has ratified all eight ILO Fundamental Labour Conventions, while the US ratified only two), the SIA clarifies that there will clearly be little impact on the EU, but for the US there are major roadblocks in terms of US law and practice that will impede ratification of these ILO conventions within the context of the TTIP negotiation. TTIP is unlikely to lead to the signing of any other ILO Fundamental Conventions (other than Convention 111, which has already been presented to Congress) as ratification by the Senate, requiring a two-thirds majority, is improbable. The EU proposal for the Sustainable Development chapter includes sustainable commitments on labour standards that are comparable to the ILO's core conventions, as well as very high standards in other areas. These will become legally binding when TTIP enters into force.

[b] Provision for a Mechanism of Permanent Monitoring on the Social Effects of the Agreement

Further, the TTIP should contemplate an adequate implementation mechanism of the agreement, aimed to monitor its effectiveness and the fulfilment of the duties deriving from it, with particular reference to provisions of *compliance* with international obligations (ILO's Declaration on fundamental social rights). In this perspective, the agreement should contemplate the constitution of an independent *committee of experts*, with an ILO member with consultative function and having the following roles: a) editing of periodic reports on the state of effectiveness of social standards, to be compiled taking into consideration the information transmitted by governments and other institutions; b) gathering and assessing any *complaint*, editing recommendations, promoting consultative forums to exchange information among governments, social

52. In this perspective *see also* T. Treu, *Labour and Industrial Relations in the Transatlantic Free Trade Agreements Guidelines*, Speech at 21 November 2013 meeting at Italian Cultural Institute in New York.
53. European Commission, European Commission services' position paper on the sustainability impact assessment in support of negotiations of the Transatlantic Trade & Investment Partnership between the European Union and the United States of America 31 March 2017. http://www.trade-sia.com/ttip/wp-content/uploads/sites/6/2017/03/TSIA-TTIP-Final-Report-03-17.pdf.

parties and other *stakeholders* (on NAALC model); c) with reference to the latter, the transatlantic communication should be duly institutionalized through the creation of a *Forum for Trade Investment and Sustainable Development*, which should regularly represent the location where the social matters linked to the TTIP should be publicly discussed. We need to observe, on the USA side, that an interest in monitoring related to promoting effectiveness profiles of the commitments undertaken in the trade field is at the basis of USA's foreign policies in *trade and investments*.

[c] Social Clause

Although the agreement in matter of labour may be conceived in wider and more ambitious terms than a mere 'social clause', and it may by all means provide for *soft* mechanisms of spreading of good praxis among the parties, my opinion is that the TTIP should contain also an actual *social conditionality clause*, to be implemented in the field of the mechanisms of enforcement of the agreement and, in particular, to be appealed before a *dispute settlement body*, on the model of WTO[54] and of what provided by the FTAs. An authoritative indication about the above-mentioned topic, relative to the adoption of a real social clause, with the contemplation of any possible trade sanctions, can be found on the *Counsel Negotiation Directives*, where it is indicated that '*the agreement must include a clause on general exceptions, inspired by Article 20 and 21 of the GATT*' (Article 12).

As we have already mentioned, thanks to art. XX of the GATT, which deals with a dispensation regime named 'general exceptions', a reserve of domestic jurisdiction in favour of the single Countries is adopted. They are authorized to propose some national politic interests to the obligations deriving from trade liberalization agreements. In particular, the norm allows the parties to adopt restrictive measures concerning exchanges that are justified by considerations relative to the protection of *public moral*, of *life and health* of people, animal and plants, to the respect of laws and internal regulations, to the defence of environment and natural resources, to the protection of the artistic heritage, and of the consumer, for reasons connected to the trading of *commodities produced in jail*. Therefore, thanks to art. XX of the GATT, States are authorized to adopt restrictive measures of international trade (restrictions to exportations: embargo, or to importations: boycott) in order to protect their markets from the introduction in the internal market of products realized with low-cost workforce.[55] Indeed, the reference contained in the *negotiation Directives* to the necessity of contemplating in the TTIP a clause on 'general exceptions' inspired to art. XX of the GATT can represent an important occasion of reflection for negotiators, in the editing of a series of general exceptions linked to the respect of the commitments undertaken in the chapter dedicated to labour and sustainability: they should recognize to the

---

54. *See* E.-U. Petersmann, The Transformation of the World Trading System Through the 1994 Agreement Establishing the World Trade Organization, in *European Journal of International Law* 6, no. 2, 1995, p. 207 The literature on this issue is extremely huge.
55. Cfr. *Wto Appellate Body 'Japan-Taxes on A/coho/ic Beverages'*, report 4th October 1996, Dor. Wl'/OS8/ABIR, e *'Canada-Certain Measures Concerning periodicals'*, Doc. Wl'/OS31/ABIR.

parties the faculty of taking the appropriate trade measures against the violation of fundamental social rights and social *dumping*.

[B] Labour Provisions on CETA: The 'Trade and Labour' Chapter

The importance of the CETA is linked both to the central position of transatlantic trade and to the historic relations also in social traditions between the two areas.[56]

In the CETA, as all the other recent FTAs, the Parties recognize that it is inappropriate to encourage trade or investment by weakening or reducing the levels of protection afforded in their labour law and standards and they shall waive or derogate from its labour law and standards, to encourage trade or the establishment, acquisition, expansion or retention of an investment in its territory, or, again, shall not fail to effectively enforce its labour law and standards to encourage trade or investment.[57]

As we can see, the Parties use, as it is for most of the FTAs recently concluded, an aspirational language, and, despite the commitment to keep the levels of protections for workers, it remains the problem to find the proof to show a link between the lowering of domestic labour standards and the intention to encourage trade or investment.

What is new is the position of these provisions in the text, which suggests, as we will see, a new function of this tool in the context of free trade.

As a matter of fact, those social clauses are inserted in Chapter 23, dedicated to 'Trade and Labour'. We should observe that the previous Chapter (22) is entitled 'Trade and Sustainable Development', while the Chapter 24 'Trade and Environment'.

Since 2008, the EU's FTAs have included 'Sustainable Development' Chapters: the first agreement was the EU-CARIFORUM Economic Partnership Agreement with the Caribbean Forum,[58] which contains numerous provisions relating to aspects of sustainability and human rights.

Partly inspired by US and Canadian FTAs, these three chapters contain obligations requiring signatory Parties to comply with labour and environmental standards (including ILO core labour standards), and, conversely, not to use labour and environmental regulation as a means of economic protection. It is worth to note that while the EU tends to combine these issues under one single sustainable chapter, the US and Canada deal with labour and environment issues in two separate chapters in their FTAs. As a result, the EU–Canada FTA contains three chapters to cover these issues: one on labour, one on the environment and one on sustainability.

The intention of EU and Canada is to recognize that economic development, social development and environmental protection are interdependent and mutually reinforcing components of sustainable development and reaffirm their commitment to

56. T. Treu, *Globalization and Human Rights: Social Clauses in Trade Agreements and in International Exchanges among Companies*, in A. Perulli, T. Treu (eds), *Sustainable Development, Global Trade and Social Rights*, Wolters Kluwer, 2018, p. 109.
57. Article 23.4 CETA, Upholding levels of protection.
58. E. Schmieg, Human Rights and Sustainability in Free Trade Agreements. Can the Cariforum-EU Economic Partnership Agreement Serve as a Model? In German Institute for International and Security Affairs, SWP Comments n. 24, May 2014.

promoting the development of international trade in such a way as to contribute to the objective of sustainable development, for the welfare of present and future generations.[59]

Consequently, the implementation of Chapters Twenty-Three (Trade and Labour) and Twenty-Four (Trade and Environment), the Parties aim to: (a) promote sustainable development through the enhanced coordination and integration of their respective labour, environmental and trade policies and measures; (b) promote dialogue and cooperation between the Parties with a view to developing their trade and economic relations in a manner that supports their respective labour and environmental protection measures and standards, and to upholding their environmental and labour protection objectives in a context of trade relations that are free, open and transparent; (c) enhance enforcement of their respective labour and environmental law and respect for labour and environmental international agreements; (d) promote the full use of instruments, such as impact assessment and stakeholder consultations, in the regulation of trade, labour and environmental issues and encourage businesses, civil society organizations and citizens to develop and implement practices that contribute to the achievement of sustainable development goals; and (e) promote public consultation and participation in the discussion of sustainable development issues that arise under this Agreement and in the development of relevant law and policies (Article 22.1, paragraph 3, CETA).

It is easy to observe that Labour and Environment are treated and considered of the same value, as it is suggested by the same concept of Sustainable Development the three dimensions (also called 'pillars') of Sustainable Development (social, environmental and economic one) are of the same importance and mutually reinforcing,[60] and it is assumed that sustainable development is only possible if all these pillars are taken account of.

[1] CETA and ILO Provisions

The CETA labour chapter 'Trade and Labour' contains also some obligations dealing with the ILO but, differently from the past FTAs, they do not refer directly to the ILO's Fundamental Conventions. Rather, reference is made to the ILO Declaration on Fundamental Principles and Rights at Work and its Follow-up (1998), to the ILO Declaration on Social Justice for a Fair Globalization (2008) and to the ILO Decent Work Agenda.

The commitment is to respect (a) freedom of association and the effective recognition of the right to collective bargaining; (b) the elimination of all forms of forced or compulsory labour; (c) the effective abolition of child labour; and (d) the elimination of discrimination in respect of employment and occupation but also (a) health and safety at work, including the prevention of occupational injury or illness

59. Article 22.1, para. 1, CETA.
60. T. Treu, *Labour Law and Sustainable Development*, WP CSDLE 'Massimo D'Antona'.INT-130/2016; V. Cagnin, *Diritto del Lavoro e Sviluppo Sostenibile*, Cedam Wolters Kluwer, Milano, 2018.

and compensation in cases of such injury or illness; (b) establishment of acceptable minimum employment standards for wage earners, including those not covered by a collective agreement; and (c) non-discrimination in respect of working conditions, including for migrant workers (Article 23.3, paragraph 4) but there is no special and direct reference to the ILO Conventions.

Despite the lack of reference or mention to the ILO Core Convention, each party reaffirms its commitment to effectively implement in its law and practices in its whole territory the fundamental ILO Conventions that Canada and the Member States of the European Union have ratified respectively and the Parties 'shall make continued and sustained efforts to ratify the fundamental ILO Conventions if they have not yet done so'.

[2] CETA and Monitoring of Implementation

In line with the soft European approach in terms of sanctions, the EU and Canada did not insert in the agreement a special mechanism for sanctions in case that labour commitments are not respected. The Parties decided to foresee a special Committee, the *Committee on Trade and Sustainable Development*, which shall oversee the implementation of those Chapters and can also carry out its duties through dedicated sessions comprising participants responsible for any matter covered by the Chapter on Trade and Labour (as well as for that on Trade and Environment). Any decision or report of this Committee shall be made public and the Committee shall present updates on the implementation of the Chapter to the Civil Society Forum.

This Forum is composed of representatives of civil society organizations established in their territories and shall be convened once a year unless otherwise agreed by the Parties. The Parties shall promote a balanced representation of relevant interests, including independent representative employers, unions, labour and business organizations and environmental groups (Article 22.5 CETA).

In particular, with the involvement of trade unions, through the Civil Society Forum, social clauses can become in this way a mean to spread practices of transnational collective bargaining at a regional level, promoting the social dialogue between European and Canadian social partners. At the same time, this Forum could be the way to overcome the aspirational language used (i.e., parties 'shall not derogate...') and would facilitate the court or the inspectorate's intervention in labour disputes, reinforcing thus the effectiveness of these social provisions, which lack, of a specific sanctions mechanism.

As a matter of fact, social dialogue is recognized as an important issue: they also recognize the importance of social dialogue on labour matters among workers and employers, and their respective organizations, and governments, and commit to the promotion of such dialogue (Article 23.1 CETA). In this perspective, the Social Clause could be considered as a tool to improve international social dialogue, as the parties of a FTA recognize the importance of social dialogue on labour matters among workers and employers, and their respective organizations, and governments, and commit to the promotion of such dialogue.

[C] Labour Provision on EPA: The 'Trade and Sustainable Development' Chapter

EU-Japan Economic Partnership Agreement (EPA)[61] is the biggest bilateral trade agreement ever negotiated by the European Union: EU firms already export over EUR 58 billion in goods and EUR 28 billion in services to Japan every year.

The EU-Japan EPA comes at a time of US President Donald Trump's erratic trade policy. This trade agreement with a strategic ally can send a strong message in favour of an open and rules-based trade order. In addition, it gives the EU trade agenda a strong opportunity to take the lead in the Asia-Pacific region. The Economic Partnership Agreement will open huge market opportunities for both sides, strengthen cooperation between Europe and Japan in a range of areas, reaffirm their shared commitment to sustainable development and include for the first time a specific commitment to the Paris climate agreement.

All the labour clauses (or provisions) are inserted in Chapter 15 'Trade and Sustainable Development', thus following the EU's approach.

This chapter is in line with the level of ambition of the chapters concluded in others recent EU FTAs. Notably, at the starting of the Chapter, EU and Japan recognize that its purpose is to strengthen the trade relations and cooperation between the Parties in ways that promote sustainable development and they clarify, first of all, that the agreement 'is not to harmonise the environment or labour standards of the Parties' (Article 16.1, paragraph 2, EPA).

Then, the Chapter provides for commitments like the prohibition of relaxing domestic labour laws to attract trade and investment ('The Parties shall not encourage trade or investment by relaxing or lowering the level of protection provided by their respective environmental or labour laws and regulations. To that effect, the Parties shall not waive or otherwise derogate from those laws and regulations or fail to effectively enforce them through a sustained or recurring course of action or inaction in a manner affecting trade or investment between the Parties', Article 16.2, paragraph 2), nor for discrimination or restrictions to trade's purpose: ('The Parties shall not use their respective environmental or labour laws and regulations in a manner which would constitute a means of arbitrary or unjustifiable discrimination against the other Party, or a disguised restriction on international trade', Article 16.2, paragraph 3).

[1] EPA and ILO Provisions

EPA refers to the commitment to the key international instruments on labour, such as the effective implementation of the four groups of ILO core labour standards as covered by the 1998 ILO Declaration on Fundamental principles and Rights at Work, a

61. The EU-Japan Economic Partnership Agreement was submitted for the approval of EU Member States on 18 April 2018. Once approved by the Council, the agreement will be sent to the European Parliament. The text of the Agreement is available here: http://trade.ec.europa.eu/doclib/docs/2017/december/tradoc_156423.pdf.

continued and sustained progress towards ratification of non-ratified fundamental ILO Conventions (Article 16.3, International labour standards and conventions).

Thus, in this case, the ratification of the ILO Convention has not been a condition, a prerequisite for the negotiations of a bilateral trade agreement with the EU.

[2] EPA and Monitoring of Implementation

The Agreement, as CETA did, constitutes a Committee on Trade and Sustainable Development (Article 16.13), which shall be responsible for the effective implementation and operation of this Chapter, (a) reviewing and monitoring the implementation and operation of the Chapter and, when necessary, making appropriate recommendations to the Joint Committee (representatives of both Parties) for its consideration, (c) interacting with civil society (independent economic, social and environmental stakeholders, including employers' and workers' organizations and environmental groups) on its implementation and (e) seeking solutions to resolve differences between the Parties as to the interpretation or application of this Chapter.

The EPA provides to include mechanisms for the involvement of civil society in the implementation of the chapter, both domestically (consultation of 'domestic advisory groups[62]') and jointly ('joint dialogue with civil society', which means independent economic, social and environmental stakeholders, including employers' and workers' organizations and environmental groups); and a tailored mechanism for the resolution of disputes, including governmental consultations and recourse to an independent panel of experts.[63]

§6.07 THE GENERALIZED PREFERENCES SYSTEM: THE EU EXPERIENCE AS AN EXEMPLAR MODEL OF POSITIVE LINKAGE BETWEEN INTERNATIONAL TRADE AND SOCIAL RIGHTS

After this reconstruction of the framework of social provisions in the latest FTAs, we can observe that it is difficult to see a real enforcement mechanism in order to oblige parties to respect all the important commitments taken in terms of social rights. If it is true that, both for CETA and EPA (as for the TTIP), labour provisions have widened and deepened compared to the past, but we need to observe that they are mostly cooperative and non-binding provisions.

FTAs use an aspirational language, and for this reason labour provisions risk to lack of an effective remedy to labour violations or of a valid deterrent. This is, unfortunately, in line with the EU traditional policies.

As a matter of fact, the only agreement where economic and clear sanctions are imposed is the EU Generalized System of Preferences (GSP), an exemplar model of positive linkage between international trade and social rights in the European external

62. Also foreseen on CETA, Art. 24.13.
63. European Commission, EU-Japan EPA – The Agreement in Principle, 6 July 2017 – report submitted to Member States and to the European Parliament, available at: http://trade.ec.europa.eu/doclib/docs/2017/july/tradoc_155693.doc.pdf.

action[64]: in this context, any of the GSP Industrialized Countries, on request by the UN, have granted a preferential and non-reciprocal treatment to developing countries in matter of trade exchanges. Such scheme (GSP), by granting a facilitated access in the European Market to commodities coming from weak territories, represents a mechanism of distributive justice in the system of international trade with a general extent. The EEC has matter-of-factly granted since 1971, notwithstanding the GATT/WTO normative that provided for a unique system of preferences, some generalized tariff preference for industrial finished and semi-finished commodities coming from developing countries, authorizing a more advantageous customs treatment compared to the one normally practiced, and consisting in the total or partial elimination of import duties.

Twenty years after the concession of the above-mentioned measure, the Council, being aware of the positive results achieved in the course of time, has adopted the Reg. 3281/1994. In the new regulation, the need to co-relate international trade with the respect of fundamental social rights overwhelmingly emerges and, in this sense, the tariff-related instrument shows great potentialities. On the same line are the following regulations.[65]

Initially, there were two types of measures provided by the 1994 Regulation.

First of all, the advantages are to be temporarily, totally or partially cancelled in case the country involved resorts to forced labour, in accordance with the ILO's Conventions on the matter,[66] as well as in case of exportation of commodities produced in jail. The temporary cancellation is not automatic, but it will be active after a procedure that may be activated through a report of the violation to the Commission.

If, in this case, we are dealing with a negative sanction, the second measure provided by the Regulation is, on the contrary, a promotional sanction, which consists in the concession of a special 'regime of stimulation', whose aim is to promote the addressee countries in the adoption of more advanced social policies.

Starting from 1 January 1998, following the Reg. n. 1154/98, some additional preferences was granted (equal to an *extra* 20%) to those countries already admitted to the GSP, which prove to have adopted – and actually implemented – the eight fundamental Conventions of the ILO.

Even though the GSP is unilaterally adopted by the EU, it is important to underline that the Council grants the potential extra-measures on the basis of criteria that must be acknowledged and shared at international level, as well as by reason of a report of the Commission that keeps into account the results of the surveys carried out by the ILO, the WTO and the OECD.

In this way, we have the promotion of an unprecedented mechanism of control based on the cooperation among several international organizations, which could be considered as the potential backbone of a system of promotion of any hypothesis of

64. A. Perulli, Clausola Sociale, Enciclopedia del Diritto, Giuffré, 2014, vol. VII, pp. 187–211.
65. Reg. n. 1154/1998, Reg. n. 2810/1998, Reg. n. 2501/2001, Reg. n. 980/2005, Reg. n. 732/2008, Reg. n. 1063/2010, Reg. n. 978/2012.
66. 1930 Convention n. 29 on forced and mandatory labour; 1957 Convention n. 105 on the abolition of forced labour.

future insertion of social clauses in trade treaties. Given the specific reference to the ILO's Conventions, the European System results as particularly virtuous and inclined towards an international trade policy complying with fundamental social rights.

The following Regulation (EC) n. 732/2008 of the Council[67] has then simplified the special regime of subsidization, by substituting the three previous regimes with the current two: the special regime in favour of developing countries and the special subsidization regime of 'sustainable development and good governance', acknowledged only to the countries that have 'ratified and effectively applied' the Conventions referring to the attachment III (among which we have the eight ILO's fundamental Conventions) and that commit themselves to 'maintain the ratification of the Conventions and of the relative laws/measures of implementation and to accept periodical assessments and re-examinations of the application, complying with the provisions of implementation of the ratified Conventions'.

Actually, Regulation n. 978/2012[68] provides for a general regime, and two special regimes, that is to say the special regime of subsidization for sustainable development and *good governance* and the one in favour of less developed Countries.

The first special regime (GSP+) is an agreement of particular subsidizations for sustainable development and good governance that recognizes total exemption from customs tariffs for commodities entering the EU's market for countries that have ratified and implemented a series of Conventions of the ILO and the UN in matter of labour and human rights, and in matter of environment and of *good governance*, and that accept a constant monitoring.

The second special regime, which provides for the cancellation of customs tariffs, is called EBA, which stands for *Everything But Arms*: such programme, reserved to less developed countries, guarantees the total cancellation of customs tariffs for all products coming from such countries, except for weapons.

With this new Regulation we see the concentration of tariff preferences 'on the support to developing Countries more in need in the field of development, trade and finance'.[69] The goal is to strengthen the subsidizations for the respect of fundamental human and labour rights, the environment and good governance norms through the GSP system, increasing its predictability, transparency and stability: in this sense, the length of the programme is increased from three to ten years, with the exception of the EBA, which has no deadline.

67. Regulation (EC) n. 732/2008 of the 22nd July 2008 Council, relative to the application.
68. EU Regulation n. 978/2012 of European Parliament and of 25 October 2012 Council, relative to the application of a system of generalized tariff preferences and that abrogates the EC Regulation 732/2008 of Council. The Regulation 732/2008 provided for a scheme of generalized tariff preferences for the period from 1 January 2009 to 31 December 2011, extended to 31 December 2013 by the GSP *Roll-over Regulation*, Regulation n. 512/2011. The new Regulation is active from 1 January 2014.
69. Recital n. 7 of Reg. 978/2012. The new Regulation intends to reduce, starting from 1 January 2014, the benefitting Countries of the preferential system, from 176 to 89. The countries that already have a different preferential access to the EU's market will be excluded, that is to say the countries that the World Bank ranked as 'high-income or medium-high-income' countries, in the course of the three consecutive years immediately prior to the update of the list of benefitting countries.

§6.08 THE US PREFERENCE PROGRAMMES

The USA adopt different agreements in order to support third countries, especially developing countries, allowing a preferential access to the USA's market.

One of the most relevant preferential programmes is the GSP (Generalized System of Preferences) instituted by the 1974 *Trade Act* to promote economic growth in the developing countries and was implemented on 1 January 1976,[70] and recently extended.[71]

The USA system of generalized preferences is a programme intended to promote economic development and growth in the developing World: it supplies a preferential exemption from customs tariffs for more than 3,000 commodities coming from 120 beneficiary Countries (including many least-developed beneficiary developing Countries (44).[72]

In the original 1974 text of the *Trade Act* were already indicated the reasons that could justify the exemption from the tariff benefit (in particular for countries with dictatorial regimes, that is to say they did not cooperate within the international war to drug trade, or they were still considered as supporters of international terrorism). With the 1984 amendment, other causes of exclusion were added: the most relevant was the social clause stating that the countries aspiring to the preferential regime must prove to being complying with internationally recognized labour *standards*. Actually, a GSP beneficiary must have taken or is taking steps to afford internationally recognized worker rights, including (1) the right of association, (2) the right to organize and bargain collectively, (3) a prohibition on the use of any form of forced or compulsory labour, (4) a minimum age for the employment of children and a prohibition on the worst forms of child labour, and (5) acceptable conditions of work with respect to minimum wages, hours of work and occupational safety and health. A GSP beneficiary must implement any commitments it makes to eliminate the worst forms of child labour.

In 1985, the USA elaborated an additional programme of tariff preferences, contained in the 1985 *Overseas Private Investment Corporation Amendment Act*. There was the constitution of a Governmental Agency, controlled by the State Secretariat, in charge of supplying services of financing and insurance of capitals coming from North American companies and employed in projects of foreign investments (most of all in developing countries). Also in this system we have a social clause stating that 'the

70. U.S. Generalized System of Preferences Guidebook, Office of the United States Trade Representative Executive Office of the President Washington, D.C., March 2017, https://ustr.gov/sites/default/files/gsp/GSP%20Guidebook%20March%202017.pdf.
71. On 23 March 2018, the President signed into law H.R. 1625 (Public Law 115-141), the 'Consolidated Appropriations Act, 2018,' which in addition to providing full-year federal appropriations through 30 September 2018, extended GSP with retroactivity, for goods entered or withdrawn from warehouse for consumption from 1 January 2018 through 31 December 2020. The new Act also provided for the retroactive refund of all duties (without interest) to the importer of record (IOR) on GSP-eligible goods entered during the 1 January 2018 through 21 April 2018 lapse period.
72. *See* General Note 4 of the U.S. Harmonized Tariff Schedule for the most up-to-date number of GSP beneficiaries: https://hts.usitc.gov/current.

company may ensure, re-assure, guarantee or finance a project only if the Country involved proves its compliance with internationally recognized labour rights'.

We need to highlight the interventions of the USA's Government in order to favour the economic development of the countries facing the Caribbean Basin. On the basis of the *Caribbean Basin Initiative (CBI)*, the missing compliance with internationally recognized social rights is impedimental to the conservation or the *ex novo* attribution of the relative tariff concessions.

In the same perspective is to be read the *African Growth and Opportunity Act*, promoted in 2000 in order to guarantee a *duty free* treatment to the commodities coming from forty States of sub-Saharan Africa, in view of the respect of a series of standards also in matter of labour.

§6.09 FUNDAMENTAL SOCIAL RIGHTS IN THE EXTERNAL ACTION OF EU

As we have seen in the previous paragraphs, if the operational justification on which the social clause is founded results as difficultly practicable by the State at a multilateral global level, on the contrary, it appears as functional to the development of the regional and/or bilateral integration. As a matter of fact, we find again important examples of social conditionality both in the field of the European construction and in the framework of the North American Trade Integration (and, in particular, central and South American), and in the bilateral Free Trade Agreements, which confirm the will of States to affirm the linkage between social rights and international trade, overcoming the several ambiguities within the previous trade treaties.[73]

In the European construction, the social harmonization has been conceived since its inception as functional to avoid forms of dumping and competition distortions founded on normative disparities, judged as inconvenient with regards to the project intended to ensure a harmonious development of the internal market. For this reason, the European social law has followed a functionalist rationality, instrumental to the service of the common market. Within a functionalistic vision of integration, the aim established by the common market's founders was to avoid a competition to the bottom in the application of social standards, contrasting the ongoing deregulation due to structural deficits and to the lack of common references to a minimum threshold of fundamental social rights.

Currently, the functionalistic vision of integration is being overcome thanks to the redefinition of the basic normative references of treaties - particularly after Amsterdam - and to the constitutionalization of fundamental social rights. The field of social rights has progressively broadened and the consideration of such rights - from being subordinate, to take part in the process of economic construction of Europe - has considerably increased to get to an equal level with the basic principles of economic

73. *See*. M.A. Cabin, Labour Rights in the Peru Agreement: Can Vague Principles Yield Concrete Change?, in *Columbia Law Review*, 2009, p. 1047 s.; for a synthetic analysis *see* K. Lukas, A. Steinkellner, *Social Standards in Sustainability Chapters of Bilateral Free Trade Agreements*, Ludwig Boltzmann Institute, Wien, June 2010.

integration. Forced to penetrate the communitarian juridical order thanks to the activity of the Court of Justice, social rights have then established themselves in the Charter of fundamental social right of the EU, becoming, with the Lisbon Treaty, common constitutional references in social matters. In this way, they were able to lay the normative basis to overcome that sort of schizophrenia consisting in the promotion of the respect of fundamental social rights in the framework of external relations, as well, as for example, with the Generalized Preference System, observing structural deficiencies in the internal field. The cyclical sequences of events of the so-called European Social model outline a scenario where the issues of labour and employment never came before the scenario of the market integration, related to strictly economic values and for these reasons at the basis of a growing mistrust and scepticism of European citizens towards Europe and its institutions.[74] Nevertheless, with the development of a 'holistic' conception of European integration,[75] culminating in the Lisbon Treaty, the goals of full employment, social progress and social cohesion are definitely relaunched in the perspective of a new 'strongly competitive social market economy', characterized by the fight against social discrimination and exclusion, and in favour of the equality between men and women, of intergenerational solidarity and of the protection of minors' rights.

[A] Social Rights in the Construction of the EU: The Perspective of the Horizontal Social Clause

In pursuing these non-trade goals, the Treaty on the Functioning of the European Union (TFEU) contemplates, for the first time in the history of the European integration, a provision, defined by commentators as a 'horizontal social clause' (Article 9), that is the expression of a new *Social Mainstreaming* in the field of a strengthening of the above-mentioned axiological orientations, expressed by the Articles 2 and 3 of the TFEU. It is evident that with such provision, to which the Commission attributes a fundamental value,[76] we are facing goals that include social and personalistic values that become part of the economic fabric and that do not result as dismissible in the intention to promote a balanced and sustainable development of the market. The clause introduces a sort of social conditionality in the 'actions' and in the 'policies' of the EU, consisting of respecting obligations deriving from the compliance with social values: it establishes, in fact, that 'in the definition and the implementation of its policies and actions, the EU keeps into account the needs linked to the promotion of an elevated level of employment, the guarantee of an adequate social protection, the fight against social exclusion and an elevated level of education, training and protection of human health'. This principle of social conditionality is reconnected with other horizontal clauses in the Treaty, relative to the equality between men and women, the

74. For a general overview *see* S. Sciarra, *L'Europa e il lavoro. Solidarietà e conflitto in tempi di crisi*, Laterza, Roma-Bari, 2013.
75. *See* P. Craig, G. de Burca, *EU Law: Text, Cases and Materials*, Oxford, OUP, 2008.
76. Communication of the Commission to the European Parliament, to the Council, to the Social and Economic Committee and to the Committee of COM Regions (2010) 608 def.

protection of environment and the protection of consumers and the fight against discrimination (Articles 8, 10, 11, 12 TFEU). Although the expression 'keeps into account' is less intense with regards to other provisions contained in these final horizontal clauses (in particular the one referring to the Article 11, according to which the needs linked to the protection of environment 'must be integrated' in the definition and in the implementation of the policies and actions of the EU), the perceptive value of the social clause is obtained both from its collocation in the title II (Provisions having General Applications),[77] and from the essentiality with regards to the action of realization of the paradigm of market social economy, otherwise destined to lacking in meaning or to being merely programmatic. Commentators should move in this perspective within the discussion whether the horizontal social clause has prevailingly political and/or interpretative orientation value for Courts and address value for the EU's organisms, or whether we may hypothesize a precise justiciability pertaining to the horizontal social clause. In fact, only if this option prevails, Article 9 of the TFEU may correctly be included among social clauses in a strict sense, characterized by a sanctionatory *lato sensu* component, which overcomes the perspective of the mere *moral suasion* in giving shape to the economic activity. In this sense, it is important to point out that the clause imposes to the institutions of the EU, and in particular to the Commission, to report on their initiatives in the framework of the obligation of providing grounds *ex* Article 296, paragraph 2 of TFEU; as if to say that an act contrary to the content of the social clause - because, for example, detrimental for employment or for social protection - may be cancelled because not complying with the Treaties, pursuant the Article 263 of the TFEU.

As being horizontal, such clause must be employed in order to introduce social goals in all relevant sectors, economic and trade policies included, as well as in order to monitor the impact of policies in a logic of integration and coordination in economic, social, employment and environmental fields. In such perspective, the social clause provides to the Institutions of the Union a wide mandate to include a series of social goals in all policies, the initiatives and the activities pertaining the EU, transforming the social development of Europe in a cross-wise task, able to overcome the historical asymmetry between development of the market's economic integration and social sphere.[78] The European Commission, to whom the Lisbon Treaty has entrusted the task to promote the general interest of the EU (Article 17 of the TFEU), must guarantee that the social clause is efficiently applied and that all documents, as well as the pertinent judiciary texts, actually refer to it and keep it into account, making sure that it effectively contributes to the pursuing of the new goals of the Treaty, both on the part

77. In this sense, *see* F. Lecomte, Embedded Employment Rights in Europe, in *Columbia Journal of European Law*, 17, p. 1 ss.
78. According to the Opinion of the European social and economic Committee on the matter *Strengthening the cohesion and the coordination of the EU in the social field thanks to the new horizontal social clause, referring to the art. 9 of the TFEU* (initiative opinion), 24 June 2012/C, lecturer Lechner, the implementation of the social clause may 'therefore contribute to reduce the sense of dissatisfaction that has long been persisting and to overcome the deeper and deeper scepticism of some Member States with regards to the added value offered by the EU, in particular in terms of economic, employment and social progress'.

of the EU and of the Member States. In particular, according to the statements of the European social and economic Committee, this clause must be applied to the general fields and to the global architecture of the new social-economic governance of the EU, provided by the 2020 Europe Strategy, and approved by the European Council in 2010. Article 9 of the TFEU therefore provides a new juridical basis to the already existing Social Impact Assessment, an *ex ante* assessment procedure of the policies inaugurated at the 2002 Laeken European Council and later confirmed with the 2005 Lisbon strategy for development and employment. With the 2009 guidelines, the Commission has adopted an ambitious mechanism of social impact assessment in the areas of labour market, standards and rights linked to the quality of labour, social inclusion, equality of treatment and non-discrimination, access to social protection, education and health system, health and public security. Particular attention is addressed to the redistributive impact on poverty and social inclusion, both within Member States and with regards to Member States, especially developing countries, concurring to the goal of guaranteeing the respect of the provisions of social policy contained in the Treaty of Lisbon (in particular the Articles from 145 to 166 and the Article 168 of the TFEU) and in the EU's Charter of fundamental rights (in particular the Chapter IV on *Solidarity*), to which the Article 6 of the European Single Act has recognized the same juridical value of the Treaties. The innovation may therefore crucially contribute to rebalance the confrontation between social rights and economic freedom that are object of a jurisprudence of the Court of Justice that tends to favour a trade-related perspective.

Recently, this tool has found another base of legitimation with the European Pillar of Social Rights, which has been proclaimed by the European Parliament, the Council and the European Commission on 17 November 2017. As a matter of fact, Article 9 TFEU is recalled on the Preamble (p. 2) of the Solemn Declaration of the Social Pillar. The Pillar, in this sense, demonstrates a new sensibility to the horizontal social clause, and this approach is in line with the recent European Court of Justice jurisprudence, which for the first time, in 2016, expressly named the horizontal social clause in a case where there was a need of balancing enterprise freedoms and social rights (C-201/15, *Aget Irarklis*, pp. 78–79).

The general comments of the doctrine have regarded the consequences that the examined horizontal social clause can and must have with reference to the internal market. However, the examined clause, as being horizontal, pertains to *all the policies of the EU* and for this reason also to the ones relative to the Union's external relations. The EU, as regional entity with a '*global vocation*' in the promotion of human rights,[79] now has a new normative basis to be employed in order to mobilize all the *governance* instruments available in the social field. A field being particularly fertile – and by all means coherent with the horizontal social clause – regards the promotion of the values contained in the *UN Guiding Principles on business and human rights* that include the *OECD Guidelines* on multinational enterprises, the *ISO 26000 Social Responsibility*

79. *See* M. Cremona, *Rhetoric or Reticence: EU External Commercial Policy in a Multilateral Context*, in *Common Market Law Review*, 2001, p. 359; T. Novitz, *In Search of a Coherent Social Policy: EU Import and Export of ILO Labour Standards?*, in J. Orbie, L. Tortell (eds), *The European Union and the Social Dimension of Globalization*, Routledge, 2009.

Standard, the UN Global Compact and other instruments of internationally recognized *Corporate Social Responsibility (CSR)*, such as the recently updated ILO Tripartite Declaration of Principles concerning Multinational Enterprises on Social Policy[80] but also the UN Agenda 2030.[81]

The involvement of the EU in the development of the project *UN Protect, Respect, Remedy* (that represents the most important point of global reference for *CSR* policies)[82] constitutes an important example of this process that involves the European Parliament and the EU delegations within international organizations. The horizontal social clause should be able to provide a greater impulse to the EU's external action, required by the NGOs that invoke the commitment of the Union within the relaunching the responsibility of multinational enterprises operating in the European territory for the violations of human rights carried out by their homologous outside the EU. In particular, these social *guidelines* should connect to the common trade policies providing, for example, a normative basis in order to realize principles of CSR in the field of initiatives (lacking perceptive value) already developed in other contexts such the '*Communication on the promotion of labour fundamental norms and on the improvement of the social governance in the context of globalization*' and the Communication '*the partnership for employment and growth: make Europe a centre of excellence in matter of CSR*'. Hence, we have the Union's commitment to promote CSR at a global level, by working in order to include within the Union's bilateral agreements norms of sustainable development and to support specific initiatives like *Global Compact* and the so-called Kimberley process. Further, Article 9 of the TFEU may provide a decisive incentive in order to implement the Resolution of the European Parliament adopted on 2 November 2010, in the field of the promotion of social values within multilateral Courts of international trade, concerning the implementation of a principle of extraterritoriality stating that a country of origin may require the compliance with its social legislation also to the enterprises operating outside their territorial field.[83] Other fields where to adopt initiatives under the sphere of the Article 9 are linked to action of coordination in areas of interest, such as the common policies on investments, which must be guided by the

80. The MNE Declaration is the only ILO instrument that provides direct guidance to enterprises on social policy and inclusive, responsible and sustainable workplace practices. It is the only global instrument in this area that was elaborated and adopted by governments, employers and workers from around the world. It was adopted close to 40 years ago (amended in 2000 and 2006) and revised in 2017. Its principles are addressed to MNEs, governments, and employers' and workers' organizations and cover areas such as employment, training, conditions of work and life, and industrial relations as well as general policies. All principles are based on international labour standards (ILO conventions and recommendations).
81. Communication from the Commission A Sustainable Europe for a Better World: A European Union Strategy for Sustainable Development (Commission's proposal to the Gothenburg European Council); COM/2001/0264 final.
82. UN Special Representative on business and human rights, UN 'Protect, Respect, Remedy' Framework, http://www.business-humanrights.org/SpecialRepPortal/Home/Protect-Respect-Remedy-Framework.
83. *See* D. Augenstein et al., *Study of the Legal Framework on Human Rights and the Environment applicable to European Enterprises Operating Outside the European Union*, Study for the European Commission, ENTR/09/045 (2010).

principles and goals of the EU's external action,[84] the specific policies on minor labour,[85] on forced labour, on human beings trade and on the *due diligence* in the mining sector. With reference to the external action, social rights start being considered as relevant issues in the field of the dialogue with third Countries, for example with Cambodia, Laos and China[86]; further, in the field of initiatives intended to guarantee the respect of the ILO's agenda on Decent Work and in the field of the relationships of international cooperation, like in the case of Bangladesh.[87] Therefore, we may expect an incentive to the promotion of fundamental social rights towards the exterior of the EU, thanks to the insertion of '*CSR* clauses' in all trade agreements stipulated by the Union on the wake of the usage of another horizontal clause, already present in the normative fabric of the prior-to-Lisbon Treaties, relative to the promotion of sustainable development (current Article 10 of the TFEU), which has contributed to insert the issue of sustainability in the field of the EU's external trade relations. According to the European Parliament, such *CSR* clauses, to be inserted in the trade agreements to come, should force enterprises to assume obligations of due diligence intended to the adoption of precautionary measures of compliance with human rights in their outsourced branches, with the obligation to periodically publish the balance sheets in matter of *CSR*.

§6.10 SOCIAL CLAUSES IN TRADE AGREEMENTS: A DISAGGREGATE ANALYSIS

At this point of the paper, I would like to propose a disaggregate analysis of some Treaties and of their social clauses, focusing in a transversal way around two essential points of the comprehension of the matter: (1) Commitments and (2) enforcement and effectiveness.

This way to proceed leads to more fruitful outcomes, compared to the single analysis of the treaties, as it permits to compare the different social clauses, in order to verify differences and similarities and to create some 'models' of social clause; it will be useful, again, to identify pros and cons of each model and thus identify the more advanced model, or, at least on paper, the more effective social clause. In the analysis I will consider some bilateral treaties (like CETA, EPA, EU–Korea, US–Jordan) and some multilateral treaties (GATT/WTO, Mercosur, NAALC, CPTPP and CAFTA-DR)

84. Communication of the Commission 'Towards a Comprehensive European International Investment Policy, COM (2010) 343 final.
85. EU Council, Council conclusion on child labour, http:www.concilium.europa.eu/eudocs/cms_Data_docs/pressdata/EN/foraff/115180.pdf.
86. *See* G. Gorska, *Mutual Influence: The Case of the EU and the UN Guiding Principles on Business and Human Rights*, in European Yearbook on Human Rights, 2012, p. 109 ss.
87. D. Augenstein, C. Behrmann, *Partnering with Civil Society: The EU's Approach to Promoting Human Rights and Decent Work in Bangladesh*, in European Yearbook on Human Rights, 2012, p. 97 ss.

and also the unilateral system of trade tariff preferences (EU GSP and US GSP), as they can be considered 'a milder approach to the social clause'.[88]

This work is useful to identify the different 'logic for action' which guided the Parties during the negotiations of social clauses and thus permits to answer, for each 'model' to a list of questions:

(i) Will the economic-mercantilist logics prevail, or the axiological ones, or a mix of those? What is the degree of social conditionality?
(ii) Is there a difference on the logics between social clauses in the agreements with developing countries and those among peer economies?
(iii) Is there any difference between the US and the EU's approach on negotiations?
(iv) Has the insertion of the social clause in the paradigm of sustainable development, which represent the last evolution of the social clause, really entailed some advantages in terms of social rights (or not?)

[A] Commitments

The first step concerning the disaggregate analysis is about the commitments. First of all, we must verify i) the allocation of the commitments in social matter in the general economy of the Treaty, ii) the literal formulas employed and iii) the content of the commitments.

[1] Allocation of Commitments

Since the signing of the North American Agreement on Labour Cooperation (NAALC), the first example of social clause adopted in the context of the multilateral agreement of free trade among the USA, Canada and Mexico (NAFTA), numerous regional or bilateral trade treaties have included provisions relative to labour, but the introduction of such provisions takes various forms and covers different aspects of social practice and labour laws.

Before starting with the analysis of the content of such provisions, we need to reflect on the possibly different 'allocation' of those provisions, as, in addition to simply being mentioned in the preamble, they may be covered in a *separate section*, that is to say in an agreement annexed to the treaty (as it is the case of NAALC, which is commonly called 'Labour side agreement), or those provisions can be *part of a specific chapter* of the agreement.

88. *See* A. Perulli, Fundamental Social Rights. Market Regulation and EU External Action, in *International Journal of Comparative Labour Law* (2014), pp. 27 ss.; F. Pantano, R. Salomone, *Trade and Labour Within the European Union. Generalized System of Preference*, Jean Monnet Working Papers (New York Univ. School of Law), 2008; L. Compa, J. Vogt, Labour Rights in the Generalized System of Preferences: A 20 Year Review, in *Lab and Policy Journal*, 22, n. 199 (2000-2001), p. 206.

In this regard, the US–Jordan (2001) was the first US agreement which introduced a special section on labour, becoming a benchmark for all subsequent agreements (Singapore, Chile, Australia, Morocco, CAFTA, Bahrain, Oman, Peru, etc.). The provision for a whole chapter of the agreement devoted to labour, integrating a clause on social issues in the body of the text, rather than in an annexed agreement, is the first step forward for the recognition of workers' social rights, in order to realize a true integration of labour concerns into the trade agreement: it is not thus a simple attachment to the treaty but a list of principles which is full part of the treaty, like any commercial provisions.

After this milestone, all the agreements have a specific chapter which regards Labour (CAFTA-DR Chapter 16 'Labour'; CPTPP Chapter 19 'Labour') or, as it is more common from the EU side, are inserted all labour provisions in a chapter entitled 'Trade and Labour' (CETA) or, more broadly, 'Trade and Sustainable Development' (as for Korea–EU FTA and EPA).

[2] Literal Meaning of Commitments

Looking at the several agreements, is it possible to observe a lot of differences concerning the language used for social clauses, which determines a great variation of the juridical and social effects of the commitments undertaken.

Often, the parties express their central obligations not in a binding way, but using an aspirational language, using verbs in their conditional form, or referring, in a 'soft' way, to the promotion of compliance: ex. NAALC, Article 1: *The objectives of this Agreement are to: (f) promote compliance with, and effective enforcement by each Party of its labour law;* US–Jordan, Article 6: 'The Parties *shall strive* to ensure that such labour principles and the internationally recognized labour rights are recognized and protected by domestic law'; CAFTA-DR, Article 16.1.1. 'Each Parties *shall strive* to ensure that such labour principle and the internationally recognized labour rights are recognized and protected by the law' or Article 16.2 'A party shall not fail to effectively enforce its labour law...'; Article 19.4 CPTPP: 'No party shall waive or derogate from its statutes and regulations'; Article 13.3 Korea-EU '(...) each Party shall seek to ensure that those law and policies provide for and encourage high levels of labour protection (...)'.

In this sense, we are not able to see a step forward in the last mega-treaties because the formula used (Article 23.3.4 CETA 'The Parties shall make continued and sustained effort to ratify the fundamental ILO Conventions if they have not yet done so') is not more binding (even if enforced in a more binding way, as we will see). We can find an approach that is still exhortative, but with a greater level of commitment, at least on paper, in the second generation USA FTAs, like for instance in the US–PERU FTA, where (Article 17.1: Statement of Shared Commitments), after stating that the parties reaffirm their obligations as members of the International Labour Organization (ILO), it is provided that 'Each Party *shall adopt and maintain* in its statutes and regulations, and practices thereunder, the following rights, as stated in the ILO Declaration'.

Those literal formulas lead to consider the social clause as a promotional tool where the commitments are often built with a regulative technique using aspirational formulas that are little binding, if not mere declarations of intentions; this weakness in the formulation of obligations does not certainly tend to a social conditionality in a strong sense.

[3] Content of Commitments

In the last two decades, labour provisions in bilateral and multilateral trade agreements have been widened and deepened. Over 80% of agreements that have come into force since 2013 contain such provisions,[89] in order to commit the parties not to lower their labour standards or derogate from labour law with a view to boosting competitiveness.

Social clauses have not only grown in number as to become a common trait of these trade agreements but have acquired great substantive and procedural complexity,[90] as they are included in different ways in FTAs.

Even if no standard model can be identified when we review these agreements, we must point out which are the most commonly included provisions, starting from the main distinction between those agreements which, as NAALC, state the commitment for each party to enforce its domestic labour law (a), on the other agreements which include also some reference to the international dimension of social rights (b) (in different ways, as we will see).

[a] No Harmonization

In most free trade agreement the Parties declare that they do not intend to harmonize the labour standards.

This is explicitly declared in NAALC, Annex 1 Labour Principles: 'The following are guiding principles that the Parties are committed to promote, subject to each Party's domestic law, but do not establish common minimum standards for their domestic law.' Also in the most recent FTA: 'the agreement is not to harmonise the environment or labour standards of the Parties (EPA, Article 16.1, paragraph 2) or 'The Parties recognise that it is not their intention in this Chapter to harmonise the labour or environment standards of the Parties' (EU-Korea, Article 13.1 3). This type of social clause, differently to what happened within the experience of European integration (as well as in the normative tradition of international labour law), does not provide for the compliance with uniform supranational minimum standards, but rather the guarantee of effectiveness of the single national standards.

Differently from this explicit negation of harmonization, MERCOSUR, through the 1998 Social Labour Declaration, states in the Preamble the objective to set a

89. ILO, Studies on Growth with Equity, Assessment of Labour Provisions in Trade and Investment Arrangements, Report July 2016.
90. T. Treu, *Globalization and Human Rights: Social Clauses in Trade Agreements and in International Exchanges among Companies*, in A. Perulli, T. Treu (eds), *Sustainable Development, Global Trade and Social Rights*, Wolters Kluwer, 2018, p. 99.

minimum floor of workers right. We could call this commitment as a 'soft' or 'small' harmonization, at least referring to the core, minimum, social standards: 'Whereas the Ministers of Labour of MERCOSUR have stated in their meetings that regional integration cannot be confined to the commercial and economic spheres, and must also incorporate social issues, as regards the adaptation of the regulatory frameworks for labour to the new circumstances resulting from integration and the process of economic globalization, as well as the recognition of a *minimum floor of workers' rights* within MERCOSUR, in line with the fundamental ILO Conventions' (Preamble, MERCOSUR).

Even if the Preamble also states that 'Whereas the States parties, as well as being Members of the International Labour Organization (ILO), have ratified the principal Conventions guaranteeing the fundamental rights of workers' at the time of writing Argentina, Paraguay and Uruguay had already ratified all the ILO Conventions, while Brazil was missing a core convention (C087 – Freedom of Association and Protection of the Right to Organise Convention, 1948 (No. 87). In this sense, the construction of a minimum floor of rights could not be referred only to the ILO core labour standards, but, more generally to some common labour standards, 'in line with' ILO Conventions and in this case the Mercosur could be considered as a pioneer in promoting the social rights in the economic relationship.

[b] Commitments to Respect Its Own Labour Law

When we are thinking about a treaty which aims to commit Parties to respect their own labour law, it is logic to refer to the NAALC Model, as it was the first example of FTA to adopt such measure.

Article 3 of NAALC testifies the intention of the parties, who promote the '*compliance with and effectively enforce its labour law through appropriate government action* (...)'. Therefore, there is no aim of harmonization or, even more, of standardization of the levels of protection in social matters, that is left to the national legislator's discretion.

This provision to respect its own domestic labour law guarantees the maximum valorization of the sovereignty of the nation State about the levels of national protections on social matters, and this model seems to be expanded, nowadays.

As a matter of fact, the formula has been adopted in the recent CPTPP: 'Article 19.5: Enforcement of Labour Laws 1. No Party shall fail to effectively enforce its labour laws', but also in the CETA Article 23.2 (Right to regulate and levels of protection), states that '*Recognising the right of each Party to set its labour priorities, to establish its levels of labour protection and to adopt or modify its laws and policies accordingly in a manner consistent with its international labour commitments, including those in this Chapter, each Party shall seek to ensure those laws and policies provide for and encourage high levels of labour protection and shall strive to continue to improve such laws and policies with the goal of providing high levels of labour protection*'. Similarly, in EPA, Article 16.2, using more or less the same words (Right to regulate and levels of protection), indicates that '*1. Recognising the right of each Party to determine its sustainable development policies and priorities, to establish its own levels of domestic environmental and labour protection, and to adopt or modify accordingly its relevant laws and regulations, consistently with its commitments to the internationally recognised standards and international agreements to which the Party is party, each Party shall strive to ensure that its laws, regulations and related policies provide high levels of environmental and labour protection and shall strive to continue to improve those laws and regulations and their underlying levels of protection.'*

This provision, as stated in NAALC, EPA and CETA, leads to some interpretation problems: how will it be possible to deal with the commitment to enforce its national labour laws, with the ideal objective of the social clause to create uniform standards, in a way to guarantee a level playing filed, and, from a point of view of values and labour, the respect of international recognized labour standards?

Will we face the risk that, in such way, the logic of comparative advantages of the different domestic levels of regulations, on which the Singapore Declaration (*We reject the use of labour standards for protectionist purposes, and agree that the comparative advantage of Countries, particularly low-wage developing Countries, must in no way be put into question*) was focused? This concern could be by-passed considering that parties 'shall strive to continue to improve those laws and regulations and their underlying levels of protection' (as it was foreseen in the NAALC, as in EPA and CETA there is a double commitment: that of enforcement of the domestic law and that of continuing to improve those laws).

A further profile of critic analysis regarding the respect of the internal legislation in matter of labour concerns the prohibition of encouraging trade or investments through the flexibility of the respective domestic regulations. This leads to the following question:

if parties should undertake to respect their labour law without any exception, is this obligation 'absolute', or is it limited to the behaviours that are capable to influence the trade relationships?

Just to mention an example, the EPA provides for commitments like the prohibition of relaxing domestic labour laws to attract trade and investment ('The Parties shall not encourage trade or investment by relaxing or lowering the level of protection provided by their respective environmental or labour laws and regulations. To that effect, the Parties shall not waive or otherwise derogate from those laws and regulations or fail to effectively enforce them through a sustained or recurring course of action or inaction *in a manner affecting trade or investment between the Parties*', Article 16.2, paragraph 2), and of discrimination or restrictions to trade's purpose: ('The Parties shall not use their respective environmental or labour laws and regulations in a manner which would constitute a means of arbitrary or unjustifiable discrimination against the other Party, or a disguised restriction on international trade', Article 16.2, paragraph 3). This clause is present also in CAFTA (Article 16.2), and in some FTAs, with reference to the internal legislation and to the related compliance with the rights as stated in the ILO Declaration on Fundamental Principles and Rights at Work and its Follow-Up (1998): for example, the US–Peru FTA states that 'Neither Party shall waive or otherwise derogate from, or offer to waive or otherwise derogate from, its statutes or regulations implementing paragraph 1 *in a manner affecting trade or investment* between the Parties, where the waiver or derogation would be inconsistent with a fundamental right set out in that paragraph'.

How should we interpret this clause?

Two explanations could be possible:

(1) According to the first interpretation, the clause confirms the existence of a minimum floor of rights which cannot be modified to attract investors or in order to facilitate trade: therefore, a floor of rights that is unconditioned and non-negotiable for trade/financial purposes. This interpretation would be coherent with the 2008 ILO Declaration on Social Justice for a Fair Globalization, according to which 'the violation of fundamental principles and rights at work cannot be invoked or otherwise used as a legitimate comparative advantage and that labour standards should not be used for protectionist trade purposes'. This interpretation is closer to the axiological logic rather than the trade one, from which, on the contrary, it seems to free itself, in order to go towards an ideal of a trade that is fair and unconditionally respectful of fundamental social rights.

(2) The second interpretation is more problematic because it seems to establish a linkage between the reduction of levels of protection and the encouragement of trade or investments. This interpretation is more coherent with the trade logic of social clause, in the sense that, in order to contrast the possible violation, the country must demonstrate that the commercial partner has adopted those behaviours (i.e., the reduction of the levels of protections) to encourage trade or investments and thus it must give the proof. This should be a very serious concern because it is not easy at all to demonstrate a direct relation between the deregulation of labour standards and the objective to encourage trade and investments.[91] This is why, in my opinion, this is a very dangerous statement, and it should be overcome enshrining the absolute obligation to respect the domestic law, and not to derogate from it, but, on the contrary, to raise the level of social rights protection, as provided in the NAALC, according to which 'each Party (...) shall continue to strive to improve those standards'.

Another concern related to the commitment of the domestic labour law regards the variety of normative references to the internal legislation. Reading the CPTPP, the parties decide to give a definition of labour law, which could be intended to limit the field of labour law which has to be promoted and respected. According to Article 19.1, 'labour law means statutes and regulations, or provisions of statutes and regulations, of a Party that are directly related to the following internationally recognised labour rights: (a) freedom of association and the effective recognition of the right to collective bargaining; (b) the elimination of all forms of forced or compulsory labour; (c) the effective abolition of child labour, a prohibition on the worst forms of child labour and

91. *See* F. Ebert, The Comprehensive Economic and Trade Agreement (CETA): Are Existing Arrangements Sufficient to Prevent Adverse Effects on Labour Standard?.

other labour protections for children and minors; (d) the elimination of discrimination in respect of employment and occupation; and (e) acceptable conditions of work with respect to minimum wage, hours of work, and occupational safety and health'. Certainly wider is the reference to the internal legislation supplied by the NAALC with its eleven labour principles that the parties commit to comply with; an omni-comprehensive list that includes also the right to strike, while no reference is made in the field of dismissal.

The matter raised by these Treaties is therefore *the field of social conditionality*, that varies in an extremely sensitive way by reason of the field of application of internal legislations recalled by each single Treaty. We may not say that the global scenario is intended to a rational identification of the object of the clauses, while it should be hoped that a research for a more homogeneous finalization of the assumed commitments, in order to build an organic network of rules about labour on a global scale, was done.

[c] Commitments to Respect International Labour Law

With reference to the commitments to respect international labour standards, which, of course, are usually added to the (possible) previous commitment to respect its own domestic labour law, we need to distinguish different types of standards mentioned, and a different degree of commitment for the signatories Parties.

[i] 'Internationally Recognized Labour Rights'

Some agreements generally refer to 'internationally recognized labour rights' without referring to the ILO Core Labour Standards, but sometimes spreading the content of the commitments undertaken, compared to those promoted by the ILO Core Conventions.

The first example of this model is the NAALC.

This agreement, which precedes the 1998 Declaration on fundamental principles and rights, makes no explicit reference to the ILO's conventions but, as prof. Bellace observed, the NAALC labour principles include the four principles in the Declaration, and more. NAALC refers to eleven principles (Article 49) which go further than the eight fundamental conventions that the nations must strive to achieve. According to the NAALC Annex 1 defines 'labour principles' as 'guiding values' that the parties commit to respect and it individuates them in the following thematic fields: (1) freedom of association and right to collective bargaining; (2) right to collective bargaining; (3) right to strike; (4) prohibition of forced labour; (5) protection of child and minor labour; (6) protection of minimum standards of employment (e.g., minimum wages and benefits for extra-hour labour); (7) elimination of discrimination on labour; (8) right to equal salary among men and women working in the same enterprise and having the same task; (9) prevention of professional illnesses and injuries on labour; (10) right to compensation in case of illnesses and injuries on labour; (11) protection of migrant workers.

Despite the content of the commitment is broader than that of the ILO Conventions, it is important to point out that such Principles, expressed in a quite vague and succinct formula, do not set common minimum standards at all, but only wide areas of interest (broad areas of concern) on which the parties have developed (each its own way) 'laws, regulations, procedures and practices' intended to the 'protection of the interests of the respective labour forces' and, further, there is no mention of the relative Conventions of the ILO.

In the case of US–Jordan, despite the commitment to respect the ILO 1998 Declaration, the parties talk about some internationally recognized labour rights but the list does not strictly correspond to the list of the core labour rights: the list is wider, mentioning among the 'internationally recognized labour rights, that of '(e) acceptable conditions of work with respect to minimum wages, hours of work, and occupational safety and health'. (US–Jordan, Article 6, *Labour* 1. The Parties reaffirm their obligations as members of the International Labour Organization (ILO) and their commitments under the ILO Declaration on Fundamental Principles and Rights at Work and its Follow-up. The Parties shall strive to ensure that such labour principles and the following internationally recognized labour rights (a) the right of association; (b) the right to organize and bargain collectively; (c) a prohibition on the use of any form of forced or compulsory labour; (d) a minimum age for the employment of children; and (e) acceptable conditions of work with respect to minimum wages, hours of work, and occupational safety and health are recognized and protected by domestic law.)

A similar commitment can be found in the recent CPTPP (2018): if the Article 19.4 states that 'it is inappropriate to encourage trade or investment by weakening or reducing the protections afforded in each Party's labour laws', Article 19.1, as already said, gives a definition of labour law, which recalls, in an identical formula to that of the US–Jordan agreement, which is included also in the CAFTA-DR (Article 16.8), demonstrating the success of this model.

Despite the broader commitment compared to the ILO Declaration, this is a critical point of the agreement, mainly for CPTPP, because (as prof. Bellace observed in her relation) it is impossible to identify definitions of these rights on which the eleven signatory nations agreed (while it could be simpler for two countries as in the case of the US–Jordan agreement). This is a limit which regards all multilateral negotiations as the countries involved could be very distant in terms of social policy and labour provisions, and thus, the more the country is involved, the less the predictability of each Party is real commitment.

[ii] Reference to the ILO 1998 Declaration

Other agreements generally refer to the ILO 1998 Declaration but do not mention the ILO Core Conventions (as CPTPP, where the members Parties have not ratified all the Core Conventions yet, or the Us–Jordan for example).

CAFTA-DR for example, in Article 16.1 states that 'the Parties reaffirm their obligations as members of the ILO and their commitments under the ILO Declaration'.

The 1998 Declaration commits Member States, in accordance with the obligations deriving from membership of the ILO, to respect and promote principles and rights in four categories, whether or not they have ratified the relevant Conventions. These categories are: freedom of association and the effective recognition of the right to collective bargaining, the elimination of forced or compulsory labour, the abolition of child labour and the elimination of discrimination in respect of employment and occupation.

The problem is that ILO Core Conventions' content is very detailed compared to the principles of the ILO Declarations, and because the ILO's organs of control guarantee interpretative uniformities of the rights sanctioned in the Conventions, differently to what happens with the 1998 Declaration, which is not submitted to any technical supervision.

[iii] Reference to the ILO Core Conventions

Other Treaties, again, refer specifically to the ILO Core Conventions, as it is usual for FTAs signed by EU. This is the case of EPA EU-Japan, at Article 16.3, with a formula that is, however, little biding: 'Each Party shall make continued and sustained efforts on its own initiative to pursue ratification of the *fundamental ILO Conventions* and other ILO Conventions which each Party considers appropriate to ratify.' The formula is a little vague, because as far as the commitment is concerned, the usual aspirational approach (shall make efforts) prevails, both with reference to core Conventions and with reference to other Conventions, leaving the parties free to identify those they believe it should be 'appropriate' to ratify. This approach to fundamental Conventions, even though it is vague, does not even recur in the Treaties signed by the US (as NAALC and US-Jordan which does not contain any reference to the ILO's Conventions). It is evident that the reference to the ILO Core Conventions should, on the other hand, be considered as a real commitment, given that the ILO requires their compliance by reason of the mere bond of affiliation. Besides, the ILO regularly examines the application of standards, thanks both to the examination of periodic reports submitted by Member States on the measures they have taken to implement the provisions of the ratified Conventions and to a representations procedure and a complaints procedure of general application, together with a special procedure for freedom of association. So the reference to the ILO Conventions is at the moment the only way to assure a control on the respect of the commitments undertaken. In most cases, Parties commit themselves to respect the ILO Conventions ratified, and to ratify those that at the moment of the signature of the treaty are not yet ratified. An example is the Korea-EU FTA: "*Article 13.4 Multilateral labour standards and agreements (...) 3. The Parties reaffirm the commitment to effectively implementing the ILO Conventions that Korea and the Member States of the European Union have ratified respectively. The Parties will make continued and sustained efforts towards ratifying the fundamental ILO Conventions as well as the other Conventions that are classified as 'up-to-date' by the ILO."* (at the time of writing Korea has ratified 4/8 ILO Core Conventions).[92]

This obligation, to ratify the Core Conventions not yet ratified at the moment of the signature of the agreement, is also present in the EU–Vietnam agreement (Article 3), and, as we have pointed out, in the EPA (Article 16.3.3: *'Each Party shall make continued and sustained efforts on its own initiative to pursue ratification of the fundamental ILO Conventions and other ILO Conventions which each Party considers appropriate to ratify'*).

This commitment towards a ratification of non-ratified fundamental ILO Conventions (even if the ratification should be on Japan's initiative) demonstrates the pressure given by the EU for a social conditionality, even if we are not in the case of pre-ratification conditionality, as it is the case, for example, of the EU SPG.

Despite this lack of pre-ratification conditionality, we can observe that this commitment has led to a progress ratification of ILO Conventions by some Countries.

I am referring, in particular, to Canada: at the time of CETA's signature, Canada had not ratified all the ILO Core Conventions: C-138 has been ratified in June 2016, and C-98 in June 2017. But we need to observe that Canada ratified 9 ILO Conventions in the last twelve months, so we can easily state that this Treaty has been for Canada a great incentive to ratify the ILO Core Conventions, while all EU Member States[93] had already ratified all the Core Conventions.[94]

92. Conventions ratified by Korea: (1) C100 - Equal Remuneration Convention, 1951 (No. 100); C111 – Discrimination (Employment and Occupation) Convention, 1958 (No. 111); C138 – Minimum Age Convention, 1973 (No. 138)Minimum age specified: 15 years; C182 – Worst Forms of Child Labour Convention, 1999 (No. 182). Conventions not ratified: C029 – Forced Labour Convention, 1930 (No. 29); C087 – Freedom of Association and Protection of the Right to Organise Convention, 1948 (No. 87); C098 – Right to Organise and Collective Bargaining Convention, 1949 (No. 98) and C105 – Abolition of Forced Labour Convention, 1957 (No. 105).

93. EU28: Austria, Italy, Belgium, Latvia, Bulgaria, Lithuania, Croatia, Luxembourg, Cyprus, Malta, Czech Republic, Netherlands, Denmark, Poland, Estonia, Portugal, Finland, Romania, France, Slovakia, Germany, Slovenia, Greece, Spain, Hungary, Sweden, Ireland and United Kingdom.

94. This is the list of countries which did not ratified at the time of writing the ILO Core Labour Conventions: *C029 - Forced Labour Convention, 1930:* Afghanistan, Brunei Darussalam, China, Korea, Republic of, Marshall Islands, Palau, Tonga, Tuvalu, United States; *C087 - Freedom of Association and Protection of the Right to Organise Convention, 1948*: Afghanistan, Bahrain, Brazil, Brunei Darussalam, China, Cook Islands, Guinea – Bissau, India, Iran, Islamic Republic of, Jordan, Kenya, Korea, Republic of Lao People's Democratic Republic, Lebanon, Malaysia, Marshall Islands, Morocco, Nepal, New Zealand, Oman, Palau, Qatar, Saudi, Arabia, Singapore, South Sudan, Sudan, Thailand, Tonga, Tuvalu, United Arab Emirates, United States, Viet Nam; *C098 - Right to Organise and Collective Bargaining Convention, 1949:* Afghanistan, Bahrain, Brunei Darussalam, China, Cook Islands, India, Iran, Islamic Republic of, Korea, Republic of, Lao People's Democratic Republic, Marshall Islands, Mexico, Myanmar, Oman, Palau, Qatar, Saudi Arabia, Thailand, Tonga, Tuvalu, United Arab Emirates, United States, Viet Nam; *C100 - Equal Remuneration Convention, 1951:* Bahrain, Brunei Darussalam, Cook Islands, Kuwait, Liberia, Marshall Islands, Myanmar, Oman, Palau, Qatar, Somalia, Tonga, Tuvalu, United States; *C105 - Abolition of Forced Labour Convention, 1957*: Brunei Darussalam, China, Japan, Korea, Republic of, Lao People's Democratic Republic, Marshall Islands, Myanmar, Palau, Timor-Leste, Tonga, Tuvalu, Viet Nam; C-111 – Discrimination (Employment and Occupation) Convention, 1958: Brunei Darussalam, Cook Islands, Japan, Malaysia, Marshall Islands, Myanmar, Oman, Palau, Singapore, Tonga, Tuvalu, United States; C-138 – Minimum Age Convention, 1973; Australia, Bangladesh, Cook Islands, Iran, Islamic Republic of Liberia, Marshall Islands,

This could be a path also for Japan, in the context of EPA: we may observe that the time of writing Japan did not ratify two Core Conventions:-C105 - Abolition of Forced Labour Convention, 1957 (No. 105) and --111 - Discrimination (Employment and Occupation) Convention, 1958. If, with regards to the latest Convention (C111), the lack of ratification is probably due to a cultural tradition, the Core Convention of Forced Labour has not probably been ratified yet, because Japan is currently under observation by the CEARC, the ILO Committee of experts about the other Conventions concerning Forced or Compulsory Labour (ratified by Japan in 1939):-C029 - Forced Labour Convention, 1930 (No. 29). The matter regards the compensation to some victims of wartime sexual slavery or industrial forced labour during the Second World War.[95] The Committee refers in particular to a decision of the Korean Supreme Court of Justice passed on 24 May 2012 which reversed the decisions of lower courts rejecting the demands for compensation by forced labour victims against two leading Japanese industries. Moreover, about the same ILO Conventions, there is a CEACR Request (on the same ILC session of 2016), related to the trafficking in humans, in particular about the low number of prison sentences imposed on perpetrators, to the fact that no perpetrators of forced labour have been brought to justice, to the decline in victim identification and to the insufficient support granted to victims.[96]

We therefore expect clear progress from Japan towards ratifying the two remaining ILO core conventions (on discrimination and on the abolition of forced labour), considering that, above all, Japan is the second largest contributor to the ILO's regular budget.[97]

A peculiar case is that of CAFTA-DR, which, in addition to a mention to the ILO 1998 Declaration, refers explicitly only to one single core ILO Convention: ILO Convention No. 182 Concerning the Prohibition and Immediate Action for the Elimination of the Worst Forms of Child Labour (1999) (ILO Convention 182). Article 16.5, focused on 'Labour Cooperation and Capacity Building Mechanism' states that: 1 1. Recognizing that cooperation on labour issues can play an important role in advancing development in the territory of the Parties and in providing opportunities to improve labour standards, and to further advance common commitments regarding labour matters, including the principles embodied in the ILO Declaration and ILO Convention No. 182 Concerning the Prohibition and Immediate Action for the Elimination of the Worst Forms of Child Labour (1999) (ILO Convention 182), the Parties hereby establish a Labour Cooperation and Capacity Building Mechanism, as set out in Annex 16.5.

Myanmar, New Zealand, Palau, Saint Lucia, Somalia, Timor-Leste, Tonga, Tuvalu, United States, Vanuatu; C-182 - Worst Forms of Child Labour Convention, 1999: Cook Islands, Eritrea, Marshall Islands, Palau, Tonga, Tuvalu.

95. Observation (CEACR) - adopted 2015, published 105th ILC session (2016) - *Forced Labour Convention, 1930 (No. 29), Victims of Wartime Sexual Slavery or Industrial Forced Labour.*
96. Direct Request (CEACR) - adopted 2015, published 105th ILC session (2016), *Forced Labour Convention, 1930 (No. 29)*, http://www.ilo.org/dyn/normlex/en/f?p=1000:13201:::NO:13201:P13201_COUNTRY_ID:102729.
97. http://www.ilo.org/wcmsp5/groups/public/---dgreports/---exrel/documents/publication/wcms_357443.pdf.

This commitment undertaken by the signatory parties could be suggested as a model to follow because in this way, choosing one or more conventions to be respected, the binding of the commitments is assured.

Finally, we need to observe that the agreements do not contain any reference to the interpretation given by the ILO about the content of the Core Conventions, so the question whether the right to strike follows from or not the Convention n. 87 on freedom of association and right to organize is not clear, as prof. Bellace underlined in her paper.

[d] Pre-Ratification Conditionality

In some cases, the social conditionality is more rigorous and it subordinates the signature of the trade agreement to the ratification of the Conventions (the so-called pre-ratification conditionality). This is the model adopted by the EU Generalized System of Preferences,[98] a regulation model which intended to combine trade liberalization and respect of social rights through the preferential and non-mutual treatment granted to developing countries in the field of trade exchanges, notwithstanding the GATT normative.[99]

According to the special incentive arrangement for sustainable development and good governance (as stated by. Article 9 of the Reg. 978/2012) a GSP beneficiary Country may benefit from the tariff preferences provided under the special incentive arrangement for sustainable development and good governance if 'it has ratified all "relevant conventions" and the most recent available conclusions of the monitoring bodies under those conventions do not identify a serious failure to effectively implement any of those conventions'.

The relevant conventions are the core international conventions on human and labour rights, environmental protection and good governance. In terms of social rights, Parties are committed to ratify and implement a list of Core human and labour rights UN/ILO Conventions, and thus, indeed, all the ILO Core Conventions.[100]

98. F. Pantano, R. Salomone, *Trade and Labour within the European Union Generalized System of Preferences*, Jean Monnet WPS, New York University School of Law, 2008.
99. *See* T.M. Franck, *Fairness in International Law and Institution*, Oxford, 1995, p. 58.; L. Bartels, C. Haberli, *Binding Tariff Preferences For Developing Countries Under Article II GATT, in Journal of International Economic Law.*
100. Annex VIII of Regulation (EU) No 978/2012 of 31 October 20121, The relevant GSP+ conventions, Core human and labour rights UN/ILO Conventions: (1) Convention on the Prevention and Punishment of the Crime of Genocide (1948); (2) International Convention on the Elimination of All Forms of Racial Discrimination (1965); (3) International Covenant on Civil and Political Rights (1966); (4) International Covenant on Economic Social and Cultural Rights (1966); (5) Convention on the Elimination of All Forms of Discrimination Against Women (1979); (6) Convention Against Torture and other Cruel, Inhuman or Degrading Treatment or Punishment (1984); (7) Convention on the Rights of the Child (1989); (8) Convention concerning Forced or Compulsory Labour, No 29 (1930); (9) Convention concerning Freedom of Association and Protection of the Right to Organise, No 87 (1948); (10) Convention concerning the Application of the Principles of the Right to Organise and to Bargain Collectively, No 98 (1949); (11) Convention concerning Equal Remuneration of Men and Women Workers for Work of Equal Value, No 100 (1951); (12) Convention concerning

In this sense the EU GSP could be considered as an exemplar model of positive linkage between international trade and social rights in the European external action[101]: any of the GSP arrangements may be temporarily withdrawn for serious and systematic violations of core principles laid down in core human and labour rights conventions and on a number of other grounds such as unfair trading practices and serious shortcomings in customs controls.

[e] The Reference to the Decent Work and to Sustainable Development

The last FTA signed by EU (CETA and EU-Korea) extends their commitment to the decent work and sustainable development.

In the EU-Korea for example all labour provisions are inserted in Chapter 13, 'Trade and Sustainable Development', where Article 13.1 states the intentions of the Parties 'to strengthen their trade relations and cooperation in ways that promote sustainable development' and (Article 13.6), the Parties recognize 'the beneficial role that core labour standards and decent work can have on economic efficiency, innovation and productivity, and they highlight the value of greater policy coherence between trade policies, on the one hand, and employment and labour policies on the other'.

In CETA, Article 22.3, paragraph 2 entitled 'Cooperation and promotion of trade supporting sustainable development' – the Parties 'affirm that trade should promote sustainable development. Accordingly, each Party shall strive to promote trade and economic flows and practices that contribute to enhancing decent work (...)'. In the following article (CETA 23.3.2), we observe the commitment to 'ensure that its labour law and practices promote the following objectives included in the *ILO Decent Work Agenda*, and in accordance with the ILO Declaration on Social Justice for a Fair Globalization of 2008 adopted by the International Labour Conference at its 97th Session, and other international commitments: (a) health and safety at work, including the prevention of occupational injury or illness and compensation in cases of such injury or illness; (b) establishment of acceptable minimum employment standards for wage earners, including those not covered by a collective agreement; and (c) non-discrimination in respect of working conditions, including for migrant workers'.

As we will point out (*see infra*), the reference to Decent Work and to the paradigm of sustainable development can represent a wider and new horizon for social clauses. Reluctant trade partners might also be more willing to accept a sustainable development chapter than a separate chapter on social rights, as Sustainable Development is a principle universally accepted[102] and proclaimed by the UN, through the

the Abolition of Forced Labour, No 105 (1957); (13) Convention concerning Discrimination in Respect of Employment and Occupation, No 111 (1958); (14) Convention concerning Minimum Age for Admission to Employment, No 138 (1973); (15) Convention concerning the Prohibition and Immediate Action for the Elimination of the Worst Forms of Child Labour, No 182 (1999).

101. Perulli A., Clausola Sociale, Enciclopedia del Diritto, Giuffré, 2014, vol. VII, pp. 187-211.

102. Van Den Putte L., Orbie J., EU Bilateral Trade Agreements and the Surprising Rise of Labour Provisions, in International Journal of Comparative Labour Law, 31, n. 3 (2015), p. 282.

Sustainable Development Goals, and by the European Commission in all the latest Communications related to the European external action to harness globalization.[103]

Moreover, the framing of core labour rights as part of a broader 'sustainable development' agenda has contributed to their unobjectable status.[104]

The questions of sustainability in those FTAs serves the goals of protection and promotion of human rights and certainly possesses model character for other, future, free trade agreements and of course can be considered as a new basis of legitimation for a new era of social and enforceable clauses.

Indeed, the majority of agreements that include such provisions are too recent to be able to stand back and assess them adequately.

[B] Carrot and Stick: Sanctions and Incentives

Whichever model of social clause may be taken into consideration, we may reaffirm that a merely voluntaristic, or founded on moral suasion choice, would not be in line with the standards of the procedures of social conditionality within both European and North American traditions. After a reasonable period of time of useless activation of the soft implementation mechanisms above-mentioned (ministerial consultations, recommendations of the experts committee, realization of consultative public forums, and so on), the *non-compliance* with *labour standards* should lead to financial or commercial sanctions, following the procedure of *dispute resolution*. For example, interruption of benefits (on the NAALC model), and/or Monetary Enforcement Assessment (on the model of some FTAs and of generalized preference systems). At the same time, this kind of *penalties* should particularly regard those sectors in which the problems about compliance with the obligations specified on the chapter on Sustainability appear repeatedly, in spite of the technical/administrative support of the experts committee and international organizations like ILO, with whom we hope for a strict collaboration.

The contemplation of sanctionatory mechanisms as a last resort does not exclude, and actually presupposes the coexistence of other compliance instruments: the cooperation and the technical support with multilateral agencies, notably the ILO. However, the TTIP should contemplate also some mechanisms founded on a promotional philosophy, under the shape of positive sanctions and 'incentives', like those who characterize in particular the GSP European Model.

103. White Paper on the Future of Europe; Reflections and scenarios for the EU27 by 2025; European Commission COM(2017)2025 of 1 March 2017; Brussels, 13.9.2017 COM(2017) 492 final Communication from the Commission to the European Parliament, the Council, the European Economic and Social Committee and the Committee of the Regions A Balanced and Progressive Trade Policy to Harness Globalisation.

104. Van Den Putte L., Orbie J., EU Bilateral Trade Agreements and the Surprising Rise of Labour Provisions, in *International Journal of Comparative Labour Law*, 31, n. 3 (2015), p. 264.

[1] A Verification of the Enforcement: The NAALC, CAFTA, EU GSP Cases

In terms of implementation, contrary to the US approach, the EU adopts a more nuanced approach, with a preference for dialogue and capacity instead of the provisions of sanctions: if it is true that, both for CETA and EPA (as for the TTIP), labour provisions have been widened and deepened compared to the past, we need to observe that they are mostly cooperative and non-binding provisions. As we saw, most EU FTAs use an aspirational language, and for this reason labour provisions risk to lack an effective remedy to labour violations or a valid deterrent. This is, unfortunately, in line with the EU traditional policies.

As a matter of fact, the only agreement where economic and clear sanctions are imposed is the EU Generalized System of Preferences (GSP) as any of the GSP arrangements may be temporarily withdrawn for serious and systematic violations of core principles laid down in core human and labour rights conventions and on a number of other grounds such as unfair trading practices and serious shortcomings in customs controls.

This 'stick and carrot' conditionality of the EU's GSP constitutes the 'flagship' of trade initiatives aimed at supporting sustainable development and human right.

In particular, if we consider the special incentive arrangement for Sustainable Development and Good Governance GSP+ granting full removal of tariffs for vulnerable low and lower-middle income Countries, its benefits may be temporarily withdrawn if the national legislation of a GSP+ beneficiary country no longer incorporates the relevant conventions or if that legislation is not effectively implemented - in other words if the underlying balance in GSP+ between additional trade preferences in the EU market and beneficiaries' acceptance and implementation of international sustainable development and good governance rules and standards is no longer properly respected. In this regard, the Commission monitors the situation in beneficiary countries on an ongoing basis primarily by drawing on material available from the relevant international monitoring bodies.

The problem is double: this regulation is only for developing countries and, as other scholars observed, the temporary withdrawal more or less has remained 'to be law in the books'.

Even in the case where sanctions for violations of the commitments in the field of labour law are clear and stated, the EU appears reluctant to apply trade sanctions for violation of labour rights: since 1995 the EU GSP has provided that 'serious and systematic violations' of labour standards could lead to a withdrawal of trade preferences but over the past two decades to date, that has only happened three times: in 1997 for Myanmar/Burma, on the grounds of serious and systematic violations of labour rights, in 2007 for Belarus, on the same grounds and in 2010 for Sri Lanka. Sri Lanka's benefits were temporarily withdrawn in 2010 due to non-effective implementation of certain human rights conventions. Thus, imports from Sri Lanka benefit only from the standard GSP preferential treatment.

This lack of sanctions demonstrates that the GSP has rarely been used for protectionism reasons, to restrict imports from developing countries, be-cause numerous calls for sanctions have not been taken into consideration.

For example, the only sanction to be adopted against China in 1989 (at that time China was a GSP beneficiary) for its violent repression of the Tiananmen Square protests was an arms embargo; in 2008, no new sanctions were added after another wave of violence in Tibet. In the same year, Russia's attack on Georgia went unpunished.

Before continuing the reflection, I would like to point out that this problem is not an only European problem.

Moreover, if we consider the US, the field of application of NAALC's sanctions is rigorously limited: they apply only if the violation of the agreement proves to be 'trade related' and 'covered by mutually recognized labour law' (NAALC, Article 49).

The NAALC requires that the NAOs (National Administrative Office in each of the three NAFTA Parties) provides for the receipt and review of submissions on labour law matters in the other two countries. The NAALC further delineates the types of issues that may be considered at the various resolution stages of the Agreement. The framers of the Agreement intended that disputes be addressed and settled through dialogue and cooperative consultations, initially at the NAO level and later at the ministerial level. At the NAO and ministerial level, there is a broad range of issues that may be considered for review.

At the time of writing (August 2018), there are thirty-nine submissions received under the NAALC: three are currently under review, four have been withdrawn by submitter, nine are declined after review, twenty-three have been reported.[105]

Considering those reported, eleven submissions were filed by the US (especially against Mexican industries, the majority for violations under the NAALC concerns freedom of association and the right to organize, collective bargaining, but there were also cases concerning violations of occupational safety and health, minimum wage and overtime pay, access to fair and transparent labour tribunal proceedings and gender discrimination), ten submission were filed by Mexico (most of the submissions concern migrant workers in the State of Washington employed in the apple industry and raises issues of freedom of association, safety and health, employment discrimination, minimum employment standards, protection of migrant workers and compensation in cases of occupational injuries and illnesses) and two submission were filed by Canada (one was also filed with the U.S. NAO and includes the same allegations of worker rights violations at two different garment factories located in Mexico, and the other raises concerns about the enforcement of labour legislation covering occupational safety and health and freedom of association of workers at the Itapsa export processing plant in the State of Mexico).

As for the results of this submissions, with regards to the last case submission reported (June 2016),[106] the U.S. Department of Labour has issued a public report

105. https://www.dol.gov/ilab/trade/agreements/naalc.htm (here the list of cases with the reports).
106. U.S. NAO Submission No. 2015-04 (UFCW).

(June 2016) in response to a submission filed under the NAALC by the United Food & Commercial Workers Local 770, the Frente Auténtico del Trabajo, the Los Angeles Alliance for a New Economy, and the Project on Organizing, Development, Education, and Research, with research assistance from Change to Win. The report determines that there is insufficient evidence, at this time, to support specific conclusions related to the Mexican government's application of labour laws at Chedraui retail stores, in light of information in the submission and additional information obtained during the review. Nonetheless, the report discusses in detail the Department of Labour's longstanding, serious concerns regarding issues raised in the submission, in particular so-called protection contracts and the primary factors that facilitate them, such as structural bias in the Conciliation and Arbitration Boards that administer labour justice in Mexico.

The previous submission had the same result (August 2007), due to the lack of evidence of proof. The submission (U.S. NAO Submission No. 2005-03, Hidalgo) was filed on October 14 by The Progressive Union of Workers of the Textile Industry, the Manufacturing, Cutting and Confection of Fabric and Garments in General and Related and Similar Industries in the Mexican Republic, a member of the 'Vanguardia Obrera' Workers Federation of the Revolutionary Confederation of Workers and Peasants, with the support of the U.S. Labour Education in the Americas Project, and the Washington Office on Latin America under the NAALC concerning the enforcement of labour laws by the Government of Mexico. The submission focuses on events at a textile plant operated by Rubie's de Mexico. In particular, the submitters allege that the Government of Mexico has failed to fulfil its obligations under the NAALC to effectively enforce its labour law under Article 3 in connection with freedom of association and protection of the right to organize, the right to bargain collectively, the right to strike, prohibition of forced labour, labour protections for children and young persons, minimum employment standards, elimination of employment discrimination, prevention of occupational injuries and illnesses, and compensation in cases of occupational injuries and illnesses, and under Article 5 with respect to fair, equitable and transparent labour tribunal proceedings.

According to Public Report of Review of Office of Trade and Labour Affairs (OTLA), 'the submitters failed to provide sufficient evidence to corroborate many of their claims and failed to pursue domestic procedures to remedy many of the alleged violations'. That is why the report included only some recommendation: the OTLA recommends NAO consultations pursuant to Article 21 of the NAALC to discuss the following: i) Compliance with procedural requirements in Mexico's labour law, and measures taken to prevent unwarranted delays and to improve coordination between federal and State authorities in the administration of labour justice procedures; ii) Transparency in the union representation process, including the establishment of a publicly available registry of unions and collective bargaining agreements; iii) Resources devoted to the periodic inspection of workplaces so that labour laws, such as those related to the protection of young people, minimum employment standards, and occupational safety and health, may be enforced effectively and consistently; iv) Clarification of discriminatory practices in Mexico and the current status of initiatives undertaken on this issue pursuant to the Ministerial Consultations Implementation

Agreement relating to U.S. Submission 9701; and v) Access to Mexican authorities responsible for relevant labour law enforcement. Despite the strict limits of operativeness which have been demonstrated by these two submissions' results, the predisposition of a social clause supported by an actual sanctionatory apparatus (which goes well beyond 'the moral pressure' and the *mobilization of shame*, in which basically the activity of the ILO can be summarized) inside a multilateral agreement of free exchange constitutes an unprecedented fact.

On the one hand, this marks a clear fracture with the past experiences of international regulation of the economy and of trade exchanges, in particular with the GATT, and on the other, it modifies the unilateral approach so far dominating the USA's trade policies, making it more suitable to international law principles and to the multilateral discipline of trade relations.

With regards to the difficulty to apply the sanctions, we may underline that in all the commitments according to the commitment of the parties not to relax their labour law 'in a manner affecting trade', the affection to trade is very hard to be demonstrated.

We must observe that this formula is very frequent: in EPA (Article 16.2.2. 'the Parties shall not waive or otherwise derogate from those laws and regulations or fail to effectively enforce them through a sustained or recurring course of action or inaction in a manner affecting trade or investment between the Parties') but also in CAFTA-DR (Article 16.2, Enforcement of Labour Laws 1. (a) A Party shall not fail to effectively enforce its labour laws, through a sustained or recurring course of action or inaction, in a manner affecting trade between the Parties, after the date of entry into force of this Agreement), in US–Jordan (Article 6.4.a A Party shall not fail to effectively enforce its labour laws, through a sustained or recurring course of action or inaction, in a manner affecting trade between the Parties) and in CPTPP (Article 19.4: Non-Derogation. The Parties recognize that it is inappropriate to encourage trade or investment by weakening or reducing the protections afforded in each Party's labour laws. Accordingly, no Party shall waive or otherwise derogate from, or offer to waive or otherwise derogate from, its statutes or regulations: (a) implementing Article 19.3.1 (Labour Rights), if the waiver or derogation would be inconsistent with a right set out in that paragraph or (b) implementing Article 19.3.1 (Labour Rights) or Article 19.3.2, if the waiver or derogation would weaken or reduce adherence to a right set out in Article 19.3.1, or to a condition of work referred to in Article 19.3.2, in a special trade or customs area, such as an export processing zone or foreign trade zone, in the Party's territory, 'in a manner affecting trade or investment between the Parties').

The difficulties to demonstrate the Party's intention to affect trade, that is to attract investors and enterprises, is clearly demonstrated by Trade Dispute issues ruling in US–Guatemala Labour Law Case, under the CAFTA-DR, finding that Guatemala's alleged failure to enforce domestic labour legislation was not done 'in a manner affecting trade'.

The Guatemala Submission under CAFTA-DR (*Arbitral Panel Decision Reached in June 2017)* was the first time a labour rights dispute had ever been filed under an FTA's dispute settlement mechanism. The US formally launched the case in 2010, following complaints made by domestic and Guatemalan labour unions two years prior. Washington officials raised concerns that the alleged treatment of Guatemalan workers (eight employers were cited for their dismissal of nearly eighty workers who had attempted to engage in union activities) was in violation of their labour rights, while also putting American workers at an unfair competitive disadvantage. The international ruling (June 2017) prevents the United States from seeking penalties on Guatemala for failing to effectively enforce its labour laws, simply because such abuses are not 'in a manner affecting trade'. Under CAFTA-DR, the panel decision is final; there is no appeal process. Any press inquiry about the case should be directed to the Office of the U.S. Trade Representative.

This decision demonstrates that it is very difficult for workers' complaints to be upheld, despite the social provisions included in the FTA. This is why we need to think to a new legitimation of the social clause.

[C] Enforcement and ISDS

A profile of particular and current interest concerns the relationship between the enforcement of social clauses and arbitral clauses on the investments (ISDS), or ICS, and their compatibility with the principles of EU's right on the external action of the Union (Articles 206 and 207 TFEU, but also Article 9 on horizontal social clause).

Such clauses could be undermined by the ISDS (*Investor-To-State Dispute Settlement*), a mechanism included in many trade and investment agreements to settle disputes.

This clause could be invoked by transnational corporations in order to protect investments and to contrast all social policies considered against financial and economic interests[107]: under a free trade agreement which include ISDS mechanisms, a company from one signatory State investing in another signatory state can argue that new laws or regulations, for example the raising of some labour standards, could negatively affect its expected profits or investment potential, and seek compensation in a binding arbitration tribunal, rather than public courts. In this way, all the commitment taken by a country in terms of social rights could be frustrated.

In reply to the criticisms to this tool, in particular due to the lack of the right to appeal, the lack of transparency or the lack of independence of arbitrators, the EU has decided to reform the traditional arbitration-based system and replace it with the ICS, the Investment Court System.

The ICS incorporates many innovative features and addresses to some of the core criticism, solving many problems like the lack of the right to appeal, the lack of transparency or the lack of independence of arbitrators, demonstrating a certain progress in developing a balanced and forward-looking approach in the international investment policy.[108]

---

107. Cfr. Lance Compa, *Labour Rights and Labour Standard in Transatlantic Trade and Investment Negotiations: An American Perspective*, John Hopkins University, Working Paper Series, July 2014.
108. Cagnin V., *New Generations Treaties and the Attempts for a Renewal of the Investor State Dispute Settlement (ISDS)*, in Perulli A., Treu T. (eds), *Sustainable Development, Global Trade and Social Rights*, Kluwer, 2018, pp. 155–168.

The first important element is the establishment of an Investment Tribunal of First Instance, composed of fifteen judges jointly chosen at random for each case, and subjected to strict ethical requirements, including a prohibition from acting as legal counsel in any investment dispute. The second important element is the creation of a permanent Appeal Tribunal, which will ensure the respect of rights and more importantly, the coherence of decisions in individual cases.

Following the EU Commission proposal to replace the ISDS with the ICS in the context of the TTIP negotiations (at the moment stopped), the ICS has been included in the CETA,[109] and in the trade agreements concluded with Singapore, Vietnam and Mexico.

The EU has discussed during the negotiations its reformed proposal on the ICS also within the Economic Partnership Agreement (EPA) between the EU and Japan, which is a well-known supporter of the ISDS[110]: the agreement is now awaiting ratification by the European Parliament and the Japanese Diet following which it could enter into force in 2019 but negotiations with Japan continue on investment protection standards and investment protection dispute resolution in order to reach convergence in the investment protection negotiations as soon as possible, in light of their shared commitment to a stable and secure investment environment in Europe and Japan.

For the EU, ISDS in EU trade and investment agreements is a thing of the past: in its recent judgment of 6 March 2018 in the *Achmea* case, the ECJ confirmed the Commission's view that investor-to-State arbitration in an agreement concluded between Member States is not compatible with EU law. The ECJ ruled that these clauses do not have legal effect.

Thus, the replacing of the ISDS with ICS is considered as a guarantee not to undermine EU's and Member States' right to adopt and apply, accordingly to their respective competences, the measures geared to non-discriminatorily fulfil legitimate interests of public policy, in social, environmental, national security, financial system

109. CETA moves decisively away from the traditional approach of investment dispute resolution and establishes independent, impartial and permanent investment Tribunals. Accordingly, the members of these Tribunals will be individuals qualified for judicial office in their respective countries, and these will be appointed by the European Union and Canada, and not arbitrators nominated by the investor and the defending State (as foreseen in the ISDS). Contrary to the traditional investment dispute settlement approach, cases will be heard by three randomly selected members. Strict ethical rules for these individuals have been set to ensure their independence and impartiality, the absence of conflict of interest, bias or appearance of bias. The Tribunal will be composed of fifteen members nominated by the Union and Canada and not by arbitrators nominated by the investor and the defending State. The tribunal will hear cases in divisions of three members appointed via a randomized procedure. CETA is then the first agreement to include an Appeal mechanism (Art. 8.28) which will allow the correction of errors and ensure the consistency of the decisions of the Tribunal of first instance. Further (Art. 8.36), CETA introduces full transparency in investment dispute settlement proceedings: all documents (submissions by the parties, decisions of the tribunal) will be publicly available on a United Nations website which the EU will finance and all hearings will be open to the public. Interested parties (NGO's, trade unions) will be able to make submissions. This will be binding and cannot be waived by the tribunal or the parties to a dispute.

110. In December 2017, the EU announced that the negotiations between the EU and Japan on the EPA had been finalized. However, for the investment chapter, some aspects remain subject to further negotiation.

stability, public health and security fields, as well as well as in social policies such as the raising of the minimum wage.

The skepticism about ISDS is growing in various parts of the world, also in the US.

This is why the renegotiations of NAFTA, including the chapter on investment, began. Canada, Mexico and the United States held several rounds of renegotiations of the treaty. Although a handful of chapters have been finalized (e.g., competitiveness, and customs and border facilitation), the investment chapter remained in flux at the time of writing. A number of proposals have been reported in the early part of 2018, including regarding the status of ISDS, since the failure by the party complained against to effectively enforce its occupational safety and health, child labour or minimum wage technical labour standards is trade related and covered by mutually recognized labour laws.

On 6 September 2017, Belgium (strong opponent to the signature of CETA) submitted to the Court of Justice of the European Union (CJEU) a request for an opinion on the compatibility of the ICS with the European Treaties.[111]

Specifically, Belgium is requesting an opinion on the compatibility of the ICS with (1) the exclusive competence of the CJEU to provide the definitive interpretation of EU law, (2) the general principle of equality and the 'practical effect' requirement of EU law, (3) the right of access to the courts and (4) the right to an independent and impartial judiciary.

The doubt of the compatibility could be overcome also with regards to the EU external action, in the ambit of which, following the Lisbon Treaty, the linkage between global trade and social rights[112] moves on, keeping the promotion of human dignity and the respect of equality and solidarity, which cannot be scarified by the free trade.

Another limit to the fairness of this clause is due to the presence of the Horizontal social clause[113] (Article 9 TFEU), which reads: 'In defining and implementing its policies and activities, the Union shall take into account requirements linked to the promotion of a high level of employment, the guarantee of adequate social protection, the fight against social exclusion (and a high level of education, training and protection of human health).'

The CJEU's response will affect future international agreements negotiated by the European Union: if, according to the CJE, the ICS is not compatible with the EU law, in the future EU's FTAs a more social logic (and less commercial) will be adopted.

In the meantime, the best solution to avoid any negative potential effect of ISDS/ICS on social rights can be found in the possibility of restricting treaty provisions that are subject to this arbitral resolution of conflict, excluding certain policy areas, such as labour law, so that those clauses cannot be invoked in social matters.

111. https://diplomatie.belgium.be/sites/default/files/downloads/ceta_summary.pdf.
112. A. Perulli, *Sostenibilità, diritti sociali e commercio globale: la prospettiva del Trans-Atlantic Trade and Investment Partnership (TTIP)*, in *WP CSDLE 'Massimo D'Antona'.INT* - 115/2015, 10.
113. On horizontal social clause, cf. A. Perulli, Fundamental Social Rights, Market Regulation and EU External Action, in *International Journal of Comparative Labour Law and Industrial Relations*, 2014, 30, 1, 33–39.

Otherwise, all social clauses, and in general, all the commitments to labour, social rights and the right to regulation, would not have reason to be inserted into Treaties.

§6.11 SOME CONCLUDING REMARKS: FROM FREE TRADE TO FAIR TRADE, THROUGH A NEW SUSTAINABLE LEGITIMATION OF SOCIAL CLAUSES

The most recent European architecture marks an important stage in the passage from *free trade* to *fair trade,* in a perspective of strong relaunch of the *linkage* between international trade and promotion of *core labour standards.*[114] Among the innovations introduced by the Lisbon Treaty is, in fact, relevant the totally unprecedented reference to the inspirational principles of the EU's external action that mark a crucial leap forward in the logic of inter-normativity between trade policies and protection of social rights. The new Article 205 of the TFEU establishes that the action of the Union on the international scene lies on the principles, pursues the goals and is conducted complying with the general provisions of Chapter I of the Title V of the EU Treaty. The reference is in particular to the Article 21 of the Chapter I, which states that the inspiring principles of the EU's action are 'democracy, the State subject to the rule of law, the universality and indivisibility of human rights and fundamental freedoms, the respect of human dignity, the principles of equality and of solidarity and the respect of the principles of the Charter of UN and of international law'.

The introduction of these general provisions applicable to the totality of the EU's external actions, international trade included, represents one of the main systematic innovations of the Lisbon Treaty, which opens unprecedented perspectives in the regulation of the global market, not only according to principles of profit but also of democracy and respect of human rights.

Another significant innovation of the Lisbon Treaty is to be read in this perspective: it is relative to the goals of the relations 'with the rest of the world' and it states that the EU affirms and promotes its values and 'contributes' to the 'sustainable development of the Earth', to 'solidarity' and to 'fair and equal trade', as well as 'to the elimination of poverty and to the protection of human rights' (Article 3 TUE). The Lisbon Treaty represents in this sense a peculiar stage towards a renewed commitment on the part of the EU in the promotion of *core labour standards*, by easing the ILO's normative action and promoting its respect in the field of its external relations, with particular (but not exclusive) reference to the trade and common investment policies. Therefore, we need to deeply ponder on the main sense of this innovation and on the operational possibilities that it opens, with particular emphasis on the notion of *free and fair* trade.

We may groundedly argue, in this sense, that behind this formula (and behind 'sustainable development') we have an idea of market and trade that is by all means opposed to the one of neo-liberalistic free market, founded on the legitimating of *social dumping*, on the Darwinian competition between social systems and juridical orders.

114. A. Lyon-Caen, *A proposito di dumping sociale*, in *Lav. dir.*, 2011.

We have a different vision of trade: a fair trade complying with the rules, the principles of equality, solidarity and correctness within exchanges; a trade (and an economic development) that is not to be founded on competitive devaluation of social regimes, but, on the contrary to become an occasion to promote the EU's values and principles, such as that of sustainable development

As a matter of fact, it is not easy to explain the meaning of the concept of fair trade. According to a more restrictive merely economic hypothesis, fair trade alludes to an organization of international trade exchanges that may ensure an equal sharing of trade flows. The right quantity of exportations and importations for each country would then be the one guaranteeing the equilibrium of the bilateral trade balance with each partner. The issue related to equality may be utilized also to claim an equal treatment of economic actors, by reason of which Governments should grant their national enterprises the same advantages of their foreign competitors. We find in this meaning of equality the idea of a level playing field among *players* that is achievable both through the elimination of unfair advantages of foreign enterprises, and through compensational mechanisms. Also in this perspective, the idea of fair trade breaks up one of the cornerstones of social *dumping*, that is to say the principle of comparative advantages as a foundation of international trade policies. As a matter of fact, social dumping, that consists in less strict labour *standards* within exporting fields, is a possible cause of distortion of trade flows, that may be caused by a 'failure' of the government in the *enforcement* of *labour rights*: basically it is definable as an 'unfair subsidy' that legitimates the activation of the procedure to impose compensational duties, according to an interpretative line suggested in the cases of environmental dumping, where the tolerance of some countries with respect to environmental degradation (particularly typical of developing Countries) would result in a sort of subsidization for national industry.

We may formulate a more extensive interpretation of the notion of fair trade in a social perspective by increasing the value of the formulation of the Havana Charter, forefather of forthcoming (however, as reminded never constituted) International Trade Organization (ITO), whereby not only was it provided the obligation to comply with 'equal labour conditions', but, even the necessity of an institutional bridge between the ILO and the ITO, in the direction of a profitable integration between liberalization and social *standards*.

Considering all this, the idea of fair trade relaunches the above-mentioned thesis according to which social dumping may be included within subsidizations granted by the State, as an attribution of an advantage to enterprises that falls on the lower cost of the product. However, in this perspective, the usage of art. XVI of the GATT in social matters – according to a perspective put forward also by the International Metalworkers Federation and analysed by the ILO's International Office of Labour – presumes such an extensive interpretation of the concept of subsidization that it would include in itself the inertia of the State that artificially (and with active will) keeps sub-standards labour conditions.

The will to promote an external action that may be coherent with the promotion and the protection of fundamental social rights is obtained from the analysis of the trade agreements with third countries.

The same methodology used in the TTIP, CETA and EPA was followed in the ambit of *free trade agreement* with Korea and the *EU–Cariforum Economic Partnership Agreement*, which could be considered as another exemplification of the EU's approach in this matter, by referring to the respect, the promotion and the effective application of *core labour rights*, the application of the ILO's Conventions and the commitment in order that the policies of *foreign direct investment* are not encouraged by compromise-oriented reductions within the internal legislation in matter of health and security in the workplace or in the deregulation of *core labour standards*.[115]

In the same way, in the Cariforum Agreement, that is operating within the relationships among the EU and all the Countries of the Caribbean Community (CARICOM), the Preamble refers to the commitment to the respect of '*basic labour rights*', with specific reference to 'rights' and not merely *standards* or principles; further, the priorities of cooperation provide for a precise commitment in order to 'facilitate the development and the respect of internationally recognized environmental and social standards' (Article 8).

In this perspective, the *compliance* with international labour law results as incorporated in the goals of growth and of development, to the extent that – and this is the most innovative part of the Agreement – 'the behaviour of investors is directly interested. Investors must comply with the ILO's *core labour standards*' (Article 72). Article 74, relative to the maintenance in activity of social *standards*, states with even greater energy that the parties shall ensure that the '*foreign direct investments are not encouraged by relaxing the labour standards in matter of labour and health in the workplace*'. Despite the *enforcement* of this provision is entrusted to single Countries, however under the control of the ILO, this clause sends a clear message to potential foreign investors, in order for them to seriously adopt praxis of 'social responsibility', instead of recurring to rhetorical as much as inoffensive calls of ethic-social principles.

Finally, we would like to point out a new tendency regarding the promotion of the compliance of social rights: the inclusion of labour provisions is more often legitimized in terms of human rights, and also increasingly in terms of sustainable development. As a matter of fact, labour standards are included in so-called chapters on 'Trade and Sustainable Development', devoted to social and environmental goals, as we saw for TTIP, CETA and EPA.

The concept of sustainable development has allowed for a large political consensus within Europe, to support the inclusion of labour standards in trade agreements. Probably social clauses have finally found an ideal and conceptual paradigm capable of providing new legitimacy and a new impetus for their incorporation into international trade treaties. This new legitimation also benefited from the legislative action of the ILO, which has become the qualified 'reference point' for the social pillar of sustainable development, and this happened also thanks to the choice made by the ILO, and that in the end proved to be right,[116] to define the core labour standards with the 1998 Declaration. This choice has in fact allowed to identify in a more specific and clear way

115. *See* Art. 72 of the *EU–Cariforum Agreement*.
116. *See* B. Langille, Core Labour Rights – The True Story (Reply to Alston), in EJIL, 16 no. 3, 2005, p. 409.

the contents of the social clause (I mean the minimum contents that should exist in any social clause), without evidently setting aside the other conventions and therefore the variety and richness of international labour law.

Sustainable Development is, indeed, an economic theory as well as juridical and ethical. Development is often understood as a synonym for economic development or economic growth. Sustainable development builds and modifies the international approach to development which needs to be understood more broadly. In the international community development in the past half-century includes at least four related concepts: peace and security, economic development, social development and national governance that secures peace and development. Each concept is reflected in major multilateral treaties that provide a common framework for relations among nations as well as a shared set of national purposes. In particular, I would like to point out the idea that social and economic developments are closely related, not only conceptually, but also in the practices of social and economic relationships. Countries that have emphasized education, health and related aspects of social development tend to have the best economic performance. Therefore, the link between economic and social sphere is not an unnatural invention and it is not related to utopia or ideology. It is not for nothing that a fundamental Treaty on human rights, The International Covenant on Economic, Social and Cultural rights contains in itself the idea of integration between economic and social sphere.

Nowadays, the UN, with its 2030 Agenda for sustainable development pursues an integrated vision with economic, social, environmental aspects; and a specific point (number 8) is related to employment and decent work, and they provide to push on the promotion of sustained, inclusive and sustainable economic growth and full, productive employment and decent work for all. In particular point 8.8 of the agenda concerns the protection of labour rights and the promotion of safe and secure working environments for all workers, including migrant workers and those in precarious employment. So, labour standards are fully present in the conceptual framework and in the political agenda of Sustainable Development, and can constitute a new important element of theoretical and practical justification for the law systems at national,[117] international and supranational level.[118] At the same time, labour law is undoubtedly an element of

117. This is why Sustainable Development can be considered as a new paradigm for Italian Labour Law, to exit from the current crisis and to stop the deregulation process. *See* A. Perulli, Il contratto a tutele crescenti e la Naspi: un mutamento di 'paradigma' per il diritto del Lavoro? in A. Perulli, L. Fiorillo, Contratto a tutele crescenti e Naspi, Decreti legislativi 4 marzo 2015, n. 22 e n. 23, Giappichelli, Torino, 2015; A. Perulli, L'idea di diritto del lavoro, oggi, in A. Perulli (a cura di), L'idea di diritto del lavoro, oggi. In ricordo di Giorgio Ghezzi, Cedam, Padova, 2016, p. XLI; H. Arthurs, Labour Law After Labour, in G. Davidov, B. Langille (eds), *The Idea of Labour Law*, Oxford University Press, Oxford, 2011; B. Langille, Labour Law's Theory of Justice, *Ibid.*, p. 101; V. Speziale, La mutazione genetica del diritto del lavoro, in Dir. lav. mer., 2016, 2.

118. *See* T. Novitz, *The Paradigm of Sustainability in a European Social Context: Collective Participation in Protection of Future Interests?*, in IJCLLIR, 2015, 243; T. Treu, *Labour Law and Sustainable Development*, WP CSDLE 'Massimo D'Antona'.INT-130/2016.

that paradigm, capable of providing a response to coordination failures and imperfections which are inherent in the labour market and contribute to economic development and growth.[119]

It is evident that, inside the Sustainable Development paradigm, the economic matter matches with the political-institutional, juridical and ethical matter. Basically, through the paradigm of Sustainable Development, some values coming from afar are reconsidered and are today rediscovered by a non-standard economic thought. Moral concepts such as prudence, social justice, equity are thus revitalized, and a particular emphasis is placed on the use of fundamental social rights in achieving Sustainable Development.[120]

The most accomplished example of this trend is offered by the European Model of Sustainable Development, from the Amsterdam Treaty of the EU that declared that one of the objectives of the European Union is to promote economic and social progress and to achieve balanced and sustainable development, to the Lisbon Declaration in 2000, where the European Council set for the Union the strategic ambitious goal of becoming the most competitive and dynamic knowledge-based economy in the world capable of sustainable economic growth with more and better jobs and greater social cohesion.[121] Another important innovation introduced by the Treaty that can be interpreted in this context, regarding the goals of relations '*with the wider world', according to which the EU upholds and promotes its values and among other things 'contributes [...] to the sustainable development of the Earth, solidarity and [...] free and fair trade' as well as to the 'eradication of poverty and the protection of human rights'* (Article 3 TUE). In order to comply with a strategy of Sustainable economic growth, when the EU replanned the regulations on GPS (the generalized preference systems which allows favourable conditions to PVS in trade matters) in the field of its external relations, it has titled this chapter 'Sustainable and Good Governance'. In the same perspective, within the TTIP negotiations between EU and USA, they are discussing the social clause within a chapter of the Treaty dealing with Sustainable Development.[122] More generally it can be surely stated that, thanks to this paradigm, the promotion of the international labour rights has become part of a wider frame on *Trade and*

119. *See* S. Deakin, *The Contribution of Labour Law to Economic Development and Growth*, Centre for Business Research, University of Cambridge, Working Paper No. 478, March 2016.
120. *See* R. Zahn & D. Mangan, *Labour Standards and Sustainable Development: Unpicking the EU's Approach*, IJCLLIR, 2015, 233.
121. The European Commission works to ensure that EU trade policy evolves to meet the Union's overarching economic and political aims, including by enhancing coherence between trade policy and other EU external and internal policies. For example, trade policy contributes to the integrated policymaking of the 2030 Agenda for Sustainable Development by focusing not only on economic aspects, but also furthering social and environmental objectives, and contributes to the European Agenda on Migration and the European Agenda on Security (Brussels, 13.9.2017 COM (2017) 492 final Communication from the Commission to the European Parliament, the Council, the European Economic and Social Committee and the Committee of the Regions: A Balanced and Progressive Trade Policy to Harness Globalisation; White Paper on the Future of Europe, Reflections and scenarios for the EU27 by 2025, European Commission COM (2017) 2025 of 1 March 2017).
122. *See* A. Perulli, *Sustainability, Social Rights and International Trade: The TTIP*, in IJCLLIR, 2015, 473.

Sustainable Development assuming the status of 'unobjectionable norm' in EU trade agreement.[123]

Inside this complex framework, there is an important evolutionary perspective to be attentively considered. As far as now, it was the social dimension to push on the trade dimension to find acknowledgement. Today, the situation is far more balanced and it is the current trade sphere to be interested in internalizing the social concerns coming from the society, as there would be a failure in achieving any sort of growth, without taking social issues into consideration. As a matter of fact, as a Nobel prize winner has recently written, the failures of globalization must be attributed to the fact that the international economic institutions have been mainly driven by commercial and financial interests and eventually, a very much peculiar vision of the role of governments and markets has prevailed; consequently, the trade agreements have been unfair because they have favoured the advanced nations to the detriment of workers, both in advanced countries and developing countries.[124] This is demonstrated by the substantial failure of the policies - dating back to the 80s - of IMF, WB and WTO. As a matter of fact, the countries which actually followed their prescriptions did not achieve any economic development nor democracy.[125] In almost all countries involved into such policies, the effect has been a massive increase of debts versus foreign creditors, and heavy cuts of public funds to the welfare, education, health system, infrastructures.

As a consequence, if up until a recent past the matter of social clause merely involved the field of a perspective of 'resistance' to the most negative effects of the liberalization of markets, with all the possible reserves on a strategy of Western economic systems accused of 'masked protectionism', the evolution of globalization, with its failures and contradictions, allows to position the matter in a wider and ambitious perspective today: as an aspect of the dynamic interrelation between the sphere of the international market's regulation and the development of non-trade,

---

123. *See* L. Van Den Putte, J. Orbie, *EU Bilateral Trade Agreements and the Surprising Rise of Labour Provisions*, in IJCLLIR, 2015, 263. The approach of the EU to social issues in the sphere of external action consists of two main perspectives. On the one hand, it has a highly developed practice in including human rights clauses in its international agreements (including regional trade agreements) which allow for the suspension of the agreement in the event that one of the parties violates human rights or democratic principles. On the other, it deals with social matters, including labour standards, by way of cooperation, entailing where necessary financial and technical assistance. For instance, concerning the Agreement which contains a type of human/social rights clause on the model of EU agreements, we can make reference to the EU-Algeria Association Agreement, the EU-Jordan Agreement, the EU-Chile Agreement, and the EU-Syria Agreement, in which the term 'fundamental social rights' is used for the purpose of 'giving priority to such rights' or to 'recognize the responsibility to guarantee basic social rights'. In the Cotonou Agreement the parties have incorporated legally binding standards 'reaffirming their commitment to the internationally recognized core labour standards, as defined by the relevant International Labour Organization (ILO) Conventions'; *see* A. Perulli, Fundamental Social Rights, Market Regulation and EU External Action, in IJCLLIR, 2014, 41.

124. J.E. Stiglitz, *Globalization and Its Discontent Revisited. Anti-Globalization in the Era of Trump*, 2002, 2018.

125. *See* S. Sassen, *Expulsion: Brutality and Complexity in the Global Economy*, Cambridge, Mass., Harvard University Press, 2014.

social and environmental policies; more generally, in the field of possible international or even global economic policies,[126] within the range of a Sustainable Development paradigm.

Considering this, the current challenge is neither to liberalize the trade regime, nor to go back to anti-historic nationalisms, but to make the existing trade openness sustainable and compatible with the idea of social justice.

126. Cf. H. W. Arthurs, *Extraterritoriality by Other Means: How labour Law Sneaks Across Borders, Conquers Minds, and Controls Workplaces Abroad*, Comparative Research in Law & Political Economy. Research Paper No. 25/2010.

CHAPTER 7

Labor and Global Trade: A U.S. Perspective

Janice R. Bellace

§7.01 INTRODUCTION

Since the end of World War II, the United States (U.S.) has been a leader in establishing and maintaining a liberal international order. For nearly thirty years, the U.S. championed free trade, and promoted the signing of free trade agreements (FTAs), both bilateral and multilateral. The election of Donald Trump in November 2016 suddenly reversed the stance of the U.S. with regard to an international rules-based trading order. Where this may lead is not yet clear as President Trump's stance may be only temporary, or it may be merely a negotiating strategy rather than a true policy reversal.

With regard to labor rights and labor clauses in FTAs, developments reached the highest point of development in 2016 with agreement on the most ambitious FTA to date: a twelve-nation multilateral free trade agreement, the Trans-Pacific Partnership (TPP). Although the U.S. is no longer a party to the TPP (or its successor, the Comprehensive Progressive Trans-Pacific Partnership (CPTPP)), the labor chapter in the CPTPP is exactly the same. Serious questions arise from the language of the TPP's labor chapter, such as whether minimum labor standards are set or whether countries can set their own minimum standards, and whether stated labor principles that repeat those in the ILO's 1998 Declaration on Fundamental Principles and Rights at Work truly are the same and are linked to the eight core conventions. Moreover, the effectiveness of the labor standards set out in the labor chapter of the TPP/CPTPP has been called into question by a 2018 arbitration decision under an earlier U.S. free trade agreement.

§7.02 TRADE IN THE POST-WAR PERIOD

The liberal international economic order which has prevailed since 1945 was the result of the Bretton Woods agreement[1] whose immediate purpose was to rebuild the shattered economies of many countries once the war ended. The worldview the Bretton Woods agreement embodied was that peace and stability can be maintained by nations' accepting a rules-based order based on certain guiding principles, notably liberal democracy, open markets, and multilateral institutions (such as the International Monetary Fund and the World Bank).[2] Led by the U.S., forty-four Allied nations were present at the 1944 Bretton Woods conference and agreed with the premise that liberal trade and free markets contribute to global prosperity and peace.[3]

With regard to trade, the main mechanism established in the aftermath of Bretton Woods was the General Agreement on Tariffs and Trade (the GATT) which was signed by twenty-three nations in Geneva on October 30, 1947. The overall objective of the GATT was to promote international trade, with its preamble stating its purpose as the "substantial reduction of tariffs and other trade barriers and the elimination of preferences, on a reciprocal and mutually advantageous basis."[4] The GATT remained in effect until the signature by 123 nations in Marrakesh on April 14, 1994, during the Uruguay Round Agreements, which established the World Trade Organization (WTO) on January 1, 1995. The transition represented a desire of the major trading countries to increase global trade which would need an organization with greater capacity. Successful in reducing tariffs and other trade barriers,[5] the GATT was simply what its name stated: an agreement. The GATT was a multilateral agreement which embodied a series of rules, renegotiated periodically in a trade "round" without significant institutional support. In contrast, the WTO was designed to be a permanent institution with its own secretariat, overseeing trade agreements and empowered to adjudicate disputes. At the end of 2017, 164 countries belonged to the WTO and the WTO trading system applied to 98% of all global commerce. China's entry into the WTO in December 2001 was a transformational moment in the global economy, marking the beginning of a new era of globalization. China's integration into the global economy has unquestionably had a significant impact on workers in many highly developed economies.

1. The meeting took place in July 1944 in Bretton Woods, New Hampshire in the United States.
2. This view goes beyond trade, into the political arena and is a topic commented on by political science academics. The European Union is arguably the most highly developed rules-based and rules-observant part of the international economic order. Discontent with the economic impact of EU financial and economic policies has extended to dissatisfaction with other policy stances, such as on migration. The non-labour aspects of the liberal international order is beyond the scope of this paper.
3. Kurt Schuler and Mark Bernkopf, *Who Was at Bretton Woods?* Center for Financial Stability. Working Paper, July 2014. http://www.centerforfinancialstability.org/bw/Who_Was_at_Bretton_Woods.pdf (last accessed October 15, 2018).
4. For a brief explanation of the GATT and documents relating to its work, *see* https://law.duke.edu/lib/researchguides/gatt/ (last accessed October 15, 2018).
5. The rationale for the GATT was the most favoured nation clause which, when assigned by one country to another, gives the selected country privileged trading rights. The GATT aimed to assist all countries in obtaining MFN status to achieve truly open markets worldwide.

Criticism of the WTO often is directed at attributes of the international trading order that pre-dated the WTO, an order which was rules based. For instance, some critics argue that the WTO infringes national sovereignty because as the body that sets the ground rules for global trade, it reserves the right to review a country's domestic trade policies. This occurred before 1995, the only difference being that the WTO was invested with competency to adjudicate disputes by use of arbitration panels. But the principle that a country that had signed the GATT was agreeing to be subject to its rules remains in effect with the WTO.

What has changed is the desire of most countries to be members of the WTO. In the 1970s, some countries may have enacted protectionist measures to enable domestic firms to grow without being subject to the competitive pressures of foreign firms that could offer products at a lower price. By 1990, most countries were members of the WTO and protectionist measures were not permitted. Thus, if a country wished to protect certain of its industries for the purpose of preserving jobs, the WTO would decide that the protectionist measure contravened the principle of non-discrimination and was a barrier to free trade.[6] By the 1990s, highly developed countries were losing jobs to lesser developed countries which could produce certain products more cheaply in large measure because of much lower wage costs and in some cases substandard working conditions. This latter fact led many to assert that free trade was not fair trade. There was nothing in the GATT or in the WTO rules[7] that addressed labor conditions.

Proposals to link labor standards to trading privileges were raised at the first Ministerial meeting of the WTO in Singapore in December 1996. While stating that it renewed its "commitment to the observance of internationally recognized core labour standards," the WTO took the position that the "International Labour Organization (ILO) is the competent body to set and deal with these standards, and we affirm our support for its work in promoting them." [8] The WTO ministers held firmly to their conviction that that economic growth and development are fostered by increased trade and further trade liberalization and that they "contribute to the promotion of these standards."[9]

Prior to 1980, most foreign direct investment involved a large firm in a developed country investing in another country because of its markets (in order to be able to sell in that market) or its natural resources. Often the large firm directly owned and operated the facility in the host country. The main labor law issues arising from this pattern related to the conduct of foreign multinational companies in the host country. Several highly publicized incidents of plant closings by American multinational

6. WTO, *Principles of the Trading System*. https://www.wto.org/english/thewto_e/whatis_e/tif_e/fact2_e.htm (last accessed October 15, 2018).
7. Technically, the GATT is part of the WTO's rules. The GATT relates mainly to agreements on trading in goods. The WTO has other agreements relating to trade in services, to intellectual property rights, etc.
8. This statement is part of para. 4 of the Ministerial Declaration adopted on December 13, 1996, the final day of the meetings. *Singapore WTO Ministerial 1996: Ministerial Declaration, WT/MIN (96)/Dec*, December 18, 1996. http://www.wto.org/english/thewto_e/minist_e/min96_e/wtodec_e.htm (last accessed October 15, 2018).
9. *Id.* They added that they rejected "the use of labour standards for protectionist purposes."

companies (MNC) in the 1970s[10] led to a spate of guidelines aimed at restraining the behavior of MNCs.[11] In general, such guidelines directed the foreign MNC to observe the national law and practice of the host country.

But the nature of foreign direct investment has changed in the last three decades. The progressive liberalization of cross-border transactions, advances in manufacturing and information technology, and improvement in transport logistics and services have provided companies with incentives to decouple production processes and to geographically disperse parts of the production process thereby effectively applying the theory of comparative advantage to the company's own operations.[12] As a UN report observed: "[b]y relocating production processes (i.e., R&D, concept, design, manufacturing, packaging, marketing, distribution and retailing) in different countries, transnational corporations (TNCs) can take advantage of the best available human or physical resources in different countries, with a view to maintaining their competitiveness by augmenting productivity and minimizing costs."[13] Global supply or production chains (GSCs), where cost reduction strategies result in goods often being produced with intermediate inputs originating from several countries, became common in many industries with the label "global" not an exaggeration.

[A] Opposing Views on Globalized Trade

The current confusing situation in the U.S. regarding trade reflects a controversy that is not recent, but one that has simmered for a very long time and has now reached a boiling point. The controversy first broke out into the national political arena in the early 1990s with the North American Free Trade Agreement (NAFTA). Negotiations on the NAFTA began under President Ronald Reagan and were continued by President George H.W. Bush. Signing this agreement became a political issue in the 1992 U.S. presidential election.

The 1993 NAFTA agreement opened a debate in the U.S. that has never ended; namely, whether free trade with a low-wage country benefits the U.S. Supporters and opponents of NAFTA have very different answers to that question, which may result from the fact that they view the relevant question differently. Supporters of trade liberalization stress that NAFTA has benefitted both the American and the Mexican economies. Opponents emphasize that the U.S. lost jobs to Mexico and that the loss of good-paying, middle-class manufacturing jobs has served as a significant restraint on

10. In one widely publicized case, an American multinational company closed its Belgian subsidiary without complying fully with Belgian law on redundancy payments. Roger Blanpain, *The Badger Case and the OECD Guidelines for Multinational Enterprises* (Kluwer, 1977).
11. The OECD and the ILO are leading examples of such action. The text of the OECD Guidelines can be accessed at http://www.oecd.org/corporate/mne/1922428.pdf (last accessed October 15, 2018). Part I, Chapter IV covers Employment and Industrial Relations. The text of the ILO Tripartite Declaration is available at http://www.ilo.org/dyn/normlex/en/f?p=1000:62:0::NO:62:P62_LIST_ENTRIE_ID:2453910:NO (last accessed October 15, 2018).
12. For a discussion of the emergence of GSCs, *see* Gary Geriffi 7 Miguel Korzeniewicz, *Commodity Chains and Global Capitalism* (Westport, Conn. Praeger, 1994).
13. Alessandro Nicita, Victor Ognivtsev & Miho Shirotori. *Global Supply Chains: Trade and Economic Policies for Developing Countries* (Geneva, UNCTAD, 2013) p. 1.

overall American wage rates, especially for the lower 40% of the labor force. In 1992, during a nationally televised presidential campaign debate, candidate Ross Perot coined an especially memorable phrase—"that giant sucking sound from the south"—to describe the job losses in the U.S. that would ensue if NAFTA were approved. Perot said:

> If you're paying $12, $13, $14 an hour for factory workers and you can move your factory South of the border, pay a dollar an hour for labor, hire young—let's assume you've been in business for a long time and you've got a mature work force—pay a dollar an hour for your labor, have no health care—that's the most expensive single element in making a car—have no environmental controls, no pollution controls and no retirement, and you don't care about anything but making money, there will be a giant sucking sound going south.[14]

In contrast, the Governor Bill Clinton (who would win the 1992 election) promised that NAFTA would create jobs in the U.S. President George H.W. Bush (who lost the 1992 election) avoided making such a claim emphasizing instead that he favored free but fair trade.

The 1992 debate prefigured the debate that continues to the present day in the U.S. Ten years ago, Professor Alan Blinder identified the perceptions that have generated intense opposition from both the right and the left today. In 2008, he noted that Americans seemed to be losing faith in globalization because "jobs destroyed by international trade are far more salient than those it creates. And with our huge trade deficit, imports do seem ... to be destroying more jobs than exports are creating."[15] Blinder noted that economists have long recognized that trade creates both winners and losers, but pointed out that American efforts to cushion the blow of job losses for the losers have "always been embarrassingly small and weak"[16] with job retraining programs inadequate and often ineffective.

More recently, Blinder presented the causes of this polarization in a more fundamental way by noting that there are two dramatically different views on the central purpose of an economy.[17] He observed that economists say it is to benefit

14. "The 1992 Campaign; Transcript of the 2d TV Debate Between Bush, Clinton and Perot. The New York Times." October 16, 1992. https://www.nytimes.com/1992/10/16/us/the-1992-campaign-transcript-of-2d-tv-debate-between-bush-clinton-and-perot.html (last accessed October 15, 2018).
15. Alan S. Blinder, "Stop the World (and Avoid Reality)," Opinion, New York Times, January 6, 2008. https://www.nytimes.com/2008/01/06/business/06view.html?ex=1357275600&en=97dd02ebc9d475c3&ei=5124&partner=permalink&exprod=permalink (last accessed 15 October 2018).
16. *Id.* Blinder, a professor at Princeton, was vice chair of the Federal Reserve Bank during President Clinton's tenure. He was referring to the Trade Adjustment Assistance Program (TAA) established under the Trade Act of 1974, Pub.L. No. 93-618. The statute provides aid to those who lose their jobs as result of increased imports. The statute was enacted at the time when the garment industry was the first to experience large-scale job losses as garment work was offshored.
17. Alan S. Blinder, "*Why, After 200 Years, Can't Economists Sell Free Trade?*" Third Annual O. John Olcay Lecture on Ethics and Economics, May 5, 2017. Peterson Institute for International Economics. https://piie.com/system/files/documents/blinder20170525ppt.pdf (last accessed October 15, 2018).

consumers with the key goal being low consumer prices, which in turn leads to the policy position that trade must be expanded. In contrast, non-economists see the economy's purpose as benefitting producers and workers, with the key goal being good jobs, which in turn leads to the policy position that jobs must be preserved.

Blinder's comments pinpoint the essential currents in American policy debates over the past quarter-century. While some might consider that the U.S. has been relentlessly pro-free trade, the picture is more complicated. There is even a difference between the views of academic economists and company CEOs. Opponents of unrestrained free trade have lobbied to insert labor clauses into free trade agreements to level the playing field and to protect human rights. In contrast, international trade lawyers, seeking to protect their clients' flexibility of operation, have endeavored to craft statutory language that seemingly guarantees labor rights but which often lack precise meaning or enforceability.

§7.03 NAFTA AND NAALC: THE FIRST INTERNATIONAL LABOR CHAPTER

Negotiations that led to the signing of the NAFTA began in the early 1980s after President Ronald Reagan proposed a North American common market. Significantly Congress in 1984 enacted the Trade and Tariff Act[18] which gives the President "fast-track" authority to negotiate FTAs, and which removes Congress's ability to change negotiating points with the result that Congress can only approve or reject the entire FTA presented. This permitted a President who was pro-trade with the ability to move forcefully to negotiate an FTA. Negotiations on NAFTA began under President Ronald Reagan and took place against the backdrop of the Uruguay Round of trade negotiations.[19] The NAFTA negotiations were concluded and the agreement was signed by President George H.W. Bush in 1992, a presidential election year, with the ratification period running past the November election. The furor that arose over NAFTA led President Clinton (who took office in January 1993) to accede to demands that conditions regarding fair competition be promoted, especially those relating to labor and the environment. This was clearly an afterthought, for this commitment was not expressed in the main body of the agreement. Formally named the North American Agreement on Labor Cooperation (NAALC), it is often (and aptly) labelled the NAFTA "side agreement." The September 1993 agreement on NAALC cleared the way for Congressional ratification of NAFTA.

Although it was akin to an afterthought, and was not part of the trade treaty itself, the NAALC is a significant milestone as it marked the first time an international labor agreement linked to a trade treaty.

18. P.L. 98-573 approved October 30, 1984.
19. The Uruguay round lasted seven years, from 1986 to 1994, and led to the creation of the WTO.

[A] Substantive Content of the NAALC

The idea of inserting a clause relating to labor in an FTA led logically to the question of what standards or principles should be included. In 1993, there was no obviously correct answer. One could argue in favor of listing general principles, or of referring to specific ILO conventions, or listing standards with reference to national law and practice (which would then have led to the question of which country's law and practice should govern).

The NAALC had two broad goals: (1) to encourage the improvement of labor conditions in North America through cooperative activities, including the promotion of a set of eleven labor principles and (2) to provide a mechanism for mediating labor disputes. To fulfill these stated objectives, the NAALC created the Commission for Labor Cooperation (CLC), composed of a Council of cabinet-level ministers from the three NAFTA countries and a Secretariat. The NAALC also requires that each government establish a National Administrative Office (NAO) within its labor ministry. The NAOs serve as a point of contact between the domestic government agencies, the NAOs of the other NAFTA countries, and the Secretariat.

NAALC has been successful in spurring cooperation and consultation. Professor Lance Compa in assessing the labor side agreement concluded that "within its limits, it has shown itself to be a viable tool for cross-border solidarity among key actors in the trade union, human rights and allied movements."[20] Because the labor rights content of the NAALC was vague, and the stated goal limited, solidarity may have been the only way to press the claim that labor rights be observed.

Compa has observed that the NAALC did not develop a strategy for upward harmonization of labor standards, but instead emphasized effective enforcement of national law.[21] This was in line with what President Clinton had proposed during the 1992 presidential campaign; namely, that the NAFTA side agreements should require each country to enforce its own environmental and labor standards and provide forums for hearing disputes regarding lax administration or enforcement of national laws. The problem that arose on the American side was the content of national labor law which establishes rights that are narrower and apply to fewer workers than set by international labor law.

The eleven labor principles set forth in the NAALC are: (1) freedom of association and protection of the right to organize; (2) the right to bargain collectively; (3) the right to strike; (4) prohibition of forced labor; (5) labor protections for children and young persons; (6) minimum employment standards; (7) elimination of employment discrimination; (8) equal pay for men and women; (9) prevention of occupational injuries and illnesses; (10) compensation in cases of occupational injuries and illnesses; and

20. Lance Compa, "*NAFTA's Labor Side Agreement and International Labour Solidarity*," 2001. Available on the Cornell University, ILR School site: http://digitalcommons.ilr.cornell.edu/articles/175/ (last accessed October 15, 2018).

21. Professor Compa was the first head of NAFTA's Secretariat for the Commission on Labor. For an assessment of the NAALC, *see* Lance Compa, "NAFTA's Labor Side Agreement and International Labor Solidarity," in Peter Waterman & Jane Wills (eds), *Place, Space and the New Labor Internationalisms* (London: Wiley Blackwell, 2001).

(11) protection of migrant workers.[22] This was agreed in September 1993, four years before the ILO's 1998 Declaration of Fundamental Principles and Rights at Work. The NAALC labor principles include the four principles in the Declaration, and more. But, none of the NAALC's labor principles is directly linked to ILO conventions. This results from the fact that the U.S. had not ratified the relevant ILO conventions,[23] often because U.S. law fell far short of the guarantees in these conventions.[24] In view of the fact that the NAALC only requires a signatory country to enforce its own laws, it was evident from the beginning that this labor side agreement would not be capable of giving workers rights as these rights are understood in international labor law.

The NAALC itself flagged this striking omission in the first sentence under "Labor Principles" which states: "The following are guiding principles that the Parties are committed to promote, subject to each Party's domestic law, but do not establish common minimum standards for their domestic law."[25]

Following this statement, there is a list of the eleven principles, with a misleading use of the label "right." For instance, under each there is a succinct definition of the principle, with the "right to strike" defined as the "protection of the right of workers to strike in order to defend their collective interests." Many of the definitions are succinct and so vague as to render meaningless the principle. For instance, "equal pay for women and men" is defined as "equal wages for women and men by applying the principle of equal pay for equal work in the same establishment." From reading this, one cannot tell whether equal pay for work of equal value is meant as guaranteed by the relevant ILO convention,[26] or the much narrower guarantee of equal pay for work that is substantially similar. Moreover, one cannot tell whether the women and men must be working in the same physical workplace, or simply for the same company.

22. Article 49, Definitions, lists these eleven and states that "labor law" means laws and regulations that are directly related to these eleven. They are repeated in Annex 1. The text of the North American Agreement on Labor Cooperation, as agreed on September 13, 1993 can be accessed at https://www.dol.gov/ilab/reports/pdf/naalc.htm (last accessed October 15, 2018).
23. The U.S. has ratified 14 ILO conventions (11 termed "technical" conventions by the ILO, seven of which relate to seamen and shipping). It has ratified two of the eight core conventions (C. 105 Abolition of Forced Labour and C. 182, Worst Forms of Child Labour). Canada has ratified 36 conventions, included all eight of the core conventions. Mexico has ratified 79 conventions, including seven of the eight core conventions. https://www.ilo.org/dyn/normlex/en/f?p=NORMLEXPUB:11001:0::NO::: (last accessed October 15, 2018).
24. For instance, the NAALC labour principles include three related to freedom of association. These rights are covered by ILO Conventions No. 87 and 98. When NAALC was agreed, the Employers' Vice Chair at the International Labour Conference was Edward Potter, a member of the U.S. employers' delegation to the ILC, and a leading labour lawyer. Potter had earlier authored a volume that argued, with detailed references to American law, that if the U.S. ratified Conventions No. 87 and 98, American law would have to be substantially amended in order to come into compliance with its obligations. *See* Edward E. Potter, *Freedom of Association, the Right to Organize and Collective Bargaining: The Impact on U.S. Law and Practice of Ratification of ILO Conventions No. 87 & 98* (Washington, D.C., Labor Policy Association, 1984). Since in 1993 there was no proposal that American law be amended, it was known that American law with regard to these fundamental rights fell far short of what the ILO conventions require.
25. Footnote 21, *supra*. Annex 1. Labour Principles.
26. ILO Convention No. 100, Equal Remuneration (1951) guarantees women equal pay with men for work of equal value. It is one of the eight ILO core conventions that gives meaning to the principle of non-discrimination.

§7.04 LINKING LABOR RIGHTS TO BUSINESS CONDUCT IN GLOBAL TRADE

Those opposed to free trade on the grounds that it was not fair trade viewed the insertion of labor clauses in FTAs as a way of achieving fair trade especially if trading rights were premised on a country's compliance with labor standards. The 1993 NAFTA-NAALC innovation led some two years later to propose tying trade privileges to adherence to labor standards in the newly established WTO. This approach was flatly rejected at the first WTO Ministerial meeting in Singapore in December 1996. The position taken by the WTO ministers was that there was a specialized UN body that handled such matters, the International Labour Organization (ILO), and as a result the WTO should not consider them.[27]

The anti-globalization movement however did compel large companies to consider responses that would indicate business' commitment to a socially responsible conduct. The WTO's rejection of any role with regard to labor rights may have been an impetus to the ILO to make progress in its work on identifying fundamental rights. Work on identifying principles acceptable to the tripartite constituents may have been spurred by the wave of anti-globalization demonstrations at that time. The adoption in 1998 at the International Labour Conference of the ILO Declaration on Fundamental Principles and Rights at Work proved over time to be the vehicle for linking trade to workers' rights. The 1998 ILO Declaration contained a succinct statement of four fundamental principles which had been agreed to and receiving overwhelming tripartite acceptance[28] at the June 1998 International Labour Conference. The 1998 Declaration set out four rights, "the principles concerning the fundamental rights which are the subject of those Conventions," namely:

(1) freedom of association and the effective recognition of the right to collective bargaining;
(2) the elimination of all forms of forced or compulsory labor;
(3) the effective abolition of child labor; and
(4) the elimination of discrimination in respect of employment and occupation.

These four fundamental principles were linked to eight conventions.

[A] Using the 1998 Declaration Language in FTAs

Those drafting an FTA and needing language for a labor clause readily turned to the principles set out in the 1998 ILO Declaration. Similarly, the "Labour" section of the June 2000 UN Global Compact lists four principles and repeats word-for-word the

27. Singapore Ministerial Declaration Adopted on December 13, 1996 WT/MIN(96)/DEC, https://www.wto.org/english/thewto_e/minist_e/min96_e/wtodec_e.htm (last accessed October 15, 2018).
28. The Employers' Group strongly supported the 1998 Declaration. At the ILC, the Employers' Vice Chair was Edward Potter, of the United States.

language of the 1998 ILO Declaration. Drafters of labor clauses in FTAs quickly seized upon the noncontroversial four fundamental principles found in the 1998 ILO Declaration. All U.S. FTAs after 1998 have utilized them. The exact relationship between the four fundamental principles and the eight core conventions[29] was not specified in the 1998 Declaration, and subsequently the difference of opinion on the exact relationship would spark a major controversy at the ILO.[30]

[B] Human Rights: The 1998 Declaration Principles and Core Conventions

The commitment of business to respect the four fundamental rights was further solidified in June 2011 when the UN Human Rights Council unanimously endorsed the Guiding Principles for the Implementation of the UN "Protect, Respect and Remedy" Framework. This clarifies the meaning of the corporate responsibility to respect human rights. To do so, there had to be clarification of what rights businesses are supposed to respect. The Guiding Principles state that this obligation "refers to internationally recognized human rights" and list the International Bill of Human Rights and the ILO's 1998 Declaration, and in the commentary expressly state these "coupled with the principles concerning fundamental rights in the eight ILO core conventions as set out in the Declaration of Fundamental Principles and Rights at Work" set the benchmarks for assessing human rights impacts. From this, it seems evident that the UN Human Rights Council viewed the meaning of the ILO Declaration's four fundamental principles as incorporating the principles flowing from the eight core conventions.[31]

In June 2012, at the International Labour Conference, the Employers in the Conference Committee on the Application of Standards (CAS) challenged the view of the ILO's Committee of Experts that a right to strike flowed from the guarantees in Convention No. 87, Freedom of Association and the Right to Organize.[32] Regardless of their reason for so doing at that point in time, it was evident that the Employers did not want to be bound by long-established views of the ILO's Committee of Experts regarding the meaning of the guarantee of freedom of association. This was not a new

29. Convention No. 87, Freedom of Association and Protection of the Right to Organise (1948) and Convention No. 98, Right to Organise and Collective Bargaining (1948); Convention No. 29, Forced Labour (1930) and Convention No. 105 Abolition of Forced Labour (1957); Convention No. 138, Minimum Age (1973) and Convention No. 182, Worst Forms of Child Labour (1999); Convention No. 100, Equal Remuneration (1951) and Convention No. 111, Discrimination (Employment and Occupation) (1958).
30. The controversy arose over ILO Convention No. 87, Freedom of Association and the Right to Organise, and whether this guarantee includes the right to strike.
31. Janice R. Bellace, 'Human Rights at Work: The Need for Definitional Coherence in the Global Governance System,' *International Journal of Comparative Labour Law and Industrial Relations*, vol. 30, no. 2, pp. 175–198 at 184 (2014).
32. For a discussion of the specific legal issue, *see* Janice R. Bellace, "The ILO and the Right to Strike," *International Labour Review*, vol. 153 no. 1 (2014) pp. 29–69. *See also* Lee Swepston, Crisis in the ILO Supervisory System: Dispute over the Right to Strike," *International Journal of Comparative Labour Law and Industrial Relations*, vol. 29, no. 2, pp. 199–218 (2013); Claire La Hovary, "Showdown at the ILO? A Historical Perspective on the Employers' Group's 2012 Challenge to the Right to Strike," *Industrial Law Journal*, vol. 42 no. 4, pp. 338–368 (2013).

position. In 1994 in a long debate on the Committee of Experts' general survey on Freedom of Association, the Employers had taken a similar, if less vehement, stance. At the 1994 Committee on the Application of Standards' session of the annual Conference, Edward Potter, the U.S. delegate, had expressed a strong preference for a greatly simplified statement on freedom of association if it were to be included in a social clause.[33] It may be that in 1998 the Employers believed that the text of the Declaration corresponded to their view of a general statement that expressed values but was not meant to lay down specific obligations. Such a belief would be in accord with the sentiments they had expressed four years earlier, in particular their disquiet regarding any social clause that would lay down obligations that would apply in trade matters and could be enforced by sanctions.[34] Some would argue that the Employers' position accords with the pragmatic reality that it is difficult to lay down precise definitions of rights in light of the variations in national law and practice among countries of widely varying economic levels and that it is preferable to agree on a general principle and move towards greater realization of that principle.[35]

§7.05 TPP: SEEMINGLY PROCLAIMING LABOR RIGHTS

After NAFTA, the drive to globalize trade led to the negotiation of many bilateral free trade agreements, with the language of the ILO's 1998 Declaration appearing in all. Because supporters of workers' rights were often disappointed with the failure of the labor clause in FTAs to result in substantial improvement, attention was paid to the exact wording of the labor clause and on the process for making complaints.[36] In the last decade, the U.S. government pushed for the most ambitious FTA yet, one with the EU and one with countries bordering the Pacific Ocean.

After a decade of negotiations, the governments of twelve nations signed the TPP a free trade agreement (FTA) on February 4, 2016. It was expected that the FTA would take effect once all twelve countries ratified the agreement. In line with his public opposition to free trade agreements, U.S. President Donald Trump announced on

33. Philip G. Alston & James Heenan, "Shrinking the International Labor Code: An Unintended Consequence of the 1998 ILO Declaration of Fundamental Principles and Rights at Work?," 36 *New York University Journal of International Law and Politics*, pp. 221–264 (2004) at 249 note 82. https://its.law.nyu.edu/faculty/profiles/representiveFiles/Alston%20-ShrinkingtheIntlLaborCode_08C3C460-B110-9BE3-1919086FF6C3D233.pdf.
34. ILO. Third Item on the Agenda: Information and Reports on the Application of Conventions and Recommendations. Report of the Committee on the Application of Standards, International Labour Conference, 81st Session, Geneva, 1994. At p. 25/69, para. 255. [The report is Document 25 in the Provisional Record. Paras. 115–148 comprise the chapter of the CAS report on the right to strike.] http://www.ilo.org/public/libdoc/ilo/P/09616/09616%281994-81%29.pdf.
35. Sean Cooney, 'Testing Times for the ILO: Institutional Reform for the New International Political Economy,' *Comparative Labor Law & Policy Journal*, vol. 20 no. 3 (1999) pp. 365–399.
36. For a review of these FTAs, *see* Jeffrey S. Vogt, 'The Evolution of Labor Rights and Trade—A Transatlantic Comparison and Lessons for the Transatlantic Trade and Investment Partnership,' *Journal of International Economic Law*, vol. 18, no. 4, December 1, 2015, pp. 827–860, https://doi.org/10.1093/jiel/jgv046 (last accessed October 15, 2018). Vogt believes that a high point was reached with the U.S.-Jordan free trade agreement, signed in October 2000 and that subsequent FTAs are not as ambitious. *Id.* at 832.

January 23, 2017 that the U.S. would withdraw from the TPP.[37] Since the U.S. had been the strongest proponent of the TPP and because it has the largest GDP of any of the TPP countries, its withdrawal threw the future of the TPP into question. Other TPP Member States, however, were loath to walk away from an agreement that took years to negotiate and which promised significant benefits to some countries.[38] In November 2017, during the Asia-Pacific Economic Cooperation (APEC) summit, the other eleven members agreed to move forward with the "Comprehensive and Progressive Agreement for Trans-Pacific Partnership" or CPTPP. On March 8, 2018, eleven nations[39] signed the CPTPP, creating a market of nearly 500 million people. The text of the CPTPP effectively is almost exactly the same as the TPP.[40] Chapter 19, the labor chapter, is exactly the same.

With the TPP generating great controversy in 2015, the Obama Administration stepped up its efforts to secure enough support in Congress to gain Congressional approval of the agreement. The Obama Administration viewed the TPP as more important than its impact on the twelve signatory countries because it believed that the TPP would serve as the template for future trade pacts. As U.S. Trade Representative Michael Froman repeatedly said, the TPP "will set the rules of the road."[41] Responding to critics, Froman stated in speeches that the TPP "raises labor and environmental standards around the world to the highest level ever, and these are fully enforceable standards."

Froman may have been technically correct in saying that the TPP has the highest level labor standards ever in an American FTA, but that is not the same as its being a "high standard" clause. Moreover, the assertion that it is fully enforceable is highly dubious as crucial rights are not only not defined but also the TPP expressly severs the link to international instruments defining these rights. It is difficult to argue that the TPP's labor clause has real meaning because it is impossible to identify definitions of these rights on which the twelve signatory nations agreed.

Chapter 19 sets forth the rights to be observed in a familiar way as it tracks the language of the ILO's 1998 Declaration, but there is an intriguing variation on the articulation of these four principles. In Chapter 19.3 it states:

> Each Party shall adopt and maintain in its statutes and regulations, and practices thereunder, the following rights as stated in the ILO Declaration: (a) freedom of association and the effective recognition of the right to collective bargaining; (b)

37. "Withdrawal of the United States From the Trans-Pacific Partnership Negotiations and Agreement." Federal Register. January 25, 2017. https://www.federalregister.gov/documents/2017/01/25/2017-01845/withdrawal-of-the-united-states-from-the-trans--pacific-partnership-negotiations-and-agreement (last accessed October 15, 2018).
38. Several of the countries already had bilateral FTAs with others among the twelve, but countries such as Vietnam did not and were predicted to benefit greatly.
39. Australia, Brunei, Canada, Chile, Japan, Malaysia, Mexico, New Zealand, Peru, Singapore, and Vietnam.
40. Less than twenty-five provisions were changed, half of which related to intellectual property. None of the changes related to labour.
41. This phrase was used consistently by the office of the U.S. Trade Representative on its website. *See*, e.g., https://ustr.gov/sites/default/files/TPP-Strategic-Importance-of-TPP-Fact-Sheet.pdf [July 29, 2016] (last accessed October 15, 2018).

the elimination of all forms of forced or compulsory labor; (c) the effective abolition of child labor and, for the purposes of this Agreement, a prohibition on the worst forms of child labor; and (d) the elimination of discrimination in respect of employment and occupation.

It is curious that the recital of the four principles is almost word-for-word the same as the recital in the Declaration itself, but with regard to child labor, it adds that "for the purposes of this Agreement" there is a prohibition on the worst forms of child labor. For those familiar with the ILO's four fundamental principles, it is clear that the meaning of child labor is set forth in ILO Conventions No. 138 and 182. A question arises about what was the reason for inserting the title of Convention No. 182 into the TPP's labor clause. Conceivably this was done simply to highlight that particular convention (which the U.S. has ratified), but there is an implication that the prohibition is limited to the worst forms of child labor and that the detailed minimum age convention, No. 138, Minimum Age for Entry into Employment, does not govern the notion of what is child labor. This is especially troubling because much of regular global trade involves manufactured goods such as garments, shoes, toys and electronic goods, often produced in Southeast Asia where wages are very low and where children are most likely to be employed in factories and workshops. The detailed provisions of Convention No. 138 regulate child labor in that type of work, not Convention No. 182.

[A] Severing the Link Between the Core Conventions and the Fundamental Principles

Without precise, agreed-upon definitions of what the standards in the labor chapter of the TPP/CPTPP mean, it will be difficult to monitor compliance. In light of the 2012 controversy at the ILO over the critical question of what ILO fundamental rights mean, it is startling to find buried in the TPP's labor clause, in footnote 3 of Chapter 19, the statement that "[t]he obligations set out in Article 19.3 (Labour Rights), as they relate to the ILO, refer only to the ILO Declaration." This means the four principles found in the ILO's 1998 Declaration have been severed from the eight core conventions. Thus, rather than linking the core conventions to the four principles as many believe the 1998 ILO Declaration does, a view with which the 2011 UN Human Rights Council's Guiding Principles on Business and Human Rights agrees, the TPP's Article 19.3 severs the link.

Without being moored to specific meanings, it appears that terms such as "freedom of association" in the TPP/CPTPP mean what any signatory nation thinks it means. This may explain the curious rephrasing of the four rights in labor clause, Chapter 19. As noted above, in the recital of child labor, there was added the phrase that the worst forms of child labor are not permitted. Now that the prohibition on "child labor" in Chapter 19 is delinked from the core conventions mentioned in the 1998 Declaration, we only know from the text itself that children under 18 should not be permitted to engage in work dangerous to their physical or moral being. We do not know at what age they are permitted to work in a factory (which is stipulated in ILO Convention No. 138).

[B] Not Permitting Existing Floors to Go Lower but Setting No Floor

Even more vague is the section on safety and health, Chapter 19.3.2 wherein it states: "Each Party shall adopt and maintain statutes and regulations, and practices thereunder, governing acceptable conditions of work with respect to minimum wages, hours of work, and occupational safety and health." That this section might have any useful meaning is undercut by footnote 5 in Chapter 19 which states: "For greater certainty, this obligation relates to the establishment by a Party in its statutes, regulations and practices thereunder, of acceptable conditions of work as determined by that Party." In essence then, "the highest standard labor clause" as proclaimed by the U.S. Trade Representative in 2016 takes the position that acceptable conditions of work are determined by each country and there is no obligation to meet any agreed upon minimum. As long as a country has not set higher standards for work conditions, it is difficult to see how any workers in that country who are aggrieved by unsafe and sweatshop conditions of work can complain under the TPP/CPTPP.

Once the text of Chapter 19 is read closely, and in particular, the footnotes are read, one is unsure what the legal meaning of the labor chapter in the TPP/CPTPP is, but there is a basis for doubting U.S. Trade Representative Froman's claim that the TPP "raises labor and environmental standards around the world to the highest level ever, and these are fully enforceable standards."

[C] The Forbidding Hurdle: Proving Violations

The enforceability of the labor rights in Chapter 19 is further weakened by a provision that appears in footnote 4 of Chapter 19 which states: "To establish a violation of an obligation under Article 19.3.1 (Labour Rights) or Article 19.3.2, a Party must demonstrate that the other Party has failed to adopt or maintain a statute, regulation or practice in a manner affecting trade or investment between the Parties." The phrase "in a manner affecting trade or investment between the Parties" had been used in other U.S. FTAs but at the time the TPP was agreed, no case under a U.S. FTA had ever gone to arbitration and as such, its meaning was unknown.

In discussing labor clauses and FTAs, most of the attention is on the labor rights set forth in the FTA. In considering whether violations of these rights can be legally challenged, the key issue is what needs to be proved before a violation is found. Unlike the FTAs of the European Union, U.S. FTAs typically have included a clause providing a forum whereby alleged violations can be challenged and remedies granted. Usually the final step is arbitration, albeit a procedure which occurs after a long process of consultation between governments over alleged violations, and after the government in question has been given time to make changes and/or to ratchet up enforcement of its laws. Since 1993, only one case under a U.S. FTA has ever reached the point where arbitration was invoked. The arbitral panel's decision was handed down nine years after the initial complaint was filed by the American central labor federation, the AFL-CIO, and nine Guatemalan unions, and nearly six years after the arbitration process was initiated by the U.S. Trade Representative.

On June 14, 2017 the first case raising the issue of a violation of a labor clause in a U.S. free trade agreement was decided by an arbitral panel in a case against Guatemala.[42] This arbitration arose under the Dominican Republic–Central America–United States Free Trade Agreement (CAFTA-DR). The key provision was Article 16.2.1(a) which states:

> A Party shall not fail to effectively enforce its labor laws, through a sustained or recurring course of action or inaction, in a manner affecting trade between the Parties, after the date of entry into force of this Agreement.

Despite severe infringements of workers' rights, well documented in complaints brought to the ILO's Committee on Freedom of Association, and noted in Observations of the ILO's Committee of Experts, and the failure of the government of Guatemala to effectively enforce or remedy these violations, the arbitral panel found that the complainants had not met the burden of proof imposed by Article 16. The arbitral panel did hold that sustained and recurring violations of workers' rights had been shown. But the panel found that the American and the Guatemalan unions had not shown cause-and-effect between these severe violations and an effect on trade: that is, the U.S. had to show that the failure to enforce labor laws affected conditions of competition by creating a competitive advantage for the enterprises in Guatemala. The panel, therefore, concluded that the U.S. had not proven that Guatemala failed to conform to its obligations under Article 16.2.1(a) of the CAFTA-DR.

This ruling was exceptionally discouraging for those who seek to utilize labor clauses in FTAs to improve labor standards. In a well-documented case of egregious labor rights violations and a showing of intransigence on the part of the government to enforce or remedy violations, it was held that the complainants were entitled to no relief because they could not show that these violations created a competitive advantage for businesses in Guatemala. The arbitral panel held this despite the fact that many believe that if employers suppress unions and collective activity, they will enjoy an advantage. With workers being unable to join together and to bargain for better terms and conditions of employment let alone strike, wages and operational costs overall will be restrained. This in turn will likely result in the employers/vendors having a cost advantage when negotiating prices with foreign companies for the supply of manufactured goods. In the case of Guatemala, the use of extreme violence, including the murder of union officials, conceivably dampened workers' enthusiasm for unions such that some probably never even supported let alone attempted to organize a union.

The arbitral panel's decision indicates that somehow the complainants must prove this, but there is no indication of how this can be done or whether it is even

42. Dominican Republic—Central America—United States Free Trade Agreement, Arbitral Panel established pursuant to Chapter Twenty. In the Matter of Guatemala—Issues Relating to the Obligations Under Art. 16.2.1(a) of the CAFTA-DR. Final Report of the Panel, June 14, 2017. Report available on the website of the U.S. Trade Representative in English and Spanish. https://www.trade.gov/industry/tas/Guatemala%20%20%E2%80%93%20Obligations%20Under%20Article%2016-2-1(a)%20of%20the%20CAFTA-DR%20%20June%2014%202017.pdf (last accessed October 15, 2018).

possible to do so.[43] From the arbitral panel's decision in the Guatemala case, it would appear that footnote 4 in Chapter 19 of the TPP/CPTPP (which uses the same exact language) will make it extremely difficult to establish a violation of rights that have been stated in the main text of Chapter 19.

[D] Granting Violators of Labor Rights the Same Trading Rights

One aspect of the TPP that must be considered now that the CPTPP is finalized is the status of the Consistency Plans. During the negotiating phase of the TPP, it was evident that certain countries fell far short of observing the fundamental principles listed in Chapter 19. To stave off criticism from unions and NGO that these countries would be permitted to benefit from this FTA, the Obama Administration devised a new approach, labeled a "consistency plan," whereby the U.S. stipulated certain actions the targeted country must take before the country would benefit from the tariff reductions in the TPP. This approach is highly unusual for a multistate FTA in that it appeared in a side agreement between the U.S. and the country concerned as a bilateral commitment. There are three separate consistency plans, tailored to circumstances in the given country, namely, (1) Vietnam, (2) Malaysia and (3) Brunei.

These plans detail changes that are to be made in the labor laws and institutions of each country so that they come into conformity with the labor standards of the TPP.[44] The U.S. is no longer part of the TPP, but no other country has indicated that it is willing to assume the U.S. role in these bilateral Consistency Plans. It appears that this means that three countries which have demonstrably poor records will still have the benefits of free trade without being monitored as to their progress on making changes in line with what was stipulated in the Consistency Plan. Some may hope that these countries' integration into free markets will lead to improvements in labor standards but that remains to be seen.[45]

If a country, such as Canada or Australia, does step forward to take the place of the U.S. in these Consistency Plans, issues will remain. As noted above, the complainant country has the burden of proof that violations have occurred and in manner affecting trade. Labor clauses in FTAs assume the signatories' willingness to guarantee the stipulated rights and to enforce them. Moreover, the enforcement provisions of a labor clause assume that one country is willing and able to monitor labor rights in

43. Eric Gottwald, Jeffrey Vogt & Lance Compa. *Wrong Turn for Workers' Rights: The US–Guatemala CAFTA Labor Arbitration Ruling—And What to Do About It* (Washington, D.C., International Labor Rights Forum, April 12, 2018). https://laborrights.org/publications/wrong-turn-workers%E2%80%99-rights-us-guatemala-cafta-labor-arbitration-ruling-%E2%80%93-and-what-do (last accessed October 15, 2018).
44. Cathleen Cimino-Issacs, "Labor Standards in the TPP," in Cathleen Cimino-Isaacs & Jeffrey J. Schott, eds. *Trans-Pacific Partnership: An Assessment* (Washington D.C., Peterson Institute for International Economics, July 2016). pp. 261–297. https://piie.com/publications/chapters_preview/7137/15iie7137.pdf (last accessed 15 October 2018).
45. The case of Vietnam is particularly interesting in this regard. For a discussion, *see* Tran Thi Kieu & Richard A. Bales, 'On the Precipice: Prospects for Free Labor Unions in Vietnam,' *San Diego International Law Journal*, vol. 19 no. 1 (2017) pp. 71–93.

another country, and to enforce the labor provisions of the FTA if labor rights are violated in that other country. Both assumptions can be questioned.

[E] Erecting a System Whereby One Country Monitors Labor Rights in Another Country

In November 2014, in studying the American FTAs then in effect, the U.S. General Accounting Office (U.S. GAO) identified challenges to worker rights and pointedly noted "weaknesses in the Office of the U.S. Trade Representative's and DOL's monitoring and enforcement of FTA labor provisions' which even with some improvements between 2009 and 2014 still lacked a 'strategic approach' and were 'inconsistent with labor provisions in the FTAs."[46] This evaluation was made during the Obama Administration. The situation is unlikely to have improved under President Trump.

There is ample evidence that labor rights continue to be violated in countries that have entered into bilateral trade agreements with the U.S. The resources for bolstering domestic enforcement of labor laws, investigating violations of trade pact labor provisions, and adjudicating complaints are often lacking. In some countries, ratifying the ILO's core conventions seems to have been the price to be paid to gain trading rights. Cambodia is one example where preferential textile trading rights were the goal. There is little indication that the Cambodian government in 2001 was truly committed to reforming its industrial relations and labor law system in view of the current adversarial and sometimes violent labor situation in Cambodia which is indicative of continuing labor struggles as workers seek to gain recognition of their rights.

More troubling is the uneven pattern of U.S. activity in supporting labor rights in other countries, in part due to the priorities of different administrations (governments) and in part due to the perception of the severity of the violation. The International Labor Affairs Bureau (ILAB) of the U.S. Department of Labor is tasked with providing technical assistance to other countries to assist them in improving labor standards and to monitor and regulate workplaces. A cursory glance at the funding of ILAB since 1990, a period when there has been a great increase in the number of countries under FTAs that need to be monitored and assisted, reveals an erratic funding pattern indicative of lack of sustained political commitment on the part of the U.S. to undertake its responsibilities under the labor clauses of FTAs.[47] The cost of hiring, training, deploying and retaining staff sufficiently knowledgeable about international labor standards, industrial relations, and conditions in lesser developed countries to work to assist those countries in improving labor standards is substantial. One must question why the government of a country would, on its own, seek to do this, especially when

46. U.S. Government Accountability Office (GAO). *Free Trade Agreements: U.S. Partners Are Addressing Labor Commitments, But More Monitoring and Enforcement Are Needed.* GAO-15-160, November 2014. p. 1. http://www.gao.gov/assets/670/666787.pdf [July 29, 2016] (last accessed October 15, 2018).

47. Callahan, David and Christina Vasile, *A Voice for Workers: Expanding U.S. Capacity to Promote International Labor Standards and Enforce Trade Agreements* (New York, Demos, 2009). http://www.demos.org/publication/voice-workers-expanding-us-capacity-promote-internatio nal-labor-standards-and-enforce-tr [July 29, 2016] (last accessed 15 October 2018).

it is duplicating work already being done by the ILO and when easy alternatives, such as contributing to a special ILO fund to permit it to intensify its efforts in certain countries, are available.

In the U.S., those who opposed the TPP did not focus on the device of consistency plans, and thus there was no critical comment about what such an approach implies. The innovation of consistency plans in FTAs for those countries failing to comply with the four fundamental rights carries its own problems. The main problem is the approach itself, whereby one country goes into another country to assist it in applying international labor standards, an approach that is somewhat redolent of a colonial power telling its colony how to have better administration. There is a danger that the more advanced country providing technical assistance will utilize the meanings attached to specific international standards as generally understood in its own country, not necessarily the same as those understood by the global system. For the U.S., this becomes particularly problematic with regard to freedom of association where the U.S. not only has not ratified Conventions No. 87 and 98, but where current law falls very short of assuring the rights guaranteed by those conventions. With regard to the TPP, particularly anomalous was the fact that U.S. has ratified only two of the eight core conventions, whereas Malaysia and Vietnam each have ratified five of the eight ILO core conventions, and are subject to oversight by the ILO supervisory bodies.

Other issues arise with this approach, such as which international labor standards the richer country focuses on. For instance, the U.S. has expended significant effort to reduce child labor in the countries with which it trades but has made much less effort to bolster freedom of association and collective bargaining. This may result from the individual rights perspective of the U.S., or simply from the realization that encouraging the formation of unions and the development of collective bargaining might be controversial at home. But it is perplexing that a country can proceed to assist another country with implementing international labor standards without fully committing to do so at home.

§7.06 CONCLUSION: REAL OR ILLUSORY PROGRESS?

It is twenty-five years since an international labor agreement which listed labor principles first was linked to a trade treaty. Since then the proponents of labor and human rights have sought in various forums to have labor rights for workers in the global supply chain guaranteed. Many labor rights activists have focused on the link between labor rights and trading privileges. In part this arose because many believed it manifestly unfair to permit free trade when fair trade was not required. But the focus also arose from the frustration of many activists that the guidelines of international organizations had no effective enforcement mechanism. In contrast, the sanction of a country's being cut off from the benefits of free trade was seen as a very strong incentive to a government to respect and protect labor rights. The severity of the sanction, however, seems to have caused business to endeavor to craft trade agreements that utilize the language of fundamental principles and rights at work but which in reality have no moorings. There is no specific meaning attached to phrases such as "equal pay" or "child labor" or "freedom of association." Moreover, anticipating that some egregious violation of labor rights might be evident despite a lack of specific definitions, business and governments have imposed an extremely heavy, almost overwhelming, burden of proof whereby the complainant must prove that the violation occurred "in a manner affecting trade or investment between the Parties."

At the present time, the U.S. appears to be retreating from its pro-free trade stance. This is likely to be a temporary phase, if only because there is a limit to a President's term of office. It may also be more of a mirage than reality, as President Trump has expressed a willingness to trade with other countries, especially through bilateral FTAs, if he believes the U.S. will benefit. For instance, the renegotiated NAFTA stipulates a much higher minimum wage for manufacturing workers than workers in Mexico currently received, such that jobs may move back to the U.S. or Canada. More importantly, American business depends on global markets and global supply chains to function and at some point it will lobby strongly to resume expanded trade. In addition foreign policy concerns may prompt the U.S. to rejoin the TPP if only to provide a counterweight to China's role in Asia. However, even if the political climate changes and reverts to what it was in 2016, it must be seriously questioned whether the American approach to labor clauses in FTAs provides a model for the realization of worker rights. Approaches that link the labor clauses to ILO conventions defining the fundamental rights and which create an international forum for the resolution of labor rights disputes are needed.

CHAPTER 8

Transnational Collective Agreements

Fausta Guarriello

§8.01 INTRODUCTION

The topic of the Transnational Collective Agreements (TCAs) is one of the most challenging issues for labour law because of its transnational dimension, the absence of a legal framework of reference, both at the national and supranational (regional and international) level. Mentioned as 'unidentified object',[1] it has fluid contours not yet well defined. Its appearance, exactly thirty years ago (1988 is the first transnational agreement of the French group BSN-Danone), gave rise to a movement of transnational agreements that has strengthened especially in the years 2000, until reaching the significant amount of more than 300 agreements, concerning about 10 million workers worldwide.[2] This is obviously a marginal figure compared to the pervasive capacity assumed by economic globalization and the occupational dimension of multinational companies, which are its main actors. However, it appears significant of a constantly rising trend, which requires (and deserves) great attention from the labour lawyers, whose studies are still predominantly anchored to the national dimension.

As other topics discussed within this Congress, it is a new and frontier theme, at the crossroads between different disciplinary paths (sociology, industrial relations, managerial sciences, international law), which requires interdisciplinary dialogue and a variety of analysis tools, as well as the support of empirical investigations that, in addition to the formal legal data, reveal both the complexity of the negotiation

1. Moreau M.A. (2017), *La spécificité des accords mondiaux d'entreprise en 2017: originalité, nature, fonctions*, Étude réalisée pour le Bureau de l'OIT pour la France, Text available on the site http://www.ilo.org/wcmsp5/groups/public/---europe/---ro-geneva/---ilo-paris/documents/publication/wcms_614879.pdf.
2. Data ETUC, 2016, according to the database of the European Commission and ILO, updated after 2015 with different sources: *see* U. Rehfeldt, 2018, who reports the figure of 330 TCAs (in April 2018), over 90% of which are signed by European multinational companies.

experiences realized and being implemented, and the reference context with strategies of the Parties. At the intersection of growing internationalization and deterritorialization of companies, outsourcing processes, organizational changes allowed by trade liberalization and information technologies, costs competition, innovation and quality of products and processes, communication strategies and customer satisfaction, respect for fundamental human rights, including labour rights, transnational collective bargaining tries to tackle issues that arise in the transnational dimension, in a global space that goes beyond the borders of national law, inventing solutions on a voluntary basis.

These are experimental forms of regulation, of a private nature but which for some traits rest on public tools. The growing hybridization between collective private and public regulatory forms, which are source of inspiration, institutional support mechanisms, base content of the agreements, support to effectiveness, is one of the main features of the current development of TCAs. The contamination between tools from different sources, mostly soft law, and their adaptation to the specific regulatory needs of the individual agreements, appears to be the result of settling experiences, learning processes and searching for more reliable mechanisms to ensure effectiveness, as well as of growing attention to the socially responsible behaviour of companies operating on a global scale, through the improvement of the voluntary mechanisms of CSR and provision of dispute settlement mechanisms that tend to raise the rate of compliance. The French law 2017 goes in this direction, providing for the responsibility of companies towards the damages caused by their violation of human rights and environmental protection occurred outside the territory of the home State. The law requires the parent company or the contractor a 'duty of supervision' on the activities of the subsidiaries, as well as of the subcontracting and supply companies, by taking care of a supervisory plan on foreseeable risks and 'due diligence' behaviour. One can consider these devices as an indirect form of enforceability of transnational framework agreements[3] that include negotiating obligations to respect fundamental labour rights both in the subsidiaries of the company, and in global supply chains (in fact about 70% of TCAs include in its scope at least the main suppliers and subcontractors).[4]

§8.02 EVOLUTION AND ACTUAL PRACTICE OF TCAs

The dynamic evolution of Transnational Company Agreements (TCAs), concluded between the management of a multinational company and one or more entities

3. Daugareilh I. (ed.) (2017), *La responsabilité sociale de l'entreprise, vecteur d'un droit de la mondialisation?*, Bruxelles: Bruylant; M.A. Moreau, 2017.
4. Hadwiger F. (2015), *Accordi quadro globali (GFA): Gli strumenti per garantire il Lavoro dignitoso nelle Catene globali di fornitura?*, Department of Social Sciences, University of Hamburg, pp. 1–14; Hadwiger F. (2018), *Contracting International Employee Participation-Global Framework Agreements*, Cham: Springer International Publishing AG; Marassi S. (2018), *Transnational Company Agreements and Management of Global Supply Chain*, Paper presented to the ISLSSL XXII Congress Turin; Murgo M. (2018), *Global Supply Chains and Labour law: What Rule for Union?*, Paper presented to the ISLSSL XXII Congress Turin; Friedrich T.S., Lopes De Oliveira F., De Oliveira Neto A.E. (2018), *Global Supply Chains, Transnational Law and Workers*, Paper presented to the ISLSSL XXII Congress Turin.

representing the workers – primarily sectoral federations, European or international, but also European Works Councils and/or one or more national trade unions – has increased and become more widespread since the year 2000. Most TCAs concern multinational companies headquartered in Europe (mainly in Germany and France), while fewer agreements are signed by companies coming from outside: USA, Canada, Brazil, Russia, South Africa, Malaysia, Indonesia, Australia, New Zealand and Japan.

These are voluntary agreements, entered into without the benefit of a binding legal framework, either European or international, in the absence of clear provisions defining the rules by which they are to be implemented (i.e., which subjects are legitimately entitled to sign them, the mandate, the form, the effectiveness of the agreement itself, as well as the tools by which their implementation is to be monitored and overseen, the provisions for dispute resolution in the absence of a relevant legal framework and also of national regulations governing the domestic effects of agreements negotiated at a transnational level). In other words, agreements like these are operating in a legal void, in which the only binding power lies in the level of obligation that the negotiating Parties decide to give to the commitments they sign up for in the agreement.

In the field of collective labour relations this legal vacuum does not prevent the social partners from creating their own legal system, according to the theory elaborated by Santi Romano of the plurality of legal systems,[5] adopted by Gino Giugni through the notion of 'inter-union order' based on the principle of collective autonomy.[6] With the collective agreement the social partners create their own rules, tools, procedures, joint institutions, through which they govern the industrial relations, also providing remedial mechanisms for the infringement of the agreement.

In fact the situation of legal uncertainty in which this kind of agreement develops should not be overestimated: these agreements possess the legal effectiveness of a contract which, both in the common law tradition and in civil law legal orders, has the full force of law between the Parties.[7] Actually, it is the Parties themselves that define the scope of application, the rights and obligations of each Party, duration and renewal terms, procedures for monitoring and supervising implementation. These are procedural rules that are typical of the compulsory part of a collective labour agreement, the purpose of which is to establish jointly the rules and procedures that the Parties agree to abide by during the negotiation and the implementation of the transnational agreement.

---

5. Romano S. (1918), *L'ordinamento giuridico*, Firenze: Sansoni.
6. Giugni G. (1960), *Introduzione allo studio dell'autonomia collettiva*, Milano: Giuffrè.
7. Van Hoeck A. (2017), *Private International Law and Dispute Resolution*, in SindNova, Fondazione Di Vittorio, Ires France, Fundaciòn 1° de Mayo, *Implementation of Transnational Agreements in Multinational Companies*, Euride Study Report, September, pp. 11–14; Van Hoeck A. (2016), *Finding a legal framework for transnational collective agreements through private international law*, Amsterdam Law School Legal Studies Research Paper, n. 2016-12; Scarponi S. (2018), *Searching for Effectiveness in Transnational Corporate Agreements: Monitoring and Sanctions Procedures*, in Guarriello F., Stanzani C. (eds), Trade Unions and collective bargaining in multinationals, Milano: Franco Angeli, pp. 96–111.

At this current stage in the evolution of transnational negotiations (more than 300 Transnational Company Agreements have been concluded), what is especially interesting is the attention devoted to their actual implementation, which until now had always been the Achilles' heel of these procedures.[8] The rules on transparency and providing information on the content of the agreements to all corporate subsidiaries and local trade unions are being strengthened, especially in terms of: joint implementation monitoring, bottom-up procedures to handle complaints, joint training exercises, mechanisms providing for periodical reporting and inspections in local subsidiaries.

Furthermore, there is a marked tendency to include in the transnational agreement's scope of application the entire supply chain and subcontractors used by the multinational enterprise, as well as laying down sanctioning mechanisms for infringements by third-party companies in fulfilling their contractual obligations: this highlights the procedural and institutional dimension of these agreements, even suggesting that the intention may be to establish a core system of transnational industrial relations.

There is a considerable variety of sources which, albeit indirectly, have contributed to the shaping of this new system. First of all, Directive no. 38/2009 on European Works Councils (EWCs), which updated Directive no. 45/1994 establishing the EWCs and strengthened the rights to information and consultation of workers' representatives in transnational corporations, and acted as the driving force for collective bargaining in agreements with multinationals, as well as promoting the voluntary extension of workers' representation to non-European subsidiaries, through the establishment of Global Works Councils. The existence of the EWCs in the European Union (EU) and the practice of regular periodical exchanges and social dialogue between the corporate management and the EWCs have favoured the development of bargaining practices *praeter legem* – that are not regulated by law – especially in multinationals under European control and management, which account for the vast majority of companies that have concluded Transnational Company Agreements.

The EU legal obligation to negotiate the establishment, composition and attributions of the EWC constituted the first nucleus of a transnational company negotiation, which contributed to the structuring of actors at this level. Nevertheless, this mark of origin has raised the issue of who is entitled to negotiate and sign TCAs on the workers' side. This is still an open question, due to diversified national systems, which attribute the power to negotiate company agreements either to representative bodies within the company, as works councils, or to union representatives. The transnational projection of the characteristics of the different national systems, already highlighted in the different mechanisms of appointment of national representatives within the EWC, is shown by the prevalence of TCAs signed by European (or worldwide) Works Councils in multinational companies of German origin, by unions in French companies.[9] The

8. I. Daugareilh, 2017.
9. Rehfeldt U. (2018), *A Mapping of the Transnational Company Agreements: Inventory and Dynamic*, in Guarriello F., Stanzani C. (eds), Trade Unions and collective bargaining in multinationals, Milano: Franco Angeli, pp. 46–59.

question deals with the different notion of company agreement, as the result of participatory dynamics within the company (e.g., information and consultation) or as a tool for the composition of conflicting interests.

In general, the concentration of a large number of TCAs in European companies is considered the result of a positive climate of social dialogue established in the parent company,[10] as well as the role that the national system of industrial relations and the European institutional framework recognize to the social dialogue at company level.[11] The situation is completely different for non-European multinationals where it rests totally on power relations[12]: often in an openly anti-union atmosphere, the agreement is the result of lengthy negotiations aimed at putting an end to mobilization campaigns and judicial strategies to denounce the company's infringements of fundamental principles within national borders or in third countries.

Second, among the international sources underpinning Transnational Company Agreements, we need to mention the following: the OECD Guidelines on Multinational Enterprises (1976), recently revised and strengthened especially in terms of States' obligations to supervise the activities of multinational enterprises; the ILO Tripartite Declaration on Multinationals (1977), revised and updated in 2017 in order to include the concept of due diligence in contractual relations with third companies, the promotion of the Decent Work Agenda, and the respect of human rights throughout global supply chains; the 2000 Global Compact and the 2011 United Nations Guiding Principles on Business and Human Rights. Although these are all instruments of non-binding soft law, these sources have promoted the development of a culture of social dialogue. They have also encouraged multinationals to endorse conventions on fundamental rights, including through the adoption of Corporate Social Responsibility (CSR) programmes entailing tools such as charters and codes of conduct, which these 'new generation' Transnational Company Agreements appear to have developed out of.[13]

---

10. Schoemann I. et al. (2012), *Transnational Collective Bargaining at Company Level: A New Component of European Industrial Relations?* Bruxelles: Etui; Telljohann V., Da Costa I., Muller T., Rehfeldt U., Zimmer R. (2009), *European and International Framework Agreements: New Tools of Transnational Industrial Relations*, Transfer, 3–4, p. 505–525; Papadakis K. (ed.) (2008), *Cross-border Social Dialogue and Agreements. An Emerging Global Industrial Relations Framework?* Geneva, ILO; Dehnen V., Pries L. (2014), *International Framework Agreements: A Thread in the Web of Transnational Labour Regulation*, European Journal of Industrial Relations, 20 (4), pp. 335–350. Among the papers presented to the ISLSSL Congress at Turin 2018 on this topic *see*: Ales E. (2018), *Transnational Collective Bargaining and European Works Councils: from Hurdle to Stepping Stone?*; Guadagno S. (2018), *Transnational Company Agreements: Opportunities in the Face of Technological Change*; Moll Noguera R. (2018), *La legitimitad negociadora de los agentes sociales a escala transnacional europea: una llamada a su complecion*; Rojas Rivero G.P. (2018), *Descentralizaciòn transnacional y negociaciòn colectiva*.
11. Treu T. (2018), *Transformation of Work: Challenges to the National Systems of Labour Law and Social Security*, General Report presented to the ISLSSL XXII Congress Turin.
12. The different institutional environment is highlighted by Smit P. (2018), *International Framework Agreements Taking the Sting out of Transnational Collective Agreements/Bargaining*, Paper presented to the ISLSSL XXII Congress Turin; Rosembaum Rimolo J. (2018), *Negociaciòn colectiva internacional. Algunas reflexiones a cerca del impulso y sus frenos en Latinoamerica*, Paper presented to the ISLSSL XXII Congress Turin.
13. The link between TCAs and CSR is widely recognized by scholars: *see* I. Daugareilh, 2017. Among the papers discussed in Turin Congress 2018, *see*: Rodriguez Gonzalez S. (2018), *El Papel*

The contents of TCAs show a fair amount of continuity with CSR practices: TCAs are based on the ILO core conventions set out in the 1998 Declaration (on freedom of association and the right to collective bargaining, on prohibition of forced labour, child labour and any form of discrimination), but also on other principles, including the protection of health and safety in the workplace, the rights of migrant workers, the right to a decent wage, including for employees of suppliers and subcontractors; on training, gender equality, data protection and even in some cases on linking certain wage items to corporate performance at the global level. In the development from unilateral CSR protocols to framework agreements negotiated with Global Union Federations (GUFs), the substance of the agreements has become the object of more detailed negotiations[14]; with auditing procedures supervising the implementation of agreements requiring a more contractual form, including full and compulsory compliance with the clauses and - at least in principle - a more stringent practical implementation. The implementation is to be overseen by the Global Union Federations through their local affiliates, and jointly by the multinational's central management exercising its influence over the company's local management.

Due to their very nature of framework agreements, TCAs are incomplete and require additional conditions, achieved through supplementary negotiation at national/local level (in fact, little practiced) or directives handed down by central management which the company's local management is obliged to comply with, in order for the contents of the agreement to be properly implemented and for the inclusion of procedures to handle complaints and sanction infringements. It is therefore especially in the implementation stage that it is necessary for the trade union involved to have strong local linkages, if it is to ensure that the agreement is managed effectively. It is at this stage that most critical difficulties occur: both because the trade union's mandate is not recognized at a local level (this is problematic in many developing countries, but also in several parts of the United States) and because of the need to oversee local suppliers and subcontractors are in compliance with the conditions agreed in the framework agreement, especially since the local suppliers or subcontractors are frequently small or very small companies.

One positive element needs to be highlighted: mostly International Framework Agreements clearly establish that observance of ILO conventions on freedom of association, as well as on the right of collective bargaining, is a crucial aspect of any agreement, since these principles are indispensable prerequisites for the correct functioning of monitoring mechanisms overseeing the successful implementation of

de los codigos de conducta en la consecucion de los objectivos de la agenda 2030 para el desarrollo sostenible; Molina Navarrete C. (2018), *Derecho de la U.E. y responsabilidad social empresarial: el 'futuro del trabajo' tambièn se juega en la 'buena gobernanza' societaria*; Giaconi M., Giasanti L., Varva S. (2018), *The Value of Social Reputation. The Protection of MNES' Workers Through Consumers' Eyes*; Erkens Y. (2018), *Dutch Sector Agreements-Innovation in Corporate Social Responsibility (CSR) and CSR Compliance*.

14. Gottardi D. (2018), *Corporate Social Responsibility. From a Unilateral Employer Choice to a Matter of Collective Bargaining: Contractual Social Responsibility*, in Guarriello F., Stanzani C. (eds), Trade Unions and collective bargaining in multinationals, Milano: Franco Angeli, pp. 60–77; S. Scarponi, 2018, pp. 96–111.

TCAs.[15] Where these monitoring and supervision procedures are properly implemented, this contributes significantly to the development and growth of unionization in many areas of the world (see the increase in union membership in the building and food sector in Latin America, in textile and garment sector in Asia).

The real challenge of these agreements lies in the relationship between the global and the local dimensions. In recent case studies it comes across clearly that the negotiating Parties are well aware of the importance of disseminating the content of any transnational agreement that is signed, ensuring that all departments in the corporation and all the local representatives of the workers are fully informed, as well as organizing appropriate training opportunities at all levels. A Transnational Company Agreement does not merely play a role by promoting the company's reputation[16]; rather, it appears to provide solutions for very practical problems, such as the prevention and management of local conflicts, production quality, improving productivity on a global scale, as well as conveying an idea of business culture.[17] And this is why the local dimension plays a strategic role, in that it is at the local level that complaints are first noted, with conflicts being addressed and solutions proposed, before they are addressed at a national than international level. Which also explains the importance attached to involving the local trade unions, as the main partner for local management in the implementation of the agreement.

The best practices in TCAs implementation clearly point to an evolution towards greater attention to soft law procedures, such as assessment and monitoring processes, conducted according to very precise and detailed voluntary regulations in order to ensure the effectiveness of the agreement. Even in the crucial phase of their implementation into the national systems, no rule requires compliance with the TCAs. National regulations and legal systems, whether they are State promoted or autonomous, tend to be totally indifferent to collective bargaining in multinational or transnational corporations. This indifference is very short-sighted, in a context in which company bargaining practices have been strongly favoured by State incentives.

§8.03 PARTIES, PROCEEDINGS, CONTENTS OF TCAs

Research studies on agreements concluded within transnational corporations have shown that negotiation leading to these agreements is the result of a deliberate strategy enacted by the main Parties: although they do not pursue the same final goals, they do have complementary objectives. On the one hand, the central management of the transnational corporation aims to improve or enhance the reputation the company

15. This aspect is notably emphasized by some scholars in the papers presented at the Turin Congress, in particular by Garcia Landaburu M.K. (2018), *Los mecanismos de participacion de las organisaciones sindicales en la verificacion del cumplimiento del codigo de conducta de Inditex*; and Rojas Rivero.
16. On the importance of this aspect, see the paper presented by M. Giaconi, L. Giasanti, S. Varva, 2018.
17. *See* lately: OIT (2018), *Entreprises mondiales et dialogue social transnational: quels enjeux pour les accords-cadre internationaux*, Paris, 7 février, pp. 1–55; Guarriello F., Stanzani C. (eds) (2018), *Trade Unions and collective bargaining in multinationals*, Milano: Franco Angeli.

enjoys nationally, extending it to a global level as well. Central management feels the need to harmonize the management style of local subsidiaries to the style of central management; to address conflicts arising in new countries at the earliest possible stage; to implement a strategy promoting the business ethics and industrial relations of the parent company within the subsidiaries and in relations with third companies; to improve production processes throughout the global value chain. Despite the fact that the phenomenon is usually studied from the viewpoint of the trade unions and/or the workers' representatives within the company, the literature that has addressed this issue has highlighted the fact that it is the company's interest in embarking on a bargaining process that triggers the multinational's response to trade union initiatives, or encourages action by management.[18]

There is no obligation, either in the regional European dimension, or on the global scale, for a multinational corporation to negotiate an agreement with a partner (often difficult to identify) which envisages implementation on a transnational level. Despite the challenges posed by economic globalization, which have weakened almost everywhere the power to govern labour relations,[19] industrial relations still appear to be firmly anchored to the national dimension. In the current situation of legal uncertainty, multinational corporations clearly feel that it is in their concrete interest to engage in the drafting and then in the compliance with a transnational agreement, though there is no legal obligation for them to do so. Although each agreement is different and no generalization is possible, empirical research confirms the essential interest of the multinational corporations' central management in negotiating transnational agreements and even more so in their implementation.

The interviews with central management (Human Resources or Industrial Relations directors) of multinational corporations confirm certain elements of analysis: first, the positive climate originating from a well-developed social dialogue within the parent company is an important starting point. An established practice of dialogue and exchange, including through the periodical information and consultation meetings with the European Works Councils (EWC), is considered essential for the development of relations based on mutual trust, and this is an indispensable prerequisite for the identification of issues of mutual interest, the backbone for the drafting of transnational agreements.

Second, prior CSR experiences are an important preparatory activity for the multinational corporation: the unilateral commitments of CSR Codes of Conduct are frequently transposed into transnational agreements, thus becoming bilateral commitments that the partners are obliged to comply with. To a large extent, the contents of TCAs reflect the unilateral commitments already undertaken by the corporation within its CSR practices, providing them with more stringent supervision and monitoring mechanisms, to be conducted jointly by the Parties or by ad hoc monitoring bodies. Incidentally, the will of supranational institutions to strengthen CSR practices (*see*

18. Platzer H.W., Rueb S. (2014), *It takes Two to Tango. Management and European Company Agreements*, Transfer, 20(2), pp. 255–270; OIT, 2018.
19. Baccaro L., Howell C. (2017), *Trajectories of Neoliberal Transformation. European Industrial Relations Since the 1970s*, Cambridge: Cambridge University Press.

below) may provide a positive incentive towards the conclusion of TCAs providing for negotiated joint monitoring and control procedures to verify compliance.

Last but not least, corporations have shown that they are fully aware of the challenge achieved with the bargaining of agreements whose clauses must be implemented in the subsidiaries and, in many cases, throughout the global supply chain as well. This is a challenge which has not yet been fully met, for it implies a huge commitment from both corporate management and the trade unions, who risk jeopardizing their credibility on this very difficult undertaking. However, if successfully met, this challenge will yield considerable improvements in labour conditions, increasing unionization rates in the countries where the multinational corporation carries out its business.

Among the workers' representatives, the negotiation of transnational framework agreements was given a considerable boost by the dynamic evolution of EWCs in Europe: the implementation mechanism envisaged in Council Directive 94/45/EC establishing the EWCs – based on bargaining between corporate central management and Special Negotiating Bodies (SNB) made up of representatives of workers employed in all the production sites involved in Europe – entrusted the establishment of the EWC and the definition of its prerogatives to inform and consult employees to an ad hoc transnational negotiation process. The revised Recast Directive 2009/38/EC further enhanced the bargaining role of the trade unions, both in the first establishment of the EWCs and in the renewal of agreements. The Recast Directive makes it compulsory to inform European trade union organizations of the beginning of negotiations, in order to ensure coordination of the process, the promotion of best practices, and full support for the SNB in its role. While trade unions are explicitly mentioned, there is no specific mention of any negotiating role to be played by the EWCs, despite the fact that EWCs had been extremely important in the negotiation of several agreements with multinational companies, not only in addressing threatened job loss crises and restructuring processes, but also on issues such as workers' health, equal opportunities, mobility and so on. This has meant that, since the entry into force of the Recast Directive, there has been a reduction in the number of transnational agreements signed by the EWCs alone, and an increase of agreements signed by sectoral federations, either European or international.

Trade unions are responding with renewed energy and this is due to a variety of different concerns. On the one hand, they fear that EWCs may become too closely involved with corporate management and they feel the need to keep the participatory role (workers' rights to be informed and consulted) distinct from the negotiating role, in compliance with the tradition of dual-channel countries. On the other hand, they need to share a joint strategy with the international trade union organizations involved in dealings with multinational corporations elsewhere, in order to engage the multinationals at a global level, so as to ensure compliance with workers' fundamental rights in every country where the corporation is present, and also throughout the supply chain. The experience of EWCs in dealing with European multinationals – or those multinationals which have instructed their European management to implement the Directive – has shown how the European regional dimension is totally inadequate for a correct analysis of the major changes affecting a multinational corporation active on a global scale. It was thus decided, on a voluntary basis, to extend membership in the EWC to representatives of workers employed by third-country subsidiaries, either as observers or as full members. In many instances, the EWC was thus transformed into a Global Works Council (GWC), since it includes representatives of workers from all countries in the world where the corporation has production plants or subsidiaries.

The periodical information on economic, financial and employment trends (now enriched with not financial information on social, environmental, human rights and fight against corruption, according to the Directive 2014/95/UE[20]), provided by corporate central management in compliance with the Directive, increasingly refers to global scenarios rather than European-scale trends. The synergy between this voluntary transformation of the EWCs into GWCs and the sectoral federations' strategy – aimed at building on the positive climate created by the implementation of the Directive on information and consultation of workers' representatives to establish a direct dialogue with corporate management to establish framework agreements on topics of mutual interest – has led to an exponential growth of the number of these agreements, whose scope extends beyond the European dimension.

We should not be surprised at the fact that sectoral federations become negotiating partners of multinational corporations in European and International Framework Agreements, even outside the context of European social dialogue processes. Sectoral production strategies are guided - or at least strongly conditioned - by multinational corporations, and it is with them that European and especially international trade union federations entertain a variety of forms of dialogue and exchange (especially in the context of implementation of the ILO Tripartite Declaration on Multinational Enterprises). In optimal conditions these forms of dialogue and exchange can lead to the conclusion of actual agreements.

The trade union federations, at a European and international level, have produced guidelines and recommendations, aimed at providing a formal framework for the rules to be followed in transnational negotiations. Among these guidelines, we shall mention: the specific mandate assigned to European federations, the requirement that the agreement be in writing, the inclusion of a non-regression clause in relation to national regulations, the approval of the final agreement by the trade unions that conferred the mandate, the indication of the applicable law for any dispute concerning the interpretation and implementation of the transnational agreement, the ways of disseminating information on the agreement itself.[21] Building on these basic rules, the attempt was made to get a European-wide regulation approved, with the purpose of providing an optional legal framework for the conclusion of transnational agreements,

20. *See* the paper presented in Turin Congress by C. Molina Navarrete, 2018.
21. Among the first to be issued: EMF, Internal EMF Procedure for Negotiations at Multinational Company Level, EMF 12/2006. For the enhancement of such guidelines through the signing of procedural sector agreements, see the paper presented in the Turin Congress by Cangemi V. (2018), *Un accord sectorial sur la procédure pour la négociation des accords cadres transnationaux*.

including dispute mediation procedures: this proposal was launched by the European trade unions, but has never been implemented.[22]

Equally, Global Union Federations (GUFs) have promoted guidelines for the negotiation of International Framework Agreements (IFAs), aimed at defining the minimum content such agreements should have in relation to: ILO's core labour standards and fundamental conventions; defining the scope of application which must extend to the entire global supply chains; control and monitoring mechanisms to oversee implementation of the agreement; the right to inspect production plants; the guarantee of an attitude of strict neutrality on the part of multinational companies' management in matters of unionization of employees in subsidiaries and throughout the global supply chain and subcontractors.[23]

In the strategy of Global Union Federations the conclusion of agreements with multinational companies is of fundamental importance: these agreements are tools for the promotion of workers' rights on a global scale. The essential prerequisites for the success of this strategy are the following: choosing multinationals characterized by a good industrial relations climate; the existence of a good dialogue between the parent company and the national trade unions, as well as established networks between the third countries' trade unions and/or the Global Works Councils, including the presence of workers' representatives from all over the world. The existence of an active network of relations between the workers in the different countries where the multinational corporation carries out its business is important because it implies that there is already an established practice of transnational dialogue and exchange with central management; but it is also important because it means that several issues and problems of common interest have been identified, and it is on these issues that negotiations can begin and agreements be concluded. It is especially important in terms of the concrete implementation of agreements, for this will require dissemination of information at all levels within the multinational company itself and within the third companies that have commercial dealings with it. This will create the basis for effective bottom-up monitoring processes, including transparent reporting procedures in cases of non-compliance, and correct handling of complaints.

The signing of a TCA is, therefore, not the conclusion of the partners' activity: on the contrary, it tends to be merely the point of departure. Once the agreement is signed a whole range of activities must be performed in order for it to be correctly implemented; the implementation will be effective to the extent that the agreement establishes the procedures that need to be followed, attributing to each partner precise obligations in terms of information, training, supervision, monitoring, reporting,

22. Sciarra S., Fuchs M., Sobczak A. (2014), *Towards a Legal Framework for Transnational Company Agreements. Report to the European Trade Union Confederation*, Brussels; ETUC (2016), *Building an Enabling Environment for Voluntary and Autonomous Negotiations at Transnational Level Between Trade Unions and Multinational Companies, Final Report*, download from the following link: https://www.etuc.org/sites/default/files/publication/files/160905_tca_final_report_en_proof_final.pdf.
23. IndustriALL, *Global Union's Guidelines for Global Framework Agreements (GFAs)*, 2012, updated in 2014.

complaints procedure, management of infringements.[24] It is in this context that Transnational Company Agreements are to be seen mostly as procedural agreements, whose purpose is to define the obligations of the Parties, which are obligations for their entire organization: this means local management in third-country subsidiaries, suppliers and subcontractors, on the company's side; local trade unions and workers' representatives in the workplace, on the workers' side.

It would not, however, be accurate to describe these agreements as merely procedural: they have a substantive content which is not purely symbolic, as some people would have it. Case studies have shown how such agreements, even with their minimal content, have become an important mobilization tool for international trade unions thanks to their inclusion of ILO core principles and fundamental conventions on freedom of association and the right to collective bargaining, on the prohibition of discrimination, of forced labour and child labour. The TCAs underscore the requirement to comply with ILO conventions, defined as fundamental tools for the active implementation of the framework agreement – especially Conventions 87/48 and 98/49 on freedom of association and the right to collective bargaining. By acknowledging the trade union as a dialogue partner for local corporate management, TCAs provide the local trade unions with new legitimacy, enabling them to benefit from authorized leaves of absence and to avail of resources needed in implementing the agreement; to provide training on the content of the agreement, to fight against anti-trade union practices. Freedom of association is a prerequisite for the mobilization of workers in the subsidiaries and throughout a multinational's production chain, especially in some States in the USA, in countries in Latin America and in Turkey, where local management or companies involved in the supply chain often enact anti-trade union practices, in breach of the TCA's clauses. In these cases, the agreement's supervision procedures oblige the multinational's central management to address the problem, remedying the critical situation by exerting pressure on local management and on the companies in the supply chain; they can also threaten sanctions and, where this is envisaged, termination of the contract with any third company which refuses to comply with the TCA's clauses.

On the positive side, ILO conventions are referred to in order to promote unionization processes in subsidiaries and in the companies in the supply chains, thanks to the role given to trade unions by the framework agreements and to the benefits related to their implementation, i.e. promoting decent work, observance of workers' fundamental rights to health and safety in the workplace, to a minimum wage, to social security. In the case of production plants located in countries known for the violation of the most elementary rights and freedoms of workers, the joint action of trade unions, non-governmental organizations (NGOs), mass media, together with the existence of a TCA, have succeeded in improving local practices and legislation; even in countries which had hitherto appeared impenetrable to actions promoting the basic rights of workers, such as in Qatar's construction sector, on the building sites for the infrastructure and sports facilities for the 2022 Football World Cup. The existence of

24. On the role of the parties in the implementation of TCAs, *see* OIT, 2018; Guarriello, F., Stanzani, C. (2018); Garcia Landaburu, M.K. (2018).

TCAs in multinational companies in the building sector has been useful in promoting international mobilization and inspections in the building sites, thanks to the alliance between multinational corporations and trade unions, partners in the TCAs.

The content of TCAs goes beyond the reference to the ILO core standards and fundamental conventions. The case studies have listed a wide range of other clauses contained in the TCAs: the promotion and supervision of workers' safety in subsidiaries and throughout the global supply chains, decent living conditions, the right to training, limits to daily and weekly working hours, supplementary pension benefits, minimum wage and wage benefits linked to productivity improvements, working and employment conditions for migrant workers, often provided by temporary employment agencies. They are for the most part minimum standards relating to wages and conditions that are of no great interest to workers in industrialized countries, but which cannot be taken for granted in developing nations, where national legislation does not guarantee adequate workers' protection standards and where salaried employment is carried out in conditions of almost slavery.

The implementation of framework agreements concluded with multinational companies in some contexts is the most important factor allowing for the introduction of decent labour conditions, especially for the workers in the supply chain, who are usually employed by small or very small local companies, relegated to the informal economy. The disaster at Rana Plaza has left their mark: it has raised the levels of global awareness among consumers and the informed general public; it has ensured greater attention to the quality of production processes on the part of corporations; it has set in motion mechanisms of solidarity bringing together both workers and trade unions, increasingly confronted by global challenges.

The urgency of the problems raised by globalization has favoured the emergence of a new generation of agreements, more interested than in the past in establishing effective implementation mechanisms. In the more all-encompassing agreements, the partners stress a whole range of obligations relating to implementation: the agreement itself shall be translated in all the languages used in the company's subsidiaries; the agreement shall be printed and distributed, its essential elements being communicated to all those involved; provisions are made for the information and training of management and workers' representatives in all production sites; periodical meetings between the Parties to the agreement shall be held, in order to examine any problems relating to implementation; inspections to be organized at production sites, including at suppliers' facilities; definition of indicators to be used in monitoring the implementation; production of periodical reports, usually drafted by management and then discussed jointly in monitoring bodies established ad hoc or in existing transnational representative bodies (EWCs, GWCs); rules for submitting complaints and bottom-up procedures for addressing them; duration of the agreement and renegotiation procedure; indication of the official language and applicable national legislation in the case of disputes. Obviously not all agreements contain all the clauses mentioned above and they are not always set out in a sufficiently precise manner. Difficulties arise when the monitoring report is drawn up entirely by management, for it can avail of the human and material resources necessary in collecting the relevant information; equally, there are problems due to the fact that trade unions cannot always be present in a timely manner at those sites where problems arise. The existence of trade union networks which can be activated when needed, and a synergy with the EWCs or GWCs which receive information and complaints from the different sites, can make up for their lack of material and organizational resources.

Can the existence of a growing number of corporate agreements, global in scope, supported by trade union strategies aimed at extending the influence of ILO core principles, to strengthen compliance with fundamental labour rights through contractual undertakings, especially compliance with freedom of association, workers' representatives in the workplace and the right of collective bargaining, become the core of a nascent system of global industrial relations, developing despite the absence of a transnational regulatory framework? The answer is yes, if we consider that historically industrial relations systems are the result of dialogue and exchange between the main players in the field, especially companies and trade unions. In civil law systems, like in common law, a contract has the binding power of law, between the Parties: through their collective autonomy they will establish the mechanisms and procedures required for their future negotiating activity. In TCAs negotiated in the last decade we can see that there has been a learning curve among the Parties who have developed this special system: if we look at the framework agreements drafted in the early years of the century, we shall see that they were still basically declarations of intent, without any adequate internal control mechanisms or monitoring procedures for implementation. Today, on the other hand, Transnational Company Agreements increasingly contain procedural machinery and control, and supervision mechanisms which are potentially capable of ensuring their effectiveness.

There is no doubt that the challenge for the Parties is still huge and the results achieved, judged positively by the partners, are by their very nature reversible, unless they are supported by continuous commitment on all parts. On the one hand, we have the economic power of the multinational company, characterized by its managerial practices which tend to prioritize financial strategies rather than productive goals. On the other, the composite group of their partners in labour relations, at a local, national, global level. The asymmetry of power between the Parties is evident: economic, financial, information, human resources and so on. The efforts of the GUFs try to exorcize the asymmetry, but there is a marked need for active synergy among the different levels of workers' representatives within the multinational and in the national, European, international sectoral federations, in order to ensure that bottom-up control mechanisms function adequately. The implicit challenge for the trade unions lies in their ability to act as a bridge between agreements reached at the top and their implementation at the local level. All the more so, when the framework agreement involves the supply chain as well, including companies that are technically autonomous from the Parties who signed the agreement: in a sense, compliance with the agreement amounts to a social clause imposed by the multinational corporation on its entire supply chain and all (or the most relevant) its subcontractors.

§8.04 HOW TO SUPPORT IMPLEMENTATION AND ENFORCEMENT OF TCAs

As has already been pointed out, negotiations on agreements within transnational corporations are to a large extent based on the hard law of the European Union's regulations on information and consultation rights through the EWCs, the establishment and functioning of which require a transnational ad hoc negotiating process. The legal obligation to establish European works councils in community-wide corporations or groups has led to the development of social dialogue practices within transnational companies, enriched by periodical exchanges of information and consultation processes enacted when the transnational corporation undergoes organizational changes, especially in restructuring processes. In compliance with the Recast Directive, the composition of the EWC must be renegotiated every time the structure of the transnational company is modified through mergers and acquisitions, according to the adjustment clause.

This particular condition in transnational negotiations – with which corporate central management (or the parent company) and a Special Negotiating Body (SNB) made up of representatives of the workers from the different production sites, assisted and coordinated by the sectoral trade union federations, are obliged to comply – ensures that the EWC is properly formed and modified when needed. In the European experience, this clause has favoured the development of a practice of social dialogue in transnational corporations, which in many cases has created the climate favourable to the conclusion of further agreements, on different issues, some more formal, others less so, negotiated outside a binding legal framework.[25] These agreements have the characteristics of voluntary agreements concluded in a situation of 'legal gap', in the absence of binding supranational rules governing the legitimacy of the signatories, the form, the scope of application, the effectiveness, the duration, the procedures for supervision, the sanctioning mechanisms.

In this situation, the will of the Parties makes up for the absence of external rules by establishing autonomously a set of shared mechanisms which the Parties undertake to observe in their joint management of the agreement (following the theory of the

25. The European Commission has defined them 'joint texts' in its Communication *Mapping of Transnational Texts Negotiated at Corporate Level*, Directorate-General, Employment, Social Affairs and Equal Opportunities, EMPL F2 EP/bp 2008 (D) 14511; and European Commission, *Commission Staff Working Document: The role of transnational company agreements in the context of increasing international integration*, Directorate-General, Employment, Social Affairs and Equal Opportunities, SEC (2008) 2155, dated 2 July 2008, referring to the variety of types of agreements concluded between the social partners. See also: Laulom S., Sciarra S. (2018), *Quel cadre juridique pour les accords transnationaux d'entreprise?* in Mélanges en l'honneur d'Antoine Lyon-Caen, Paris: Dalloz, pp. 517–532; Leonardi S. (ed.) (2012), *Transnational Company Agreements. A stepping stone towards a real internationalization of Industrial Relations?* Roma: Ediesse; EURACTA 2 (2015), *The transnational company agreements. Experiences and prospects. Final Report*, Text available on the site www.fondazionedivittorio.it/sites/default/files/content_attachment/Euracta2_Final%20report_0.pdf.

'collective autonomy' elaborated in the '60 by Gino Giugni).[26] This explains why the procedural and institutional elements of TCAs have evolved and become more elaborate in recent years, in order to meet the needs of the effective implementation of the agreement's clauses, ensuring that the agreement does not remain a mere declaration of intent, with no effective consequences. The absence of binding rules does not, however, mean a total absence of all rules for Parties operating transnationally, especially not for multinationals.

Ever since the 1970s, a range of international codes of conduct, non-binding in nature, i.e., soft law, have been addressed to multinational corporations with the goal of guiding their conduct in the various countries where they establish production plants. They are: the 1976 OECD Guidelines on Multinational Enterprises, the 1977 ILO Tripartite Declaration, the 2000 United Nations Global Compact, the 2011 United Nations Guiding Principles on Business and Human Rights. All of these instruments have recently been revised and updated, with the addition of mechanisms ensuring technical assistance, expertise and supervisory obligations to ensure compliance with recommended conduct. Alongside these instruments, addressed to multinational companies, another highly significant source of inspiration for IFAs is, of course, the 1948 Universal Declaration of Human Rights, which is frequently recalled amongst the guiding principles of the agreements.

Until recently these soft law tools advanced on a parallel path to the negotiation experiences of agreements within transnational companies. Now they are increasingly being seen as an international reference framework, which will favour the transition from unilateral CSR practices, moving beyond those charters or codes of conduct on fundamental rights whose nature is merely that of declarations of intent, which have no reliable mechanisms for monitoring or control with respect to labour issues; a transition towards procedures of social dialogue and concertation, which can assure more effective control mechanisms, when the multinational company is called upon to implement the commitments taken with the unions. The question of control mechanisms is, in fact, the weak point in unilateral CSR practices, managed entirely by a company's Departments of Human Resources or Quality Control, entirely separate from the real-life conditions of industrial relations. In recent years these two pathways have tended to meet, to strengthen each other, to benefit mutually from the complementarity of the different instruments.

The most relevant instrument addressed to multinational companies are the OECD Guidelines, revised on 25 May 2011, providing recommendations 'for responsible business conduct in a global context', to be followed in the country of corporate headquarters and in all countries where there are subsidiaries and commercial partners, especially in those countries where there are no efficient administrative offices capable of ensuring full compliance with internal and international regulations. The Guidelines recall a list of ethically correct behaviours to be observed. In particular, Chapter IV of the Guidelines addresses the observance of Human Rights based on the

26. Adhere to this setting Sobzack A. (2012), *Ensuring the effective implementation of transnational company agreements*, European Journal of Industrial Relations, 18 (2), p. 139–151; Moreau M. A. (2017); Daugareilh I. (2017).

United Nations (UN) 'Protect, Respect and Remedy' Framework, following the principles enunciated by John Ruggie; whereas Chapter V addresses Employment and Industrial Relations. In this field, apart from recalling the core principles and fundamental rights in the 1998 ILO Declaration, the Guidelines recommend that multinational companies comply with laws, regulations and customary practices in the host countries, as applicable to employees and labour relations,[27] as well as collaborating with the social partners in order to conclude collective agreements, applying standards in no way less favourable than those offered by comparable employers in that country or, when comparable employers are not present, applying the best salaries and the best working conditions in relation to the local socio-economic context; the adoption of provisions capable of ensuring health and safety in the workplace, even when this may not be a compulsory legal requirement in that country; the hiring of local employees, including managerial staff, and the provision of training aimed at improving employees' skills; information to be provided in a timely manner to workers' representatives and public authorities on important organizational changes; and the commitment to mitigate the social and employment consequences of any such changes; refraining from threatening to transfer production plants or workers out of the country in the effort to influence unfairly any negotiations, or in order to prevent trade unions from organizing effectively; provide protection to any worker who may – in good faith – report situations of abuse or violations.

Compared to the contents of TCAs, the OECD Guidelines are especially interesting in the section on the principles of freedom of association and the right to collective bargaining, which a multinational company should try to ensure 'through appropriate provisions' even in those countries where freedom of association is not guaranteed. There is a similar correlation and strengthening between the two instruments – the first being unilateral (CSR), the second being bilateral (TCA) – to be found in some general recommendations: that a company should implement due diligence based on risk assessment and integrated in the corporate risk management systems, in order to identify, prevent and mitigate any negative impact, either potential or actual, of its business activities on any of the issues addressed by the Guidelines (especially in relation to the new chapter on human rights, inspired by the United Nations 2011 Guiding Principles on Business and Human Rights), and be accountable as to how this impact is managed (point 10); and further, through this obligation to monitor and supervise, extend the scope of application of these principles to the multinational company's commercial partners, i.e., suppliers and subcontractors, so as to ensure that they, too, observe the principles of responsible business conduct in compliance with the Guidelines (point 13). The inclusion of these new chapters is due to the realization that there is considerable global competition from non-OECD countries' companies; to

27. The notion of employee or employed worker is intended to have the same meaning as in the ILO Tripartite Declaration. In case of doubt as to the existence of an employment relationship, one can refer to the indicators given in para. 13 of ILO Recommendation 198/2006. The OECD Guidelines recommend that employers do not support disguised employment practices or resort to the informal economy, whereas in the case of civil and commercial relations (excluding relations with employees), companies shall act according to due diligence based on risk and on the supply chain, in compliance with items 10 and 13 in the General Principles (*see* below).

the concerns raised by such stakeholders as NGOs and trade unions over the risk of serious human rights abuses perpetrated in emerging economies and elsewhere, as a result of cost-cutting competition, a 'race to the bottom' fought by stripping workers of their rights, especially in times of economic crisis. The issue of global supply chains, made up predominantly of local SMEs, has for many years been the subject of discussion in the trade union component of ILO.[28]

The voluntary and non-binding endorsement of the Guidelines by the multinational enterprises of OECD countries, and not only,[29] is today supported by the shared commitment of governments to promote their effective application through the establishment of National Contact Points (NCPs).[30] The NCPs, as non-judicial grievance mechanism whose establishment is compulsory for governments, are intended to meet the need to disseminate information on the content of the Guidelines, to respond to requests, to guarantee full interpretation and correct application, to solve issues related to implementation and to address 'specific instances' raised by trade unions, NGOs and individuals as to the violation of the Guidelines' clauses by multinational companies or their suppliers.

The NCPs must respond to all requests for action submitted 'in good faith' by any one of the subjects legitimately entitled to act, proposing itself as a mediator to favour positive dialogue between all interested parties, if needed with the assistance of the NCPs from other countries involved, treating the matter in an entirely impartial manner, acting fairly, in a timely and foreseeable and transparent manner, with a view to obtaining a formal declaration on the importance of the matter, a report on the issue and on the result of the mediation, accompanied by any recommendations to be made to the company and by a clear indication of deadlines for the monitoring and assessment of the implementation of the agreed solution.

Attention to the procedures through which complaints are managed ('specific instances' in the jargon OECD), including the detailed definition of the procedures followed by the NCPs, is one of the issues that was most discussed during the recent review of the Guidelines, with the aim of equipping the CSR mechanism with effective and harmonized Alternative Dispute Resolution (ADR) procedures, to match the voluntary nature of the commitments undertaken.[31] The solution of reported issues is reached through a procedure of concertation and dialogue amongst all the Parties involved, in order to find an agreement, the implementation of which will be monitored

---

28. *See*: Papadakis K. (2018), *Lessons Learnt and On-Going Debates on the Implementation of IFAs in Global Value Chains*, in Guarriello F., Stanzani C. (eds), Trade Unions and Collective Bargaining in Multinationals, Milano: Franco Angeli, pp. 112–124.
29. As of 25 May 2011, the governments of all OECD Member States had endorsed the Guidelines, as well as Argentina, Brazil, Egypt, Latvia, Lithuania, Morocco, Peru and Romania.
30. The obligation to establish a NCP aims at improving information on the content of the Guidelines and to guarantee access to remedial mechanisms in case of infringement. The NCP is a non-judiciary State body providing a platform for discussion and for the resolution of a broad range of issues linked to the application of the OECD Guidelines within multinational companies and throughout their global supply chains. OECD Member States have considerable freedom as to the configuration of the NCP, but must observe shared criteria of visibility, accessibility, transparency and responsibility.
31. J. Schneider, L. Siegenthaler, *Les principes directeurs de l'OECD: pour une conduite responsable des entreprises multinationales*, in La vie économique, 9, 2011, pp. 63 ss.

by the NCPs. As mentioned above, the intention is not to sanction conduct in violation of the Guidelines, but rather to recommend that in the future the company may adopt conduct more consistent with the Guidelines and also remedy any damage caused.

The obligation to perform due diligence vis-a-vis the companies in the supply chain extends the scope of application of responsible conduct beyond the boundaries of the multinational corporation and its subsidiaries, to the entire network of its commercial partners from different countries, including non-OECD members or which have not endorsed the Guidelines; these are companies of all different sizes, including local SMEs. The multinational company is encouraged to use its influence in order to promote conduct compatible with the Guidelines by their suppliers, thereby contributing to the improvement of local standards. In the case of serious violations, a procedure of concertation and dialogue is envisaged, which will bring together the companies and the stakeholders in order to agree on a gradual alignment with the recommendations; should this not be achieved, the commercial relationship will be temporarily suspended, or totally terminated if serious violations persist.

In relation to the multiplication of risk factors in the supply chains, and the different geographical and sectoral contexts, the OECD recommends that multi-stakeholder platforms are established, like the one on mineral extraction in conflict-affected or high-risk areas (2010), or in the supply chains in the garment and footwear sector (2017), which commit multinational companies to involving trade unions and workers' representatives in the due diligence process at every single stage of the platform's implementation, including in the evaluation of suppliers, remedial actions, monitoring of impact and planning of operational mechanisms to handle complaint management and resolution.[32]

Global Framework Agreements (GFAs), agreements negotiated between multinational companies and international and local trade unions, are considered by OECD and ILO particularly suitable tools to strengthen the processes of due diligence throughout the supply chain, thus creating a relationship of trust between the various stakeholders: that is what occurred in the garment sector with the Agreement on Fire and Building Safety in Bangladesh in 2013 after the Rana Plaza tragedy, with the Honduras Labour Framework and the Indonesia Freedom of Association Protocol, just as with the IFAs signed between the multinational corporations Inditex and H&M and the Global Union IndustriALL.

The handling of complaints in the supply chains through the establishment of concertation and dialogue processes amongst all the Parties involved (social partners, governments, local government authorities, embassies, NGOs) is of fundamental importance since it promotes the conclusion of agreements[33] and the enactment of monitoring mechanisms and follow-up. The relationship between the different instruments enhances the synergy between them, on the one hand promoting negotiated solutions in the handling of social responsibility procedures, on the other providing new instruments to remedy violations of TCA clauses connected to the Guidelines.

32. *See* the different contributions in I. Daugareilh (ed.), 2017.
33. Examples of such procedures as they are applied in practice are reported in: Global Deal, ILO, OECD, *The Global Deal for Decent Work and Inclusive Growth Flagship Report*, 2018, pp. 78 ss.

A similar correlation of goals and instruments can be found in the evolution of the ILO Tripartite Declaration of Principles concerning Multinational Enterprises and Social Policy and the current developments in TCAs. Alongside the 1998 Declaration on Fundamental Principles and Rights at Work, the 2000 Decent Work Agenda and the 2008 Declaration on Social Justice for a Fair Globalization, the ILO has also worked on a review of the Tripartite Declaration on Multinational Enterprises with the goal of harmonizing this instrument - voluntary in nature - with the changes that have occurred on the global economic stage. In particular, the general discussion undertaken at the 2016 International Labour Conference on the topic of Decent Work in global supply chains,[34] following a request submitted sometime earlier by the workers' group in the ILO Governing Body: the request was to ensure transparency and to define procedures for corporate responsibility throughout the entire subcontracting, supply, production and distribution chains. After the conference a working group and a select committee were appointed to draft the conclusions of the discussion and in March 2017 the revised Tripartite Declaration of Principles concerning Multinational Enterprises and Social Policy was released.

The changes concerned essentially the inclusion of the entire supply chain into the multinational company's sphere of CSR; by endorsing the Declaration, the multinational enterprise undertakes to exercise due diligence on the operations of its suppliers and subcontractors, in order to ensure that each of them shall comply with the goals of the Decent Work Agenda and shall observe the core labour standards, including in those countries that have not ratified ILO fundamental conventions or which do not have suitable administrative offices to ensure they are respected.

The revised version of the Declaration assigns to States the task of ensuring that human rights are respected, protected and implemented, through the establishment of Tripartite National Contact Points, whose function is to raise the awareness of trade unions and employers' organizations, to facilitate social dialogue and the establishment of networks with the countries in which the multinationals are operating. In the ILO perspective, due diligence processes are preferably devised and implemented through bilateral agreements, reached between corporate management and trade union federations, involving in this process suppliers and national/local trade unions; such agreements further envisage periodical monitoring and assessment, as well as complaint handling procedures. The pressure exercised by workers' group within the ILO Governing Body, demanding that arbitration procedures be established for breaches of the Declaration by multinational corporations or by companies in the supply chain, has led to the role of the ILO as a trusted dispute settlement mediator, thus extending its role of technical assistance, and providing the resolution to issues relating to the interpretation of the Declaration.

As compared to other soft law instruments, founded on mechanisms related to the unilateral commitment on the part of the company, the ILO Tripartite Declaration presupposes the existence of a structured social dialogue between the social partners,

34. *See* K. Papadakis, 2018.

both internationally (through the parent company's central management), and locally (with the local management and the global supply chains).

There is widespread disappointment due to the lack of effectiveness of the monitoring and auditing mechanisms envisaged in CSR – for they are considered totally inadequate in monitoring the level of compliance relating to social goals and especially to the respect of human rights. Conversely, the mechanisms based on direct dialogue between the Parties in the industrial relations system (although the system is still not very well structured and lacks supranational regulations) are considered more relevant and more promising in the ILO context, thanks to the tripartite dialogue and structure on which the organization is founded. It should therefore not surprise us that TCAs concluded in recent years have given special attention to monitoring and evaluating implementation of agreements, extending the scope of application to include the supply chains.[35]

The attention devoted by the ILO to negotiation and implementation of IFAs, the constant and direct dialogue with the companies that have endorsed the Declaration and with Global Union Federations, which have their main offices in Geneva, the technical assistance provided through the ILO dedicated help desk, the confidential resolution of interpretation disputes raised by the stakeholders and, lastly, the activity of consciousness raising, support to social dialogue and facilitation in the establishment of networks provided by the Tripartite National Contact Points (TNCP), all together provide a near-institutional support structure to IFAs, offered by the UN organization specialized in labour issues. Nor should we forget that the ILO, through these actions, is working to extend the scope of application and to strengthen the effectiveness of its core labour standards, since serious and persistent violations of the standards can be ascertained by the usual control mechanisms provided by its Committee on Freedom of Association or its Committee on the Application of Standards, where the conduct of a State – in terms of either commission or omission – can be assessed: in the final analysis, it is the State that is responsible for the application of ILO standards.

Thanks to the dialogue between international organizations, the various soft law instruments addressed to multinational corporations have begun to interact and to implement decentralized supervision procedures; since the multinational corporations endorse them on a voluntary basis, these soft law tools tend to call upon the active surveillance of States, to detect human rights abuses and violations of the ILO fundamental conventions in their own territory, but also in countries where a multinational operates or where the global supply chains are active.

§8.05 CURRENT PROBLEMS AND PROSPECTS

The variety of transnational agreements is such that it is impossible to generalize about the existing experiences, since each one has its own rational approach, which could not

35. Hadwiger, F., 2015; Hadwiger F. (2017), *Looking to the Future: Mediation and Arbitration Procedures for Global Framework Agreements*, Transfer, 23/4, pp. 409–424; Hadwiger, F., 2018; OIT, 2018.

easily be borrowed for a different situation. Even the distinction between European Framework Agreements (EFAs) and International Framework Agreements (IFAs) only really grasps one aspect of the situation, i.e., its scope of application. It actually tells us very little about the nature of the agreements, whether they are prevalently about substance or procedure; or about their content, if they focus on the interests of individual workers, or on prerogatives that can be exercised by trade union or workplace representatives. The only element they have in common is the transnational dimension of the issues involved, projecting beyond the traditional national dimension of industrial relations systems.

The absence of rules at the transnational level leads the partners to build their agreements based on an incremental, do-it-yourself putting together of experiences, of previously unilateral commitments, currently negotiated with the trade union partner, of national regulations adapted to the transnational dimension, or the adoption of guidelines issued by European and Global Union Federations, adapting the follow-up procedures envisaged for CSR to the bilateral nature of collectively negotiated obligations. The toolbox that can be used has grown considerably in recent years, with the addition of new instruments and new opportunities, as well as a greater awareness that States play an essential role in the transnational dimension, too.

As the number of agreements with corporations at the global dimension is increasing, as compared to agreements covering only the European dimension, the time has come to ask ourselves how relevant a European-based Optional Legal Framework is today. The European Trade Union Confederation (ETUC) firmly believes that there is great urgency for such a legal framework, which would provide regulatory support to company agreements including the new dimension of social dialogue envisaged by the Treaty and so far implemented exclusively at the inter-professional and sectoral dimension; and further, it would allow agreements to fight more effectively against social and wage dumping practised in Europe by multinationals in their race towards relocation and cost reductions, in European countries with lower labour costs and reduced social rights. For this reason the trade unions decided to propose an Optional Legal Framework for Transnational Company Agreements, as a tool providing those agreements with a legal status, laying down the necessary formal and procedural prerequisites ensuring their legal effectiveness in the context agreed upon by the signatories. A legal framework, albeit voluntary in nature, supporting company agreements would provide negotiators with a regulatory reference parameter, formalizing the obligation to respect certain essential conditions and acknowledging the legal effectiveness of the commitments undertaken by corporate management, accepting them as binding for all subsidiaries and/or controlled companies listed in the agreement; and, where specifically envisaged, also including suppliers and subcontractors. The legal basis of this initiative could be the acknowledgement of the role of social dialogue, as stated in the Treaty on the Functioning of the EU.[36]

36. Article 152 of the TFEU states: 'The Union recognises and promotes the role of the social partners at its level, taking into account the diversity of national systems. It shall facilitate dialogue between the social partners, respecting their autonomy.'

Should such a legal tool be introduced, within the context of promoting social dialogue we might wonder whether it could effectively facilitate the conclusion of TCAs, to start with, in the European dimension but, moving forward, on a global scale. There is no easy answer to this question: many scholars raise doubts about the opportunity of this initiative, arguing that it's too early to press this new development in a fixed frame, because it could freeze the spontaneous blooming of agreements[37]. Others doubt the effectiveness of a purely optional legal framework, which could encourage companies to prefer informal agreements or not to negotiate at all. A positive attitude considers the adoption of an optional legal framework as a useful tool to give transparency and legal certainty to TCAs, overcoming the current phase of agreements that follow different regimes in each country.

Another question we need to examine in depth concerns the enforceability of procedural obligations envisaged in TCAs. It is a matter here of establishing a procedural machinery which could support the self-regulatory capacity, i.e., the ability of the social partners to ensure their interests are upheld. On a global scale, and in relations with multinational corporate management, the position of trade unions is far weaker than in more traditional contexts, where it is regulated by national industrial relations practices. In such a context, the implementation of a collective agreement – especially as concerns the different national systems in the countries covered by the agreement – becomes a question that raises a variety of problems. Implementation can become objectively difficult both for the multinational corporation and for the Global Union Federations (and, to a different extent, for the European federations). Domestic legal mechanisms capable of ensuring that the framework agreement is complied with in the various countries (the mandate being conferred by the national trade unions, negotiations to be held at a local level, directives issued by corporate central management and then applied by local management, the duty to influence affiliate trade unions, etc.) all suffer from absence of regulations and challenges in application. No system envisages the precise legal effects that a TCA can have at a national level, although the problem has occasionally been addressed (e.g., the Italian trade union confederations document on collective bargaining 2016, or French Combrexelle Report 2015) in documents outlining the new horizons of collective bargaining at company level.

In this context, a system supporting the effective implementation of transnational agreements by means of procedures establishing the State's obligation to supervise – where the State's duty to supervise is clearly regulated – with follow-up mechanisms included in CSR undertakings, would be beneficial: it would offer the advantage of putting the State back into the process of overseeing the activity of multinationals. This could add effectiveness to the agreement between the Parties, both in the company's country of origin (through the obligation to make supervision arrangements, to ensure the respect of human rights and reparations for damages caused), and in the countries where they have established plants and subsidiaries. This debate and the initial solutions proposed in recent years by international organizations bear witness to the

37. Meissner D., Transnational Collective Agreements (2018), Paper presented to the ISLSSL XXII Congress Turin.

fact that there is a clear determination to establish a correlation between the different legal tools, in order to work towards a fair globalization.

TCAs have provided a significant contribution to these developments: experiments with autonomous methods of monitoring and implementation of agreements on global scale, by means of a whole range of procedural obligations and creating opportunities for dialogue, for sharing results achieved and complaint handling mechanisms. The lesson learned from the experience of implemented TCAs is that there is a need to link the global dimension to the local dimension, meaning subsidiaries, but also all the companies in the subcontracting and supply chains. The effective implementation of TCAs presupposes efficient and transparent communication at all stages (both bottom-up communication, i.e., when the agreement is still being negotiated, and top-down, when agreed contents need to be communicated to the subsidiaries and, if envisaged, throughout the supply chains) and with all subjects involved, within the multinational corporations and throughout the partner organizations.

Different procedures and methods can be envisaged, depending on how the corporate command chain is structured; and, on the trade union side, depending on the internal relations as well as relations between trade unions and workers' representation in the workplace. Implementation is the crucial stage: if successful, it needs to demonstrate the active participation of all subjects involved in the concrete application of the undertakings in the agreement. Agreements reached at the top which are not then concretely applied in the daily life of the company – and its subsidiaries and supply chains – are destined to be merely symbolic statements of intentions. The negotiators of second-generation IFAs, fully aware of this risk, have taken great care in providing agreements with all instruments necessary to ensure their correct implementation, allowing all sections of their organization to take over the agreement and implement it in their concrete daily practice. The range of these instruments varies considerably: presentation and dissemination of the agreement, translation into a variety of languages, training opportunities on the content of the agreement, periodical inspections to production sites, preparatory meetings and follow-up sessions before and after meetings with management, complaint handling procedures, indicators for implementation monitoring, etc. And it is this wide-ranging toolbox that is the most innovative aspect of TCAs, with their multilevel implementation and monitoring, which will lead to the development of a sustainable system of global industrial relations, capable of meeting the needs of present-day challenges.

CHAPTER 9

Safeguarding the Rights of Migrant Workers: Another Challenge for Labour Law?

Kübra Doğan Yenisey[*]

§9.01 MIGRATION AS A PHENOMENA

[A] Facts and Figures

If the human migration is not a new phenomenon, its extent and speed lead researchers to investigate transnational migration closely. According to the International Migration Report of 2017, the number of international migrants reached 258 million in 2017, up from 220 million in 2010.[1] In 2017, only twenty countries were hosting two-thirds of all international migrants. The United States of America, Saudi Arabia, Germany and the Russian Federation are the first four countries residing the largest number of migrants in the world. According to the UN Refugee Agency, 65.6 million people were displayed forcefully from their home around the world, and this is the highest levels of displacement on record in 2016.[2] 22.5 million refugees were coming from three countries: South Soudan, Afghanistan and Syria. With 3.1 million refugees and asylum seekers, Turkey became the largest host country worldwide, followed by Jordan (2.9

* Acknowledgement: I would like to thank F. Columbu from Brazil, K. Koldinska from Czechia, C. Hayakaw from Japan, E. Binay from South Africa, F. Camas Roda from Spain, P. Herzfeld Olsson from Sweden who prepared national reports which were helpful to make this study possible.

1. United Nations Department of Economic and Social Affairs, Population Division (2017). International Migration Report 2017: Highlights (ST/ESA/SER.A/404).
2. http://www.unhcr.org/uk/figures-at-a-glance.html.

million), the State of Palestine (2.2 million), Lebanon (1.6 million) and Pakistan (1.4 million).[3]

Northern America and Europe are two regions wherein almost half (48.5%) of migrant workers are intensified. The Arab States host 11.7% of the world's migrant workers.[4] Migration flows are changing, and many migrant-sending countries of the twentieth century become transit or migrant-receiving countries. Spain, Italy, Turkey, South Africa which were country of emigrants become country of immigrants in the twenty-first century. However, for example, Brazil which was a migrant-receiving country in nineteenth and twentieth century becomes a migrant-sending country. Migrants' contribution to their national states under the form of remittances is significant in some countries, e.g. Pakistan, Bosnia and Herzegovina and Ecuador.[5]

Ageing populations and declining workforce in some parts of the world are met by the labour surplus in other countries. Migrant workers are used to maintaining the labour supply and filling labour shortages in emerging and developed economies. The factors which shape contemporary migration patterns are identified as follows: '*(1) migration to developed countries, largely for economic gain (about 70 percent of all migration); (2) migration from one developing country to another, or "South-South" migration, again for largely economic reasons (almost one-third of migration); (3) intra-regional migration, with almost 50 percent of migrants remaining in their region of origin, while some 40 percent cross just one border into a neighboring country; (4) migration as the result of changing national boundaries and the political and economic turmoil that can result; (5) migration as a result of the recruitment of low-skilled workers to fill labor gaps, especially for domestic and manual labor; and (6) special entry for high-skilled workers to increase international competitiveness.*'[6]

In addition, the potential number of migrants, who wish to move permanently in another country if they could, is estimated as 500 million adults.[7] The effects of climate change will certainly increase these numbers in the future. If not only, the primary reason behind the migration is to seek good employment.[8] Not only those who are unemployed or underemployed but also those who have an employment status in some parts of the World, for example East Africa, Southern Africa and West Africa, interviewed adults are likely to migrate. However, in other parts of the world such as developing Asia, which covers China and India, the employment status of people is less likely to affect their desire for migration.[9] Seeking a life in a more liberal political environment and cultural intimacy may also be among reasons for migration.

3. United Nations Department of Economic and Social Affairs, Population Division (2017). International Migration Report 2017: Highlights (ST/ESA/SER.A/404).
4. ILO, Promoting fair migration, Report of the Committee of Experts on the Application of Conventions and Recommendations (Arts 19, 22 and 35 of the Constitution), International Labour Conference, 105th Session, 2016, para. 12.
5. ILO, Promoting Fair Migration, para. 50.
6. E. L. Berg/D. J. Besharov, 'Patterns of Global Migration', Adjusting to a World in Motion, ed. by J. B. Douglas/M. H. Lopez, 59-60.
7. N. Esipova/R. Srinivasan/J. Ray, 'Global Desires to Migrate', Adjusting to a World in Motion: Trend in Global Migration and Migration Policy, ed. by B. Douglas/M. H. Lopez, Oxford 2016, 25.
8. ILO, Promoting Fair Migration, para. 11.
9. N. Esipova/R. Srinivasan/J. Ray, 'Global Desires to Migrate', 43.

Policymakers keep on developing active policy measures to manage transnational labour migration. International and regional efforts focus on developing an efficient migration policy which provides a sustainable development and efficient migration management.[10] At the regional level, the EU has developed the foremost harmonized model concerning migration from third countries and freedom of movements for the citizens of Member States. The European Agenda on Migration in 2015 is based upon four pillars: (1) Reducing the incentives for irregular migration; (2) saving lives and securing external borders; (3) strengthening the common asylum procedure; (4) developing a new policy on legal migration. The European Union thus adopted a serial of directives.[11]

The African Union (AU) adopted a Migration Policy Framework in 2006. A programme document on Labour Migration Governance for Development, which was issued in 2017, sets out principles to strengthen the governance and regulation of labour migration. The Union Economic Community of West African States (ECOWAS) has created an integrated region with a free movement of persons, which is one of the pillars of African Economic Community. The Commission of the ECOWAS adopted the Common Approach on Migration on 18 January 2008 declaring the principles among others the free movement of persons, combatting human trafficking and the protection of rights of migrants, refugees and asylum seekers. The Southern African Development Community (SADC) adopted Labour Migration Policy Framework in 2014.[12]

In Asia, the Association of Southeast Asian Nations (ASEAN) adopted Cebu Declaration on the Protection and Promotion of the Rights of Migrant Workers in 2007. The ASEAN Committee on the Implementation of the ASEAN Declaration implemented several initiatives including developing a Compendium on Migrant Workers' Education and Safe Migration Programmes in 2017.[13] In the Kathmandu Declaration, Member States of the South Asian Association for Regional Cooperation (SAARC) agreed to

10. For international developments on the migration and sustainable development *see* ILO, Promoting fair migration, paras 29–43.
11. Directive 2011/98/EU on 13 December 2011 on a single application procedure for a single permit for third-country nationals to reside and work in the territory of a Member State and on a set of rights for third-country workers legally residing in a Member State (hereinafter, the Framework Directive), Directive 2009/50/EC of 25 May 2009 on the conditions of entry and residence of third-country nationals for the purposes of highly qualified employment (hereinafter, the EU Blue Card Directive); Directive 2014/36/EU of 26 February 2014 on the conditions of entry and residence of third-country nationals for the purpose of employment as seasonal workers (hereinafter, the Directive on Seasonal Workers); Directive 2014/66/EU on the conditions of entery and residence of third-country nationals in the framework of an intra-corporate transfer and the Directive 2016/801/EU of 11 May 2016 on the conditions of entry and residence of third-country nationals for the purposes of research, studies, training, voluntary service, pupil exchange schemes or educational projects and au pairing (hereinafter, Recast Directive); For the historical background *see* P. Herzfeld Olsson, 'The Legal Basis and a Historical Overview', National Effects of the Implementation of EU Directives on Labour Migration from Third Countries, Bulletin of Comparative Labour Relations 91, 2016, 1–7.
12. *See* E. Biney, 'Labour migration as a social protection mechanism in Sub-Saharan Africa: Reflections on the EAC and SADC', Research paper for ISLLSSL.
13. Compendium on Migrant Workers' Education and Safe Migration Programmes, A Project of the ASEAN Committee on the Implementation of the ASEAN Declaration on the Protection and the Promotion on the Rights of Migrant Workers.

commitment *'to collaborate and cooperate on safe, orderly and responsible management of labour migration from South Asia to ensure safety, security and well-being of their migrant workers in the destination countries outside the region'* in 2014.

The Caribbean Community (CARICOM) has stated by the Havana Declaration of 2016 the profound commitment to the upholding of the human rights of migrants, irrespective of their migration status. The Caribbean Community countries reiterated their commitment *'to the upholding of human rights of migrants, irrespective of their migration status and to ensure an effective struggle against the illegal traffic of migrants and trafficking in persons, as well as all discrimination against them, independently of their national or ethnic origin'*.

MERCOSUR, as a single common market, founded with an aim to promote free trade, free movement of goods, people and currency, adopted in 1998 the Social and Labour Declaration, which states in its Article 4: *'The States Parties undertake to adopt measures to establish rules and procedures relating to the movement of workers in and to take the necessary actions to improve employment conditions and the working and living conditions of these workers.'* MERCOSUR aiming to implement a single labour market has not adopted yet any binding labour and social security instrument.

One may see that despite the multitude of policy documents, not many binding legal instrument regulating the rights of migrant workers exists. In spite of the widely debated nature of the phenomenon, it is hard to tell that labour laws, in general, have developed particular responses towards the problems of migrant workers. In many countries, e.g. Brazil, Czechia, South Africa, Sweden, Japan and Turkey, migrant workers constitute a part of debated topics in labour law. However, except Sweden which has adopted three new acts due to EU requirements, there exists no specific regulation relevant to the rights of migrant workers.[14]

Migration is, in general, perceived as falling out of the realm of labour law. However, either forcefully or intentionally displaced, the employment appears as the primary survival and integration channel to the host society. Each immigrant is a potential candidate for employment in a national labour market. Costello and Freedland aptly show the 'intersection and interaction' between migration and labour law.[15] Migration and migration law have a 'divisive' impact on both the objectives and subjects of labour law; the objectives of labour law in the sense of worker protection regime and labour market regulation in particular labour supply regulations and the subjects of labour law in the sense of the application of labour law to particular individuals on the base of their statuses.[16]

14. P. Herzfeld Olsson, Questionnaire-Sweden: The Act (1999:678) on posting of workers, The Act (2013:644) on a right to wage and other remuneration for work performed by a foreigner that is not authorized to be in Sweden. Act (2018:318) on right to remuneration when a seasonal worker permit is withdrawn.
15. C. Costello/M. Freedland, Migrants at Work, Oxford University Press, 2014.
16. M. Freedland/C. Costello, 'Migrants at Work and Division of Labour Law', Migrants at Work, Oxford University Press, 2014, 8–11.

[B] Who is 'Migrant Worker'?

If the term 'migrant worker' can encompass different groups, it has certain blurriness when it comes to drawing its borders. It is a general observation that the legislation in many countries does not have the concept of 'migrant worker'. Overseas workers, immigrant workers, foreign workers, employment of aliens, foreigners, foreign nationals, non-national workers, in some countries non-nationals and third-country nationals are among the terms used by national legislations.[17] It is quite common to have the term 'foreign' workers in labour legislations, such as Belgium, France, Germany and Turkey. In many legislations, e.g. Brazil, South Africa, Sweden, Japan and Turkey,[18] the term 'migrant workers' does not cover refugees, asylum seekers and those who are under other international protection regimes.

Article 11 of the ILO Convention No. 97 on Migration for Employment Convention (Revised) of 1949 defines the term 'migrant for employment' as '*a person who migrates from one country to another with a view to being employed otherwise than on his own account and includes any person regularly admitted as a migrant for employment*'. The same definition is given by Article 11 of Convention No. 143 on Migrant Workers of 1975. The Committee of Experts states that Convention No. 97 applies to international migrants for employment, as well as refugees and displaced persons and the family members of migrant workers.[19] Article 1(2) of the Recommendation No. 86 concerning the Migration for Employment states that '*For the purpose of this Recommendation, references to the Government or competent authority of a territory of emigration should be interpreted as referring, in the case of migrants who are refugees or displaced persons*'.

Article 2 (1) of the 1990 UN Convention on Migrant Workers provides that '*The term migrant worker refers to a person who is to be engaged, is engaged or has been engaged in a remunerated activity in a State of which he or she is not a national*'. Regardless of the main motivation in immigrating, such as family unification, seeking employment, or fleeing war, the UN Convention on Migrant Workers takes the engagement in a remunerated activity as a base to define migrant worker.

Likewise, the International Organization of Migration gives a general definition of migrant '*as any person who is moving or has moved across an international border or within a State away from his/her habitual place of residence, regardless of (1) the person's legal status; (2) whether the movement is voluntary or involuntary; (3) what the causes for the movement are; or (4) what the length of the stay is*'.[20]

In this study, I would prefer to use the term 'migrant workers' to refer those persons who are engaged in a remunerated activity in a state without having its nationality. It should be underlined that no legal difference is aimed at the terms 'worker' and 'employee'.

17. ILO, General Survey on Migration, 33.
18. F.Columbu, Questionnaire-Brazil; C. Hayakaw, Questionnaire-Japan; E. Binay, Questionnaire-South Africa; P. Herzfeld Olsson, Questionnaire-Sweden.
19. Comm. Exp., Conv. No. 97, Kyrgyzstan, 2016, 106th ILC Session 2017.
20. IOM, Glossary on Migration, International Migration Law Series, No. 25, 2011; https://www.iom.int/key-migration-terms.

The primary aim of this report is to give a general picture of the legal status of migrant workers and show the challenges that labour law face while regulating their rights. Part 2 provides an overview of the international instruments, which specifically regulate the rights of migrant workers. A general look at international instruments may help to understand the level of protection provided to migrant workers. In addition, I believe this picture will help us to determine criteria which encompass different migrant statuses in a holistic way and to explore in Part 3 different statuses from the perspective of labour law. Part 4 explores a tentative methodology while labour law dealing with the regulation of migrant workers. I will try to show how migration regulation affects the risk mutualization/demutualization in work relationship. This may help to better capture the insights of the problem. Finally, Part 5 explores some reintegrative responses of labour law to specific problems of migrant workers. The report does not attempt a comprehensive analysis of all problems: it focuses on several of the major issues, which in my belief, represent the complexity of the regulation of migrant workers. I admit that a survey piece such as this must take a broad-brush approach, and does not claim to be comprehensive. Rather, it selects some typical regulation pieces and country examples.

§9.02 INTERNATIONAL INSTRUMENTS PROVIDING PROTECTION TO MIGRANT WORKERS

In this part of the study, I will map the international instruments through the lenses of labour rights,[21] without denying the importance of general international instruments in the protection of migrants' rights.[22] Aleinikoff has classified international law on migration in three different categories: treaties that see the migration regarding labour flows; treaties that see the migration regarding human rights and those related to state control and security,[23] and Thomas has clearly shown 'convergences and divergences' within these treaties.[24] I will focus only on those which directly regulate the rights of migrant workers.

[A] The Declaration on the Human Rights of Individuals Who Are Not Nationals of the Country in Which They Live, 1985

The Declaration on the Human Rights of Individuals Who are Not Nationals of the Country in which They Live, 1985, as a non-binding instrument, aims to recognize the protection of human rights and fundamental freedoms of non-nationals resumes by

21. *See also* R. Cholewinski, 'International Labour Migration', International Migration Law, ed. B. Opeskin/R. Perruchoud/J. Redpath-Cross, CUP 2012, 283–311.
22. *See* B. Ryan/V. Mantouvalou, 'The Labour and Social Rights of Migrants in International Law', Human rights and Migration, ed. R. Rubio-Marin, Oxford University Press, 2014, 177–211.
23. T. Aleinikoff, 'International Legal Norms on Migration: Substance without Architecture' in International Migration Law: Developing Paradigms and Challenges, ed. R. Cholewinski, R. Perruchoud and E. MacDonalds, T.M.C. Asser Press 2007, 467.
24. C. Thomas, 'Convergences and Divergences in International Legal norms on Migrant Labour', 32 Comparative Labour Law and Policy Journal, 2011, 405–441.

ensuring the rights of States. Following the definition of 'alien', Article 2 (1) states that '*Nothing in this Declaration shall be interpreted as legitimizing the illegal entry into and presence in a State of any alien, nor shall any provision be interpreted as restricting the right of any state to promulgate laws and regulations concerning the entry of aliens and the terms and conditions of their stay or to establish differences between nationals and aliens.*'

Article 5 of the Declaration provides the fundamental rights for all aliens, whereas Article 8 lays down 'lawful reside' as a condition to enjoy from labour rights. The Declaration modestly recognizes the labour and social rights for those who lawfully reside in the host state, without mentioning the right to work. Article 8 of the Declaration sets out the right to safe and healthy working conditions, fair wages, equal remuneration, the right to join trade unions, the right to health protection, medical care, social security and social services, education, rest and leisure.

[B] The International Convention on the Protection of the Rights of All Migrant Workers and Members of Their Families (UNCMW)

The UN Convention on the Protection of the Rights of All Migrant Workers and Members of Their Families adopted on 18 December 1990 has a broad personal scope including both workers as well as self-employed persons and their family members.[25] The term 'migrant worker' refers to '*a person who is to be engaged, is engaged or has been engaged in a remunerated activity in a State of which he or she is not a national*'.

The UN Convention on Migrant Workers considers, among others, '*that workers who are non-documented or in an irregular situation are frequently employed under less favourable conditions of work than other workers and that certain employers find this an inducement to seek such labour in order to reap the benefits of unfair competition*'. Moving from the base that '*to recourse the employment of migrant workers who are in an irregular situation will be discouraged if the fundamental human rights of all migrant workers are more widely recognized*', the Convention guarantees fundamental rights to undocumented migrants.

Even if the Convention covers both regular and irregular migrants, the scope of rights guaranteed to each group is different. Part III of the Convention regulates the human rights of all migrant workers and their families, and Part IV rights for regular migrants. A dualism, therefore, takes place on the base of migration status.

Both regular or irregular migrants benefit from the protection of basic human rights, e.g., the right to leave the state of employment and the right to enter and remain in their state of origin (Article 8), the right to life (Article 9), not to be held in slavery

25. B. Ryan, 'In Defence of the Migrant Workers Convention: Standard Setting for Contemporary Migration', Ashgate Research Companion to Migration Law, Theory and Policy, ed. S. S. Juss, Routledge 2013, pp. 493–494; B. Ryan/V. Mantouvalou, 'The Labour and Social Rights of Migrants in International Law', Human rights and Migration, ed. R. Rubio-Marin, Oxford University Press, 2014, 185.

or servitude (Article 11), the freedom of thought, conscience and religion (Article 12), the right to privacy (Article 14). Article 25 prohibits the less favourable treatment of migrants in respect of remuneration and working conditions, that is to say, overtime, hours of work, weekly rest, holidays with pay, safety, health, termination of the employment relationship and any other conditions or terms of work. Article 26 sets out right to join trade unions, and Article 27 the right to social security under certain conditions.

The Convention, thus, considers the irregular migrant workers to a great extent. Despite its duality model, Article 25 (3) states that '*States Parties shall take all appropriate measures to ensure that migrant workers are not deprived of any rights derived from this principle by reason of any irregularity in their stay or employment. In particular, employers shall not be relieved of any legal or contractual obligations, nor shall their obligations be limited in any manner by reason of such irregularity*'. It is an important advancement to state that irregularity of the migration status does not relieve employers of their any legal or contractual obligations.[26] Nevertheless, the Committee on Migrant Workers has relied upon Article 83 of the Convention rather than Article 25, which states an effective remedy to those whose rights or freedoms are violated as a base for its remarks.[27]

Part IV of the Convention regulates the specific rights guaranteed only to migrants documented or in a regular situation. The right to liberty of movement in the territory of the state of employment and freedom to choose their residence there (Article 39), the right to form associations and trade unions (Article 40), access to social services, unemployment benefits, training, and housing (Article 43) are among the rights afforded only regular migrants.

The UN Convention on Migrant Workers, adopted after ten years of the negotiation process, has been ratified only by fifty-one states as of May 2018.[28] Many of the countries, e.g., Latin American, North and West African states, the Philippines and Sri Lanka, Albania and Turkey, who have ratified the UNCMW are the migrant-sending countries. The changing nature of migration destinations, in the sense that migrant-sending countries of the past becoming transit or destination countries gives hopes for an increasing influence of the Convention in the future.[29]

---

26. B. Ryan, 'In Defence of the Migrant Workers Convention: Standard Setting for Contemporary Migration', 498; comp. L. S. Bosniak, 'Human Rights, State Sovereignty and the Protection of Undocumented Migrants Under the International Migrant Workers Convention', The International Migration Review, Vol. 25, No. 4, Special Issue: U.N. International Convention on the Protection of the Rights of All Migrant Workers and Members of Their Families (Winter, 1991), 759.
27. About the work of the Committee *see* B. Ryan, 'In Defence of the Migrant Workers Convention: Standard Setting for Contemporary Migration', 504–510, 508.
28. For the evaluation of alleged obstacles *see* A. Desmond, 'The Triangle That Could Square the Circle? The UN International Convention on the Protection of the Rights of All Migrant Workers and Members of Their Families, the EU and the Universal Periodic Review', European Journal of Migration and Law, 17 (2015), 48–49.
29. B. Ryan, 'In Defence of the Migrant Workers Convention: Standard Setting for Contemporary Migration', 502–503.

[C] The 1951 Geneva Convention Relating to the Status of Refugees (The Refugee Convention)

The Geneva Convention of 28 July 1951 and the Protocol of 1967 provide an important exemption to an international principle that states have no obligation to admit non-nationals to their territories. The status of refugee imposes nation states a duty to admit foreigners into their territory. Before the New protocol of 1967, the Convention has applied only to refugees of Europe as a result of events prior to 1 January 1951. The New York Protocol removed the geographical and temporal restrictions. Nevertheless, there are still few countries who have ratified the Geneva Convention but not the Protocol of 1967.

Article 1 of the Convention defines the refugee as '... *owing to well-founded fear of being persecuted for reasons of race, religion, nationality, membership of a particular social group or political opinion, is outside the country of his nationality and is unable or, owing to such fear, is unwilling to avail himself of the protection of that country; or who, not having a nationality and being outside the country of his former habitual residence as a result of such events, is unable or, owing to such fear, is unwilling to return to it*'. Thus, the Geneva Convention restricts the grounds on which the well-founded fear of persecution could be based.

The Convention Governing the Specific Aspects of Refugee Problems in Africa of 1969 reflects Africa's approach to asylum seeking, and places itself as a complementary instrument to the Geneva Convention. It gives a refugee definition in a more expanded way comparing with the one in the Geneva Convention. Nevertheless, there is no additional right as regards the rights of refugees to access to wage-earned employment.[30]

The Cartagena Declaration, which was adopted by a group of experts and representatives from Governments at the Colloquium on the International Protection of Refugees in Central America, Mexico and Panama on 19–22 November 1984, recommends the use in the region of a '*definition or concept of refugee ... which, in addition to containing the elements of the 1951 Convention and the 1967 Protocol, includes among refugees persons who have fled their country because their lives, safety or freedom have been threatened by generalized violence, foreign aggression, internal conflicts, massive violation of human rights or other circumstances which have seriously disturbed public order.*'

Therefore, the definition of the refugee concept, as well as the asylum seeking procedure, show large discrepancies throughout the world. National adjudicators enjoy large discretionary powers while determining who will stay under cover of the Convention because of the absence of a single international authority or dedicated court of international refugee law.[31] While defining refugee, the impact of human rights

30. *See* A. Abbas/D. Mystris, 'The African Union Legal Framework for Protecting Asylum Seekers', Regional Approach to the Protection of Asylum Seekers an International Legal Perspective, ed. A. Abass/F. Ippolito, 2nd ed., Routlage 2016, 19 et seq.
31. C. Costello, The Human Rights of Migrants and Refugees in European Law, Oxford 2016, 175.

law is widely recognized.[32] The jurisprudence of the ECtHR about the guarantee of non-refoulement provides important legal protection to refugees.[33] However, many states are not a party to an internationally binding convention. The goodwill of the host states thus becomes determinant in the protection of refugees rights.

The Geneva Convention establishes a system of duties owed by the state parties depending on the bond between the concerned state and the refugee. While all refugees benefit from core rights, the nature and the attachment to the asylum state enable them additional rights.[34] In fact, there exists a very limited core of refugee rights granted to those who reach a state's territory; the duty of non-discrimination (between and among refugees) and the right to non-refoulement.[35]

Refugees who have a 'lawful presence' in a state party are entitled to the right to engage in self-employment. Lawful presence entitles refugees only the right to self-employment, a right to engage independent economic activity in agriculture, industry, handicrafts and commerce and to establish commercial and industrial companies (Article 18 of Con.).[36]

Under the Geneva Convention, refugees (or so-called asylum seekers while their refugee status has not been recognized yet) who stays lawfully benefit from the freedom of association (Article 15), the right to engage in wage-earning employment (Article 17), the right to access to public housing and welfare (Article 21), and the right to have the same treatment as nationals in respect of labour and social security legislation (Article 24). In order to work with an employment contract or to engage in professional practice, the Convention requires more dense tights, which means lawfully staying, with the host state. That also explains the frequency of sham self-employment relations with refugees.

In addition to those who are granted asylum consequent to formal recognition of refugee status, refugees 'lawfully staying' also encompass all those who benefit from temporary protection regime or another durable protection regime. To be considered as 'staying lawfully', there is no need for the formal declaration of their status as refugees, the grant of the right of permanent residence, or the establishment of domicile.[37] Persons, only those who had not applied or whose applications had been refused are considered in an 'irregular position' under the Geneva Convention.[38]

The difference among national systems is striking when it concerns the refugee's right to work, freedom of association and other rights. In most of the less developed world, the access of refugees to the labour market is denied, there may have formal bans on their employment or required work authorization process, which takes a long time. In most developed states, the right to work is formally recognized to refugees,

32. B. Burson/D. J. Cantor, 'Introduction: Interpreting the Refugee Definition via Human Rights Standards', Human Rights and the Refugee Definition, 2016.
33. *See* C. Costello, The Human Rights of Migrants and Refugees in European Law, Oxford 2016, 180 et seq.
34. J. C. Hathaway, The Rights of Refugees under International Law, Cambridge University Press, 154–155, 156 et seq.
35. Hathaway, The Rights of Refugees under International Law, 160–171.
36. *See* Hathaway, The Rights of Refugees under International Law, 723–729.
37. Hathaway, The Rights of Refugees under International Law, 730.
38. Hathaway, The Rights of Refugees under International Law, 175 et seq.

immediately after their refugee status has been granted.[39] Many European countries set a period of time during which the asylum seekers are denied from labour markets. In addition those who are subject to temporary protection regimes are not entitled to the right to work in many cases.[40]

[D] The ILO Conventions

The preamble of the ILO Constitution refers to the 'protection of the interests of workers when employed in countries other than their own'. Since 1919, the ILO has adopted many instruments which regulate the migration.[41] I will only mention the very few ones directly related to the migrant workers' rights.

Article 2 of the Convention No. 29 of 1930 on Forced Labour provides that '*forced or compulsory labour* shall mean all work or service which is exacted from any person under the menace of any penalty and for which the said person has not offered himself voluntarily', therefore applicable both nationals or non-nationals.

The Convention No. 97 of 1949 concerning Migration for Employment and the Recommendation No. 86 of 1949 were adopted with an aim to facilitate migration for employment. According to the Convention No. 97, Member States undertake to maintain an adequate and free service to assist migrants for employment (Article 2), take all appropriate steps against misleading propaganda relating to emigration and immigration (Article 3), facilitate the departure, journey and reception of migrants for employment (Article 4), to maintain appropriate medical services (Article 5) and to apply the principle of non-discrimination as regards remuneration and working conditions, trade union membership, accommodation, social security, taxes and legal proceedings (Article 6). The Convention aims to guarantee no less favourable treatment to migrants compared to nationals. In the following period, a series of ILO instruments, such as the Protection of Migrant Workers (Underdeveloped Countries) Recommendation, 1955, the Employment Policy Convention and Recommendation of 1964 dealt with the recruitment and placing of migrant workers.

The Convention No. 143 of 1975 concerning Migrations in Abusive Conditions and the Promotion of Equality of Opportunity and Treatment of Migrant Workers and the Recommendation No. 151 of 1975 primarily aim to prevent illegal immigration considering '*the evidence of the existence of illicit and clandestine trafficking in labour calls for further standards specifically aimed at eliminating these abuses*' (Preamble of Convention No. 143). Each member shall determine whether there are illegally employed workers in its territory (Article 2) and adopt measures to suppress clandestine movements of migrants (Article 3). Article 9 of the Convention provides important

39. Article 26 (1) of the Council Directive on minimum standards for the qualification and status of the third-country nationals and stateless persons as refugees or as persons who otherwise need international protection and the content of the protection granted states that 'Member States shall authorise beneficiaries of refugee status to engage in employed or self-employed activities subject to rules generally applicable to the profession and to the public service, immediately after the refugee status has been granted.'
40. *See also* Hathaway, The Rights of Refugees under International Law, 733–737.
41. *See* ILO, Promoting fair migration, paras 57–73.

protection to migrants in an irregular situation in the sense he/she enjoys the equality of treatment in respect of basic human rights.

As regards social security rights, two conventions seem particularly pertinent. The Convention No. 102 of 1952 on Social Security (Minimum Standards) and in particular, the Convention No. 118 of 1962 on Equality of Treatment (Social Security) Convention deals with the social security of migrants, the correct term 'non-nationals'.

The main principle dominates all ILO conventions is to implement the equality of the treatment between nationals and migrants as regards employment and social security rights. However, the Convention No. 97 has been ratified by forty-nine countries out of 186 and The Convention No. 143 ratified only by twenty-three countries. Considering the importance of the topic, at its 321st session (June 2014), the Governing Body of the International Labour Organization (ILO) decided to conduct a general survey concerning the migrant workers instruments, in particularly the Migration for Employment Convention (Revised), 1949 (No. 97), and the Migration for Employment Recommendation (Revised), 1949 (No. 86), the Migrant Workers (Supplementary Provisions) Convention, 1975 (No. 143), and the Migrant Workers Recommendation, 1975 (No. 151).[42]

[E] The European Convention on the Legal Status of Migrant Workers

The European Convention on the Legal Status of Migrant Workers entered into force on 1st May 1983 is another treaty with a very low ratification rate which aims to regulate the legal status of migrant workers so as to ensure that they are treated no less favourably than workers who are nationals of the receiving State in all aspects of living and working conditions (Preamble). The total number of ratification is eleven as of May 2018. Article 1 of the Convention defines the 'migrant worker' as '*a national of a Contracting Party who has been authorised by another Contracting Party to reside in its territory to take up paid employment*'. Since the Convention requires both sending and receiving countries to be signatory to find a place of application, it hardly plays a role in migration debates.

[F] The Revised European Social Charter

The European Social Charter of 1961 and the Revised Social Charter state in their preamble the right to protection and assistance for migrant workers and their families. The main headlines of Article 19 of the both charters could be summarized as assistance and information on migration and protection against misleading propaganda; departure, journey and reception; co-operation between social services emigration and immigration states; equality regarding employment, the right to organize and accommodation; equality regarding taxes and contributions; family reunion; equality

42. ILO, Promoting fair migration, Report of the Committee of Experts on the Application of Conventions and Recommendations (Arts 19, 22 and 35 of the Constitution), International Labour Conference, 105th Session, 2016.

regarding legal proceedings; guarantees concerning deportation; transfer of earning and savings; equal treatment for the self-employed; teaching language of the host state and teaching the language of the mother state to their children.

The difficulty arises from its restricted personal scope of application. Only those migrants who are nationals of a party state and legally residing and/or legally working in the territory of a contracting state enjoy protections offered by the Charters. Refugees and stateless persons if lawfully staying in the territory of the state enjoy the treatment as favourable as possible and in any case not less favourable than the protections provided by the Charter (paragraphs 2-3 of Appendix).[43] Nevertheless, irregular migrants thus fall mainly out of the personal scope of the Social Charter. This restricted personal scope of the Charter creates tension among the fundamental values protected by the Charter and provide complex situations as regards the nationals of the non-party States.[44]

[G] The American Convention on Human Rights

The American Convention on Human Rights states that '*Every person has the right to the nationality of the state in whose territory he was born if he does not have the right to any other nationality.*' (Article 20 (2)). This provision demonstrates a clear different approach towards migrants' rights comparing to the European Convention on Human Rights.[45]

Regarding asylum seekers, the American Convention provides that '*Every person has the right to seek and be granted asylum in a foreign territory, in accordance with the legislation of the state and international conventions, in the event he is being pursued political offences or related common crimes*' (Article 22 (7)). The Court of Inter-American Human Rights admits the importance of access to employment for asylum seekers. Asylum seekers like other migrant workers acquire labour rights regardless of their regular or irregular status in the state.[46]

§9.03 TWO DIFFERENT PARAMETERS TO ANALYSE THE LEGAL STATUS OF MIGRANT WORKERS

An overlook of international treaties reveal two parameters which directly affect the rights of migrants: the voluntary/forced nature of migration and the regularity. Article

43. Digest of the Case Law of the European Committee of Social Rights, 1 September 2008, 183–184; S. Clauwaert, 'Article 19§4 The Right of Migrant Workers and Their Families to Protection and Assistance', The European Social Charter and the Employment Relation, ed. N. Bruun/K. Lörcher/I. Schömann/S. Clauwaert, Oxford: Hart Publishing, 2017, 345–346.
44. C. O'Cinnéide, 'Migrants Rights under the Social Charter', Migrants at Work, Oxford University Press 2014, 288, 289–292.
45. M.-B. Dembour, When Humans Become Migrants: Study of the European Court of Human Rights with an Inter-American Counter Point, Oxford University Press, 2015, 56–57.
46. D. J. Cantor/S. Barichello, 'Protection of Asylum Seekers under the Inter-American Human Rights System', Regional Approach to the Protection of Asylum Seekers An International Legal Perspective, ed. A. Abass and F. Ippolito, 2. ed., Routlage 2016, 287–288.

11 of the ILO Convention No 97 on Migration for Employment Convention defines 'migrant for employment' as '*a person who migrates from one country to another with a view to being employed otherwise than on his own account and includes any person regularly admitted as a migrant for employment*'. The same definition is adopted by Article 11 of Convention No 143 on Migrant Workers Convention of 1975. Obviously migrants who cross borders for the purpose of employment have been the primary concern of labour law. But as regards those who forcedly displaced, even if their primary motivation to cross borders is not to seek better employment, any person within a state away from his/her country of origin needs to work regardless of the motivation behind immigration. Thus, once they enter into another state, their status in labour market need to be explored.

The regularity of migrants also operates as a significant determinant in determining the scope of migrants' rights. Likewise, migrants forcedly displaced enjoy different protections until their legal status is regularized.

A diagram based on two axes may be helpful to depict the general picture of the legal statuses and the level of protection provided to different migrant groups. It may also enable to detect the most vulnerable groups under the current system. In simplified terms, a basic analysis calls for the following parameters: the regularity/irregularity in a broad sense, which would be refined further, and the voluntary/forced nature of migration. Therefore, four different categories are to be covered through the lenses of labour rights:

(1) Forced and regularly admitted migrants.
(2) Forced migrants in an irregular status.
(3) Migrants for the purpose of employment and regularly admitted.
(4) Migrants for the purpose of employment and in an irregular status.

Figure 9.1 Categories of Migrants

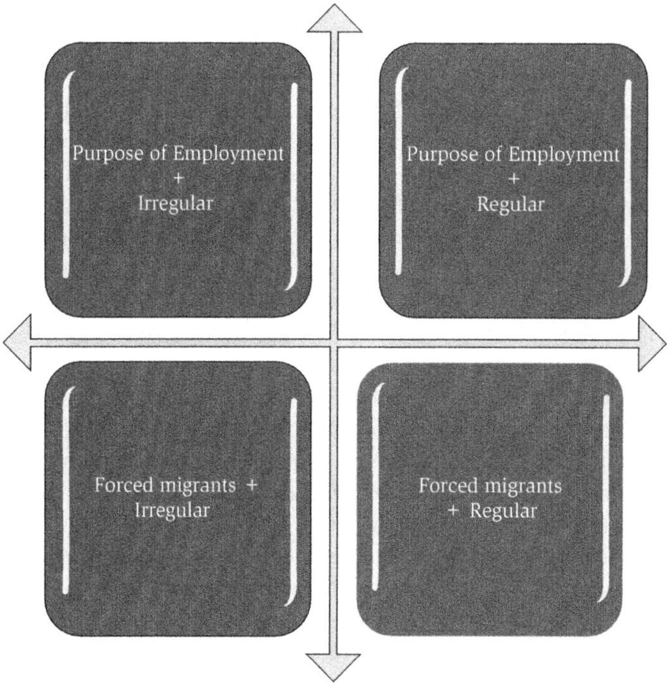

[A] Forced Migrants

Migrants displaced for humanitarian reasons constitute an important part of the migrant population in some countries. The International Organization for Migration defines forced migration as '*A migratory movement in which an element of coercion exists, including threats to life and livelihood, whether arising from natural or man-made causes (e.g. movements of refugees and internally displaced persons as well as people displaced by natural or environmental disasters, chemical or nuclear disasters, famine, or development projects)*'.[47] Comparing with the above mentioned international protection regime, this definition encompasses a larger scope covering not only man-made causes but also environmental disasters, famine or development projects. Displacements related to climate changes are expected to increase in the future, and neither national nor international instruments do not provide sufficient protection. That is why the UN Refugee Agency is engaged with the process of implementation and action pursuant to the United Nations Framework Convention on Climate Change

47. https://www.iom.int/key-migration-terms.

(UNFCC).[48] In addition, even those who are covered by international protection regime are subject different statuses when it comes to their access to the right to work.

[1] Access to the Labour Market by Refugees and Asylum Seekers

The Geneva Convention makes a difference as regards the access of labour market by asylum seekers: 'lawful presence' grants, thus the right to engage in an independent activity, where 'lawful staying' the right to engage in wage-earning employment. Debates on the meaning of 'lawfully staying' touch to the core of the problem: if refugees who undergo status verification procedure can be considered staying 'lawfully' after a certain lapse of time.[49] The preparatory work of the Geneva Convention shows the reluctance from the part of nation states.[50] Nevertheless, in accordance with Article 17 (1) of the Geneva Convention, within the first three years, the Refugee Convention satisfies with the 'most favourable treatment of foreign nationals' standards.[51] The circumstances in which refugee even if not yet lawfully staying may claim a right of exemption from the restrictions imposed non-nationals are regulated under paragraph 2 of Article 17. If a refugee has been present in the asylum state for at least three years or has a spouse or children with the host state's nationality, no further question about lawfully staying in the asylum country. Only after three years of residence in the country, they enjoy the right to wage-earning employment, and they are exempted from reciprocity.[52] Once the refugee status is recognized, they, in principle, enjoy the right to work. However, in some states, the work permit regulations also encumber refugee's access to the labour market.

In fact a legal dilemma arises from the fact the recognition of the refugee status has a declarative nature. Thus, a person does not become a refugee because of the recognition.[53] Due to this legal frame, asylum seekers must be treated on the assumption that they may be refugees.[54] Moreover apart from the EU, there is no binding international instrument which sets deadline for the asylum procedure.

48. http://www.unhcr.org/uk/protection/environment/5a215eb67/2017-unhcr-engagement-united-nations-framework-convention-climate-change.html.
49. Hathaway, The Rights of Refugees under International Law, 186–188, 730; *see also* L. Slingenberg, 'Equal Treatment under the Refugee Convention', The Reception of Asylum Seekers under International Law: Between Sovereignty and Equality, London: Hart Publishing, 2014, 128–132; B. Ryan/V. Mantouvalou, 'The Labour and Social Rights of Migrants in International Law', Human rights and Migration, ed. by R. Rubio-Marin, Oxford University Press, 2014, 182; However, Grahl-Madsen argues for a refugee who has a residence permit entitling him to remain there more than three months or who is lawfully present in a territory more than three months is lawfully staying: A. Grahl-Madsen, The Status of Refugees in International Law, Vol. II, A.W. Sijthoff-Leiden 1972, 354.
50. The Refugee Convention 1951, Travaux préparatoires analysed with a commentary by Dr Paul Weis, http://www.unhcr.org/uk/protection/travaux/4ca34be29/refugee-convention-1951-travaux-preparatoires-analysed-commentary-dr-paul.html.
51. B. Ryan/V. Mantouvalou, 'The Labour and Social Rights of Migrants in International Law', Human rights and Migration, ed. by R. Rubio-Marin, Oxford University Press, 2014, 182.
52. For more details *see* Hathaway, The Rights of Refugees under International Law, 755–761.
53. UNHRC, Handbook on Procedures and Criteria for Determining Refugee Status (1979 re-edited 1992), para. 28.
54. Hathaway, The Rights of Refugees under International Law, 158–159.

The European Union establishes common asylum procedures at the EU level by the Recast Asylum Procedures Directive 2013/32/EU. It states that an asylum procedure is normally concluded within six months of the lodging of the application (Article 31 (3)). Applicants are allowed to remain in the Member State until the determining authority has made a decision at first instance. Nevertheless, that right to stay shall constitute an entitlement to a residence permit (Article 9 (1)). With regard to employment rights, the Recast Reception Conditions Directive 2013/33/EU, on the one hand, puts the states under a duty to ensure that applicants have access to labour market no later than nine months (Article 15 (1)). On the other hand, the Directive grants Member States a large discretionary power to decide the conditions for granting access to the labour market (Article 15 (2)). Therefore, it is hard to say that there exist accurately common standards throughout the Union.[55]

It should also be noted that asylum seeking procedure is regulated on the individual base and there is a strong incentive to week out abusive asylum claims. However, due to large inflow experienced during last years, the length of asylum procedure seems increased enormously comparing to previous years. Even in the EU, this process, in practice, takes much longer than six months in many countries.[56] In many cases the extinction of these deadlines does not give an automatic right to work to asylum seekers that they are required a work permit. Table 9.1 shows the heterogeneity among legal systems.

Table 9.1 Access to the Labour Market by Asylum Seekers

	When do asylum seekers have access to the labour market?	Does the law allow access to employment only following a labour market test?	Are there restrictions to accessing employment in practice?
Belgium	4 months	No	Yes
Germany	General time limit 3 months Max. time limit (in initial reception centres) 6 months	No	Yes
France	9 months	No	Yes
Italy	2 months	No	Yes

55. V. Chetail, 'The Common European Asylum System: Bric-a-brac or System?', Reforming the Common European Asylum System, The new European Refugee Law, ed. V. Chetail/P. De Bruycker/F. Maiani, Brill 2016, 28–29.
56. European Council on Refugees and Exiles, The Length of Asylum Procedures in Europe, October 2016, Asylum Information Database, https://www.ecre.org/wp-content/uploads/2016/10/AIDA-Brief-DurationProcedures.pdf.

Hungary	No As a result of the March 2017 amendments, asylum seekers no longer have access to the labour market.		
South Africa	6 months	No	Yes
Sweden	1 day	No	Yes
Turkey	6 months	Yes	Yes
UK	1 year	Yes	Yes

Retrieved from Country reports of Asylum Information Database, http://www.asylumineurope.org/reports *and Questionnaires*.

Therefore, as regards of refugees and asylum seekers, the legal framework relevant to the labour rights is quite heterogeneous throughout the world and their access to the right to work takes much longer than regulated in practice.

[2] Access to the Labour Market by Beneficiaries of Complementary/Subsidiary[57] and Temporary Protection

The concept of 'refugee' is quite narrow in many senses: In addition to geographical and temporal limitations of the Geneva Convention, the well-founded fear of '*being persecuted for reasons of race, religion, nationality, membership of a particular social group or political opinion*' are numerous which entitle the displaced person the refugee status. It is hard for people fleeing armed conflicts to demonstrate the individual persecution.

Despite the established jurisprudence of the ECtHR relevant to the principle of non-refoulement, those who fall out of the scope of refugee and asylum seekers do not enjoy an international protection regime. The European Union Qualification Directive of 2004[58] lays out the main principles relating to those who are excluded the refugee status.

Pursuant to the Qualification Directive, the person eligible for subsidiary protection means a third-country national or a stateless person who does not qualify as a refugee but in respect of whom substantial grounds have been shown for believing that the person concerned, if returned to his or her country of origin would face a real risk of suffering serious harm and is unable, or, owing to such risk, unwilling to avail

57. The UNHRC prefers the use of term 'complementary protection' referring to the complementary nature of this status to the Geneva Convention.
58. Council Directive 2004/83/EC of 29 April 2004 on Minimum Standards for the Qualification and Status of Third Country Nationals or Stateless Persons as Refugees or as Persons Who Otherwise Need International Protection and the Content of the Protection Granted [2004] OJ L304/12 and Directive 2011/95/EU of 13 December 2011 on standards for the qualification of third-country nationals or stateless persons as beneficiaries of international protection, for a uniform status for refugees or for persons eligible for subsidiary protection, and for the content of the protection granted (Recast).

himself or herself of the protection of that country (Article 2 (e)). Serious harm consists of the death penalty or execution, torture or inhuman or degrading treatment or punishment of the applicant; serious and individual threat to a civilian's life or person by reason of indiscriminate violence in situations of international or internal armed conflict (Article 15).

This definition is a source of inspiration for other states who grants a protection status for those persons. Under Turkish law, according to Article 63 of Act No. 6458 on Foreigners and International Protection, a foreigner or a stateless person, who neither could be qualified as a refugee nor as a conditional refugee, shall nevertheless be granted subsidiary protection upon the status determination because if returned to the country of origin would be sentenced to death, or face the execution of the death penalty or face torture or inhuman or degrading treatment or punishment, or face serious threat to himself or herself by reason of indiscriminate violence in situations of international or nationwide armed conflict.

Article 26 of the Qualification Directive sets out their access to employment that '*Member States shall authorise beneficiaries of international protection to engage in employed or self-employed activities subject to rules generally applicable to the profession and the public service, immediately after protection has been granted.*' Their access to employment in the Member States are protected despite the reduction of the content of this article during the drafting process. An important acquis is that the right to access the labour market is granted immediately after protection has been granted whereas there were six months of the waiting period in the original proposal. In addition, the Recast Directive removed the provision which enables the situation of the labour markets in the Member States may be taken into account while authorizing the beneficiary of subsidiary protection to engage in employment.[59]

Under Turkish law, Article 89/4-b of the Act No. 6458 provides that '*the refugee or the subsidiary protection beneficiary, upon being granted the status, may work independently or be employed, without prejudice to the provisions stipulated in other legislation restricting foreigners to engage in certain jobs a profession. The identity document to be issued to a refugee or a subsidiary protection beneficiary shall also substitute for a work permit and this information shall be written on the document.*' Therefore, subsidiary protection owners need a work permit. Nevertheless, the identity document substitutes this permit. In addition, the following subparagraph of Article 89 shows the reflection to keep labour market to nationals: Where the situation of the labour market and developments in the working life as well as sectoral and economic conditions regarding employment necessitate, in agriculture, industry or, service sectors or a certain profession, line of business or, administrative and geographical areas, access of the refugee and the subsidiary protection beneficiary to the labour market may be restricted for a given period.

Both the Refugee Convention and the Qualification Directive require an individualized status determination which short of meeting the urgent need for the protection

59. For the discussions about Art. 26 of the Directive of 2004 *see* J. McAdam, 'The European Union Qualification Directive: The Creation of a Subsidiary Protection Regime', International Journal of Refugee Law, 2005, Vol. 17, Issue 3, 508–510.

of large numbers of people fleeing human rights abuses and armed conflict in their country of origin. In Article 16 of the Guidelines on Temporary Protection and Stay Arrangements by UNHRC, 'self-sufficiency or work opportunities' is among the minimum standards of treatment. The conflicting interests of nation states and the complexity of the problem explain the difficulty in reaching internationally binding agreements which regulate the issue.[60]

The EU Temporary Protection Directive (2002/55/EC) adopted on 20 July 2001 broadens the narrow definition of a refugee under the Geneva Convention. As regards the obligation of Member States towards persons enjoying temporary protection, Article 12 of the Temporary Protection Directive states that '*The Member States shall authorise, for a period not exceeding that of temporary protection, persons enjoying temporary protection to engage in employed or self-employed activities, subject to rules applicable to the profession, as well as in activities such as educational opportunities for adults, vocational training and practical workplace experience*'. However, Member States have the right to give priority other groups for reasons of labour market policies. The general rules relating to remuneration, access to social security systems relating to employed or self-employed activities and other conditions of employment apply to those who are under temporary protection status. Nevertheless, the non-implementation of the Directive and large discrepancies between Member States show the difficulty of finding a consensus.[61]

With 3.1 million displaced persons from Syria, Turkey became the largest hosting country worldwide. Syrians who have crossed the border in a mass influx are under temporary protection status. According to Article 91 paragraph 1 of Act No. 6458, '*temporary protection may be provided for foreigners who have been forced to leave their country, cannot return to the country that they have left, and have arrived at or crossed the borders of Turkey in a mass influx situation seeking immediate and temporary protection*'.

[3] International Protection Regimes Through the Lenses of Labour Law: Weak and Fragmented Protection

One of the common grounds of the three international instruments which could be considered the most significant ones in the sense of laying out a comprehensive set of civil, political, economic, social and other rights, the International Convention on the Protection of the Rights of All Migrant Workers and Members of Their Families and the ILO's Conventions on the Migration Employment and the Migrant Workers (Supplementary Provisions) Convention, is that they are among the least ratified treaties.

60. UNHCR Executive Committee of the High Commissioner's Programme, 32nd session, Protection of Asylum Seekers in Situations of Large-Scale Influx, No. 22(XXXII), 1981; UNHCR Executive Committee of the High Commissioner's Programme, 45th session, Note on International Protection, A/AC.-96/830, 7 September 1994, UNHCR Executive Committee of the High Commissioner's Programme, 55th session, Conclusion on International Cooperation and Burden and Responsibility Sharing in Mass-Influx Situations, No. 100(LV) (2004); UNHCR, Guidelines on Temporary Protection or Stay Arrangements (2014).
61. *See* European Commission, Study on the Temporary Protection Directive, January 2016.

There exist many reasons to explain the low ratification of migrant conventions.[62] With respect to the UN Convention on Migrant Workers, Part III, which regulates the human rights of all migrant workers and their families, is cited as an obstacle to its ratification.[63] In fact, the Convention with the aim of balancing the states' sovereign powers and the fundamental human rights of irregular migrants[64] has no aim to regularize the irregular migrants but only to provide basic human rights. Thus, Article 35 of the Convention states itself that '*Nothing in the present part of the Convention shall be interpreted as implying the regularization of the situation of migrant workers or members of their families who are non-documented or in an irregular situation or any right to such regularization of their situation, nor shall it prejudice the measures intended to ensure sound and equitable-conditions for international migration...*'. In addition, Article 79 of the Convention underlines explicitly the sovereign powers of nation states while admitting the migrant workers and their families as '*Nothing in the present Convention shall affect the right of each State Party to establish the criteria governing admission of migrant workers and members of their families...*'. But these provisions do not seem suffice to convince nation states to ratify the Convention. The low number of the binding international instruments comparing with the multitude of policy document shows that migrants-receiving high-income states are reluctant to be bound by international conventions.

Moreover, many workers fall out of the scope of these treaties and are therefore excluded from the international protection: Frontier workers, artists and members of the liberal professions who have entered the country on a short-time basis; seamen; persons coming specifically for purposes of training or education; employees of organizations or undertakings operating within the territory of a country who have been admitted temporarily to that country to undertake specific duties or assignments, for a limited and defined period of time (Article 11 (2) of Convention No. 143). ILO Convention No. 97 does not apply to frontier workers, short-term entry of members of the liberal professions and artists, and seamen (Article 11 (2)). The UN Convention on Migrant Workers excludes persons sent or employed by international organizations and agencies or persons sent or employed by a state outside its territory to perform official functions; persons sent or employed by a state or on its behalf outside its territory who participate in development programmes and other co-operation programmes; persons taking up residence in a state different from their state of origin as investors; refugees and stateless persons under certain conditions; students and

62. For the obstacles and theirs evaluation *see* A. Desmond, 'The Triangle That Could Square the Circle? The UN International Convention on the Protection of the Rights of All Migrant Workers and Members of Their Families, the EU and the Universal Periodic Review', European Journal of Migration and Law, 17 (2015), 48–49; M. Ruhs, The Price of Rights, Princeton University Press 2015, 16–23.
63. A. Desmond, 'The Triangle that could Square the Circle? The UN International Convention on the Protection of the Rights of All Migrant Workers and Members of Their Families, the EU and the Universal Periodic Review', European Journal of Migration and Law, 17 (2015), 45.
64. *See* L. S. Bosniak, 'Human Rights, State Sovereignty and the Protection of Undocumented Migrants Under the International Migrant Workers Convention', The International Migration Review, Vol. 25, No. 4, Special Issue: U.N. International Convention on the Protection of the Rights of All Migrant Workers and Members of Their Families (Winter, 1991), 737–770.

trainees; seafarers and workers on an offshore installation who have not been admitted to take up residence and engage in a remunerated activity in the state of employment (Article 3).

International human rights instruments focus on the circumstances of concerned individuals in their countries of origin and mainly regulates the admission criteria and statuses in another country. Thus, the protection provided by the international human rights instruments contains subtle differentiations and restrictions as regards labour rights of displaced persons. The conditions to their access to the labour market depend upon extra-labour circumstances, such as the grounds of their fear, the individual or collective nature of fleeing. Apart from asylum seekers, people who are under an international protection status do not benefit any labour right during the recognition process. The length of the process depends on the numbers of arrived persons and the infrastructure of the host country.

Another difficult issue is the fact that each economic migrant can try to claim to be an asylum seeker. The host state is under obligation to assess this claim and to recognize the exact legal status of the person. Legal systems are far from providing a satisfactory solution both protecting forced migrants and preventing abuses. Regulations aiming to prevent abusive practices aggravate the situation of forced migrants. This point also shows the blurry line between the two groups of migrants; those who cross the borders for the purpose of employment and those who forcedly displaced. In addition, migrants displaced due to natural disasters fall out of the scope of international protection. It seems displacements related to climate change will increase in the future and for the moment, these people who suffer from the climate warming have no legal bases to claim rights in the host country.

Moreover, the formal recognition of the migrants' status under international law does not, in most of the cases, grant an automatic right to work in the host states. The three steps of the settlement in a host state, entry, stay and work, are subject to different legal preconditions. Many people could stay lawfully in a state without having a right to work. Having the right to work does not mean having a work permit in practice. The states such as the case in Turkey may ask for further labour market tests to grant work permit.

The regularity or irregularity of the migrant's status affects their rights arising from the employment relationship. The question of regularity seems complicated when one considers that people who escape from persecution, war, natural disasters cross the borders of another state in both regular and mainly in irregular ways. The person may enter into another state and ask for asylum, as well as just cross the border without having travel and identity documents. In cases of mass influx, it takes time to recognize the identity of people forcedly displaced. As shown above, the recognition process of their status varies considerably from state to state. The impact of their irregular status on the labour relationship will be examined below.

Therefore, there are groups of people forcedly displaced and who have right to stay but do not benefit from the right to work. The nation states keep the sovereign power to grant the right to work/a work permit. The basic assumption is either all these people fleeing from war, persecution or disasters have necessary means to live or all host countries have financial sources to provide them with a life with dignity. Both cases seem far from being realistic. Facing the huge number of displacements, even economically strong countries have difficulties. On the other hand, all legal requirements, setting aside the practical integration problems, e.g., lack of language, professional certificates, relating to the access the labour market increase the vulnerability of these people. Having the right to stay lawfully without having the right to work would increase the vulnerability in the labour market and indicates the need for the labour law's approach to the problem. Table 9.2 can give an idea about the heterogeneity of legal systems.

Table 9.2 Refugees and the Right to Work

		The Number of Refugees	*The Right to Work*
Bangladesh	Not party to the 1951 Convention relating to the Status of Refugees or the 1967 Protocol	31,958 refugees and approximately 200,000 people in refugee-like situations. (The government categorizes the 300,000–500,000 unregistered Rohingyas as 'illegal economic migrants.')	Registered refugees and undocumented Rohingyas are officially denied the right to work. Informal employment has been tolerated.
Ecuador	Party to the 1951 Convention and the 1967 Protocol, and party to the Cartagena Declaration	53,191 refugees, 68,344 people in refugee-like situation, and 11,583 asylum seekers totalling 133,11851 = 0.82% of a total estimated population	Since 2012, refugees have not been required to have work permits, further easing access to labour markets.
Ethiopia	Party to the 1951 Convention relating to the Status of Refugees (but with reservations), the 1967 Protocol, and the 1969 Organization of African Unity Convention	736,086 refugees and 2,131 asylum seekers totalling 738,217 = 0.74% of a total estimated population	Reservation to the 1951 Refugee Convention, notably to Article 17.2. Refugees in Ethiopia are only allowed to work and access education insofar as Ethiopia's laws allow other foreign nationals in Ethiopia to do. Large informal employment.

		The Number of Refugees	*The Right to Work*
Germany	Party to the 1951 Convention relating to the Status of Refugees and the 1967 Protocol	316,115 refugees and 420,625 asylum seekers totaling 736,740 = 0.9% of a total estimated population	Once refugees are recognized and issued a residence permit, there are no limitations on their access to the labour market, self-employment, training and education. Since November 2014, asylum seekers are authorized to reside in Germany but awaiting a decision on their status to take up employment three months after their arrival. Those whose deportation is suspended (Duldung) are also entitled to work; they can also be self-employed after three months with a priority review and after 15 months without such review.
India	Not party to the 1951 Convention relating to the Status of Refugees or the 1967 Protocol	201,381 refugees and 6,480 asylum seekers totalling 207,861 = 0.01% of a total estimated population	No need for work permit. Refugees having residence permit have right to work
Italy	Party to the 1951 Convention relating to the Status of Refugees and the 1967 Protocol	147,370 refugees and 99,921 asylum seekers totalling 247,291 = 0.41% of a total estimated population	Those who have been granted refugee status have the right to work. Asylum seekers can also work within 60 days of having filed their application, while they are awaiting a decision on their status.
Jordan	Not party to the 1951 Convention relating to the Status of Refugees and the 1967 Protocol	664,118 refugees and 24,935 asylum seekers totalling 689,053 = 10.4% of a total population	Except, refugees who entered Jordan through unofficial borders or who are residents of refugee camps, refugees have right to have a work permit Large informal economy

		The Number of Refugees	*The Right to Work*
Kenya	Party to the 1951 Convention relating to the Status of Refugees, the 1967 Protocol, and the 1969 Organization of African Unity Convention	553,912 refugees and 39,969 asylum seekers totalling 593,881 = 1.2% of a total estimated population	Refugees have the right to work but they need a work permit Informal employment
Lebanon	Not party to the 1951 Convention relating to the Status of Refugees and the 1967 Protocol	1,070,854 refugees and 12,139 asylum seekers totalling 1,082,993 = 18.5% of a total estimated population	Strict legal restrictions on the employment of Palestinian refugees. All other non-Palestinian refugees need a work permit Informal employment
Pakistan	Not party to the 1951 Convention relating to the Status of Refugees and the 1967 Protocol	1,561,162 refugees and 6,442 asylum seekers totalling 1,567,604 = 0.83% of a total estimated population	Registered Afghan citizens living in Pakistan have been subject to Pakistani labour and employment laws, and were legally authorized to work in the country Informal employment
South Africa	Party to the 1951 Convention relating to the Status of Refugees, the 1967 Protocol, and the 1969 Organization of African Unity Convention	121,645 refugees and 1,096,063 asylum seekers totalling 1,217,708 = 2.21% of a total estimated population	Refugees and asylum seekers have right to work Informal employment
Turkey	Party to the 1951 Convention relating to the Status of Refugees and the 1967 Protocol, but applies geographical limitation by providing 'refugee status' only to individuals fleeing events occurring in Europe	2,541,352 refugees and 212,408 asylum seekers totalling 2,753,760 = 3.5% of a total estimated population	Refugees and those under temporary protection status have the right to work but need a work permit They can apply for a work permit six months after applying for international protection status. Informal employment

		The Number of Refugees	*The Right to Work*
United Kingdom	Party to the 1951 Convention relating to the Status of Refugees and the 1967 Protocol	123,067 refugees and 45,870 asylum seekers totalling 168,937 = 0.25% of a total estimated population	Refugees have the right to work Asylum seekers have no right to work while their applications are being considered, although this constraint may be waived after 12 months if their initial claim has not been decided.
United States	Party to the 1951 Convention relating to the Status of Refugees and the 1967 Protocol	273,202 refugees, and 286,168 asylum seekers totalling 559,370 = 0.17% of a total estimated population	Refugees have the right to work Asylum seekers need Employment Authorization Document and they can only apply for an EAD: (1) 180 days after filing their asylum claim and (2) if an application for asylum has been pending for more than 150 days without decision.
Venezuela	Party to the 1967 Protocol, and to the 1984 Cartagena Declaration on Refugees	6,694 refugees, 167,060 people in a refugee-like situation, and 235 asylum seekers totalling 173,989 = 0.54% of a total estimated population	Refugees have the right to work without need for a work permit Informal employment

Retrieved from KNOMAD Study, Refugee's Right to Work and Access to Labour Markets - An Assessment, Part II, Country Cases, by R. /H. Ruadel, September 2016

[B] Migration for the Purpose of Employment

Migrants who seek to have employment in another state may be divided into two categories: those who have a permanent residence permit in a foreign state and those who work under temporary residence and work permits. In 2013–2014, a growth in the number of temporary workers, including seasonal workers, was recorded in Canada, Republic of Korea, New Zealand and Unites States and also Brazil. The Gulf States receives almost exclusively temporary migration.[65] The vulnerabilities of both group and the protection requirements are different from each other.

[1] The Diversity of Legal Instruments

The reciprocal interests of the both sending and receiving states are implemented through migration management policies. The international community develops new instruments while trying to deal with the complexity of the transnational migration. According to recent research conducted by the ILO, the diversity of legal instruments, e.g. bilateral agreements, memorandum of understanding, memorandum of agreements, framework agreements, protocols, inter-agency understandings, cross-border worker agreements, bilateral social security agreements, anti-trafficking agreements, is outstanding.[66]

The bilateral agreements, as a binding legal instrument, constitute the main legal tool to regulate the migration. The agreement between France and Italy in 1904 is its first example. The main aim of the bilateral agreements was the labour recruitment which were largely used during the post-war reconstruction period in Europe,[67] whereas post 1990's bilateral agreements have many other aims than recruitment, such as promoting regional integration, controlling irregular migration and promoting regular migration and ensuring readmission, promotion of cultural ties, ensuring temporariness in stays, protecting rights and promoting welfare of migrants.[68]

The long list of good practices in bilateral agreements such as explicit reference to upholding rights of migrant workers or to international instruments concerning migrant workers; specific reference to the equal treatment of migrant workers; gender concerns; provisions to promote fair recruitment practices; coverage of wage protection measures; concrete provisions relating to the employment contract, concrete provisions relating to social dialogue and implementation and monitoring procedures and so on[69] show that these agreements could be used in a very effective manner to protect migrant workers' rights. The more comprehensive and concrete references to the labour rights of migrants and more effective monitoring procedures, ensuring the involvement of employers' and workers' trade unions will increase the benefits of these agreements.[70]

---

65. ILO, Promoting fair migration, paras 20–21.
66. ILO, Bilateral agreements and memoranda of understanding on the migration of low-skilled workers: a review, Report prepared by P. Wickramasekara, ILC-Geneva: ILO-2015, box 2, 13–14.
67. The need for labour in Belgium, France, the Federal Republic of Germany (West Germany) and the Netherlands concluded agreements with one or more countries in southern Europe (Greece, Italy, Portugal, Spain), Turkey, Ireland, the former Yugoslav Republic and the north Africa (Algeria, Morocco, Tunisia).
68. ILO, Bilateral agreements and memoranda of understanding on the migration of low-skilled worker, 17–18.
69. *See* ILO, Bilateral agreements and memoranda of understanding on the migration of low-skilled worker, 24–32.
70. *See* R. Cholewinski, 'Evaluating Bilateral Labour Migration Agreements in the Light of Human and Labour Rights', The Palgrave Handbook of International Labour Migration: Law and Policy Perspectives, 2015, 231–246.

[2] Strictly Regulated Patterns

The political borders of the nation states also draw the borders of their labour markets, in a sense open to nationals and restricted to non-nationals. In each country, migration legislation determines different categories of migrants whose migration pathways are clearly defined: for example in the UK, five-tier visa system is valid: tier 1 visa is for 'high-value migrants', tier 2 visa for 'skilled workers, tier 4 visa for 'students', tier 5 visa for six sub-tiers of temporary work.[71] Tier 3 visa for 'low-skilled workers' filling specific temporary labour shortages was never implemented and discontinued. Under Turkish law, there exists four types of working permit: Permanent working permit, temporary working permit, turkuaz card for skilled foreigners and work permit for self-employed persons.

Many countries have labour immigration programs which refer to a set of policies that regulate the admission, employment and rights of migrant workers. Ruhr summarizes demand side restrictions in these programs as job offer, labour market test, sectoral and occupational restrictions as appear in many seasonal agricultural programs, work permit fees, wage restrictions, and in rare cases trade union involvement. Supply-side restrictions are nationality and age, gender and marital status, skill requirements, language skill requirements, self-sufficiency.[72]

The nation states strictly regulate the entrance conditions into their labour market. The application for residence and work permits are two different steps of the process. By the implementation of the Single Permit Directive (2011/98/EU), these two steps have been unified in the EU, but in many other states, residence permit and work permit are two different steps of the migration process. In some cases work permit fees reaches an important amount. The application for these permits, at least for the first time, must be done before entering the host state. Migration legislation which aims to provide labour supply to sectors suffering from the shortage of workforce put restrictions on the work permits which prevent working in other sectors.

In many national laws, the work permit is subject to a condition to have a job offer or an employment contract. In Germany, a residence permit for employment will be granted if a concrete job offer exits (section 18 paragraph 5 of Residence Act). If there is no need a valid employment contract, the applicant is expected to present a solid offer, a draft employment contract. The potential employer is required to provide the Federal Employment Agency with the information about pay, working hours and other terms of the employment relationship. The permit is granted only if the employment of foreigner does not result in adverse consequences in the labour market. However, the approval of the Federal Agency is not necessary for highly qualified

71. M. Zou, 'Employer demand for "skilled" migrant workers: regulating admission under the United Kingdom?' Tier 2 (general) Visa', Temporary Migration in the Global Era, ed. J. Howe/R. Owens, Oxford: Hart Publishing 2016, 120–121.
72. Ruhs, The Price of Rights, 60–64.

workers, executives and employees in science, research and specialists.[73] In Brazil, temporary work visas are granted if migrants provide evidence of a job offer formalized by a legal entity active in the country (Article 14, I, § 5, Law 13.445/2017).

Under the Tier 2 (general work visa) visa regime of the United Kingdom, the applicant must have an offer for a skilled job in the UK. Job offer is a precondition for entry. In addition, such a migrant could only be employed by a licensed sponsor. The employer should give the migrant a certificate of sponsorship that the candidate migrant could apply for a Tier 2 visa. Therefore, it is under the control of the authorities for which job the visa application is granted.[74] In the UK, the employer needs to have a sponsor licence to recruit a migrant. The sponsor licence which enables the recruitment of a foreigner in a specific job in the workplace to someone outside the country makes possible to monitor both sides of the employment relationship.

A labour market test is also another precondition for entry in many countries. Sweden presents an interesting exemption to this practice. The migrant should also provide a job offer including the terms of employment and salary that are on par with those set by Swedish collective agreements or which are customary within the occupation or industry. Nevertheless, there is no labour market test in the Swedish system. It is the employer who decides about the need for the recruitment of third-country nationals.[75]

[3] Discrepancy of Rights

A general overview of different legislative models reveals that nation states combine measures to control immigration with those of juridical status of immigrants in the host states. Migration studies show clearly the discrepancy of rights granted to different migrant statutes. A recently published study contains an empirical analysis of 104 labour migration programs in forty-six high and medium-income countries, which provide important insights as regards the regulated migration patterns in 2009.[76] According to Ruhr's study, the legal rights of migrants vary from region to region. As a general observation, labour immigration programs in Gulf Cooperation Council countries and Southeast Asia contain more restrictions as regards the rights of migrant workers compared with the ones in Latin America, Europe and North America.[77]

---

73. C. Shaubert/L. Schmitt, 'The German Regulations on Labour Migration and the Impact of the EU Directives on Labour Migration thereon', Bulletin of Comparative Labour Relations, National Effects of the Impelementation of EU Directives on Labour Migration from Third Countries, 91, 2016 (35-76), 40-41.
74. For the details of the system *see* M. Zou, 'Employer demand for "skilled" migrant workers: regulating admission under the United Kingdom?' Tier 2 (general) Visa', Temporary Migration in the Global Era, ed. J. Howe/R. Owens, Hart Publishing Oxford 2016, 113-130.
75. P. Herzfeld Olsson, 'The Swedish Regulation on Labour Migration and Impact and Possible Impact of Three EU Directives on Labour Migration', Bulletin of Comparative Labour Relations, National Effects of the Impelementation of EU Directives on Labour Migration from Third Countries, 91, 2016 (35-76), 78-81.
76. M. Ruhs, The Price of Rights: Regulating International Labor Migration, Princeton University Press, 2015.
77. Ruhs, The Price of Rights, 89.

The defining parameter affecting the scope of migrant's rights seems the skill level of the migrant. Countries are, in general, more open to admitting high-skilled workers, with important exceptions such as GCC countries wherein low-skilled migrants constitute the large majority of the workforce (over 50% in Saudi Arabia to 95% in Qatar).[78]

The research of Ruhs elucidates the extent of rights at work in the labour migration programs.[79] Different policies for high and low-skilled migrants flesh out different admission criteria and rights for migrants. The admission conditions and work permit regimes are easier as regards high-skilled migrants than low-skilled migrants. All existing migration programs with permanent residence status target high-skilled workers. They enjoy, at least in theory, the right to equal working conditions, equal wage and their enforcement. As regards social rights, unemployment benefits and social housing are two restricted social rights.[80] It should also be noted that high-skilled workers often do lower skilled work in high-income countries.[81] Rights granted to workers under temporary migration programs are much more limited comparing to permanent residence status, and low-skilled workers are, in general, admitted under temporary migration programs. Temporary migrants suffer from considerable restrictions on their freedom to choose and change their employer. In many cases, changing employer requires a new work permit.[82]

The comparison of the EU Blue Card Directive and the EU Directive on Seasonal Workers leads to similar conclusions: High-skilled blue card owners are entitled to strong protections both in terms of employment relations, social security and family reunification rights. However, as regards seasonal workers, if the principle of equality with national workers is valid in terms of employment rights and the freedom of association, the level of social security is much lower, since the aim of the EU Directive is to ensure that the seasonal workers return their homes as soon as their permits expire.[83] Likewise, the Caribbean Community (CARICOM) Treaty provides a free movement only for skilled nationals.

In order to prevent illegal migration, it is argued that the regular migration channels should be left open. Temporary workers, guest or visa workers, have a right to work under predetermined conditions. The fact is that their rights to reside and work, generally visas, depending on a specific employment with a particular employer

78. Ruhs, The Price of Rights, 91 et seq., 97.
79. Selected rights at work are as follows: Free choice of employment, equal pay, equal working conditions (e.g., overtime, hours of work, weekly rest, paid holidays, sick pay, health and safety at work, protection against dismissal), right to join trade unions; the right to redress if the terms of their employment contract have been violated by their employer, Ruhs calls these rights as economic rights. However, we prefer to call them as labour rights: *see* Ruhs, The Price of Rights, Appendix 3, 222. The selected social rights are as follows: the right to equal access to unemployment benefits, to public retirement pension schemes, public education and training, public housing and public health services, The Price of Rights, Appendix 3, 223–224.
80. Ruhs, The Price of Rights, 88.
81. Ruhs, The Price of Rights, 51 et seq., 88–89; ILO, Fair Migration, paras 105–106.
82. Ruhs, The Price of Rights, 67–68.
83. P. Herzfeld Olsson, 'Introduction to Directives', Bulletin of Comparative Labour Relations, National Effects of the Implementation of EU Directives on Labour Migration from Third Countries, 91, 2016, 24–30.

prevent them to choose another job in the labour market. This system carries a risk of causing certain vulnerabilities.[84] The main aim of these programs is to supply workforce to employers and these programs are demand driven programs by their nature.

[C] Migration and the 'Regularity': Triangle Between Labour Law, Migration Law and Human Rights Law

A general overview of the international instruments reveals that the regularity of the migrant's status has a determinant effect on the scale of the protection provided to migrants. The UN Convention on Migrant Workers provides the principle that migrant workers shall not deprived of any rights derived by reason of any irregularity in their stay or employment (Article 25 (3)). However, an important part of the vulnerability suffered in the labour market arises from the irregularity of the migrant. Thus, the term 'irregularity' needs a further investigation as regards migrant workers. What is the irregularity which affects the validity of the contractual relationship?

Labour laws, in general, make no distinction as regards the cause of irregularity. And as an independent legal discipline, labour law plays little role in determining the destiny of the work relationship. The question is whether each irregularity on the immigration procedure should have the power to invalidate the contract of employment. Does the combat with illegal migration justify such legal destruction?

[1] Deconstruction of Legal 'Irregularity'

Illegal, undocumented or irregular migrants, three terms conveying different connotations, have overlapping meanings. Even though terms illegal/irregular/undocumented migration finds an important place on the policy agendas, there is no clear legal definition. Both ILO Conventions Nos. 143 and 97 refer to the criteria 'regular admission'. It is, therefore, the host state which defines the conditions of the regularity in the admission process. However, the UN Convention on Migrant Workers has a broader concept of irregularity: According to Article 5 (1) of the Convention, migrant workers '*are consideredas documented or in a regular situation if they are authorized to enter, to stay and to engage in a remunerated activity in the State of employment pursuant to the law of that State and to international agreements to which that State is a party*'.

The Appendix of the European Social Charter determines the personal scope of application as '*foreigners only in so far as they are nationals of other Parties lawfully resident or working regularly within the territory of the Party concerned*'. In order to be covered by the Charter, the nationality of the migrant and being lawfully resident or working regularly become determinant. This wording implies that workers who are not

84. M. Ontiveros, 'Migrant Labour in USA', Migrants at Work, ed. C. Costello/M. Freedland, Oxford University Press, 2014, 187–188.

lawfully residing in a contracting state but who are working regularly fall within the scope of the Charter and enjoy the full protection of rights.[85]

The Employer Sanctions Directive 2009/52/EC defines 'illegal employment' as '*the employment of an illegally staying third-country national*' and 'illegally staying third-country national' as '*third-country national present on the territory of a Member State, who does not fulfil, or no longer fulfils, the conditions for stay or residence in that Member State.*[86] The Directive should not apply to third-country nationals staying legally regardless of '*whether they are allowed to work in its territory*' (Recital 5 of the Preamble).[87] Therefore, the illegal employment is related to the conditions for stay and residence. And Article 3/3 of the Directive states that ' *A Member State may decide not to apply the prohibition referred to in paragraph 1 to illegally staying third-country nationals whose removal has been postponed and who are allowed to work in accordance with national law.*'

The illegal/legal presence and legal/illegal work are thus related each other in international instruments. The irregular employment, in most of the cases, overlaps with the informal employment. However, there may exist cases wherein the migrant who has a social security number is able to stay legally and works with this social security number without having a work permit. Thus, there is a possibility that an irregular migrant is recruited in a formal employment relationship. Nevertheless, the number of irregular-formal employment cases has been reducing, while a growing number of states adopting immigration legislation which imposes upon the employer new duties.

The migration legislation makes a distinction between the conditions of entry and stay. In order to maintain an effective immigration control and to prevent illegal immigration, the states impose upon employers stricter duties to check the immigration status of the employee. Offences concerning documents constitute an important part of immigration offences. Either the submission of a valid document that relates to someone else or the presentation of a forged document is introduced as an offence. But in any case, the employer is under obligation to check the list of documents, which evidence the right to work. It is important to have the correct documents to prove the non-national's right to stay in many cases. Therefore, not only having the right but also having the required documents, which demonstrate the right to stay is determinant to have a valid contractual relationship. In this legal framework, every kind of irregularity has the potential to render the contractual relationship invalid.

Before examining the migrant worker's legal situation comparatively, I believe rather develop a basic typology consisting of main axes of irregularity to better capture the impacts of migration legislation on the labour rights of migrants. Such a deconstructivist approach to the irregularity will show the large range of irregularity.

85. C. O'Cinnéide, 'Migrants Rights under the Social Charter', Migrants at Work, Oxford University Press 2014, 291–292.
86. *See* S. Peers, 'Legislative Update: EC Immigration and Asylum Law Attracting and Deterring Labour Migration: The Blue Card and Employer Sanctions Directives', European Journal of Migration and Law 11 (2009), 387–426, 411–426.
87. S. Peers, 'Legislative Update: EC Immigration and Asylum Law Attracting and Deterring Labour Migration: The Blue Card and Employer Sanctions Directives', 412.

Table 9.3 Irregularity in Migration Process and the Employment Relationship

Entrance	*Stay*	*Irregular Employment*		*Legal Employment Formal + Informal*
		Formal	*Informal*	
Illegal (transiting a border without having a residence/work and necessary documents)	Illegal		x	
Illegal (transiting a border without having a residence/work and necessary documents)	Illegal	Formal (paying taxes and social security contributions but working without having a work permit)		
	Illegal (children of illegal migrants born country of residence)	x	x	x
Illegal (asylum seekers without access to the right to work)	Legal		x	
Illegal (Refused asylum seekers who do not return, are not removed and/or who are de facto non-removable because of lack of documents, unclear identity, unsafe country of origin, family links or health, age and gender-related constraints.	Semi-Legal (e.g., person in respect to whom removal order has been formally suspended)	x	x	x
Clandestine entry Illegal	Often apply asylum and regularize their stay		x	
	x			
Legal (Tourists working without permission)	Legal		x	

Entrance	*Stay*	*Irregular Employment*		*Legal Employment Formal + Informal*
		Formal	*Informal*	
Legal immigrants without right to work, e.g., students, family members	Legal		x	
Legal (visa overstayers)	Illegal		x	
Legal (persons whose residence work permit has expired but continue to be formally employed)	Illegal	x		

Adopted from A. Kraler, Regularization; "A Misguided option or part and parcel of a comprehensive policy to irregular migration", IMISCOE Working Paper No. 24, February 2009, Table 1.

Table 9.3 shows the great variety of irregularity, which may affect the validity of the employment relationship. The irregularity may occur on each step of the immigration process. The employment relationship of a foreigner, such as a foreigner arriving clandestinely on to the territory of the host state; a foreigner crossing the borders without required visa documents whereas having the right to stay; a foreigner legally residing but working without having a work permit; a foreigner working over the limits of his/her visa; or a foreigner working having the right to work but without possessing the required documents, seems tainted with irregularity. It would, thus, be wrong to see the irregular migration as an independent social phenomenon. The illegality of the migration has strong ties with state policies and social, political and legal construction.[88] In addition, the irregularity has a temporal nature that following the expiry date of the visa/work permit, the legality of the employment relationship is questioned. Costello shows the 'multi-level legality' and 'temporal shifts' in the status of migrants.[89]

The pathways to irregularity lead to questioning the legal attitude towards contractual validity.[90] Each irregularity on the migration process should have the power to render the employment contract invalid? The migration legislation seeking to combat irregular migration directly affects the validity of the employment contract.[91] It

88. F. Düvell, 'Paths into Irregularity: The Legal and Political Construction of Irregular Migration', European Journal of Migration and Law 13, (2011), 275-295; B. Anderson, 'Migration, immigration controls and the fashioning of precarious workers', Work, Employment and Society, Vol. 24 (2), 312.
89. C. Costello, The Human Rights of Migrants and Refugees in European Law, Oxford University Press 2015, 64-67.
90. F. Düvell, 'The Pathways in and out of Irregular Migration in the EU: A Comparative Analysis', European Journal of Migration and Law 13 (2011), pp. 245-250; and also *see* F. Düvell, 'Paths into Irregularity: The Legal and Political Construction of Irregular Migration', European Journal of Migration and Law 13 (2011), 275-295.
91. C. Costello, The Human Rights of Migrants and Refugees in European Law, 67.

is a general worry that providing labour rights to those who work without having a valid work permit will risk the incentives of immigrants to cross borders and work irregularly. Restricting the access of migrants to labour markets reveal an important step in managing migration. It seems important at least to make a distinction between those cases wherein the migrant has no right to work with the cases wherein irregularity arises from the procedural infractions.

[2] The Validity of the Employment Contract

The labour law turns to its contractual origins in order to deal with such irregularity, an old problem of employment law. The invalidity of the employment contract and its effects on the employment relationship are among the very first topics that labour lawyers discussed while determining the borders of employment law with the law of contracts.

In general, a contract is void if its terms breach the mandatory rules of law or contravene to public policy or morality. Labour law, by its nature, convey a large number of mandatory provisions aiming to restrict the freedom of contract of the parties. However, in many cases, these mandatory rules have an aim to protect the employee as the weaker party to the employment contract. The illegality of an employment contract may basically arise from two hypothesis: an employment contract with an object of committing an illegal act and an employment contract prohibited by the statute with an aim to protect the employee as the weaker party to the contract such as underage employees or women in some cases or to protect third parties or general public interest. When it concerns the employment contracts concluded with an irregular employee, another policy concern is included: the prevention of illegal migration. How to reconcile this policy consideration with the aim of protection the weaker party to the employment contract?

There exist mainly two sorts of approaches: legal systems wherein the contract of employment concluded by an irregular migrant is invalid, in many cases the invalidity ends up the contractual relationship automatically and legal systems wherein the irregularity of the migration status gives to the employer a cause to terminate the contractual relationship.

In the first case, the invalidity of the employment contract which is concluded by an irregular migrant has not been subject to specific legal regulations, therefore, the general rules about contractual invalidity apply. The invalidity of employment contract depends on the *ratio legis* of the broken norm. If the norm aims to protect the public order, the invalidity has a retrospective, *ex tunc* effect. However, in cases wherein the protection of the worker is the primary goal of the norm, the invalidity will have *ex nunc* effect. Considering the need for the protection of the irregular migrants, even if the legal norm is considered related to the public order, the invalidity may have *ex nunc* effect.[92] That is the case in Sweden, Turkey, Brazil, Spain[93] whereas in the Czechia *ex*

92. J. Pélissier/G. Auzero/E. Dockes, Droit du travail, 27th ed., Dalloz 2013, no. 175.

tunc effect.[94] The negligence or intentionality of the worker generally does not count on while determining the invalidity.

In both cases, the right to back pay is protected e.g., Germany, France, Italy, Spain, Turkey, South Africa, Japan and Brazil.[95] The irregular migrant benefit from the same rights as local employees, at least in theory. Even in some cases, the contractual terms are presumed. The EU Employer Sanctions Directive provides any outstanding remuneration to the illegally employed third-country national (Article 6/1-a): '*The agreed level of remuneration shall be presumed to have been at least as high as the wage provided for by the applicable laws on minimum wages, by collective agreements or in accordance with established practice in the relevant occupational branches, unless either the employer or the employee can prove otherwise, while respecting, where appropriate, the mandatory national provisions on wages*'.[96]

Regarding indemnities related to the termination of the contractual relationship, if the contract ends up by the invalidity, migrant workers do not enjoy any indemnity related to the termination in the absence of a specific regulation. However, in certain countries such as France, the legislator provides that in case of the termination of the contract, the irregular migrant will be eligible to a lump sum equal to one month of salary, unless there exist statutory or contractual provisions which are more favourable, without prejudice to the provisions related to the additional compensation (L 8252-2 CT).

The contractual invalidity approach which considers the requirements of both labour and immigration law provides a middle ground in the sense that the irregular migrants are entitled to labour rights, however, they are exposed to the sanction of immigration law.[97] The shortcoming of this system is that since it is judge-made law, the access of the contractual claims by the irregular migrant requires a judicial process. The system provides remedies for the performed work in past, thus *ex post* protection. Theoretically, migrant workers benefit from health and safety measures, and may claim for the damages in case of an industrial accident. Nevertheless, it is hard to predict the judgment. The extent of legal rights always consists of a margin of uncertainty. The provisions related to the unjust enrichment or compensation find a place of application. However, in other cases, In French law, for example, the legislator takes a positive action facing with the hesitations of the courts. An act adopted on 17 October 1981 put the irregularly recruited migrant with the same legal status as those

93. F.Columbu, Questionnaire-Brazil; F. Camas Roda, Questionnaire-Spain; P. Herzfeld Olsson, Questionnaire-Sweden.
94. K. Koldinska, Questionnaire-Czechia.
95. P. Herzfeld Olsson, Questionnaire-Sweden; F. Camas Roda, Questionnaire-Spain; E. Binay, Questionnaire-South Africa; C. Hayakaw, Questionnaire-Japan; F. Columbu, Questionnaire-Brazil; E. Dewhurst, 'The Right of Irregular Immigrants to Back Pay The Spectrum Protection in International, Regional and National Legal Systems', Migrants at Work, ed. by C. Costello and M. Freedland, Oxford University Press 2014, 234–235.
96. About critics N. Selberg, 'The Laws of 'Illegal' Work and Dilemmas in Interest Representation on Segmented Labor Markets: A Propos Irregular Migrants in Sweden', 35 Comp. Lab. L. & Pol'y Journal, 2013–2014, 257–259.
97. E. Dewhurst, 'The Right of Irregular Immigrants to Back Pay The Spectrum Protection in International, Regional and National Legal Systems', Migrants at Work, ed. C. Costello and M. Freedland, Oxford University Press 2014, 219–220.

who are regular.[98] The irregular migrant benefits from provisions of the Code du travail related to the hygiene, security, working time and poses and vacancies, the protection of maternity and the inclusion of the periods passed under an employment contract for the calculation of the employee's length of service in the company (L. 8252-1 CT). The employer of the irregular migrant is under obligation to pay the whole amount of the wages, contractual wage or minimum wage), as well as supplemental wages (L. 8252-2 CT).

The strict illegality doctrine seems particularly prevalent in the UK and the Republic of Ireland wherein the maintaining of the integrity of the legal system is the main argument in questioning the validity of the contractual relationship. Thus if tainted with illegality, the contract will automatically be unenforceable, and the employee will have no legal right to claim his contractual and statutory rights.[99] The culpability of the victim, the nature of the rights affected by the illegality and the public policy have all nature of affecting the legal reasoning.

Nevertheless, important developments should be noted. Under the UK law, In *Hounga v. Allen* (2014) UKSC 47, the question was whether an irregular migrant could bring a claim for race discrimination.[100] The appellant was a minor when arrived in the UK from Nigeria to undertake domestic work with a fraudulently obtained visitor's visa. The Supreme Court in the UK shows the possibility to distinguish between the permitting a claim for discrimination and condoning the plaintiff's illegal conduct. Bogg argues that the doctrine of implied statutory prohibition must take into account the migrants' human rights and that will provide a legal technique for confining the illegality doctrine within legitimate bounds. The common law doctrine of illegality finds a way to function in a 'worker-protective' mode.[101]

A distinction operates on the nature of the rights: contractual rights and statutory rights.[102] Even though the contractual claims are denied because of the illegality, the statutory rights remain claimable. The rights being claimed by the migrant employee could be related to statutory rights, such as fundamental rights, the statutory right to be unfairly dismissed, the right not to be discriminated, the right to have a minimum wage.[103]

98. J. Pélissier/G. Auzero/E. Dockes, Droit du travail, no. 175.
99. A. Bogg, 'Illegality, Public Policy, and the Contract of Employment', The Contract of Employment, eds. by M. Freedland/A. Bogg/D. Cabrelli/H. Collins/N. Countouris/A.C.L. Davies/S. Deakin/J. Prassl, Oxford University Press: 2016, 398 et seq.; Dewhurst, 'The Right of Irregular Immigrants to Back Pay', 232–233.
100. *See* C. Monaghan, 'Hounga v. Allen at the Supreme Court: The defence of illegality in race discrimination cases and the competing public interest in preventing the exploitation of illegal immigrants', International Journal of Discrimination and the Law, 2015 1(Vol. 15) 3, pp. 178–188; A. Bogg/S. Green, 'Rights are not Just for the Virtous: What Hounga Means for the Illegality Defence in the Discrimination Torts', ILJ, Vol. 44, No. 1, March 2015, 101–122.
101. A. Bogg, 'Illegality, Public Policy, and the Contract of Employment', 414–415.
102. About the operation of illegality doctrine in employment claims *see* A. Bogg, 'Illegality, Public Policy, and the Contract of Employment', 409 et seq.; M. Pilgerstorfer, 'A Dog's Dinner? Reconsidering Contractual Illegality in the Employment Sphere', ILC, September 2008, 279 et seq.
103. A. Bogg, 'Illegality, Public Policy, and the Contract of Employment', 400–401.

In *Hoffman Plastic Compounds, Inc. v. National Labor Relations Board,*[104] the United States Supreme Court held that certain remedies which are available to regular migrant workers are not available to irregular migrant workers. The case concerned undocumented workers who were dismissed because of his union activities. Though in cases wherein a documented worker is dismissed due to trade union activities the NLRB orders reinstatement of the employee to his former position and be given the back pay, in Hoffman, the NLRB did not order the reinstatement because the employee did not have the legal right to work in the USA. Nevertheless, the undocumented worker had been given back pays. The United States Supreme Court reversed the order because the NLRB did not have the authority to award back pay to undocumented workers. The legal reasoning was based on the argument that such an award would contradict the immigration laws prohibiting the employment of undocumented workers. Therefore, since *Hoffman,* it seems undocumented workers are protected against discrimination, however, they are not entitled to receive the remedies of the reinstatement or back pay.[105] The Hoffman decision is criticized because it decreases the deterrent function of employment law and increases the possibility of more discrimination against undocumented workers. Moreover, the lack of monetary sanctions makes the employment of undocumented workers less expensive comparing to documented workers.[106]

Following the Supreme Court decision in the case of *Hoffman Plastic Compounds v. National Labor Relations Board,* The American Federation of Labor and the Congress of Industrial Organizations (AFL-CIO) and the Confederation of Mexican Workers (CTM) made a complaint to the ILO alleging that on the basis of their immigration status, millions of workers have lost the only protection that had been available to ensure respect for their freedom of association rights and challenged the decision with the principles of freedom of association. The Committee on Freedom of Association considered that '*the remedial measures left to the NLRB in cases of illegal dismissals of undocumented workers are inadequate to ensure effective protection against acts of anti-union discrimination*'.[107]

Recent research shows the legal picture in the USA is much more heterogeneous than it is predicted. The research is based on courts opinion held between 2002–2012 and asks the question that how often courts use immigration status against suspected or known unlawful foreign plaintiffs in work-related disputes. The results are interesting that 80% of the courts disregarded the immigration status of migrants: As regards injury complaints, many courts rule that the worker's immigration status did not bar him from recovering worker's compensation benefits. The plaintiffs were awarded

104. *Hoffman Plastic Compounds, Inc. v. National Labor Relations Board* [2002] 535 US 137, *see* M. Ontiveros, 'Immigrant Workers' Rights in a Post-Hoffman World-Organizing around the Thirteenth Amendment', 18 Geo. Immigr. L.J. (2004), 651–680.
105. M. Ontiveros, 'Migrant Labour in USA', Migrants at Work, ed. C. Costello and M. Freedland, Oxford University Press: 2014, 185–186.
106. M. Ontiveros, 'Migrant Labour in USA', 186.
107. Case No. 2227 (United States), 332nd Report, para. 610.

monetary damages, or rules eligible for this remedy. Their success rate is in wage actions (77.1%), state wage and hour claims (70.8%), and contract cases (69.1%).[108]

These results show us the importance of the labour law approach in dealing with the irregular migration. Once there is a vulnerability and exploitation in an employment relationship, each system tries to prevent these injustices by referring to different legal tools. Nevertheless, when it turns to the efficiency question, French model seems the most predictable and provides more protection. Nevertheless, it should be borne in mind the difficulties to reach justice by irregular migrants.[109]

[3] Administrative and Criminal Sanctions

Preventing the illegal migration require the collaboration of labour law and migration law. Pursuant to Article 6 (1) of the ILO Convention No. 143 on Migrant Workers, '*Provision shall be made under national laws or regulations for the effective detection of the illegal employment of migrant workers and for the definition and the application of administrative, civil and penal sanctions, which include imprisonment in their range, in respect of the illegal employment of migrant workers...*'. The ILO Convention No. 143 was adopted in 1975, and the first employers' sanctions were introduced in France in 1972, in Germany in 1972, in the USA and the UK in 1986.[110] Article 68 (2) of the UN Convention on Migrant Workers refers to sanctions on employers and workers. The Employers Sanction Directive also provides some penalties upon employers.[111]

There exists an increasing tendency to hold employers responsible while recruiting a migrant employer. For example, under the UK law, Immigration Act 2016 Act replaced the former offence scheme under section 8 of the Asylum and Immigration Act 1996 which first made it a criminal offence to employ illegal workers.[112] A migrant who is disqualified from working because of his immigration status and if he knows or has a reasonable cause to believe this situation, commits an illegal working offence pursuant to section 24B of Immigration Act. The migrant worker is disqualified from working by reason of the person's immigration status is the one who has not been granted leave to enter or remain in the United Kingdom, or the migrant's leave to enter or remain in the United Kingdom is invalid, or has ceased to have effect (whether by reason of curtailment, revocation, cancellation, passage of time or otherwise), or is

108. M. H. Le Roy, 'Remedies for Unlawful Alien Workers: One Law for the Native and for the Stranger who Resides in your Midst? An Empirical Perspective', 28 Geo. Immigr. L.J. (2014), 623-655.
109. *See* C. Barnard, 'Enforcement of Employment Rights by Migrant Workers in the UK: The Case of EU-8 Nationals', Migrants at Work, Oxford University Press, 2014, 193-215.
110. P. Martin / M. Miller, 'Employer Sanctions: French, German and US Experiences', International Migration Papers 36, ILO 2000; B. Ryan, 'The evolving legal regime on unauthorized work by migrants in Britain', Comp. Labour Law and Policy Journal, 27, 2005-2006, 27-58.
111. Council Directive (EC) 2009/52 providing for minimum standards on sanctions and measures against employers of illegally staying third-country nationals (Employer Sanctions Directive). The Directive applies to the twenty-four EU Member States other than Denmark, Ireland, and the United Kingdom.
112. *See* B. Ryan, 'Employer Enforcement of Immigration Law after section 8 of the Asylum and Immigration Act 1996', ILJ, Vol. 26, No. 2, June 1997, 136-148.

subject to a condition preventing the person from doing work of that kind. This new offence seems to enable the earnings of illegal workers to be seized.[113] Moreover, the employer who employs a migrant who is disqualified from employment by reason of the person's immigration status and has reasonable cause to believe that the employee is disqualified commits also the offence of employing an illegal worker. There is no need of recruiting these migrants knowingly. Having 'reasonable cause' is enough to commit that crime.

Employers are not only checking the documents before the recruitment but also they are under obligation to recheck the documents during the employment relationship, and the content of checks is becoming tighter.[114] Article 4 of Employer Sanctions Directives imposes upon employers the duty to require a valid residence permit or authorization for his/her stay before taking up the employment and keep for at least the duration of the employment a copy or record of the residence permit or other authorization for stay available for possible inspection by the competent authorities of the Member States and also notify the competent authorities of the start of employment of third-country nationals within a period laid down by each Member State. Therefore, in order to combat illegal migration, nation states adopt immigration legislation which criminalizes the employment procedures.

[4] Protection of Irregular Migrants Through Human Rights

The irregularity in the migration process has a depriving effect on the employment rights of the migrants. The fundamental rights are the most countervailing principle against public policy concerns. In *Hungo* cases, the claimant, who had been trafficked into the UK at the age of 14 years old and was working illegally, was seeking an award to compensate her for injury to feelings as a consequence of the race discrimination. The approach based on the plaintiff's potential status as a victim of human trafficking permitted the migrant to recover her damages.[115]

Even if the ECHR does not require the grant of secure migration status,[116] the ECtHR has developed a jurisprudence protecting the migrants' right to protection of their family and private life and also the right to non-removable, if there are a serious human rights violations in another country. Nevertheless, the obligation to let migrants stay and the obligation to create a secure status differ from each other.

Mrs Mendizabal, having a Spanish nationality resides in France, had obtained asylum in France in 1976 and following her political refugee status has been withdrawn, she has been given a one-year temporary residence card during fourteen years. The applicant alleged that the precariousness of her status and the uncertainty over her

113. Immigration Act 2016, Explanatory Notes.
114. For example *see* B. Ryan, 'Employer Checks of Immigration Status and Employment Law', Migrants at Work, ed. C. Costello and M. Freedland, OUP 2014, 241–243.
115. *See* C. Monaghan, 'Hounga v. Allen at the Supreme Court: The defence of illegality in race discrimination cases and the competing public interest in preventing the exploitation of illegal immigrants', International Journal of Discrimination and the Law, 2015 1(Vol. 15) 3, 178–188.
116. *Slivenko v. Latvia*, App No 48321/99 (ECHR, 9 October 2003); *Sisojeva et al. v. Latvia*, App No 60654/00 (ECHR, 16 June 2005) (Grand Chamber ECHR, 15 January 2007).

fate have had significant consequences for her in material terms and (precarious and disqualified employment), social and financial difficulties, impossibility for lack of a residence permit to rent a room and to exercise the professional activity for which it had undertaken a training. The European Court of Human Rights ruled that the fact that the applicant had not been granted a residence permit for such a long period, whereas she had regularly been residing in France for more than fourteen years, undeniably constituted an interference with his private and family life and caused a material, as well as non-material damage.[117]

In the case of *Siliadin v. France*, the applicant who was a victim of trafficking lived in Paris and served as an unpaid servant for several years as minor, and her passport was confiscated. She argued that the criminal-law provisions in force at the material time had not afforded her adequate protection from servitude or forced or compulsory labour in their temporary forms. The Court considered that the applicant had been subjected to forced labour and held in servitude within the meaning of Article 4 of the Convention, but not in slavery in the traditional sense of that concept and held France had been a violation of the respondent State's positive obligations under Article 4 of the Convention.[118]

A recent case *Chowdury v. Greece* depicts the strong links between the labour law aspects of the problem. 42 Bangladeshi nationals with undocumented status who worked in a strawberry farm in Manolada in Greece under the supervision of armed guards. They worked picking strawberries every day from 7 a.m. till 7 p.m. in return for a wage of 22 euros for seven hours labour and 3 euros for each overtime hour, less 3 euros for food. They lived in makeshift tents of cardboard boxes and nylon without running water and toilets. Since their wages have not been paid, the Bangladeshi nationals went on strike to demand their wages, and they were responded by armed guards who opened fire and seriously harmed them. The guards were convicted for the harm, however, acquitted of the charge of trafficking in human beings. The 42 Bangladeshi migrants claimed that they were subjected to forced labour and human trafficking and that Greece has failed to fulfil its positive obligations under Article 4 to protect them against these abuses, to conduct an effective investigation, and to prosecute the perpetrators. The Court of Human Rights stated that Greece had criminalized the human trafficking at the national level, nevertheless the Court considered that the operational measures taken by the authorities were not sufficient to prevent trafficking in human beings and to protect the applicants from the treatment they received, while the authorities were aware of the situation of the migrant workers in the Manolada region and the abuses to which they are exposed.[119]

Article 4 of the Convention provides an important tool in the legal reasoning. Pursuant to Article 4, '*No one shall be held in slavery or servitude*' and '*No one shall be required to perform forced or compulsory labour*'. The decisions pose challenges as

---

117. *Aristimuno Mendizabal v. France*, App No. 51431/99 (ECHR, 17 January 2006), para. 72.
118. *Siliadin v. France*, App No. 73316/01 (ECHR, 26 July 2005).
119. *Chowdury and others v. Greece*, App No. 21884/15 (ECHR, 30 March 2017).

regards the definition of forced labour and servitude.[120] The jurisprudence of the European Court shows, however, an important step for the protection of the rights of irregular migrants.

An important aspect of the *Chowdury* relates to the remedies. The Bangladeshi migrants argued that their employers did not keep a record of the hours worked by each of them and unpaid wages have a cause and effect relationship with the violation of Article 4 of the Convention. The government argued that the applicants do not prove the amount that they claimed did not explain why they had not seized the domestic to claim the corresponding sums pursuant to Article 904 of the Code Civil, relating to unjust enrichment. The European Court stated that there is no doubt at the applicants suffered pecuniary damage because of the unpaid wages held a sum of EUR 16.000 to be awarded to each of them.[121] In *Rantsev v. Cyprus and Russia*, the ECtHR maintained similar reasoning as regards the state's positive obligations against trafficking and exploitation in general.[122]

The Inter-American Court of Human Rights Advisory Opinion about the rights of undocumented migrants provides guidelines that any migratory policy or legislation must conform to the international and regional standards in force with regard to legitimate restrictions to human rights. The Thirteenth Amendment which bans slavery and the badges and incidents of slavery is a legal tool to protected undocumented migrants in the USA.[123]

Another significant attempt to enlarge protection to irregular migrants came from the European Committee of Social Rights.[124] In the collective complaint 14/2003 *International Federation on Human Rights Leagues (FIHD) v. France,*[125] the Committee provided a certain level of protection to illegally resident nationals of non-state parties by an expansive interpretation of the Charter following that France had ended the exemption of illegal immigrants with very low incomes from all charges and introduced special charges for inpatient hospital treatment for foreigners illegally residing in France and excluded the children of illegal immigrants and unaccompanied minors from the French universal medical coverage. The Committee decided that legislation or practice which denies entitlement to medical assistance to foreign nationals, within the territory of a State Party, even if they are there illegally is contrary to the Charter. The Committee has kept the same approach in a subsequent collective complaint *Defence of Children International v. the Netherlands*[126] that the denial of access to the house of an adequate standard to children unlawfully present in their territory. Therefore, the Committee extended the personal scope of the Charter when it is about the access to

120. *See* V. Stoyanova/R. Söderbeg, 'Sweet Taste with Bitter Roots – Forced Labour and Chowdury v Greece', (2018), E. H. R.L. R., Issue 1, 67–75.
121. *Chowdury and others v. Greece,* App No 21884/15 (ECHR, 30 March 2017).
122. *Rantsev v. Cyprus and Russia,* App No 25965/04 (ECHR, 7 January 2010).
123. Ontiveros, 'Migrant Labour in the USA', 189–191.
124. Council of Europe, Digest of the case law of the European Committee of Social Rights, 1 September 2008, 183–184.
125. International Federation of Human Rights Leagues (FIDH) *v.* France CC 14/2003, European Committee of Social Rights, Decision of 8 September 2004.
126. Defence of Children International *v.* Netherlands CC 47/2008, European Committee of Social Rights, Decision of 20 October 2009.

emergency health care, shelter and social assistance, which are essential to maintaining human dignity.[127]

Human rights approach enables to acknowledge the role of the states as duty-bearers, therefore prevails the dignity of the migrants. Such an approach facilitates the protection of migrants' social security rights. But except cases wherein exist severe forms of exploitation, it is hard to predict effectiveness of the labour rights' protection through human rights tools. Therefore, the labour law's approach is indispensable to prevent vulnerabilities in the labour market.

[D] Migrant Workers under Two Parameters

The legal status of migrant workers through the lenses of two parameters shows the absence and the need for the labour law's approach towards migrant workers.

[1] Patchwork Legal Order

Regulation of the legal status of migrant workers reveals a great diversity both at national and international levels. The number of international instruments which directly set out principles in the treatment of migrant workers is not many, and their low rate of ratification shows the lack of international commitment towards the protection of migrant workers.[128] Nations states aim to keep their sovereign powers in dealing with this problem. Considering the wide variety of policy documents in respect of migration management, this reluctance is an issue of concern. However, the non-ratification of international instruments aiming to protect migrant workers does not prevent the intervention of the human rights law to protect fundamental rights at work. The European Court of Human Rights and the Inter-American Court of Human Rights, as well as the European Committee of Social Rights, have recorded important achievements as regards the protection of migrant rights.

Looking through the lenses of labour rights, international instruments provide weak protection to migrants forcedly displaced. The Geneva Conventions recognizes the right to work only to those who lawfully stay in a state. Even after the recognition of refugee status, in most of the less developed world, the access of refugees to the labour market is denied. There may have formal bans on their employment or required work authorization process which takes a long time. In most developed states, the right to work is formally recognized to refugees, immediately after their refugee status has been granted. As regards the entrance of asylum seekers to the labour market, even among the Member States of the EU with the utmost harmonized asylum protection

127. O'Cinnéide, 'Migrant Rights under the European Social Charter', 289–292.
128. The International Covenant on Civil and Political rights, the International Covenant on Economic, Social and Cultural Rights, the International Convention on Elimination of Racial Discrimination, the Convention on the Freedom of Association and Protection of the right to organize, the ILO Convention on discrimination ILO Declaration on Fundamental principles and Rights at Work: the 2000 UN Convention against Transnational organized Crime (Palermo Convention) and its three protocols.

system, there exist legal barriers. Despite the time limits set by the law to the assessment of the asylum applications, it takes much more time than predicted at first instance and in appeals. People displaced due to environmental reasons fall out of the international protection regimes.

At the national level, migrant workers are at the intersection of migration law, labour law, human rights law, criminal law and trade law. Different legal disciplines interact with each other, which certainly affects the use of migrant labour. Each discipline with its principles and goals (protection the worker, punishment, compensation), concepts and techniques (such as burden of proof) regulate one part of the phenomenon and does not always operate harmoniously.

[2] Migrants for 'Jobs' and Regulated Precarity

The international law recognizes the state's powers to make a distinction among persons while admitting them into their territory, except refugees. The visa regimes and migration programs show bifurcation of policies towards the skills of migrants.

Depending on the labour market in a given country, migration regulations determine the legal pathways of the migrants. The labour and skill shortages in certain sectors are mainly satisfied by migrant workers admitted under temporary visa regimes. The first step of these process is to determine which jobs are available in the labour market either because of the labour shortage or because the local workers do not prefer to work in these jobs. Caps and quotas are very common demand side restrictions. Therefore, the regulated migration pathways provide migrant workforce for jobs.

The second step focuses on the admission of the migrant and assures that he/she keeps the targeted job during his/her stay. By bilateral agreements, nation states control who will apply for which jobs. Since the aim is to supply the labour shortages in the labour market, many of these programs are employer-driven and temporary. It is obvious that these systems are based on the efficacy of the visa regimes rather than the protection of workers.[129]

Temporary migration status requires fixed-term contracts for precarious jobs. Workers, in the majority of legal systems, do not benefit from job security and indemnities related to the termination. The precarious work is characterized by various degrees of uncertainty and insecurity such as the work performed in the formal and informal economy, uncertainty as regards the duration of employment, the multiple employers or agencies, disguised employment relationship, low wages, low protection from the termination of the contract, substantial obstacles to enjoying trade union and collective bargaining rights, the lack of access to social protection.[130] Trade unions

129. J. Howe/R. J. Owens, 'Introduction', Temporary Labour Migration in the Global Era, ed. by J. Howe/R. J. Owens, Oxford hart Publishing 2016, 9.
130. ACTRAV, From precarious work to the decent work, Outcome document to the Worker's Symposium on Policies and Regulations to Combat Precarious Employment, ILO 2012, 27–29.

have different policies about the temporary migration programmes[131] and in many cases migrant workers fall out of the concern of trade unions. Some studies refer to hyper-precarity of migrant workers to the extent of forced labour.[132]

Immigration status significantly determines one's position while entering into work relations.[133] Migration and asylum law create a particular migrant status composed of a set of rights and duties. This status often determines the rights in other parts of life, political or family life, as well as in workplace and economy.[134] The personal status of a migrant worker is introduced by migration legislation, which leads to the 'division' as called by Mark Freedland and Cathryn Costello of subjects of labour law. Migration legislation imposes certain types of working conditions by creating different categories of entrants,[135] and an old discussion of 'status from the contract' seems to come back as regards migrant workers.[136]

I acknowledge that there are certain vulnerabilities that are intrinsic in the fact of being migrant, even having the permanent residence permit does not prevent to suffer from such vulnerabilities. The only fact of being a migrant, particularly in the early periods of migration, causes a sort of vulnerability. The language, the cultural differences, the fact of being foreigner create a certain inhibition towards the counterparties. However, among many reasons causing migrant's vulnerability in the labour market, the most striking one is the law, itself, is becoming a source of vulnerability in some cases.[137]

[3] Instrumentalization of Labour Law

The aim of combatting irregular migration leads nation states to increase the level of protection in the admission of new migrants. The migration legislation regulates the access to the labour market in a detailed way and imposes new duties upon employers and property owners to prevent the recruitment of irregular migrants. New offences are

131. T. Basok/A. Lopez Sala, 'Rights and Restrictions: Temporary Agricultural Migrants and Trade Unions Activism in Canada and Spain', Int. Migration & Integration (2016) 17:1271-1287.
132. M. Zou, 'The Legal Construction of Hyper-Dependence and Hyper-Precarity in Migrant Work Relations', The International Journal of Comparative Labour Law and Industrial Relations 31, No. 2 (2015): 141-162; H. Lewis/P. Dwyer/S. Hodkinson/L. Waite, 'Hyper-precarious lives: migrants, worked and forced labour in the Global North', Progress in Human Geography, 2015, Vol 39 (5), 580-600.
133. N. Kountouris, 'The Legal Determinants of Precariousness in Personal Work Relations: A European Perspective', 34 Comparative Labor Law and Policy Journal, 2012, 27-28.
134. C. Costello, The Human Rights of Migrants and Refugees in European Law, Oxford University Press, 2015.
135. B. Anderson, 'Migration, immigration controls and the fashioning of precarious workers', Work, Employment and Society, Vol. 24 (2), 300-317, 306-312.
136. M Freedland and C Costello 'Migrants at Work and the Division of Labour Law' in C Costello and M Freedland, Migrants at Work: Immigration and Vulnerability in Labour Law (OUP 2014); C Costello, 'EU Migration and Asylum Law: A Labour Law Perspective', Research Handbook on EU Labour Law, ed. by A. Bogg/C. Costello/A.C.L. Davies, Edward Elgard Publishing: 2016, 299-334.
137. V. Mantouvalou, 'The Right to Non-Exploitative Work', The Right to Work, Legal and Philosophical Perspectives, Hart Publishing 2015, 49-51.

introduced as regards irregular migrants taking up employment and employers recruiting them. Immigration law controls illegal migration through the use of the criminal law, now through the labour law and even with the help of rent law. The mandatory rules and offences of migration law become a part of labour law.[138] The increasing number of such rules makes evident that migration law instrumentalizes labour law in its combat against illegal migration. Therefore, the validity of the employment contract is put under scrutiny to protect the interests falling out of the scope of labour law.

In addition, the instrumentalization of the labour law affects the implementation of the principle of equality between nationals and non-nationals which is one of the founding principles while regulating the legal status of migrant workers. All main regulations in international instruments regulating the migrants' rights are based on the principle of equality (e.g., Article 7 ICMWR, Article 9 of ILO Convention No. 143; Article 6 of Convention No. 97).[139]

Having a particular interest in the equality regarding remuneration and other employment and working conditions, in many EU Member States there exists specific anti-discrimination acts implementing the EU Directive 2000/43/EC on the principle of equal treatment on the grounds of racial and ethnical origin and 2000/78/EC establishing a general framework for equal treatment in employment and occupation.[140] The Committee of Social Chart regularly states that *'it is not enough for a government to prove that no discrimination exists in law alone but that it is obliged to prove, in addition, that no discrimination is practised in fact or to inform the supervisory organs of the practical measures taken to remedy it'*.[141]

The detailed legal charges upon the employer to check the immigration status of a migrant job applicant allows the employer to investigate the personal status of migrants. This investigation causes important questions with regard to discrimination law. The problem does not concern only immigrants having a temporary visa, but all immigrants even those who have the nationality of the host state. Ryan shows the multiple questions: what if an employer asks the nationality of an employee based on the someone's appearance, accent, name and ask for the proof of their rights to work from those who are assumed to be non-national? Or since the immigration statuses are directly related to the nationality, what if an employer prefers certain immigration statuses, or adopts a policy to consider only applicants for whom there is no need for a work permit? It should be borne in mind that the lodging work permit applications require time and money for employers. Likewise, similar questions are valid for the check during the employment. And also if the employer reaches the wrong conclusion

---

138. L. Lamarche, 'Human Rights, Social Security and Migrant Workers', Bulletin of Comparative Labour Relations, Social Security and Migrant Workers, 84, 2014, 9–30; A. Bogg, 'Illegality, Public Policy, and the Contract of Employment', The Autonomy of Labour Law, ed. by A. Bogg/C. Costello/A.C.L. Davies/J. Prassl, Hart Publishing 2015, 399.
139. *See* S. Olney/R. Cholewinski, 'Migrant Workers and the Right to Non-Discrimination and Equality', Migrants at Work, Oxford University Press, 2014, 259–281.
140. ECSR, European Social Charter (Revised), Conclusions 2011, Vol. 2, Conclusions (2011): France – Art. 19, pp. 464–465; Conclusions (2011): Ireland – Art. 19, 579–580; Conclusions (2011): Italy – Art. 19, 632–633.
141. Statement of interpretation, Conclusions III, 1973; Digest of the Case Law of the European Committee of Social Rights, 1 September 2008, 131.

about the immigration status of migrants or considering the difficulty in hiring an immigrant, just refuse to hire migrants? These questions show the very problem that employment check may create in terms of discrimination on the ground of nationality or ethnic origin.[142]

It is hard to claim that each legal discipline has its own district field of regulation. That has never been the case. However, it seems also obvious that the introduction of certain duties to the contractual relationship may affect the power balance between the parties to the contract. That is the reason for using labour law as a tool may result in some adverse or intended effects. A shift from an employment agenda to immigration control agenda may ultimately turn out to be damaging to the interests of the majority of the workers.[143] Fudge aptly shows the severe exploitation of domestic workers when the role of the labour market and immigrating institutions are ignored.[144]

These conflicting interests among different workers require closer co-operation between migration law, human rights law, criminal law and labour and social security law. The correction of power imbalances between the parties to a contractual relationship and reallocation of risks are a particular interest of labour law. It seems important to see how these regulations affect the power relationship in the employment contract.

[4] Lack of Protection for the Most Vulnerable Groups

It is obvious that some migrant workers encounter much more difficulty than the others. Domestic workers or migrants working in agriculture are the first ones coming to mind.

The sectoral working conditions appear as the primary reason for their vulnerabilities. In many countries, agriculture and domestic works fall out of the scope of protective labour legislation. They are vulnerable to human rights violations. In addition, domestic work is the main migration channel for women, therefore have gender, and also in many cases, racial dimension.

The ILO Convention No. 189 Concerning Decent Work for Domestic Workers with its accompanying Recommendation also provides protection to migrant domestic workers. Article 8 states that '*... migrant domestic workers who are recruited in one country for domestic work in another receive a written job offer, or contract of employment that is enforceable in the country in which the work is to be performed, addressing the terms and conditions of employment*'. Article 2 of the Convention declares that the Convention applies to all domestic workers, regardless of their

142. B. Ryan, 'Employer Checks of Immigration Status and Employment Law', 243-256.
143. A.C.L. Davies, 'Migrant Workers in Agriculture', Migrants at Work, ed. by C. Costello and M. Freedland, OUP 2014, 79.
144. J. Fudge, 'Migrant Domestic Workers in British Columbia, Canada Unfreedom, Trafficking and Domestic Servitude', Temporary Labour Migration in the Global Era, ed. J. Howe, R. Owens, Oxford Hart Publishing 2016, 151-172.

migration status. The Domestic Workers' Convention is an important step in the protection of all domestic workers, despite the difficulties in enforcement.[145]

It is debatable whether sectoral approach is apt to protect these workers. However, the sectoral approach might help to reduce vulnerabilities encountered by migrants. For example in Sweden a specific collective agreement has entered into force for the wild berry picking sector.[146]

[5] Obstacles in Use of Collective Labour Rights

A recent study which examines the differences in unionization rates between migrants and natives in twenty-three European countries shows that the unionization gap between migrants and natives is related to the industrial relation system rather than individual characteristics of migrants, such as age, gender, educational background and or different distributions of migrants over occupations, types of labour contracts or company rate. The unionization rate of migrants is determined by the overall unionization rate in the country of destination: in countries with an organized corporatist regime (i.e., the Nordic countries), the gap is large, which means migrants have a lower unionization rate comparing to one of the natives, whereas the gap is virtually absent in countries of the central and eastern European countries. Nevertheless, the number of unionized migrants is higher in the corporatist regimes than any other regime in Europe. Apart from the characteristics of the industrial regime in the host country, the union density in their home country, the length of their stay in the host country, if the country of origin is a former colony of the country of destination seem affecting the unionization of migrants.[147]

Regular migrants, though their collective rights are guaranteed, suffer from practical obstacles on the full enjoyment of their rights to join a trade union and benefit from collective bargaining. The policies of trade unions towards migration and their attitudes towards irregular migrants vary from country to country depending upon many factors, e.g., the institutional framework, the nature of migration policies, sectoral characteristics, the identity of union and organizational structure and institutional power.[148]

---

145. *See* S. Fredman, 'Home from Home: Migrant Domestic Workers and the International Labour Organization Convention on Domestic Workers', *Migrants at Work*, ed. by C. Costello/M. Freedland, OUP 2014, 399–421.
146. P. Herzfeld Olsson, Questionnaire-Sweden.
147. M. Kranendonk/P. de Beer, 'What Explains the Union Membership Gap between Migrants and Natives', British Journal of Industrial Relations, 54:4, December 2016, 846–869; another study about the gap between local and foreign workers in 14 Western European countries, A. Gorodzeisky/A. Richards, 'Trade unions and migrant workers in Western Europe', European Journal of Industrial Relations, 19(3), 2013, 239–254.
148. M. Kahmann, 'Trade Unions and Migrant Workers: Examples from the Unites States, South Africa and Spain', European Trade Union Institute 2002, DWP 2002.02.03; E. Bengtsson, 'Swedish Trade Unions and European Union Migrant Workers', Journal of Industrial Relations, 55(2) 174–189; S. Marino, 'Trade unions, special structures and the inclusion of migrant workers: on the role of union democracy', Work, employment and society 2015, Vol. 29(5) 826–842.

As regards irregular migrants, the legal obstacles in respect of union membership are not absent. The UN Convention on Migrant Workers guarantees the right to join trade unions and take part in their activities to all migrants regardless of irregularity (Article 26), whereas only regular migrants have the right to form trade unions (Article 40). In some states such as Sweden, Japan and Turkey, irregular migrants, on a theoretical level, have the right to join trade unions and to claim benefits arising from the collective agreements applicable in the workplace. However, in Brazil or the Czechia, the legal situation seems more complex. In both cases, legal and practical difficulties exist in union membership.[149]

The right to organize is one of the fundamental rights in the 1998 ILO Declaration of Fundamental Principles and Rights at Work. The ILO Convention No. 87 on Freedom of Association and the Protection of the Right to Organize provides that workers and employers 'without distinction whatsoever' shall have the right to establish and join organizations of their own choosing (Article 2). ILO Convention No. 98 on the Right to Organize and Collective Bargaining Convention provides that workers should have adequate protection against acts of anti-union discrimination (Article 1), and workers organizations against any acts of interference (Article 2). The Committee of Experts has considered the rights of migrant workers to exercise trade union rights without risk of deportation, to elect union representatives, to be founding members and leaders of trade unions and employers' associations. As regards irregular migrant workers, the Committee on Freedom of Association has considered that the denial of their rights conflicts with Article 2 of the Convention No. 87.[150] Article 11 of the ECHR can also be interpreted in a way to protect the right to organize of irregular migrants.[151]

On the national level, Alan Bogg and Tonia Novitz show how individual employment law could operate as an obstruction in the active use of collective labour rights by irregular migrants in the UK.[152] Even if the invalidity has an *ex nunc* effect, the migrants, as well as trade unions, may have no information about his/her status. In our survey, we also found in South Africa or Brazil, though their contractual rights are protected, irregular migrants do not enjoy the right to join trade unions or benefit the collective agreement.[153] On the other hand, there may be some practical obstacles in their access to enjoy union membership. In Turkey, the trade union membership has acquired via an electronic application system (Article 17/5 of Act No. 6356). However, the worker needs a social insurance number to use this system. Thus, migrants, who work informally, have no opportunity to join a trade union in practice.

149. F. Columbu, Questionnaire-Brazil; K. Koldinska, Questionnaire-Czechia; P. Herzfeld Olsson, Questionnaire-Sweden; C. Hayakaw, Questionnaire-Japan.
150. Case No. 2121 (Spain), Digest of decisions and principles of the Freedom of Association Committee of the Governing Body of the ILO, 5th edition, ILO 2006, para. 214; Case No. 2620 (Republic of Korea), Report No. 374.
151. V. Mantouvalou, 'Organizing against Abuse and Exclusion The Associational Rights of Undocumented Workers', Migrants at Work, ed. by C. Costello and M. Freedland, OUP 2014, 381–398, at 390–396.
152. A. Bogg/T. Novitz, 'Links between Individual Employment Law and Collective Labour Law Their Implications for Migrant Workers', Migrants at Work, ed. by C. Costello and M. Freedland, OUP 2014, 361–380.
153. F. Columbu, Questionnaire-Brazil; E. Binay, Questionnaire-South Africa.

§9.04 'RISK MUTUALIZATION' AND REGULATION OF LABOUR MIGRATION

Migration consists of complex and dynamic interactions between economic, social policies and legal regulations. In addition, the intervention of different legal disciplines, e.g., migration law, human rights law, labour law, international and also trade law, complicates further the regulation of migrants' legal rights.

[A] A Labour Law Approach Based on the Risk Mutualization

Considering the number of legislative initiations from immigration law and the decisions of human rights courts, the absence of an approach from the labour law to migration specific problems is obvious. Fudge[154] and Shamir[155] demonstrate how important to develop a labour law approach in combatting human trafficking and forced migration. The Protocol of 2014 to the Forced Labour Convention 1930 states labour law regulation, labour inspection and trade unions among the measures to be taken for the prevention of forced and compulsory labour. Trade unions are becoming an important actor in the prevention of human trafficking and forced labour.[156]

Despite all its importance, it is not the human right law to prevent the vulnerabilities in the labour market. Human rights law has an individualistic and victim-centred approach that the victims play a passive role and receive *ex post* protection. If the human rights may be effective in treating the severe forms of labour exploitation such as forced labour, servitude or slavery, labour law has the capacity to protect migrants against vulnerabilities which have not been reached to that point. Considering migrants for employment, migrants are 'agents' in the labour market rather than victims. When it comes to correct the inequalities in the labour market, it is the labour law having a wide range of tools.[157] Labour law is opted to probe and redress the inequalities created by other legislation in the labour market and focus on the reintegrative solutions.

Economic theory supports the migration in the sense that the movement of labour from the countries wherein they produce less value than to the countries wherein they produce more value will increase the net gains for the world as a whole. Workers move towards states wherein they earn higher wages, which also signifies that they create more value. Wages of the workers in the receiving country may fall, but migration will

154. J. Fudge, 'Migrant Domestic Workers in British Columbia, Canada Unfreedom, Traficking and Domestic Servitude', Temporary Labour Migration in the Global Era, ed. J. Howe, R. Owens, Oxford Hart Publishing 2016, pp. 151–172.
155. H. Shamir, 'A Labor Paradigm for Human Trafficking', UCLA Law Review, 60 (2012), 76–136.
156. About the ILO's Tripartite Action to Protect Migrant Workers within and from the Greater Mekong Subregion from Labour Exploitation Project *see* E Marks & A Olsen, 'The Role of Trade Unions in Reducing Migrant Workers' Vulnerability to Forced Labour and Human Trafficking in the Greater Mekong Subregion', Anti-Trafficking Review, Issue 5, 2015, pp. 111–128, www.antitraffickingreview.org.
157. Shamir, 'A Labor Paradigm for Human Trafficking', 80–82; 105–106.

operate in favour of employers, as well as ultimate consumers.[158] Employers in a labour market prefer a model, which enables them to decide freely who and how many migrants to admit. This perspective leads to the conclusion that migration is no longer attractive if migrant workers enjoy equal working conditions as local workers. Therefore, migrant-sending countries may follow migration policies satisfied with lower working conditions, compared to local workers, provided to their emigrant nationals. Ruhs argues for a trade-off between the openness of the labour markets and the rights of migrants in the high-income countries' migration policies, endorsing a pragmatic approach that the temporary rights restrictions in exchange for more migration.[159] Migrants labour is attractive if only it is cheaper than local workers unless it is high-skilled.

This approach jeopardizes the fundamental approach of labour law, the principle of equality as regards labour rights, while dealing with migration. It also shows the complex nature of the protection of migrant workers. Labour law faces another dilemma protection *v.* employment, in the sense that increasing legal protections to migrants risks their chance of taking up employment. If labour law protects workers against themselves in the sense of restricting their withdrawals from mandatory provisions, this protection does not encumber the access of local workers to work.

The complexity of the migration problem and the legal structure which enables receiving states with a large power of discretion show tense relationships between migration law and labour law.[160] I suggest that an approach based on the 'mutualization and demutualization of risks' developed by Mark Freedland and Nicola Kountouris to labour migration may help us to capture better insights of the phenomenon in the search for a fair mutualization of risks which will be base for a regulation.

The legal construction of work relations is based on a mutualization of risks.[161] Many aspects of the migration legislation have an impact on the given risk allocation determined by the national labour regulations. The regulation of personal work relationships mutualizes and demutualizes different risks such as having (or not having) access to decent employment, the continuity of the work relationships, the security of income, the health and safety. Labour law regulations allocate these risks among workers, between workers and employers and other actors. In a fair risk mutualization, some risks particularly the health and security should be dispersed away from the individual worker.[162]

Migration legislation inserts 'migrant workers' into the risk allocation of each system as another group out of local workers. The classical idea has its heart the assumption that nation states have all the power to decide who can or cannot take a

158. H. F. Chang, 'Introduction', Law and Economics of Migration, Ed. by H. F. Chang, Edward Elgar Pub. 2015, XI–XLIII.
159. M. Ruhs, The Price of Rights: Regulating International Labour Migration, Princeton University Press 2013.
160. M. Freedland/C. Costello, 'Migrants at Work and the Division of Labour Law', Migrants at Work, OUP 2014, 1–20.
161. M. Freedland/N. Kountouris, The Legal Construction of Personal Work Relations, OUP 2011, 439–446.
162. M. Freedland /N. Kountouris, The Legal Construction of Personal Work Relations, 440.

role in their labour markets. Therefore, the labour side of the equation is divided into two, having in some cases conflicting interests. Local workers, both nationals and permanent migrants, and migrants become competitors in the labour market.

This fact presents a conflict of interests at the heart of labour law: to protect which worker? The principle of equality and the non-discrimination is one of the basic principles while regulating the legal status of migrant workers. The principle serves not only to protect the migrant workers in the labour market but also prevents the unjust competition towards local workers, thus also protect the local workforce. However, in sectors wherein the receiving states have poor working conditions the principle of equal treatment is far from providing protection.[163] That is the case in agriculture and domestic work. An approach based on the risk mutualization may provide a satisfactory way of addressing analytical shifts between the migration and labour law.

The term 'risk' conveys the possibility of vulnerability but does not necessarily entail vulnerability. The vulnerability depends on the legal, economic and social structure of each country. Risk refers to the expected loss of migrants as well as local workers. Therefore, the term 'risk' seems a better way of formulating different interests without denying the migrant's vulnerability. Moreover, this approach enables the involvement of other actors in the evaluation of legal structure.[164] The role of receiving and sending states, labour agencies, unions should take into account while seeking better regulation.

Freedland and Kountouris suggest three kinds of risks in the regulation of personal work relations: The vertical mutualization of risks consists of the risk allocation between employers and workers. The horizontal mutualization of risks consists of allocation and reallocation of risks between workers and lastly the diagonal mutualization is the reorganized risk allocation by the introduction of intermediaries.[165]

Migration legislation affects the given risk mutualization which exists between worker and employer. By 'given risk mutualization', I refer to the ideal situation in the sense that migrants and local workers are treated equally. Therefore, the same risk allocation between national workers and employers will be valid as regards migrant workers. If one admits the vulnerability is intrinsic in the migration, migrants will always carry a certain of risks of vulnerability. Under the principle of non-discrimination, each deviation from this point seems legally questionable, if particularly it creates vulnerability on the part of migrant workers. Not only legislative intervention but also the construction of legal norms, for example the large interpretation of invalidity by courts, may affect the risk mutualization. As shown in the diagram below, the large interpretation of the irregularity increases the risks over migrants.

163. J. Fudge/P. Herzfeld Olsson, 'The EU Seasonal Workers Directive: When Immigration Controls Meet Labour Rights', 464.
164. M. Freedland/N. Kountouris, The Legal Construction of Personal Work Relations, 440.
165. M. Freedland/N. Kountouris, The Legal Construction of Personal Work Relations, 440–441.

Figure 9.2 Risk Mutualization and Migrants

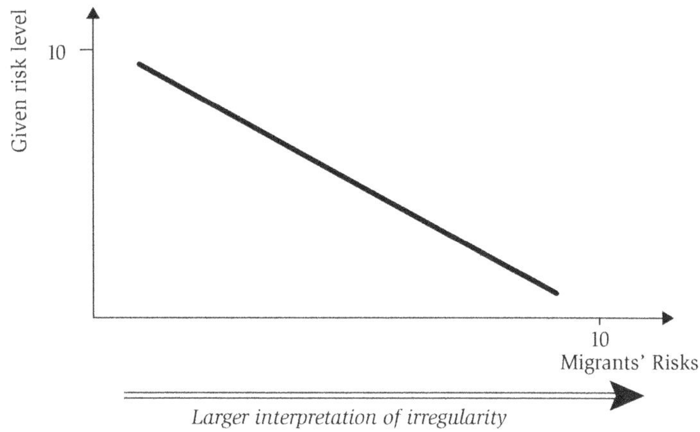

At this point, I will try to illustrate this approach with different examples taken from migration legislation.

[B] Admission Process and Horizontal Risk Mutualization

One of the established practice throughout the world is that migrants should lodge their work permit applications, at least for the first time, from their homeland. Nation states rarely open their borders to non-nationals who seek employment.

At first sight, one may find difficult to justify many restrictive rules such as quotas, increasing skill requirements, labour market tests and employer sponsorships, while migrants are seeking for employment, which is not available in the home country and employers are looking for a worker in the host country. However, many provisions of the migration legislation aim to protect local workers against the competition coming from migrants.[166] As regards migrants for the purpose of employment, nation states assure by the requirement of a job offer or an employment contract that migrants are recruited in the sectors wherein the shortage of workforce exists, therefore also protects local workers. On the other hand, such requirements may serve to different aims. This procedure provides security to migrant workers considering the difficulty of seeking employment in a foreign country, particularly in their first admission. Crossing borders without having a job offer place migrants at risk of not finding proper employment in a foreign country. Therefore, these regulations allocate risks between migrants and local workers, and mainly operate in favour of local workers. Risk of not having employment is a risk and consists entirely upon the individual migrant worker who has not yet crossed the borders.

166. M. Zou, 'Employer demand for 'skilled' migrant workers: regulating admission under the United Kingdom?' Tier 2 (general) Visa', 113.

If such a privilege is justifiable to a certain extent regarding non-nationals immigrating with the purpose of employment, it seems me hardly justifiable as regards migrants forcedly displaced. The work permit regulations and requiring labour market tests result in that who have a legal right to stay in a country may have a limited to access its labour market. Migrants staying in their home country have the legal right, and an opportunity to find employment, whereas migrants forcedly displaced have no legal right to access to work. Those who are the most vulnerable bear the greater part of the risk. That also shows that the particular conditions of migrants should be taken into account to reach a normative fair risk mutualization.

Such legislation also becomes questionable when they affect the vertical risk allocation in the work relationship. The weakness of the employee at the conclusion of the contract of employment is a well-known fact by labour lawyers, which directly affects the bargaining power of the one who seeks to take up employment. Requiring a job offer or valid employment contract from migrants who stay in the home country rather than the country of employment, will reduce further their bargaining power over working conditions. The power of the social networking to which the migrant belongs and the relatives in the host country helps to get better contractual terms. Migrant workers are in between two risks: either face the difficulty of seeking employment in a foreign country or accepting limited bargaining power over working conditions. There is certainly need some legal interventions to redress this power imbalance. To what extent imposing some contractual standards is helpful to protect migrants needs further analysis.

Having preference for local workers may be justified, at least the power of nation states has not been challenged by international law. Regional co-operations and bilateral agreements create a second group of workers who have preferential access to the labour market in comparing to third-country nationals that all countries which are out of these co-operations. Migrants of some countries receive more advantageous positions comparing to migrants from other countries.

Nevertheless, once the employment relationship is concluded, the principle of equality should govern the relations between national and migrant workers. Termination of the employment relationship due to labour shortage requires particular attention in the selection of who will be dismissed. In Brazil, the legislation provides that the dismissal of foreign workers should precede nationals when the dismissal is on the ground of labour shortage.[167] It seems us difficult to justify such legislation under the principle of non-discrimination.

As regards migrants who have already crossed the borders, the access of migrants to job also becomes a risk for receiving states. Migrants are widely affected by the economic crisis, and they have more difficulty in finding good jobs than nationals. Though states are not obliged legally to provide a job to each resident in their territory, unemployment is a responsibility of governments. This shows the importance of labour market integration programs. For example in Spain, immigrants are regarded as a particularly vulnerable group with difficulties in accessing employment. Therefore

167. F.Columbu, Questionnaire-Brazil.

they benefit from the active (or aid) policies which make it easier for them to find work. States should also bear certain risks in this process to provide a fair risk allocation.[168]

[C] Migration Legislation and Vertical Risk Mutualization

The power relationship in employment relationship is structured under the contractual prerogatives of the employer. Migration legislation aims to assure that migrants entering into the borders take up the employment for which the authorization is given and carry out this job. On the other hand, determining a citizen who will carry responsibility towards national authorities for the irregularities and conducts of migrants facilitates the monitoring of the migration. Therefore, migration law, by involving employer in the migration process, aims to assure that the migration operates in the way officially declared. However, such employer tied or occupation tied visa regulations may affect the established vertical risk mutualization in the contract of employment.

The range of employer tied regimes in the migration system operates on a large scale. On the one hand, there exists kafala system in the countries member to the Gulf Cooperation Council (GCC)[169] provides that a sponsor (the kafil) is required to take full economic and legal responsibility of the migrant worker. Sponsor is responsible for the employee's recruitment fee, medical examination and the issue of a national identity card, etc. The system protects local workers and also state by putting all responsibility upon the employer. Having such a large responsibility, the sponsor thus uses a complete control over the mobility of the migrant workers to the point that the employee needs an exit visa from the sponsor to leave the country in some cases.

On the other edge of the spectrum, there exist visa regimes tied to an occupation, sector or employer. Temporary and seasonal workers generally work under tied visa regimes. In cases wherein the work permit of the migrant is tied up to solely one employer, the migrant worker will have no right to end up a contractual relationship without taking the risk of being removed to the homeland. A migrant worker who ends up the employment relationship risks of being deported or restart a difficult admission process. Such rules have an effect of empowering the employer beyond the contractual structure and put additional risks over migrant workers. It becomes difficult for a migrant worker not to abide by orders and instructions in the employment relationship. The compulsory ties enable employers to deduct replacement expenses from monthly wages of migrants.[170]

Contrary to employer tied visa regimes, in the frame of occupation tied visa regimes migrant workers should have a right to remain in the same sector even if their initial contractual relationship ends up. At first sight, occupation tied visa regimes do

168. F. Camas Roda, Questionnaire-Spain.
169. Qatar, Saudi Arabia, the United Arab Emirates, Bahrain, Kuwait, Oman.
170. Maria Platt, Brenda S.A. Yeoh, Grace Baey, Khoo Choon Yen, Theodora Lam, Dhiman Das and Miriam Ee, 'Financing Migration, Generating Remittances and the Building of Livelihood Strategies: A Case Study of Indonesian Migrant Women as Domestic Workers in Singapore', Working Paper, 10, November 2013, web: http://migratingoutofpoverty.dfid.gov.uk.

not affect the vertical risk allocation. Considering the protection of the local workers affiliated out of the occupation and the protection of employer's interest, occupation tied visa regimes seems to provide more acceptable risk mutualization.

Therefore, migration legislation may vest the employer extra-contractual powers over the personal life of migrants.

[D] Labour Agencies: Diagonal Risk Mutualization

Labour agencies have controversial roles as regards the protection of migrant workers. They may increase the vulnerability in the market as well as help the implementation of legal protection. Article 7 of the ILO Convention No. 97 provides that '*Each Member for which this Convention is in force undertakes to ensure that the services rendered by its public employment service to migrants for employment are rendered free*'. In many states, such as Brazil, Japan, Turkey, South Africa, Sweden,[171] there exists no specific protection as regards migrants recruited by intermediaries.

Finding a decent job in a foreign country is almost impossible without the help of some intermediaries, if not some relatives or social network. The agencies have an important function to facilitate the introduction of migrants to a foreign market. Sometimes their functions go beyond the simply finding a vacant job. For example, in the case of Indonesian domestic workers, they provided necessary training, some domestic skills and basic English, to enable them to take up jobs in Singapore. Migrants paid the fees to the agency in the form of monthly deductions after they started to work in Singapore. The vulnerability occurs at the moment of reimbursement. In addition to the high amount of these fees, many women move without knowing the real amount of their debts. These fees are deducted from their monthly salary by employers.[172]

The labour agencies may also provide an important tool to secure a decent work to employees in sectors, which fall out of the scope of employment regulations. Licencing labour providers enable migration and labour authorities to check whether the relevant standards are fulfilled and take action when there is evidence of a breach. Just licensing labour providers does not suffice to assure the compliance with the relevant standards. In the United Kingdom, the Gangmasters Licencing Authority was established by Gangmasters (Licencing) Licencing Act in 2004 to operate the licensing scheme for labour providers in the regulated sectors. The Immigration Act of 2016 renamed this authority as Gangmasters and Labour Abuse Authority and extended its powers to cover all sectors outside the agriculture.[173] Therefore, thinking about the

171. F.Columbu, Questionnaire-Brazil; C. Hayakaw, Questionnaire-Japan; E. Binay, Questionnaire-South Africa; P. Herzfeld Olsson, Questionnaire-Sweden.
172. Maria Platt, Brenda S.A. Yeoh, Grace Baey, Khoo Choon Yen, Theodora Lam, Dhiman Das and Miriam Ee, 'Financing Migration, Generating Remittances and the Building of Livelihood Strategies: A Case Study of Indonesian Migrant Women as Domestic Workers in Singapore', Working Paper, 10, November 2013, web: http://migratingoutofpoverty.dfid.gov.uk/.
173. For an assessment of the act *see* A.C.L. Davies, 'The Immigration Act 2016', Industrial Law Journal, Vol. 45, No. 3, September 2016, 431-442.

labour providers and their role may give helpful tools to protect migrant workers in certain sectors.[174]

§9.05 RESPONSES FROM LABOUR LAW

Migrant workers present new challenges to labour law. On the labour law's classical conflict of interest scheme, the employer has mainly economic benefits in recruiting migrant workers both regular and irregular. On the other hand, either regular or irregular migrant workers have intrinsic vulnerabilities in this relationship, the later certainly much more vulnerable than the former. Migrant workers urge labour lawyers to relook to the well-established concepts and institutions of labour law from another perspective. The risk allocation under the migration legislation explains why and where the classical mechanisms of labour law fall short of protecting migrant workers. The protection of labour rights, both institutionally and collectively, relates to the expertise and knowledge that labour law can provide.[175]

[A] Rethinking the Right to Work: A Right Subject to Permission?

One of the main reasons for the vulnerability in the labour markets as regards irregular migrants is the lack of the right to work. The legal status of the migrants displaced forcedly shows us that those who have the legal right to stay do not always have the right to work in a host state. Nation states have wide sovereign powers not only in deciding on who will enter and stay in their territories but also on who will work in their labour markets. In fact, the latter is less underlined in international law.

In human rights law, the division between the first-generation rights as civil and political rights and the second-generation rights as economic, social and cultural rights is widely accepted. The right to work as being part of the economic and social rights presents particular challenges in its theoretical bases as well as its implementation. The vagueness intrinsic in the right of work leads to gloss over the fact that the citizenship posits as a precondition as regards migrant workers' right to work.

[1] The Distinction Between the Right to Work and the Right to Stay

The legal status of the migrants forcedly displaced shows us that those who have the legal right to stay do not always have the right to work in a host state. Nation states have wide sovereign powers not only in deciding on who will enter and stay in their territories but also on who will work in their labour markets. In fact, the latter is less underlined in international law.

174. *See* A.C.L. Davies, 'Migrant Workers in Agriculture', Migrants at Work, ed. C. Costello and M. Freedland, OUP 2014, 79-97.
175. C. Costello, 'EU Immigration and Asylum Law: A Labour Law Perspective', EU Labour Law, ed. A. Bogg/C. Costello/A.C.L. Davies, Edward Elgar Publishing 2016.

The single permit regime in the Member States of EU combines the right to stay with the right to work. Pursuant to Article 2/c of the Directive 2011/98/EU on a single application procedure for a single permit for third-country nationals to reside and work in the territory of a Member State and on a common set of rights for third-country workers legally residing in a Member State, 'single permit' means a residence permit issued by the authorities of a Member State allowing a third-country national to reside legally in its territory for the purpose of work. Third-country nationals reside for the purpose of work will need a single permit rather than two different permits. Under the EU Directive, Germany abolished two separate permit regime in 2005. Foreigners may pursue an economic activity only if the residence title so allows (Residence Act, section 4).[176] Therefore, the residence permit determines, in general, whether the immigrant may take up employment.

However, the right to stay and the right to work are separated from each other in many states. In addition, legal requirements to have a work permit may prevent the access to the jobs by migrants who have a right to work. For example, Syrians in Turkey are under temporary protection regime and have the right to work under certain conditions. According to statistics of Ministry of Labour, 13.290 work permits have been given to Syrians in Turkey.[177] This number is increased to 20.970 in 2017.[178] The number of given work permits is not low itself. However, considering 2.5 million Syrians, these numbers show also the vulnerability and informal work. And Turkey is not alone having such legislation.

From the labour law perspective, it seems questionable whether there exists a reasonable justification to explain the discrepancy exists between the right to work and the right to stay. My main concern is the binary structure in relation to the right to work of migrants. Those who are lawfully residing in a country, should they need to have a work permit in order to have a legal employment contract? It may be helpful to first examine the protection provided by international instruments.

[2] The Right to Work: A Citizen Right?

Article 23 of the Universal Declaration of Human Rights states that '*Everyone has the right to work, to free choice of employment, to just and favourable conditions of work and to protection against unemployment*'. The following paragraphs refer to the right to equal pay, right to just and favourable remuneration, the right to form and join trade unions for 'everyone'. Likewise, Article 15 of the African Charter on Human and Peoples' Rights provides '*Every individual shall have the right to work under equitable and satisfactory conditions, and shall receive equal pay for equal work*'.

The International Covenant on Economic, Social and Cultural Rights dealing with more comprehensively with the right to work proclaims in its Article 6 (1) that '*The States Parties to the present Covenant recognize the right to work, which includes the*

176. https://www.gesetze-im-internet.de/englisch_aufenthg/englisch_aufenthg.html# p0058.
177. https://www.csgb.gov.tr/media/7315/yabancilarin-%C3%A7ali%C5%9Fma-%C4%B0z%C4% B0nler%C4 %B0-2016.pdf.
178. http://multeciler.org.tr/turkiyede-calisma-izni-verilen-suriyeli-sayisi/.

right of everyone to the opportunity to gain his living by work which he freely chooses or accepts, and will take appropriate steps to safeguard this right.' The Covenant as a binding instrument grants the right to work to 'everyone', moreover develops the individual dimension of this right in its Article 7 about just and favourable conditions of work, and the collective dimension in its Article 8 about the right to form and join trade unions.

Article 6 of the Additional Protocol to the American Convention on Human Rights in the Area of Economic, Social and Cultural Rights states that '*Everyone has the right to work, which includes the opportunity to secure the means for living a dignified and decent existence by performing a freely elected or accepted lawful activity*'. The UN Convention on Migrant Workers grants both regular and irregular migrants the protection of basic rights, but it is hard to find a right to work for both groups. Some other treaties recognize the right to work referring to the 'employment'[179] or the principle of non-discrimination.[180]

The subject of the right to work in international instruments is universal: 'everyone' in the Article 22 (1) of the UDHR, also in Article 6 (1) of the ICESCR.[181] However, Article 15 of the EU Charter of Fundamental Human Rights makes a clear distinction stating in its paragraph 1 that '*Everyone has the right to engage in work*' and in its 2 paragraph, '*Every citizen of the Union has the freedom to seek employment, to work*'.[182]

It is the Committee on Economic, Social and Cultural Rights giving a systematic analysis of the right to work declares the general nature of this right under the title of '*Migrant workers and the right to work*': '*The principle of non-discrimination as set out in article 2.2 of the Covenant and article 7 of the International Convention on the Protection of the Rights of All Migrant Workers and Members of Their Families should apply in relation to employment opportunities for migrant workers and their families. In this regard, the Committee underlines the need for national plans of action to be devised to respect and promote such principles by all appropriate measures, legislative or otherwise*'.[183] The Committee is referring implicitly to the fact that 'everyone' has the right to work and taking the principle of non-discrimination as the ground ends up with a modest claim for national plans of action.

On the national level, some constitutions grant explicitly the right to work to citizens. The German Basic Law in its Article 12 (1) states that '*All Germans shall have*

179. The ILO Convention No. 122 of Employment Policy of 1964; The European Social Charter of 1961 and the Revised European Social Charter of 1996 (Part II, Art. 1).
180. Article 5, para. (e) (i), of the International Convention on the Elimination of All Forms of Racial Discrimination; Art. 11, para. 1 (a), of the Convention on the Elimination of All Forms of Discrimination against Women; ILO Convention No. 111 on Discrimination in respect of Employment and Occupation of 1958.
181. M. Freedland/N. Kountrouris, 'The Right to (Decent) Work in a European Comparative Perspective', The Right to Work, Legal and Philosophical Perspectives, Hart Publishing 2015, 123, 126.
182. *See* D. Ashiagbor, 'The Right to Work', Social Rights in Europe, ed. G. De Burca and B. De Witte, Oxford University Press 2005, 241–259.
183. CESCR, General Comment No 18: Art. 6 (The Right to Work), Adoption 24 November 2005, para. 18.

the right freely to choose their occupation and profession…',[184] or the Constitution of the Kingdom of the Netherlands of 2008 in its Article 19 (3), '*The right of every Dutch national to a free choice of work shall be recognised…*'.[185] In other constitutions, the right to work having a universal nature is recognized for 'everyone'. According to the Article 49 of the Turkish Constitution of 1982, '*everyone has the right and duty to work*' or in its Article 27 (1) of the Constitution of Japan, '*All people shall have the right and the obligation to work*',[186] or in the Preamble of the French Constitution of 1958, '*everyone has a duty to work, and a right to employment*'. Nevertheless, regardless of the constitutional wording, migrant workers need a permit to use their right to work in all of these countries.

Despite the universalism in national and international instruments, the right to work appears as a right granted to citizens in principal and sometimes to a limited number of states citizens, as in the case of EU.[187] Regarding non-nationals, in every case, the right to work depends on the migration status.[188]

Moreover, different approaches to the right to work in international treaties reveal that the right to work is fraught with definitional problems and hard to talk a consensus on its core components.[189] The Committee on Economic, Social and Cultural Rights in its General Comment No. 18 gives a very comprehensive overview of the right to work combining its different components.[190] According to the Committee, the right to work certainly meant a decent work includes '*… the right of every human being to decide freely accept or choose work. This implies not being forced in any way whatsoever to exercise or engage in employment and the right of access to a system of protection guaranteeing each worker access to employment. It also implies the right not to be unfairly deprived of employment*'.[191]

The Committee underlines the duties of the states that '*States parties are under the obligation to respect the right to work by, inter alia, prohibiting forced or compulsory labour and refraining from denying or limiting equal access to decent work for all persons, especially disadvantaged and marginalized individuals and groups, including prisoners or detainees, members of minorities and migrant workers*'.[192] Even modest,

184. https://www.btg-bestellservice.de/pdf/80201000.pdf.
185. file:///C:/Users/K%C3%BCbra/Downloads/the-constitution-of-the-kingdom-of-the-netherlands-2008.pdf.
186. http://www.ndl.go.jp/constitution/e/etc/c01.html#s3.
187. *See* M. Freedland/N. Kountrouris, 'The Right to (Decent) Work in a European Comparative Perspective', The Right to Work, Legal and Philosophical Perspectives, Hart Publishing 2015, 123–136.
188. V. Mantouvalou, 'The Right to Non-Exploitative Work', The Right to Work, Legal and Philosophical Perspectives, Hart Publishing 2015, 43.
189. *See* G. Mundlak, 'The Right to Work-The Value of Work', Exploring Social Rights: Between Theory and Practice, ed. D. Barak-Erez/A.M. Gross (London Hart Publishing 2007), 341–366.
190. Committee on Economic, Social and Cultural Rights, General Comment, No. 18, The Right to Work (adopted 24 November 2005,E/C12/GC/18); about the General Comment *see* Colm O'Cinneide, 'The Right to Work in International Human Rights Law', The Right to Work, Legal and Philosophical Perspectives, Hart Publishing 2015, 99, 105–111.
191. Committee on Economic, Social and Cultural Rights, General Comment, paras 6–7.
192. Committee on Economic, Social and Cultural Rights, General Comment, No. 23.

the achievement is important. Migrant workers should have equal access to decent work.

Mantouvalou asserts that the denial of the right to work to undocumented migrants guarantees their exploitation and immigration rules cannot and should not be enforced through the exclusion of human rights.[193] The meaning of exploitation seems determinant. Mantouvalou defines the exploitation as 'abuse of a person's vulnerability that is created or exacerbated by law, to make a profit'.[194]

I would prefer to argue on the base of the close relationship between the right to work and other civil and political liberties. Work is the main means to generate income which is crucial to meet the basic needs.[195] If the right to work provides the necessary preconditions for other necessities of life there exists a close link between the civil and political liberties and the right to work.[196] As part of economic and social rights, the right to work appears as the main means to secure human dignity and liberty, fundamental conditions for all rights. In addition, work is a mean of self-esteem, esteem for others, self-development or self-realization.[197] The Committee on Economic, Social and Cultural Rights states that '*The right to work is essential for realizing other human rights and forms an inseparable and inherent part of human dignity. Every individual has the right to be able to work, allowing him/her to live in dignity. The right to work contributes at the same time to the survival of the individual and to that of his/her family, and insofar as work is freely chosen or accepted, to his/her development and recognition within the community*'.[198] The Committee recognizes the work encompassing all forms of works, both dependent and independent.[199]

Collins aptly shows another legal base, Article 8 of the ECHR.[200] The European Court of Human Rights has developed a case law in respect of legislation which bans some individuals from the labour market. In *Sidabras and Others v. Lithuania*, former KGB employees were refused to take up some private sector jobs for ten years. Reiterating that '*there is no watertight division separating the sphere of social and economic rights from the field covered by the Convention*', the Court held that '*the impugned ban affected, to a significant degree, the applicants' ability to pursue various professional activities and that there were consequential effects on the enjoyment of their*

193. V. Mantouvalou, 'The Right to Non-Exploitative Work', The Right to Work, Legal and Philosophical Perspectives, Hart Publishing 2015, 39–60.
194. V. Mantouvalou, 'The Right to Non-Exploitative Work', The Right to Work, Legal and Philosophical Perspectives, 49.
195. V. Mantouvalou, 'Introduction', The Right to Work, Legal and Philosophical Perspectives, Hart Publishing 2015, 1.
196. H. Collins, 'Is There a Human Right to Work', The Right to Work, Legal and Philosophical Perspectives, ed. by V. Mantouvalou, Oxford Hart Publishing, 2015, 18.
197. About the values and the right to work *see* G. Mundlak, 'The Right to Work – The Value of the Work', Exploring Social Rights, Between Theory and Practice, Ed. by D. Barak-Erez and A. M. Gross (Oxford, Hart Publishing 2011) 341, 343–345; H. Collins, 'Is There a Human Right to Work', The Right to Work, Legal and Philosophical Perspectives, ed. by V. Mantouvalou, Oxford Hart Publishing, 2015, 17, 28–37.
198. Committee on Economic, Social and Cultural Rights, General Comment, para. 1.
199. Committee on Economic, Social and Cultural Rights, General Comment, para. 6.
200. H. Collins, 'Progress Towards the Right to Work in UK', The Right to Work: Legal and Philosophical Perspectives. ed. Virginia Mantouvalou. London: Hart Publishing, 2014, 250–254.

right to respect for their 'private life' within the meaning of Article 8. It follows that Article 14 of the Convention is applicable in the circumstances of this case taken in conjunction with Article 8'.[201]

In Campognano v. Italy, the Court gave a decision about an automatic exclusion of a bankrupt person from a large number of types of work and professions for a period of five years. According to the Court, '*on account of the fact that entry in the bankruptcy register was automatic and that the application of the resulting restrictions was not examined or reviewed by the courts, and given the length of time before rehabilitation could be obtained, the interference under section 50 of the Bankruptcy Act with the applicant's right to respect for her private life was not 'necessary in a democratic society' within the meaning of Article 8 § 2 of the Convention*'.[202] Therefore, the European Court of Human Rights has shown strong bonds between the right to work and the right to respect for private and family life and hold exclusion from the labour market is a penalty which requires justification under the light of Article 8.[203]

If the financial and technical capacity of states is limited to create jobs for everyone who aims to have one, as regards the negative aspect of the right to work, the goal is easier to achieve: The right of everyone to gain his living by a decent work which he freely chooses and accepts. Migrants are deprived of this basic aspect of the right to work. In addition, not only those who have entered irregularly but also those who have a legal right to stay are in some cases excluded from the right to have a decent work in the host country.[204] In many cases, the right to work is subject to the work permit regulations, which leads a practical exclusion from the labour market.

It seems hard to justify the exclusion of migrants forcedly displaced from the right to work in the sense of freedom to pursue a job for long periods. The protection of local workers does not justify such exclusion from the labour market. Those who have a right to stay in a foreign country have also fundamental rights, including the development and fulfilment of personality, which is a part of the right to private life.

Caruso while discussing the impact of globalization and migration on the nation state argues for the reinterpretation of the right to work in the light of the multi-ethnic and multi-racial labour markets and the universal recognition of the right to work.[205] If some restrictions aiming to protect local workers could justify the restrictions to the migrants for the purpose of employment, as regards forcedly displaced migrants, it seems difficult to find justification.

201. *Sidabras and Dziautas v. Lithuania*, Apps Nos. 55480/00 and 59330/00 (ECHR, 27 July 2004), para. 50.
202. *Campagnano v. Italy*, App No. 77955/01 (ECHR, 23 March 2006), para. 66.
203. H. Collins, 'Progress Towards the Right to Work in UK', The Right to Work: Legal and Philosophical Perspectives. Ed. Virginia Mantouvalou. London: Hart Publishing, 2014, 250–254.
204. Mantouvalou argues for non-exploitative work, V. Mantouvalou, 'The Right to Non-Exploitative Work', The Right to Work, Legal and Philosophical Perspectives, Hart Publishing 2015, 39–60.
205. B. Caruso, 'Immigration Policies in Southern Europe: More State, Less Market?', Labour Law in an Era of Globalization, Oxford University Press, 2002, 317–319.

[B] Re-examine Contractual Tools

Contractual tools of labour law may also help to redress certain vulnerabilities of migrant workers.

[1] Invalidity of the Employment Contract

The irregularity of migrants in the labour market has a complex nature taking into consideration multi-disciplinary regulations and temporal shifts. As have shown above, the irregularity of the migrant, either in the admission process to a host state or during its stay in the residing country, affects his/her status in the labour market.

Moreover, it is very difficult to distinct to have a clear-cut between regular and irregular situations; such as a student working beyond the working hours allowed by its visa. Thus, regularity/irregularity binaries are not sufficient to cover the whole details of the system. The migration literature uses different terms such as semi-legality, legal illegality, formal informality or semi-compliance to refer to that phenomenon.[206]

Two responses seem prominent: Selberg argues for the reconsideration and redefinition of the concept of 'worker' in the sense that 'work-performing bodies' regardless of his/her migration status, in a similar way of the opinions that the citizenship should be based on individual's personhood or social participation.[207] This approach puts aside the contractual validity as a precondition for labour rights.

A more conventional approach is to be based on the contractual relationship. Migration legislation with a set of detailed mandatory provisions, usually involving the imposition of a criminal penalty for a statutory offence, puts labour lawyers with a difficult task of deciding about the validity of the contractual relationship. Each legal system has its tools while dealing with this problem. The purpose of law or the nature of the legal rules could be a helpful device in some countries. Nevertheless, in the absence of a clear legal provision stating the contractual relationship invalid, the legal question whether the employment contract concluded with an irregular migrant is implicitly prohibited by the statue is a complex interpretative task. Regardless of the legal tools, it should be bear in mind that a large interpretation of the invalidity has an effect of increasing the risks upon migrant workers, which seems questionable.

Also in some cases, an administrative fine could be a satisfactory response without touching the validity of the contract. In *Sharma v. Hindu Temple,*[208] an Indian National having a work permit to work as a priest with one Hindu temple, changed employment to the second temple without obtaining a new work permit and claimed unfair dismissal against the second employer. The administrative system may need to

206. *See* for all Düvell, "Paths into Irregularity", 292, notes 80–83.
207. N. Selberg, 'The Laws of 'Illegal' Work and Dilemmas in Interest Representation on Segmented Labor Markets: A Propos Irregular Migrants in Sweden', 35 Comp. Lab. L. & Pol'y Journal, 2013–2014, 280–287.
208. *See* Ryan, 'The Evolving Legal Regime on Unauthorized Work by Migrants in Britain', 45–46.

track the migrants on their employment. Nevertheless, this fault should not cost all dismissal rights.

[2] Different Types of Employment Contract

The general assumption of labour law is that the contract for indefinite period provides more protection than fixed-term contracts. Certain rights, e.g. job security, severance indemnity, are related to the seniority in the employment relationship. Migrants under seasonal work programs hardly enjoy these legal protections.

Herzfeld Olsson shows that in some cases, legal institutions presumed to be more protective regarding labour rights may result in adverse effects as regards migrants. Within the terms of open-ended employment contracts, the employer has a right to end an indefinite contract just by giving a notice in many states and workers are entitled to job security at the end of a waiting period. Migrants who do not enjoy job security and whose visa regimes will be affected by a termination carry higher risks arising from the termination of the employment contract. Herzfeld Olsson argues for a particular type of employment contract, fixed-term contract, which could be ended if only for just reasons or gross negligence's of migrants, and which will provide migrants job security during the duration of their work permit. Moreover, such a contract may facilitate the enforcement of their contractual rights.[209] This approach also shows the importance of a labour law approach to migrant workers in the sense of providing more effective protection.

[C] Trade Unions and Collective Agreements

Unionization of migrant workers, in some cases hyper-mobile, requires changes in the structure and strategies of unions,[210] and a change in union's policies to concern the vulnerabilities of migrant workers.[211]

In 2017, Syrian shoemaker workers with local workers went on strike for two days and asked for 25% increase in their wages in Adana, Istanbul, Gaziantep, Konya, Izmir, Manisa, Hatay and Bursa, mainly the all big cities of Turkey, without being organized under a trade union. They received 21% of the increase. If Syrian workers gained lower wages than Turkish workers at the beginning, the wage discrepancy seems to decrease nowadays. They are still working informally, like many workers having Turkish nationality. But this movement seems the importance of the collective rights in labour law and opportunities that trade unions must take facing with the migration.

209. P. Herzfeld Olsson, 'Empowering Temporary Migrant Workers in Sweden A Call for Unequal Treatment, Temporary Migration in the Global Era, ed. J. Howe/R. Owens, Hart Publishing Oxford 2016, 203-222.
210. I. Greer/Z. Ciupijus, 'The European Migrant Workers Union and the Barriers to Transnational Industrial Citizenship', European Journal of Industrial Relations, 19 (1), 5-20.
211. G. Alberti/J. Holgate/M. Tapia, 'Organising Migrants as Workers or as Migrant Workers? Intersectionality, Trade Unions and Precarious Work', The International Journal of Human Resource Management, 2013, 24 (22), 4132-4148.

Migrants are capable humans with their social networks. They may show the power to alter given risk mutualization and reduce their vulnerabilities under suitable legal circumstances. Collective labour rights present an important legal tool to improve working conditions. The irregularity in their migration process also affects their active use of collective labour rights. Legislation could also be used in a more constructive way to prevent irregularity. For example in Sweden, trade unions are an active part of the migration process in the sense that they may verify whether the terms laid down in the offer of employment are in accordance with the collective agreements or custom.

§9.06 CONCLUSION

'Migrant labour is not a commodity' as stated by Kountouris and Freedland.[212] Migration as a global social justice phenomenon challenges borders and institutions of labour law. Nation states prefer to regulate migration in the service of the specific needs of their labour markets and try to avoid forcedly displaced migrants. The legal status of migrant workers is being forged at the intersection of migration law, labour law, international law, and criminal law.

To implement the principle of equality between migrants and nationals as regards labour and social security rights, labour law should develop a specific approach, which will prevent vulnerabilities and exploitation in the market and strengthen labour law institutions. The risk mutualization may help to capture the insights of the complex migration phenomenon.

212. N. Kountouris/M. Freedland, 'Epilogue Resocialising Europe – Looking Back and Thinking Forward', Resocialising Europe in a Time of Crisis, Cambridge University Press 2013, 493, 502–503.

CHAPTER 10

The Role of the State and Labour Relations

Jesús Cruz Villalón

§10.01 THE INITIAL AND EXTENSIVE CENTRALITY OF STATE INTERVENTION

The sovereign power of nation states in the critical point of the industrial society is the benchmark of the emergence and development of Labour Law as an organizing tool for subordinate work. State power has designed key institutions regulating subordinate work for decades, especially in the economically most developed countries, but also in market economies as a whole. Moreover, it has been also the public power that, by means of judges and courts or by means of administrative authorities' action, has controlled to a large extent the effective fulfilment of labour standards set by the State legislative power itself.

This phenomenon is even more acute in continental Europe and other non-European countries markedly influenced by German and Latin legal culture. In these countries, a constitutional and social conception of the rule of law has led to an attribution to public authorities, whether it the legislature or the government, a decisive leadership in the regulation of labour relations and its implementation. Probably, this leadership is not as distinct in legal orders with an anglosaxon legal culture but it cannot be denied the influential role of political actors in labour relations during the industrial period through the application of economic and social measures distant from the classic liberal statements characterising the 'laissez faire, laissez passer' doctrine.

Complementarily, in practical all legal models inserted in the industrial society, it was for the public power, by the means of the judicature or the administrative authorities, to control in a large extent the enforcement of labour standards previously determined by the national legislature, including private commitments between individuals and entrepreneurs, in individual as well as in collective affairs.

Notwithstanding that, in many occasions, all the foregoing has been carried out thanks to the impetus provided by various supranational organism, Manila as the result of the influence of the International Labour Organization, the decisive role has been played by the State in such a way that labour relations models have been set up at the national level, presenting each one their own political, economic, social and cultural peculiarities.

Considering that decisive influence, the State has become the protagonist par excellence in the development of the balance of interest function between workers and entrepreneurs in labour relations. Both the contents and the methods of intervention have been notably different in every country, but, in any event, it can be said that both have also shared as a common guiding thread: the decisive influence of the nation state playing a role as the lawmaker as well as playing a role deploying orientation public policies in the evolution of the labour market.

That intervention of the State has been particularly intense when it comes to the setting of minimum standards of labour conditions aim at applying uniformly to the whole working population. In contrast with this, it cannot be said the same concerning the intervention of the State in the design of collective labour relations. Indeed, in that particular aspect of labour relations, it can be observed different options between one country and others. Certainly, in the majority of developed economies during the expansive period of the *fordist* model of production, the intervention of trade unions and enterprise organizations have been really relevant and it has triggered an intervention, complementary to the State intervention, especially by the means a decisive collective bargaining adapting minimum legal standards to the peculiarities of the companies or the productive sectors.

The development of the trade union's activity and collective bargaining in some models have taken place on the basis of a state regulatory framework of trade union freedom as well as collective bargaining, even in cases which reference rules for the development of other typical manifestations of collective autonomy: participation in the company, exercise of the right to strike, conciliation and arbitration proceedings. In sum, it is a model in which the State has played a major role setting the collective labour relations system. It is also possible to identify, during this long period of economic expansion in developed economies, other countries which have prevailed another model favouring a more legal abstentionism when it comes to the collective relations system design, leaving room enough to trade unions and enterprise organizations to set the previously mentioned rules, notably in the case of collective negotiation regime and labour conflicts resolutions. That said, even in models more inclined to some legal abstentionism, it is possible to observe the role of the State in the background that, in one way or another, has set up the labour collective relations system. Collective bargaining has had a decisive role in the labour collective relations system in industrialized countries influencing the labour market in the framework of a national model of collective relations, with its own peculiarities, due to the legal culture of every country and, more specifically, due to the specific model of State intervention in the collective labour relations.

If, after all, collective bargaining in industrialized countries had an influential role in the labour market, it was due to the outcome of two factors: first, a national model of collective bargaining - every one of them with their particular features and legal culture - and, second, the specific model of State intervention in the field of collective labour relations, whether this intervention is through legal, judicial or administrative means.

To conclude, it can be said that States, even with different economic and legal profiles, including those countries ascribed to the common law tradition have induced or determined relations of exchange between entrepreneurs and workers. It was a regulation with a clear tendency towards uniformity. On the one hand, it was exclusively centred in subordinated work whereas autonomous work could not be protected by a regulation acting as a guardian of its interests because it was considered sufficient the recourse to the traditional rules of liberal contracting which rendered parts on an equal footing. On the other, considering that the *fordist* model of production was the salient model universally, it had to prevail a homogeneous regulation for all the salaried population, not being necessary to introduce legal differences.

§10.02 A QUALITATIVE CHANGE OF SCENARIO: TRIGGERING FACTORS

Various factors have contributed to a qualitative change in the previous overview in the last decades. It cannot be denied that the panorama turned more complicated and, in particular, it is observed an evident weakening in the capacity of the State to govern and manage completely by itself labour relations as it was accustomed to do in the past.

That change cannot be explained exclusively by the influence of one specific cause, but there are plenty of factors influencing the changing process that can be noticed from the decline of the *fordist* model of production in the 1970s. Some of those factors are present in labour relations from the emergence of the first industrial revolution more than two centuries ago. Nevertheless, not only have these transformations been increased lately but also they have been universalized in all territories, sectors and professions, not to mention that a clear influence over the capacity of ruling on labour relations by the State.

Besides, it must be underlined that the different factors that influenced and still influence trigger a qualitative change of scenery and they feed each other, that is there is a bidirectional influence between these factors. It all leads to a much more intense effect of those factors in such a way that a strong synergy acts.

In some cases, we refer to factors that act as causes that accelerate and intensify the weakening process of national interventionism. In other situations, it can be the case of phenomena that, undoubtedly, have a long presence in different models of labour relations, but are more profound in their intensity and scope provoking a reinforced effect in the preceding tendencies towards the lesser capacity of leadership that the State plays in the intervention of labour relations. In other cases, it could be considered those phenomena are at the same time cause and effect of the new reality we are sketching.

We can underline the following prominent factors in this changing scenery.

[A] Globalization of the Economy

Among the various factors that have led to this outcome, it has been commonplace to underline one of them: the process of globalization of national economies that affects developed countries as well as those located in inferior relative positions in the macroeconomic and microeconomic level. In all cases, trade transactions, production of goods and service provision go beyond national borders in such a way that competition among companies is taking place mainly in the international arena. Not only is this process of globalization influencing the business domain but also it is leaving its mark in the labour market, employment and working conditions. Under these circumstances, the risk of social dumping increases at the international level and, accordingly, the capacity of the State to manage labour relations are reduced. The State loses its pre-eminent position designing the rules applicable to relations between entrepreneurs and workers in such a way that its leadership is more and more complex. It cannot be argued a withdrawal of the intervention of the State, but at the same time it is undeniable that the State finds higher technical and political difficulties to achieve that his interventions are as effective and have the same impact than they had in the past.

Globalization raised the level of business competence, so that it is not confined to the local sphere. Initially, it was considered it would only affect companies acting in the field of international trade which would amount to a limited impact. However, nowadays – apart from the exponential increase of the number of people acting in the supranational trade ambit – the phenomenon is influencing indirectly over the whole productive sector and services. This indirect influence is verifying through diverse means: interconnection of businesses with those operating in the international sphere, outsourcing expectation of certain activities even if they are not initially within the international trade sector, globalization on the part of the consumer that alternatively selects the product to purchase, the service to enjoy or his personal destiny between those located in plural nations. Not only can globalization be held responsible for a higher pressure on labour costs but also it generates uncertainty regarding its evolution which creates more job rotation and, more generally, increases the requirements for work flexibility from the point of view of human resources. In other words, the abandonment of a labour model based on stable working conditions, that requires a continuing process of business reorganization with the focus on labour instruments of change management that must take into account techniques anticipating the change to present business crisis.

In the framework of collective labour relations, there are no signs of deregulations on the part of States traditionally protagonist in this respect, but the existing regulations are conceived for traditional model – not a globalized one – in such a way that it can differ its capacity to make an impact.

It is necessary to underline the fact that a globalized economy acts in a scenery where economic disruptions are more and more marked and, especially, where there is a tendency for a decrease in the average time of consumption of products and services offered by companies. It even reduced the lifetime of companies and, consequently, the average time of the legal bond between workers and companies. In doing so, it is increasing in many countries non-typical labour formulas and, especially, a significant rise of part-time work and a reduction of labour day in the case of indefinite work. Overall, the result is an intensification of the rotation of the occupied population with an intense flow of people in and out unemployment situations. We are also interested in highlighting its repercussions on the traditional model of collective labour relations. As it was already mentioned with regard to dimension of companies, the more conventional model of workers' participation in the company and, generally, of union activity is built on relatively stable workforce. When, on the contrary, we are dealing with a different scenario where workers are well aware that their expectation of continuity reduces, their implication in collective participatory processes is weakened and it gets more complex the application of certain traditional models of collective relations and it is also noticeable the difficulties of maintaining new models of collective bargaining models focused on the company level.

[B] Digitalization of Productive Processes

Second, it should be noted the huge impact of the generalization of technologies of information and communication, economy digitalization, artificial intelligence and robotization in the last decades. These technologies, as a manifestation of the technical revolution of the post-industrial society, have expanded universally in all companies, productive sectors and countries with no exception. One of the most significant traits of such technologies, in contrast with previous technological changes, is that they are not concentrated in certain activities or specific fields, but they have a general impact. It is also worth noting the impact of these technologies over some legal institutions and traditional rules whose effectivity is decreasing or, at least, they have some functionality.

This process has experienced an exponential increase in the recent years. In so doing, it is harder and harder to react to the effects they entail. At the outset, one of its most clear upshots is the extinction of certain labour activities, which used to require the presence of human intervention leading to a significant destruction of jobs without the creation of an alternative that may compensate it. It is even possible that technical and professionalized work to be substituted by robotization. In some cases, we assist to an incorporation of automated processes in the short term of that may lead to the disappearance of a mass of traditional jobs. These technologies make possible that some residual and manual activities are replaced to users and consumers (prosumers), which, indirectly, substitute traditional jobs. The sum of all of these factors has led to some experts to consider that the extinction of professions in the short term that may trigger massive destruction of jobs practically unknown till now.

Even those technologies are already creating important changes in jobs that still persist or in newly created jobs. Others are also being altered in their content, function and way of execution which entails a qualitative transformation in labour conditions, provision of services and they even impinge on obligational tie between workers and employers.

It is especially worth mentioning the important impact technologies are having when it comes to the intervention of certain institutions and traditional rules in the labour sphere whose effectiveness is being reduced or they simply play a different function. Suffice it to mention how these technologies do influence the place for providing services, the functionality of certain rules regarding work time, the intensity of pattern of work, instruments protecting security at the workplace, procedures and instruments of control on the part of the employer and its impact on the employee's privacy. It all provokes that labour rules, without changing its content, deploy a functionality and efficacy rather different than those in the past.

This kind of changes do not limit themselves to the sphere of labour standards of work conditions, but they can project themselves to collective labour relations. In this vein, trade union's activity is forced to adapt to this new context as well as collective bargaining experience the impact of transformations happening within the companies as a result of the intense presence of technologies of information and communication. Besides, these technologies are a reinforcement for globalization in such a way that its generalized presence all over the world is attributable to those technologies. The result, once again, is a more complex interplay of the classic rules of the labour legal order in this new technological scenario.

[C] Organization Changes: Flexibility and Decentralization

Globalization and digitalization have had an impact on business organization and, in particular, due to its general repercussion on the productive decentralization and outsourcing of services. In some cases, it has been carried out via specialization which contributes to add value to the activity executed by contracting companies or it provides a superior capacity of quick adaptation to change. In other cases, this kind of decentralization is preferred in the intent of reducing labour costs, employment stability or as a means to avoid salaried labour. In those national models where there is traditionally a strong leadership of sector collective bargaining or where trade unions have a major influence in the case of leading companies, the process of decentralization is more acute with the aim of provoking an effect of reducing labour costs thanks to an exit from sector bargaining or through the application of the main company's collective bargain by contracting companies.

It can also be observed synergies as a result of that accumulative application of the three above-mentioned phenomena: (1) globalization, (2) technological processes and (3) organizational transformations. In this vein, these phenomena of decentralization, that were not feasible on grounds of the technology employed or the impossibility of acting in the supranational sphere with total or partial relocation, are perfectly feasible presently as a consequence of the interplay of economic globalization and the implementation of technologies of information and communication. As a result, there has been an expansion of 'jobs on demand' and micro jobs entrusted and executed just in time.

The synergic effect of the three previous factors which push for a reduction of labour costs is responsible for the emergence of phenomenon unknown till now, à savoir: poor workers. In the past, having a job was tantamount to a certainty regarding a minimum level of income guaranteeing a decent livelihood whereas it is presently emerging a certain volume of workers that even if they are able to connect different options of micro-occupation, their income is not sufficient to face their economic necessities.

[D] The Settlement of Small Companies and Informal Economy

Fourth, it is equally necessary to underline the expansion of small and very small companies, in terms of the number of employees, in many national economies. Consequently, this has led to a greater weight of these kinds of enterprises in national economies. Again, it is a deep-rooted and widespread phenomenon in some countries that it is general to all productive sectors. At first sight, it could be thought that a contradiction lays in the phenomenon inasmuch as it could be hypothesized a more stable model of a globalized economy with a marked presence of international companies should be conducive to an increase of the average size of companies if we consider the number of employees. Nevertheless, the trend is actually the opposite since globalization is not only compatible but it also is enhanced with formulas of flexible organization of companies. In so doing, the sum of formulas of network corporate association, the expansion of models of productive decentralization and the deep penetration of TICs in the field of small and micro companies allows the incorporation of small business corporations in a globalized economy. In this way, the typical model of legal intervention over labour relations is specially designed to be applied to companies with medium and big size. Anyhow, it is out of question that an intensification of the weight of very small companies will make more difficult the applications of the traditional model of labour relations. In particular, it is of the utmost importance to evaluate the impact of these circumstances over rules promoting trade union's action and, in particular, of the tendency to promote collective bargaining in the corporate field which requires organization with a minimum number of employees.

It cannot be overlooked the strong presence in many countries of the so-called informal economy, that is, to be precise, informal employment. It is true that the term informal employment encompass very different realities. Besides, it is understood differently in one country or others. In any event, this term covers at least two diverse phenomena, notwithstanding they can be closely linked in certain occasions. On the one hand, this term is referred to labour activities that escape from the control exercised by labour rules enacted by the State. As a result, that labour activities are developed in the framework of irregular employment that does not comply with labour minimum standards. On the other, it refers to self-employment situations that are also apart from State intervention in the management of labour market. Both phenomena are an expression of informal employment and not only do they affect individual labour relations but also they have an impact on trade union's activity as well as collective bargaining. It is indisputable that informal employment is a common feature in some countries a long time ago. This circumstance shares space with the new scenario of a globalized economy and, in addition, informal employment is increasing a percentage in relation with the total. Some have raised a major concern that the high rate of salaried workers, which is considered as one of the most characteristic traits of a developed economy, can be reduced progressively in some labour markets, especially enhanced by new ways of labour organizations, network enterprises schemes and the implementation of technological transformations. However, it must be warned that statistical data known till now do not confirm this foreseen trend towards a reduction of the rate of salaried workers in the labour market. All these factors enable some more extended forms of self-employment without altering productivity, efficiency and enterprise productivity. Naturally, if this tendency is verified, we will be witnessing a more complex State intervention in the management of labour market.

[E] Migration Flows

Fifth, there is a process of migration flows which is the result of structural elements (unbalanced economic growth and job opportunities) as well as cyclical (war conflicts and humanitarian crisis). Among structural elements, we should underline those phenomena emerging from globalization which project its effects to the field of economy and society. In particular, it is important to emphasize the existence of workers with ample information concerning change expectations about their personal life conditions even at the risk of the uncertain results of transnational movements. The truth is that those strong migration flows trigger pressure effects over the labour market in immigration-receiving countries and even on those where immigrants come from. At times, it is about bi-directional flows within the same territory given that meanwhile there are tendencies of receiving external population with low professional qualification, there are also workers with higher level of qualification leaving our borders with better job expectations – normally, this is the case young generations and highly qualified professionals – but undoubtedly this may cause a notorious damage on the labour force in those countries suffering emigration. The phenomenon is so complex that, not surprisingly, some countries are simultaneously exporting migrants and importing migrants with all the difficulties that lie therein.

With respect to the matter that concern us at the moment, we are dealing with migration flows that are rather difficult to handle by public powers apart from the imposition of border controls by the States affected. The public power's weakness managing migration flows in the supranational sphere and, primarily, in the European Union. Again, it is confirmed a clear decline on the part of national and supranational executives in their traditional task of managing these flows in order to favour their labour market. In the end, the national sphere is able to manage the effect of migration processes but cannot cope with the intensity of these flows.

[F] Cultural Changes

Finally, all the previous factors lead to labour market perceived in a less uniform way on the part of workers; therefore, that is conducive to undebatable social and cultural changes regarding the way the population faces their incorporation and permanence to the labour market. The traditional dualist conception of a system struggling in a contrast of interests of two parts has been replaced by a pluralist and, consequently, less uniform. Traditional elements of concentration of interests between salaried workers are diluted, and it emerges phenomena of labour market segmentation, identity crisis of the occupied population and resisting tendencies to the full delegation when it comes to collective representation. The worker tends to assume diverse identities' roles as a result of very different factors: related to territory, family ties, professional career, type of labour contracts, gender, age, nationality, race, vital or religious conceptions without ruling out the possibility of the sum of some of these elements at the same time. Ultimately, all the previous circumstances lead to a diversity of personal and cultural conceptions not very favourable for a unitary response on the part of the protagonists of the system of labour relations and for a uniform action on the part of public powers through the traditional legal technique of a general legal norm.

§10.03 DETERIORATION AND COMPLEXITY IN NATIONAL LABOUR GOVERNANCE

Without considering that the influence of the State is playing a residual role in the design of labour politics, as time goes by and the influence of the previously mentioned transformations, there is no doubt that the situation we are living in is getting more and more complex. In particular, it is confirmed a marked decline in the capacity of the State by its own to manage labour relations fully as it was the case in the past. Initially, this process of decay in the determining role of the State governing labour relations was concealed owing to three considerations. First, a progressive which was not easy to advert. Second, the State has not stopped adopting measures even if they were losing effective. Third, it was considered to be just a cyclical matter that would not last forever. However, it is undeniable that we are dealing with a general and permanent trend that can be perceived all over the world.

The modification of classic relations between politics and economy has altered a scenario where the State and the market have been acting in the past decades and where the balance between economic power and political power was the result of the hegemony of States. Today, the economy has gained its independence from politics in many senses.

The ways through which it perceived this weakness are plural but, in brief, we can enumerate some of them, not to mention the paramount influence of globalization. Certainly, it is beyond the reach of the national norm to be effective over situations that transcend the national territory in such a way that there is exogenous factor that has an impact on our national reality but cannot be controlled by the national power. The result can be very different: labour norm does not change but it loses or reduces its functionality, and there are legal reforms reactive to new scenarios but those modifications have no real impact. The result is a *lampedusian* effect: norms do not go beyond the official diary because they are not applied. In other words, the norm is formally applied but it is not capable to produce effects. In other cases, the norm is applied and it achieves its ends but at the same time it produces side effects in other spheres with an even boomerang effect.

It is observed a major complexity in the intervention of the labour norm as a result of the fact that it needs to act over a more diffuse reality. For example, those difficulties are the result of a transition of the *fordist* model to the present one. As opposed to one reality focused on subordinated work, as a separated space with reference to autonomous work, the latter starts to present a bigger influence and, above all, a pressure effect on employment conditions in subordinated work. In turn, in the case of autonomous work, there is a change from uniformity to fragmentation with complex processes of segmentation of the labour market. Additionally, there is also change from business and contractual stability to a general uncertainty panorama where transitions are permanent. Finally, certain realities that were perceived as cyclical in the past in the development of labour relations are becoming more normal. It all forces us to get a new approach to labour regulation.

§10.04 THE UNAVOIDABLE CONTINUING EXISTENCE OF NATIONAL POWER

Regardless of the acknowledgement of the existence of a novel weak and complex reality governing labour relations, it must be affirmed the overarching role of the State in any case. Not only is it not vanishing in the new scenario but also it still maintains its transcendence managing labour relations in very different aspects.

Above all, globalization, technological changes and the rest of factors intervening in this changing period are not disappearing, but they can even exert the eternal distortions in the functioning of labour market as a result of the mere application of the law of offer and supply under the premise of laissez faire. Consequently, an external power is needed that can counter-attack those results of economic and labour disruption.

What is more, the process of economic globalization, leaving aside some specific experiences, has not caused the emergence of entities of organizations alternative to State power. The confirmation of regional or international organizations in this new scenario of globalized economy has not determined the substitution of the traditional role played by the State in the last decades.

Experiences conforming supranational entities – paradigmatically, the European Union – have had a significant impact on the construction of a model capable of managing in certain fields the mark left of regional globalization from the perspective of labour market functioning. Nevertheless, when the process of globalization has been universalized to further territories it has been attested the limitations of the European project. In any event, the intervention in the field of the European Union did not carry out with the aim of substituting the role of the nation state; instead its purpose is to perform a complementary function, by means of sophisticated technics of European Union intervention. Suffice it to say, without elaborating in detail, on the complex matter of dialogue between the European Union and Member States via Directives, open method of coordination and other diffused techniques of soft law.

Social partners have not been able to create spaces of interlocution at the international level that can balance the State's loss of relevance. It is noted in some territories some novel experiences in this framework of globalized economy. In some cases, different formulas of worker participation and representation are being tested within transnational companies. In addition, some experiences in the field of transnational collective bargaining are noticeable. With regard to these cases testing transnational collective relations, its design is only to a minimum degree the result of the State intervention or international organizations. Consequently, it can be verified again the deeper complexity of the intervention of the State in the field of labour relations.

Finally, certain phenomena, described below in more detail, are social clauses in Free Trade Agreements and collective transnational agreements. Both require, whether we are concerned about their scope or their implementation, State intervention. In the end, States are responsible for their signature and control their application. Likewise, it is observed that transnational agreements achieve great success in those situations where administration boards are located and adopt a legal culture embracing collective bargaining, not to mention that their implementation depends on the national model of labour relations prevailing in each case.

In the light of all the foregoing, notwithstanding the noticeable weakening of State intervention in order to manage labour relations, given that there is no public interlocutor at the international level, it can be considered that nation states are still unquestionably a reference in the development of labour relations correcting the distorting effects of the law of supply and demand which are distinctive of a capitalist economy. It is true that an adjustment to the new globalized scenario is required, and it is also observed that a more complex intervention and different legal methods would be needed, but we cannot overlook the pre-eminent role of the State in this respect.

§10.05 NEW CHALLENGES AND OLD DEBATES

From the simplified diagnosis of the most important transformations occurred within labour relations, due to this new context of a globalized economy, it is for us to assess the new forms of State intervention implications to manage the labour market and, particularly, collective labour relations. If possible, such evaluation should not restrain itself exclusively to a mere diagnosis and identification of the changes that are taking place. It is of the utmost importance that we introduce several action proposals to face the new scenario.

[A] Global Trade Agreements, Transnational Companies and Social Clauses

The first question to deal with relates to the fact that a global economy is not the simple outcome of undertaking activities in the field of transnational trade. Much of it has to do with the approval of a transnational Free Trade Agreement between more than two big economic areas, such as the present negotiation between Europe and The United States of America, as well as other in the Pacific area. At the beginning, WTO did have a great influence on the liberalization of these transnational agreements, especially on commercial trade activity and their customs systems, but it also affected many other aspects of economy functioning in a globalization model, among which employment and labour conditions must be highlighted, especially when we talk about agreements in different countries with diverse models of labour and Union relations.

That is precisely why this type of agreements includes some social clauses, even though their real influence has been rather modest up to now. Furthermore, these social clauses are sometimes written ambiguously and not always accompanied by any mechanisms of control.

In this context it would be necessary to get to know how different countries have introduced these social clauses in their own national regulations and their effectiveness inside the Free Trade Agreements as well as the impulse role of national economies on them. The first task to undertake would be a deep insight into the contents of these clauses in order to provide them with a higher effectiveness degree. A comparative study could be useful because we will be able to ascertain the result of a more intensive use of these clauses within a global economy and the measures to be taken to avoid social dumping. In this sense it could be quite interesting to analyse transnational posting of workers through countries where free commercial trade are applicable, to check in what way the implementation of free trade areas improve the number of workers moving from one country to another.

It is common knowledge that there are certain loyalty practices from a social point of view among global trade transnational undertakings where an interesting experience of social corporative responsibility is being carried out. It would be advisable to study whether this responsibility comes from the undertakings themselves with workers representatives understanding or free trade agreements and national political measures on global economy mean a progressive development of these good practices. In the same way, the connection between these elements and the evolution of transnational collective bargaining hand out some supportive measures.

Another issue to address in this context regards to the State intervention on the requirements demanded to foreign investments and their connection with labour mobility. Nowadays there are some attempts to establish some sort of structural funds to compensate undertakings for labour impacts in certain areas or sectors due to modifications and changes occurred within the enterprise as a consequence of the implementation of this new 'scenario' of free trade originated by the transnational agreements. Production and workers are many times compelled to move from some territories to others, and it is necessary to tackle the question of workers reduction searching for public measures to be put forward to secure the situation and reduce the negative effects for undertakings under these conditions.

[B] Impact on National Labour Relations

The effects of this global process on collective labour relations are particularly noticeable: on the one hand realizing how traditional rules have been transformed because of this new reality in a different setting and on the other working to introduce some innovations in national regulations.

Singularly important is to verify what is happening in terms of participation in the undertaking organization and in settled legal institutions as collective workers representation.

It is important to pay attention to collective bargaining in this area: the tendency to maintain or change workers percentage to be ruled under collective bargaining; negotiation structures transformation particularly focused on the proposals to address the undertaking as a preferential space to develop collective bargaining; where it exists, this is the natural space to improve sectorial collective bargaining and keep alive the process of individual negotiation about labour relations; the comparative law vision regarding the compulsory elements of what has been negotiated, the *erga omnes* efficacy of collective bargaining and finally the definite role of judges on their fulfilment.

When it comes to speak about the right to strike and other expressions of labour dispute, it is essential to take into considerations the three following aspects: (1) the point of view of the legislative power, which can opt for a more interventionist or more passive approach, (2) the use of the right to strike as a method of control in a context of transnational scenario and (3) to what extent national collective bargaining applies to posting workers. It will necessarily be useful to see how the legislative deals with the problem of work stoppage in case of public services essential to the community. Here, consumer's reaction to this question must be taken into consideration.

Lastly, it is also important to analyse how different national models of arbitration procedure try to solve some labour disputes, specifically the ones trying to promote them and whether they accept the questions when they take place in a transnational context.

[C] New Ways of State Intervention on Industrial Relations

As we all know, the most classical forms of legal State intervention on labour law have taken place putting into force some minimum legal standards of working conditions, in such a way that the most common juridical technique has consisted of establishing a block of some necessary rules that cannot be changed by the contracting parties, commonly named under the expression 'hard law'. Although more frequently used for individual labour relations, from the initial engagement till the extinction of the employment contract, including working conditions, it has also had a long way within the area of collective working relations, where the use of 'hard law' rules has been intensive as well.

By contrast, some experiences of 'soft law' have been appearing and spreading lately in different ways, such as diagnosis reports, positioning, recommendations, instructions, good practices in certain areas attempting to extend to some other ones, outcome evaluations.

Under this perspective, to test the evolution of State intervention through this hard law technique to verify if there has been either a decrease or any changes in public intervention about its use and efficiency would be of great interest.

Furthermore, the same analysis should be carried out about the 'soft law' experience to check the depletion degree and its real impact on working relations.

In the end, the question laid before is in what way mutual influences can be identified between both techniques, hard and soft law, and if so they act as an alternative, to trade one against the other, or, on the contrary, must be considerate complementary options that enhance each other.

As a consequence of the aforementioned, it is clearly visible that a deep insight into the new State tools used to allow the parties of the labour relations to face the new challenges must be done as soon as possible: green economy; digital economy, professional training, young people integration, social inclusion, balance between working and family life time, active ageing, migration, etc.

CHAPTER 11

The Role of the State and Industrial Relations in Latin America[1]

Maria Katia Garcia Landaburu

Although data is not available for all countries in the region and the productive structure and labor markets are heterogeneous,[2] which makes it difficult to reach general conclusions, the information from Argentina, Mexico, Panama, Peru and Uruguay can give us an idea of how industrial relations are being configured in the area, and what is the impact of globalization and free trade agreements (FTAs) in this part of the world. According to information from the World Bank, for the countries mentioned, in 2017 they had a labor force of more than one hundred and twenty million people.[3] This represents more than a third of the labor force of Latin America and the Caribbean, which amounted to 309,820,576.

1. For the preparation of this report, various Latin American labor law societies were asked to answer a questionnaire. Answers from Argentina, Mexico, Panama and Uruguay are consolidated in points 1 and 2 of this document (together with comments about Peru).
   The participation of Mariela Lucia Fernandez, Julieta Zagari and Oscar Eduardo Benitez (Argentina); Tomas H. Natividad Sanchez (Mexico); Margarita Ibets Centella, Carlos Ayala and Carlos Membreño (Panama); Juan Raso Delgue and Fernando Delgado (Uruguay) are gratefully acknowledged. Likewise, the participation of Katerine Bermúdez, Director of the Labor Research Center of the Universidad Externado de Colombia, who answered the questionnaire providing information of her country is gratefully acknowledged.
2. Although as indicated by the International Labour Organization (ILO) in the 2017 Labor Overview for Latin America and the Caribbean, and despite the fact that economic cycles in the region over the past four decades have generated a heterogeneous impact on labor markets, the impact of the variation in the price of commodities exported by the countries of the region in the employment rate follows a relatively similar pattern, growing during the expansionary phase and contracting during the economic slowdown. Available at: https://www.ilo.org/wcmsp5/groups/public/---americas/---ro-lima/documents/publication/wcms_613957.pdf.
3. According to the World Bank, the labor force of these countries in 2017 was as follows: 19,901,854 (Argentina), 26,421,872 (Colombia), 58,072,554 (Mexico), 1,992,357 (Panama), 17,902,674 (Peru) and 1,769,211 (Uruguay). Available at: http://api.worldbank.org/v2/es/indicator/SL.TLF.CACT.ZS?downloadformat=excel.

§11.01 GENERAL INFORMATION

In general terms, it should be mentioned that the statistics on unionization and collective bargaining are not very accurate and have certain distortions and there is controversy regarding the information on the subject. In any case, it is estimated that the unionization rate in Argentina is around 37% and in Uruguay 25%, while in the other countries it is much lower. Panama has a rate of 10.73% and Mexico of approximately 10%, although in the latter case, according to Natividad, the aggressive exercise of the right to strike has resulted in companies signing collective agreements because of the threat of stoppages in cases that do not have unions operating. Peru has a very low rate of unionization in the private sector. In 2016 it was 5.2% while in the public sector, it was 15.6% (with the highest number of affiliates in health and education). The same happens in Colombia, where the unionization rate is 4.6%, with most of the workers belonging to the public sector.

With respect to the number of workers covered by a collective agreement, it is estimated that in Argentina and Uruguay[4] the coverage reaches 80% and 95% respectively while in Panama it reaches 12% and in Colombia 6.3%. There is no precise information in the cases of Mexico and Peru.

The great difference between the figures of Argentina and Uruguay and those of Panama, Peru and Colombia can be explained, among other reasons, by the different bargaining unit predominant in those countries.

In Argentina, historically and normatively, the union organization has been promoted by activity regardless of the craft that the workers perform (this can be seen in Articles 29 and 30 of the Union Associations Law 25.871), although there may exist different levels of bargaining, there are coordination strategies that allow the coexistence of bargaining by activity and enterprise level. The same happens in Uruguay, a country in which the collective bargaining system of Wage Councils that establishes bargaining by activity predominates, although bargaining by enterprise or any other level is also possible. However, it is not allowed to make agreements for work and wage conditions lower than the ones agreed to by activity.

Panama and Peru have a decentralized model at the enterprise level. In Colombia, most of the unionized workers are affiliated to craft (49.4%) and enterprise (23.2%) unions, while only a little more than a quarter (26.8%) are affiliated to activity unions.[5]

There are several factors that have influenced the type of bargaining structure, but in Peru for instance, it is the relevant position adopted by the State which requires

4. As of 2005, coverage was extended to the domestic and rural sectors (which were excluded by the Wage Council system provided in Law 10.449 of 1943) and in 2009 with the approval of Law 18.508 of collective bargaining in the public sector – which establishes a specific system for public employees – almost all of them are covered by agreements, with the exception of a few departmental governments.
5. As Bermúdez informs, according to the Trade Union and Labor Information System (Sistema de Informacion Sindical y Laboral-Sislab), in 2016 there were 506,352 affiliates of craft unions, 238,401 were affiliated with enterprise unions, 274,606 with industry unions and 6,395 with various crafts unions.

an agreement with the employers to set the bargaining level – who refuse to negotiate by activity – and that those who negotiate to represent the absolute majority of workers and employers involved. This and other factors have resulted in a few cases of collective bargaining at the sectoral level (such as civil construction), in which the bargaining had to be restored by the Constitutional Court (which in the case of stevedores, ordered that an arbitration tribunal must decide the level of bargaining).

The decentralized model is the most widespread in Latin America with exceptions, such as those of Uruguay, Argentina and also Brazil (in the latter two cases the State promoted the bargaining by activity), which generates less coverage of collective bargaining, that determines bargaining working conditions and no other matters that could be dealt with at the sectoral level.

As already mentioned, the model of industrial relations in Latin America is diverse, ranging from one such as Uruguay, traditionally qualified as "abstentionist" (although Raso and Delgado have reported that in the last decade it has become one of "moderate interventionism"). In others, like the Peruvian one, the State occupies a central role and its level of intervention prevents employers and workers from properly assuming the role that should correspond to them. Also, the bargaining units have been set (a "closed list" of the types of unions), preventing social actors from directly dealing with the issue. This is reflected in workers participation and representation systems.

In Argentina, although the National Constitution promotes a "free and democratic organization" of unions, infra-constitutional regulation (the Union Associations Law 23.551 and its Regulatory Decree 467/88) restricts the freedom of association in that the Ministry of Labor, Employment and Social Security has the power to grant union status. This favors vertical union organizations as opposed to the ones of enterprise and craft. Thus, in the opinion of some scholars and practitioners, organizations that do not have this status would in essence be nonfunctional as unions in this context.

In Panama, according to Centella, Ayala and Membreño, the Labor Code specifies the number of workers representatives allowed to negotiate collectively (except for the Panama Canal Authority). The same happens in Peru, but not in Uruguay, where the State does not play a part in workers' participation and representation systems.

Generally speaking, in connection with collective bargaining, there is a certain level of State intervention which varies in each country. In Argentina the State intervenes by making it necessary for administrative approval of collective bargaining agreements (a validation which does not allow its contents to be altered) which is required to confer upon its legal status *erga omnes*, based on an analysis of its legality, timing and suitability.[6]

In Mexico, the Contract Law[7] still governs four branches: textiles, radio and television, sugar and rubber; in them the Contract Unit Law of the Ministry of Labor coordinates and manages the revision and updating of these contracts. In everything

6. The administrative approval is not applicable to company collective agreements, but that instrument has a reduced presence in the Argentine reality.
7. Collective labor contracts declared compulsory in the industry that they regulate.

else of federal matter and large industries of local (state) matter prevails a direct bargaining of the parties.

In Panama, the Labor Code describes the minimum contents of the collective agreement, limiting the mediation of the State (through the Ministry of Labor and Labor Development) to the overseeing of bargaining without actually participating in it.

The situation is very different in Uruguay because the system of Wage Councils - created in 1943 and convened again in 2005 - determines that the setting of wages and working conditions is carried out in a tripartite way (State, employers and unions) by activity. Currently there are approximately 240 trading units in this context in the private sector.

These types of tripartite organizations made up of employers, workers and government have spread in the region, with different levels of success.[8]

Argentina has a National Council of Employment, Productivity and Minimum, Vital and Mobile Wages created in 1991, whose function is to constitute an institutional environment for permanent dialogue between representatives of workers, employers, the national and provincial governments (through the Federal Labor Council).[9] This tripartite body of national scope has, among others, the objectives of: (i) fixing the vital and mobile minimum wage; (ii) determination of the minimum and maximum amounts and the percentages corresponding to the first months of unemployment benefit; (iii) approve the guidelines, methodology and norms for the definition of a "basic needs basket" that becomes a reference element for the determination of the minimum, vital and mobile wage (iv) to formulate recommendations for the elaboration of policies and programs of employment and vocational training; and (v) to propose measures to increase production and productivity. According to Fernandez, Zagari and Benitez, in general, the normative activity of this National Council has been limited to the determination of the minimum, vital and mobile wage and of the unemployment benefit which has had little effectiveness in terms of social dialogue.

Mexico has a National Council of Minimum Wages (Consejo Nacional de los Salarios Minimos-CONASAMI) that since the 1960s has determined the minimum wage. In 2015 CONASAMI unified the minimum wage into a single one for the entire country. In 2016 it separated it from more than 690 federal, state and municipal laws that previously used it as an economic indicator. Panama has a National Minimum Wage Commission (Comision Nacional de Salario Minimo). In Peru, the National Council for Labor and Employment Promotion (Consejo Nacional de Trabajo y Promocion del Empleo-CNTPE) is the mechanism of social dialogue and labor agreement that aims to coordinate policies on (i) the promotion of labor employment and job

8. Raso and Delgado mention that the long tradition of social dialogue and tripartite bodies in Uruguay can be seen not only in the existence of the Wage Councils, but also in the Tripartite Higher Council, and in the participation of representatives of workers and employers in the Board of Directors of the Social Security Bank and the Employment and Vocational Training Institute, as well as in various tripartite consultation bodies.

9. Although the decisions of the Council are taken by a two-thirds majority, and if this is not achieved in two sessions, its president (appointed by the Ministry of Labor and Social Security) decides the points in controversy. The latter occurred in 2017, when Resolution 3-E / 2017 established the Minimum, Vital and Mobile Wages and the minimum and maximum amounts of unemployment benefits.

training and (ii) social protection for national and regional development. It also participates in the regulation of the minimum wage. To date, effectually speaking, the Council has fomented more of a social dialogue rather than social agreement. This is because it has not passed important regulation, for instance, a General Labor Code. Owing to the fact that though the representatives of both employers and workers in the CNTPE reached a consensus on a large number of issues, no agreement was reached on the most controversial matters. Colombia has a Permanent Commission on Concertation of Wage and Labor Policies (Comisión Permanente de Concertación de Políticas Salariales y Laborales), among whose functions it is to set, in a concerted manner, the wage policy and the monthly legal minimum wage in December of each year. However, as indicated by Bermudez, its effectiveness in fixing of the minimum wage has not been very high, since to date consensus on the matter has been reached on only seven occasions. On all other occasions, the government fixed the minimum wage unilaterally.

Thus, the situation described above shows that in most Latin American countries the role of the State is decisive in the regulation of labor relations. Although the economic, social and technological transformations that are being experienced all over the world have reached Latin America, it seems to me that the perspective is different, insofar as our societies are still in the process of development and have not yet gained access to the Welfare State for the majority of its population as is found in Europe and other parts of the world.

The factors decisively influencing the transformation of work, such as the globalization of the economy, digitization of productive activity, productive decentralization, environmental and climate change, immigration flows and cultural changes, have also impacted Latin American countries, although in different ways. It is not my intention to refer specifically to each of these issues, but it is of interest to analyze the impact of economic globalization as well as FTAs.

§11.02 ECONOMIC GLOBALIZATION AND THE IMPACT OF FTAs

[A] Economic Globalization Processes

In general terms, economic globalization has occasioned the improvement in the standards of protection afforded to workers. Furthermore, international competition is requiring companies to improve their production processes. As Bermudez says, it leads to the improvement in union guarantees, greater protection for union leaders and the promotion of collective bargaining.

Following this, we will analyze the impact of the presence of multinational companies and the intervention of international trade union organizations, especially in terms of social dialogue (although they have also participated in specific situations to solve labor problems arising from noncompliance codes of conduct and global framework agreements) and their effect on collective bargaining.

Globalization has caused multinational companies to extend their activities in countries of the region.[10] However, this has not had a great impact on the industrial relations model in each country. The structure of unions has been maintained and the multinationals have adapted to it. However, in some cases, as in the Peruvian mining sector (in which there is considerable foreign investment), service provider workers have constituted their unions as allowed by legislation. To improve their working conditions, each service providers' union – as a negotiating strategy – negotiates with their respective managements at the same time while submitting similar demands. This, in effect, results in collective bargaining by the unions with their management while the mining company looks on only as an observer. Likewise, in Colombia, Bermúdez mentions that in export sectors like mining, an attempt has been made to extend the effects of collective bargaining to indirect workers whether they belong to mining or other sectors of the economy.

What has happened is that multinational companies have incorporated a series of new policies and procedures, greater use of technology, etc. In addition, as already indicated, global competition determines that companies need to improve their processes to optimize their costs and having a structure that allows them to adapt to a changing environment. This favors the use of civil and commercial contracts to the detriment of direct contracting of workers.

Besides the activity of multinational companies in the region, there have also been actions taken by international trade union organizations. Fernandez, Zagari and Benitez mention the case of UNI Global Union, which through its American regional arm has further developed its practices of dialogue and action at the regional level. This has been done through (i) the UNI-Wal Mart Hemispheric Network consisting of unions from the United States, Brazil, Argentina and Chile and (ii) the UNI-Cencosud Network, consisting of trade union representatives from Argentina, Brazil and Chile (the Board of Directors of which has two seats to be occupied in the future by Peru and Colombia).

With regards to the development of collective bargaining, economic globalization has not generated significant changes either. In Peru, for example, although there are a greater number of multinational companies (especially in sectors such as mining, energy and telecommunications), this fact has not led to important changes in the development of collective bargaining. The subsidiaries of these companies have relied on local legislation to negotiate at the company level in the cases in which workers have formed unions. In Uruguay, collective bargaining is done through the Wage Council system and bipartite bargaining; although Raso and Delgado mention a novel labor pre-agreement entered into by the Finnish company UPM which will put into place a large paper mill and the unionization of the sector as a whole even before the company begins any activity. This can be considered as an example of "bargaining in the future."

10. In Argentina, for instance, as mentioned by Fernandez, Zagari and Benitez, in 2012 there were 1719 subsidiaries of multinational companies (one-third of them are German, French and Spanish origin), and all of these firms employ approximately 700,000 workers, which represents 12% of registered private employment.

There is no development of collective bargaining at the international level, despite the fact that we have some subregional integration processes such as the Andean Community and MERCOSUR. In the case of MERCOSUR, although Article 13 of the Social Labor Declaration urges the State Parties to promote social dialogue at the national and regional levels, the States have not yet promoted instances of collective bargaining at that level. However, a case of collective bargaining involving more than one country is the Volkswagen Collective Agreement of 1999, signed by its subsidiaries in Argentina and Brazil and their respective unions. This however would not qualify as a global framework agreement given the parties and its scope (although it is open to the inclusion of other units of the business group in MERCOSUR).[11]

As can be appreciated, until now economic globalization has not had a major impact on the industrial relations model of the countries mentioned in this report. Its influence has been in line with the level of participation of each country and the specific sector in the global market. Nor has it caused a decrease in public interventionism in the use of the hard law technique. State intervention through traditional regulation is maintained or even increased in some cases, through the issuance of legal and regulatory standards. The use of soft law techniques by the State has not been widespread and, when used, has only been in certain areas. For instance, instruments to prevent harassment may be mentioned, such as the "Protocol of action against cases of labor violence, harassment and sexual harassment, directed at the companies of the Mexican Republic." Another instance is the protocols of action in Uruguay, agreed to between the State and the unions. This was created for the prevention of moral and labor harassment (as in the protocol signed in public banking in December 2016). Furthermore as Bermudez observes, this technique has also been used in Colombia to develop concepts, circulars and memos which are used as additional or interpretive criteria of the norms.

Perhaps what can be emphasized is the interest that exists in some cases to achieve consensus standards on specific issues. For instance, Centella, Ayala and Membreño report that in 2012 the Panamanian government signed the "Tripartite Agreement of Panama" with the ILO and the social actors (CONEP, CONATO and CONUSI). This was the result of the meetings of the Technical Assistance Mission of the ILO to promote an effective dialogue on the exercise of freedom of association in Panama which in itself was the result of constant complaints about its noncompliance together with the recommendations of the ILO supervisory bodies. This Agreement established (i) the "Tripartite Agreement Commission of Panama" to harmonize the legislation with Conventions 87 and 98 and (ii) the "Commission for the Rapid Treatment of Complaints on Freedom of Association and Collective Bargaining." To date, discussion is pending before the National Assembly of Deputies of the Draft Law regulating Collective Industrial Relations in the Public Sector which, in itself, was the result of the tripartite consensus achieved with the support and guidance of the ILO.

11. This agreement does not refer to specific wage conditions. What it seeks is to extend labor relations at the regional level, and promote communication, information and dialogue between the parties.

[B] Free Trade Agreements

The State has not significantly reduced its role owing to the signing of FTAs. It is also necessary to take into account that there are subregional integration processes such as the Common Market of the South (MERCOSUR). These are negotiated as a block, allowing for a better negotiation position. Furthermore, not all FTAs have social clauses. These are incorporated in agreements with countries such as the United States or the European Union. Also, these clauses have not been fully utilized in all cases. MERCOSUR, amongst whose members are Argentina and Uruguay, does not allow the celebration of FTAs by its parties unless expressly authorized. MERCOSUR has signed some FTAs, as in the case of Israel and Egypt, but these agreements do not include social clauses. There exist agreements such as the one between Argentina and Chile (complement of the Economic Complementation Agreement 35 of MERCOSUR) and the one between Uruguay and Chile, but they are very recent to analyze their consequences effectively.

The signed FTAs have not had a direct impact on the development of industrial relations in Latin America. However in Mexico, as Natividad points out, the twelve FTAs with forty-six countries have promoted foreign investment, generating jobs in the formal economy. In addition, they have prompted the most important reform at the constitutional level to Mexican labor law in February 2017. Regulations under this law, which are still pending, will determine the transfer of the labor courts from the Executive Branch to the federal and state Judicial Branch.

According to Centella, Ayala and Membreño, in Panama the FTAs have had little impact because direct foreign investment is encouraged and only agreements with the United States and Chile include social clauses which have not yet been fully applied. However, this cannot lead us to ignore the fact that in some cases certain changes in the labor legislation have been made before or even after the signing of an FTA. Besides the direct effect of the FTAs on labor legislation, the social clauses can be used by trade unions and Non-Governmental Organisations (NGOs) to sue the State to comply with the labor legislation, using the mechanism of control provided in the FTA. This includes a dispute resolution system that is triggered by a violation of the labor provisions, which in turn affects the trade or investment between both countries.

As Bermúdez reports, in Colombia the FTA with the United States not only generated reforms to labor legislation and inspections but also to the signing of a Labor Action Plan in 2011. The object of the reforms was the promotion of direct contracting and control of outsourcing processes that affect workers' rights, such as the right to association and collective bargaining. Under the Plan, Colombia had to meet certain obligations within a deadline, in order that the United States Congress approve the FTA. In this way, the effect of the social clauses of the FTA turns out to be high because, when modifications are made in the labor legislation, the reforms acquire a general and binding character.

This did not happen in Peru, which failed to adopt the legislation to the standards required by the FTA with United States. The social clause of the FTA was accepted by the Peruvian government so that Peruvian products could continue entering the North American market (which was previously achieved under a system of preferences).

During negotiations with the U.S. government, the Peruvian Congress enacted new legislation (e.g., the new law on labor inspection that led to the creation of the Inspection System of Work). However, only the norms under Law No. 29157 were the ones enacted for the actual implementation of the FTA. As Canessa points out, Peru did not comply with the adaptation of its legislation to the labor standards required by the FTA. The majority of these laws regulated labor relations between the State and the workers in the public sector. Only two did so with respect to the private sector (the regulation on outsourcing and the regulation on microenterprise and small business), although in both cases what was accomplished was to make existing legislation more flexible.[12]

However, the FTA has served in demanding that the State complies with labor legislation. For example, in Peru, among the cases presented by way of a public petition to the Office of Trade and Labor Affairs (OTLA) of the United States Department of Labor (in accordance with the provisions of the FTA) is that of the National Union of the SUNAT (Superintendencia Nacional de Administración Tributaria, the Peruvian Tax Agency) for the violation of their rights to collective bargaining. Refusal by the SUNAT to negotiate with its National Union, the terms of remunerative and non-remunerative conditions resulted in nonfulfillment of the labor chapter of the FTA. Consequently, the Peruvian government issued a new rule permitting both parties to request discretionary arbitration in certain cases.

Therefore, although the State, as a result of the FTA, has not significantly reduced its role, it has had to adjust its labor legislation in certain cases.

§11.03 IMPACT OF NEW TECHNOLOGIES

As can be seen from the topics discussed above, the leading role of the State in trying to balance the interests of workers and employers is maintained. Economic globalization or FTAs have not had a great impact on the industrial relation models adopted by the countries of the region. Perhaps what has happened – due to a series of factors – is the increase in the difficulty of the State in controlling compliance with its rules, a situation that could worsen with new forms of economic development brought about by extended uses of new technologies.

The countries of Latin America are not seriously concerned with the impact of new technologies in the workplace. The main concerns continue to be informality, underemployment and unemployment. Structural failures which persist in complicated political environments of a high level of confrontation and, in many cases, instability.

Right now, low wages in this part of the world do not make the incorporation of new technologies in many sectors of the economy attractive. Rather, this situation has generated the development of new activities, such as call centers, which have moved from developed countries to countries in the region and other areas of the world with

12. Canessa Montejo, Miguel F. "El impacto del capítulo laboral del Tratado de Libre Comercio entre Perú y Estados Unidos en el mundo del trabajo peruano." Available at: http://www.relats.org/documentos/GLOB.Canessa.pdf.

lower labor costs. This, however, can change in the short or medium term, as new technologies expand and reduce costs, in the same manner as communications and the internet. Changes and their impact on society will be much faster than those produced by previous industrial revolutions, and their effects will be more widespread.

The disappearance of jobs and the emergence of new jobs is not possible to foresee. However, it is obvious that more skilled workers, with greater capacity to adapt to changing environments, will be required. Not all Latin Americans are prepared for that. According to a UNESCO report of September 2017, in Latin America and the Caribbean, 36% of children and adolescents cannot read with proficiency; 53% of adolescents (approximately 19 million) will be unable to meet minimum proficiency levels by the time they should be completing lower secondary school. This, despite the fact that in general terms, governments of the region currently devote a greater part of the public budget to education now compared to that of a few decades ago. Consequently, it would seem that the situation of young people and adults who currently comprise the labor force is more complicated.

Therefore it is very likely that it will be increasingly difficult to find qualified workers for the new jobs that are being created. This, in turn, could cause more jobs in technology to move to other countries, especially if geographical location is not relevant.

In any case, the level of inequality in Latin American societies could increase considering the existing gap between workers with greater adaptation skills (to technological changes and new jobs), and workers without them. The latter, would therefore, look for new activities to generate an income. These activities would normally be outside the scope of the protection of labor and social security laws, as happened in some countries decades ago. There the privatization of public companies (and the reduction in the size of the State) forced workers, formerly of the public sector, to look for other activities that could generate an income. The abovementioned protections can also be elusive to workers who offer/render services directly to their customers through the use of digital platforms.

Considering the tendency that characterizes our governments, it is very possible that in the future they will try to regulate these new activities. However, the difficulties in the application and compliance of such rules will be greater.

From the previously discussed topics, it may be concluded that the leading role of the State, trying to balance the interests of workers and employers, will be maintained. Even economic globalization and FTAs have not had a great impact on the models of industrial relations adopted by the countries of the region. Furthermore, it is likely that this role will be maintained in the future, even when technological changes may entail a necessary adaptation of the legislation to this new reality.

CHAPTER 12
Organization, Productivity and Well-Being at Work

Takashi Araki & Sylvaine Laulom

§12.01 INTRODUCTION

All countries are currently confronting common issues such as the globalized economy and accompanying financial crises, remarkable technological innovation (ITC, IoT, AI, etc.), reform of business structures resulting in a fissured workplace[1] and diversification of workers and working formats. The post-WWII labour law model called the 'social compact'[2] with stable standard employment is unravelling. How to handle these issues properly is becoming an increasingly urgent agenda item for social policy and industrial relations in every country.

Theme four 'Organization, Productivity and Well-being at Work' of this World Congress is comprehensive and covers various social policy issues mentioned above. However, the outline suggested by President Tiziano Treu clarifies what should be discussed under theme four: (1) new forms of work organization and their impact on labour and labour law and (2) the role of decentralized collective bargaining in regulating organization, productivity and well-being at work.

This General Report will discuss these two independent themes in sections 2 and 3 respectively. However, these two themes deal with the common social issues, namely how to strike a better balance between flexibility and security or social protection for the diversified workforce in a rapidly changing work environment. In the final section, the report will examine the roles of the state, law, social partners and the market in

1. *See* David Weil, *The Fissured Workplace* (Harvard University Press, 2014).
2. Wilma B. Liebman and A. Lyubarsky, 'Crowdworkers, the Law and the Future of Work: The U.S.' in Bernd Waas et al., *Crowdwork – A Comparative Law Perspective*. HSI-Schriftenreihe Band 22, 32 (Bund Verlag, 2017).

striking a better balance between flexibility and security and attaining well-being at work in this new era.

§12.02 NEW FORMS OF WORK AND THEIR IMPACT ON LABOUR AND LABOUR LAW

[A] New Forms of Work and Their Impact on Labour

New forms of work developing under the so-called gig economy, digital economy, platform economy, crowd work, or more broadly the fourth industrial revolution, triggered by the rapid development of information and communication technologies and Artificial Intelligence (AI), have attracted much attention.

Here we face two different issues: (1) whether new technologies replace human work or not and (2) legal and policy issues concerning new forms of work in a digital economy.

[1] Do New Technologies Replace Human Work?

Because of dramatically developing technologies including AI, not only routine tasks that have been automated but also cognitive tasks that until recently were considered non-automatable are now at risk. Thus, unlike in the former industrial revolutions, it is feared that jobs themselves may be entirely replaced by machines under the fourth industrial revolution.

A much-quoted article by Frey and Osborne in 2013[3] contends that 47% of the workforce in the US would be at high risk due to computerization or automation. By applying Frey and Osborne's framework, a similar high risk of replacement in other countries has been reported. For instance, Nomura Research Institute (NRI), in collaboration with Frey and Osborne, estimates that 49% of the Japanese workforce could be replaced by AI or robotics.[4]

Frey, C.B. and M.A. Osborne, 'The Future of Employment: How Susceptible are Jobs to Computerization?' Oxford Martin School Working Paper, 37 (2013).

However, many counterarguments denying the persuasiveness of such estimations have also been publicized. For instance, in their OECD working paper, Arntz, Gregory and Zierahn estimate that just 9% of jobs on average are at a high risk of being automated, ranging from around 12% of jobs in Austria, Germany and Spain to around 6% or less in Finland and Estonia.[5] Differing from Frey and Osborne's assumption that occupations are displaced by machines, Arntz, Gregory and Zierahn argue that it is

3. Carl B. Frey and Michael A. Osborne, '*The Future of Employment: How Susceptible Are Jobs to Computerisation*', Oxford Martin School Working Paper (2013). https://www.oxfordmartin.ox.ac.uk/downloads/academic/The_Future_of_Employment.pdf.
4. Nomura Research Institute (NRI), '49% of the Japanese workforce can be replaced by AI or Robots' NRI News Release, 2 December 2015. https://www.nri.com/jp/news/2015/151202_1.aspx
5. Melanie Arntz, Terry Gregory and Ulrich Zierahn, '*The Risk of Automation for Jobs in OECD Countries: A Comparative Analysis*', OECD Social, Employment and Migration Working Papers,

certain tasks that can be displaced. To an extent, bundles of tasks differ across countries and also within occupations, so occupations at risk of being automated according to Frey and Osborne may well be less prone to automation when considering the fact that most occupations contain tasks that are difficult to substitute, at least in the foreseeable future. Similarly, the German White Paper Work 4.0[6] quotes the results of research that only 12% of workers in Germany today are at a high risk of being automated.[7] Therefore, the discussion of nearly half of human jobs being taken over by machines might be somewhat exaggerated.

While new technologies would cause displacement of certain jobs, new jobs would be created as we experienced in the past industrial revolutions.[8] According to the German White Paper 4.0, if policymakers and the business communities were to take on a pioneering technological role and systematically align education and infrastructure policies with the digital transformation (the scenario of 'accelerated digitalization'), an additional 750,000 jobs in total would be lost in twenty-seven sectors (e.g., retail, paper and printing, public administration), but this would be more than offset by the growth in employment of a million jobs in total in thirteen sectors (e.g., IT services, research and development). Overall, the labour force could grow by around a quarter of a million people by 2030.[9]

If new jobs could be amply created, 'technological unemployment' would be further limited.[10] However, job creation in the digital economy depends on whether appropriate policies are taken. It is certain that job displacement and changes to occupational structure will take place. According to OECD research, jobs with automatable risk between 50–70% will not be substituted entirely, but workers need to adapt as jobs will be significantly retooled (*see* Figure 12.1).[11] Therefore, it is more important how we deal with new challenges caused by technological changes entailing job changes, mismatch of skills, and possible polarization by skill level.

This leads to the second issue: what should be done to deal with new forms of work under the digital economy?

No. 189, p. 8 (OECD Publishing, Paris, 2016). https://www.oecd-ilibrary.org/the-risk-of-automation-for-jobs-in-oecd-countries_5jlz9h56dvq7.pdf?itemId=%2Fcontent%2Fpaper%2F5jlz9h56dvq7-en&mimeType=pdf.

6. Federal Ministry of Labour and Social Affairs, White Paper Work 4.0, 47 (2017).
7. Bonin, Holger; Gregory, Terry; Zierhan, Ulrich (2015).
8. *See* James Bessen, 'How computer automation affects occupations: Technology, jobs, and skills' Boston University School of Law, Law and Economics Research Paper (2016); Simon Deakin and & C. Markou, 'The Law-Technology Cycle and the Future of Work' University of Cambridge Faculty of Law Research Paper No. 32/2018 (2018).
9. *See* OECD, 'Automation and Independent Work in a Digital Economy, Policy Brief on the Future of Work', 3 (OECD Publishing, Paris, 2016).
10. It is not clear whether job destruction caused by technological developments, especially by AI including machine learning and deep learning, can be followed by sufficient job creation. Discussion would need to continue.
11. OECD (2016), 'Automation and Independent Work in a Digital Economy, Policy Brief on the Future of Work', 2.

Figure 12.1 Percentage of Workers in Jobs at High and Medium Risk of Automation

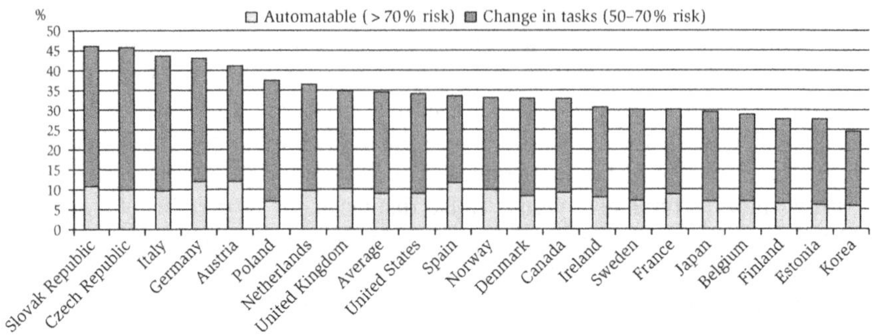

OECD, 'Automation and Independent Work in a Digital Economy, Policy Brief on the Future of Work', 2 (OECD Publishing, Paris, 2016).

[2] New Forms of Work in a Digital Economy

[a] New Forms of Work in Europe

As for new forms of work, a large body of research has been published in Europe.[12] The most recent and comprehensive Eurofound research on new forms of employment[13] provides an overview of nine types of new forms of employment: Strategic employee sharing,[14] job sharing,[15] interim management,[16] casual work,[17] ICT-based mobile

12. For example Eurofound, New forms of employment (Publications Office of the European Union, 2015); IndustriAll, Digitalization for equality, participation and cooperation in industry, Position Paper (2015); European Commission, 'A European agenda for the collaborative economy' COM(2016)356; European Parliament, 'The situation of workers in the collaborative economy' PE 587.316 (2016); J. Drahokoupil and B. Fabo, 'The platform economy and the disruption of the employment relationship' (ETUI, Brussels, 2016); Austrian Chamber or Labour et al., Frankfurt Paper on Platform-Based Work (2016).
13. Eurofound, Overview of new forms of employment-2018 update (Publications Office of the European Union, 2018).
14. Employee sharing, where an individual worker is jointly hired by a group of employers to meet the HR needs of various companies, resulting in permanent full-time employment for the worker.
15. Job sharing, where an employer hires two or more workers to jointly fill a specific job, combining two or more part-time jobs into a full-time position.
16. Interim management, in which highly skilled experts are hired temporarily for a specific project or to solve a specific problem, thereby integrating external management capacities in the work organization.
17. Casual work, where an employer is not obliged to provide work regularly to the employee, but has the flexibility of calling them in on demand (e.g., intermittent work and on-call work).

work,[18] voucher-based work,[19] portfolio work,[20] platform work,[21] collaborative self-employment[22] (*see* Figure 12.2). As the Eurofound research covers 'new' developments since 2000 and those considered 'new' in the national context, it contains various forms of work that are not necessarily caused by new technologies or digitalization.

Figure 12.2 Nine Types of New Forms of Employment

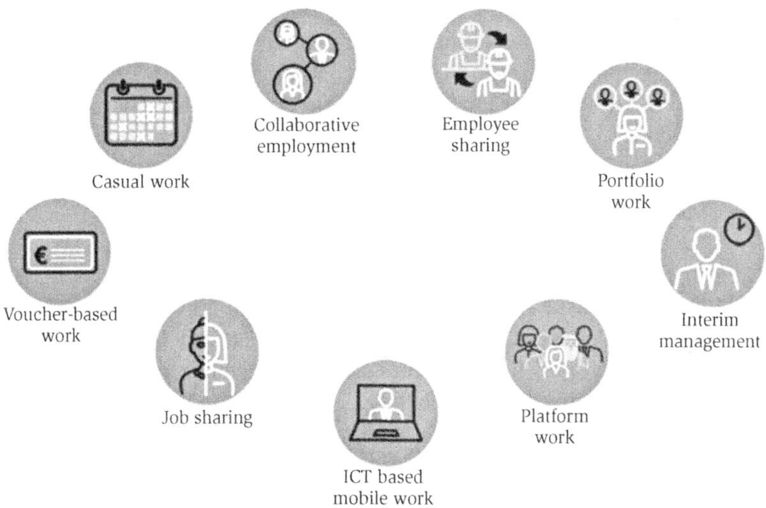

Among the analysed new forms of employment, Eurofound concludes that job sharing, employee sharing and interim management seem to provide the most beneficial working conditions and labour market implications. ICT-based mobile work brings about some positive working conditions, while the labour market effects might be partly negative. However, voucher-based work has some good labour market potential, while working conditions show room for improvement. Casual work raises the most concerns in terms of labour market and working conditions.[23]

18. ICT-based mobile work, where workers can do their job from any place at any time, supported by modern technologies.
19. Voucher-based work, where the employment relationship is based on payment for services with a voucher purchased from an authorized organization that covers both pay and social security contributions.
20. Portfolio work, where a self-employed individual works for a large number of clients, doing small scale jobs for each of them.
21. Platform work, where an online platform enables organizations or individuals to access other organizations or individuals to solve specific problems or to provide specific services in exchange for payment.
22. Collaborative employment, where freelancers, the self-employed or micro enterprises cooperate in some way to overcome limitations of size and professional isolation.
23. Eurofound, Overview of new forms of employment – 2018 update, 21 (Publishing Office of the European Union, 2018).

Eurofound confirms that, with the exception of casual work, the flexibility inherent in most new forms of employment can be considered as positive for the working conditions of affected workers, enabling them to achieve a better work–life balance. In addition, the increased level of autonomy, responsibilities and content of tasks are assessed positively by workers.[24]

However, flexibility in these new forms of employment brings about various social problems: job insecurity and social/professional isolation as well as higher stress levels and work intensity. The lack of workers' representation might also be attributed to the enhanced flexibility, resulting in a fragmented workforce where workers' representatives have difficulties in identifying and approaching workers. Such problematic situations are typically found in platform work, which has attracted much attention worldwide.

[b] Platform Work and Its Problems

In the 2010s, the presence of platform companies, such as Uber, Lyft, Amazon Mechanical Turk and TaskRabbit, became conspicuous in many countries, and some litigations were filed alleging that platform workers should be given labour law protection. Accordingly, new forms of work are most often discussed in the context of the platform economy, gig economy, sharing economy or on-demand economy.

Platform work is a form of work arrangement that uses an online platform to enable organizations or individuals to access other organizations or individuals to solve specific problems or to provide specific services in exchange for payment. In the literature,[25] platform work is usually understood as two different forms: (1) 'crowdwork', which refers to working activities that imply completing a series of tasks through an online platform (e.g., Amazon Mechanical Turk); and (2) 'work on-demand via apps', which is a form of work in which the execution of traditional working activities, such as transport, cleaning, running errands as well as clerical work, is channelled through apps managed by a platform company (e.g., Uber, TaskRabbit).

Although there are varieties of platform arrangements, some common features of platform work can be pointed to: (1) the organization of paid work through online platforms; (2) the involvement of three parties – online platform, client (requester) and worker; (3) its use to conduct specific tasks or solve specific problems; (4) its operation

24. With regards to access to training and skills development, the picture is mixed. While positive effects are found in employee sharing, job sharing, platform work and collaborative self-employment, less favourable effects are reported in interim management, casual work, voucher-based work and portfolio work. Eurofound, Overview of new forms of employment – 2018 update, 19 (Publishing Office of the European Union, 2018).
25. *See* Valerio De Stefano, 'The Rise of the "Just-in-Time Workforce": On-Demand Work, crowd-work, and labour protection in the "Gig-Economy"', Condition of Work and Employment Series No.71, 1 (ILO, 2016); Antonio Aloisi, 'Commoditized Workers: Case Study Research on Labor Law Issues Arising from A Set of 'On-Demand/gig Economy' Platforms', 37 Comp. Lab. L. & Pol'y J. 653, 660-661 (2016).

as a form of outsourcing/contracting out; (5) 'jobs' are broken down into 'tasks'; and (6) services are provided on an on-demand basis.[26]

These features lead to both positive and negative aspects for platform workers.[27] As for the positive aspects, workers enjoy autonomy regarding freedom to choose when and where to work, how long to work, and what work to perform, which enables better work-life balance and provides better chance for workers to engage in multiple jobs to gain additional earnings.

However, the following negative aspects can be pointed to: low and insecure payment or remuneration as jobs are broken down into small tasks, and refusal to accept the work workers have done; information asymmetry such as workers' lack of information about employers and tasks to be performed; possible privacy violation; lack of support from colleagues and managers as platform workers work in isolation; and lack of reliable dispute resolution systems.

Most of these negative elements stem from the fact that platform workers are generally considered to be self-employed or freelancers and, thus, not to be covered by companies' employee benefits programs and states' labour protective regulations. Consequently, even if platform workers such as Uber drivers or Uber Eats deliverers suffer from accidents in the course of work, they are not compensated under the workers' compensation insurance as they are not employees.

[B] Extending Labour Law Protection to Nonemployee Workers?

As seen above, whether platform workers or other workers in the new forms of work can be regarded as employees or not surfaces as the most important legal issue. However, the positive features for platform workers, and to some extent, other workers in new forms of work, are that they enjoy autonomy regarding the freedom to choose when and where to work, how long to work, and what work to perform. When we assume that these workers have such autonomy in providing their work, it is not easy to deem platform workers employees under the traditional notion of employee.[28]

Then, how shall these 'nonemployee workers' be protected? There could be four approaches: (1) to expand the notion of employee; (2) to introduce an intermediate category between employee and self-employed; (3) to extend protection to nonemployee workers by legislation; and (4) to utilize other measures than labour law.

---

26. *See* Eurofound, Overview of new forms of employment-2018 update, 15 (Publishing Office of the European Union, 2018).
27. *See* Eurofound, Overview of new forms of employment-2018 update, 15 (Publishing Office of the European Union, 2018); Alek Felstiner, 'Working the Crowd: Employment and Labor Law in the Crowdsourcing Industry', 32 Berkeley J. Emp. & Lab. L, 143 (2011); Miriam Cherry and Winifred Poster, 'Crowdwork, corporate social responsibility, and fair labor practices', Saint Louis University School of Law, Legal Studies Research Paper Series, No. 2016-8 (2016); The Taylor Review of Modern Working Practices, *Good Work* (2017) https://assets.publishing.service.gov.uk/government/uploads/system/uploads/attachment_data/file/627671/good-work-taylor-review-modern-working-practices-rg.pdf.
28. *See* Bernd Waas et al., *Crowdwork – A Comparative Law Perspective*. HSI-Schriftenreihe Band 22, 262 (Bund Verlag, 2017).

[1] Expanding the Notion of Employee

The first approach is to expand the traditional notion of employees to cover platform workers and other new types of workers. In many countries that adopt the employee *v.* self-employed (independent contractor) dichotomy, this is the most common interpretative measure to extend labour law protection to those who are not yet regarded as employees.

However, it is not easy for judges to modify the established notion of employees. For instance, several cases[29] were filed in the US where Uber and Lyft drivers sought protection under the labour protective regulations, but these cases were settled without giving any clear answers. On 11 April 2018, US District Court[30] decided that Uber drivers are not employees under the Fair Labor Standards Act relying on the six-factor test established by the Donovan case,[31] and granted the summary judgement that Uber requested.

By contrast, in a judgement on 30 April 2018, the California Supreme Court[32] adopted a notable interpretation called the ABC test[33] to expand the notion of employees concerning the application of California's wage and hour laws. Under the ABC test, in order to establish that an individual is not an employee but in fact an independent contractor, an employer must prove that: A) it does not control how the individual performs the work; B) the individual provides a service that is not part of the employer's usual business; and C) the individual customarily engages in an established business, trade, or profession that is independent of the employer's business. In the case, the California Supreme Court ruled that Uber failed to meet the ABC test to classify individuals into independent contractors and, thus, Uber drivers shall be deemed employees under the Californian wage and hour laws.

It remains to be seen whether such shifting of the burden from the plaintiff (worker) to the defendant (employer) with strict criteria to establish independent contractor status will be adopted by other state courts and Federal courts in the US where both the traditional common law (control) test (narrow interpretation of the notion of employee) and the 'economic realities' test (broader interpretation adopted in the FLSA) requiring the plaintiff to establish employee status seem to be generally supported.

---

29. *O'Connor v. Uber Techs. Inc*, 82 F. Supp. 3d 1133 (N.D. Cal. 2015); *Cotter v. Lyft, Inc.*, 60 F. Supp. 3d 1067 (N.D. Cal. 2015).
30. *Razak v. Uber Technologies Inc*, U.S. District Court for the Eastern District of Pennsylvania, No. 2:16-cv-00573.
31. *Donovan v. DialAmerica Marketing, Inc.*, 757 F.2d 1376 (3d Cir. 1985). The six factors are: (1) the degree of the alleged employer's right to control the manner in which the work is to be performed; (2) the alleged employee's opportunity for profit or loss depending upon his managerial skill; (3) the alleged employee's investment in equipment or materials required for his task, or his employment of helpers; (4) whether the service rendered requires a special skill; (5) the degree of permanence of the working relationship; and (6) whether the service rendered is an integral part of the alleged employer's business.
32. *Dynamex Operations W., Inc. v. Super.* Ct., No. S222732 (Cal. 30 April 2018).
33. The ABC test is first established by the New Jersey Supreme Court in 2015 in *Hargrove v. Sleepy's*, LLC. 612 Fed. Appx. 116, 2015 U.S. App. LEXIS 7832 (3d Cir. N.J., 2015).

In France, where the employee/self-employed dichotomy is adopted, food deliverers (bikers) of Take Eat Easy were regarded as not being employees by recent decisions.[34]

In Japan, which also maintains the employee/self-employed dichotomy, employee status is determined by applying the use-dependency (subordination) test in the individual labour law. Currently, the Japanese courts rather narrowly interpret the scope of employees. However, the Supreme Court in Japan admits that the notion of employees in the Labour Union Act or collective labour relations is broader than that in the individual labour law.[35]

Germany has introduced the third notion of 'employee-like persons (*arbeitnehmerähnliche Personen*)' that sits in between employee and self-employed. However, as far as the notion of employees is concerned, the German Federal Labour Court principally maintains the traditional 'dependent-test',[36] which is narrower than the risk assessment test proposed by Rolf Wank.[37]

Here, it should be confirmed that the legal notion of employee is mandatory and cannot be disposed of by the parties' agreement or intent.[38] This is a universal understanding for labour lawyers as labour law provides mandatory regulations rectifying the imbalance of negotiating power between the parties to the employment contract. The objective criteria range from the narrower control test to the broader economic realities test depending on respective legislation in the US and on individual or collective labour relations laws in Japan. Generally speaking, the control test, subordination test or dependency test remains the key concept to determine employee status in many countries as labour law itself is often defined as law to protect subordinate labour. Consequently, platform workers tend to be denied their employment status.

In determining employment status, various factors surrounding this key concept are taken into consideration. As a result, the demarcation line between employee and self-employed is not clearly drawn. The lack of legal clarity triggers abusive misclassification by purported employers on the one hand, and brings about legal disputes on the other. If the elements for determining employment status are not suitable for new forms of work, which appreciate flexibility and freedom from direct control by employer concerning place, time and manner of performing work, it is not surprising that a new approach is sought after.

Discussions on the notion of employee become further complicated because they overlap with another discussion concerning the basic idea of whether the notion of employee should be universal throughout all labour regulations in a country, as in

34. E.g., Paris, pôle 6, 2e ch. 20 avr. 2017 n° 17/00511, confirmant une décision du cons. prud'h. Paris, 17 nov. 2016.
35. Kezuka, K, 'Crowdwork and the Law in Japan', Bernd Waas et al., *Crowdwork – A Comparative Law Perspective*. HSI-Schriftenreihe Band 22, 187 (Bund Verlag, 2017).
36. *See* Bernd Waas et al., *Crowdwork – A Comparative Law Perspective*. HSI-Schriftenreihe Band 22, 260 (Bund Verlag, 2017).
37. Rolf Wank, *Arbeitnehmer und Selbständige* (1988).
38. *See* Bernd Waas et al., *Crowdwork – A Comparative Law Perspective*. HSI-Schriftenreihe Band 22, 261 (Bund Verlag, 2017).

Germany, or can be interpreted differently in each labour legislation, as in the USA, or should be two uniform notions respectively in individual and collective labour laws, as in Japan.[39]

[2] Introducing an Intermediate Category Between Employee and Self-Employed

Another approach often contended is to introduce the intermediate category between employee and self-employed. In several countries, such as Germany (employee-like person [*arbeitnehmerähnliche Person*], the UK (worker whose notion is broader than employee), Canada (dependent contractor), the intermediate category has already been introduced.[40]

The purpose is to extend certain protections to individuals who would otherwise not fall under the protection of labour law but who suffer from some of the same vulnerabilities as those classified as employees. Theoretically, partial extension of labour protection to the intermediate category persons (nonemployee workers) by interpretation would not be impossible, but usually this is made possible through legislative measures to explicitly extend labour law protection to those nonemployee workers.

In the UK, the notion of worker is defined more broadly than that of employee. In the Employment Right Act 1996, worker is defined as 'an individual who has entered into or works under (or, where the employment has ceased, worked under) –

(a) a contract of employment [= this is the definition of 'employee']), or
(b) any other contract, whether express or implied and (if it is express) whether oral or in writing, whereby the individual undertakes to do or perform personally any work or services for another party to the contract whose status is not by virtue of the contract that of a client or customer of any profession or business undertaking carried on by the individual;...'

Therefore, the notion of worker covers not only employee, who works under an employment contract, but also an individual, who undertakes to do or perform personally any work or services for another party to the contract.

Employment Right Act 1996, National Minimum Wage Act 1998, the Working Time Regulations 1998, Employment Relations Act 1999, the Part-time Workers (Prevention of Less Favourable Treatment) Regulations 2000 apply not only to employees but also to workers.[41] The UK Government's Taylor Review issued in July

39. As to this fundamental issue, *see* Guy Davidov, *A Purposive Approach to Labour Law* (Oxford, Oxford University Press, 2016).
40. According to Bernd Waas et al., *Crowdwork – A Comparative Law Perspective*. HSI-Schriftenreihe Band 22, 160 fn. 80 (Bund Verlag, 2017), Austria, Switzerland, and Spain also have a similar intermediate category.
41. Stephen Hardy, Labour Law and Industrial Relations in Great Bulletin, 93 (3rd. ed., 2007); Deakin & Morris, Labour Law.

2017 suggests renaming 'worker' as 'dependent contractor' and proposes measures to clarify the notion.[42]

In Germany, employee-like persons are defined by section 12a of the Act on Collective Bargaining Agreements as 'persons who are economically dependent and in need of social protection comparable to an employee (...), work on the basis of a contract of service or a contract for work and services for other persons, perform the services they are obliged to perform personally and essentially without collaboration with employees and *a)* predominantly work for one person, or *b)* on average, more than half of the total remuneration they are entitled to for the performance of work is paid by one person'.

The Act on Collective Bargaining Agreement, the Federal Paid Leave Act (*Bundesurlaubsgesetz*), the Act on Health and Safety of Workers (*Arbeitsschutzgesetz*), the General Equal Treatment Act (*Allgemeines Gleichbehandlungsgesetz*), and the Labour Court Act apply to employee-like persons.

In Canada, a 'dependent contractor' category was created for the purpose of collective bargaining eligibility under provincial labour laws. The intent was to cover a class of workers who are legally independent but economically dependent, 'in order to provide some degree of protection to very small businesses – mostly those operated by a single person – that depend economically (to a large extent) on a single client.[43]

Referring to these examples, scholars advocate the creation of a third legal category of workers in the countries that have not yet introduced it.[44] However, in response to such a proposal for introducing the intermediate category, strong opposition exists. First, introducing the third category would make the current difficult determination of the status of workers even more complicated and unpredictable. Second, the third category might trigger the misclassification of employees into dependent worker status and deprive them of their full protection as employees.[45]

Instead of introducing the third category, therefore, critics propose assuming that above a minimum threshold of hours worked, the default classification would be an employment relationship.[46] The aforementioned ABC test, which shifts the burden of proof from the worker to the purported employer in establishing independent contractor status, belongs to this position.

42. The Taylor Review of Modern Working Practices, *Good Work*, 9, 32ff (2017).
43. Guy Davidov, 'Who is a Worker?', 34 Industrial Law Journal 61 (2005).
44. *See* Seth Harris and Alan Kruger, *A Proposal for Modernizing Labor Laws for Twenty-First-Century Work: The 'Independent Worker'*, The Hamilton Project, Discussion Paper 2015-10 (December 2015); James Surowiecki, 'Gigs with Benefits', *The New Yorker* (6 July 2015), http://www.newyorker.com/magazine/2015/07/06/gigs-with-benefits; *See also* Andrei Hagiu, 'Work 3.0: Redefining Jobs and Companies in the Uber Age', Harvard Business School, Working Knowledge (29 September 2015) https://hbswk.hbs.edu/item/work-3-0-redefining-jobs-and-companies-in-the-uber-age.
45. De Stefano, V (2016), 'The Rise of the "Just-in-Time Workforce": On-Demand Work, crowdwork, and labour protection in the "Gig-Economy"', Condition of Work and Employment Series No.71, 19–20 (ILO, 2016); Bernd Waas et al., *Crowdwork – A Comparative Law Perspective*. HSI-Schriftenreihe Band 22, 105f, 265 (Bund Verlag, 2017).
46. Miriam Cherry and Antonio Aloisi, ''Dependent Contractors' In the GIg Economy: A Comparative Approach', American University Law Review Vol. 66 Iss. 3, Art. 1, 653, 682ff (2017).

[3] Legislative Measures to Provide Necessary Protection

Another possible approach is to introduce necessary protection to certain categories of self-employed or independent employees or dependent workers directly by specific legislative measures. Differing from the above-mentioned two approaches that demarcate the scope of labour law protection by relying on the notion of employee or employee-like person, this approach directly provides or prepares protection to the worker who needs protection by legislation.

For instance, under the Japanese Act on Workers' Compensation Insurance, it is possible for the self-employed, such as managers of small and medium-sized enterprises, solo-entrepreneurs in automobile transportation or civil engineering and construction, to enrol in the workers' compensation insurance even though they are not employees in the sense of labour protective law. The reason is that an independent contractor, such as a solo master who runs his own construction business, will be exposed to the same risk of industrial accidents as other employees working on the same construction site. Thus, the law provides same opportunity for the independent contractor to be covered by the protective workers' compensation insurance. However, enrolment is voluntary, not compulsory. It is up to the independent contractor to be covered by enrolling in the insurance and by paying insurance premiums him/herself.

Recently, in France, the 2016 Labour Code Reform Act known as '*El Khomri* Act' introduced special provisions to extend social protection to platform independent workers (*travailleurs indépendants*). First, when an independent worker voluntarily enrols in workers' compensation insurance, the platformer is to bear the insurance premium within a certain maximum amount. Second, the cost for vocational training guaranteed by the Labour Code to dependent workers, which is normally borne by the dependent workers, shall be paid by their platform company. Third, dependent workers may organize and join trade unions and contend their interest collectively through the unions. Furthermore, they may collectively refuse to provide their service in order to protect their contention so long as this is not regarded as abusive, and such an action shall neither be the grounds for resolving their relationship with the platforms nor justify the penalty measures.[47]

Although the Act does not deem platform workers to be employees, it provides them with certain workers' protections and purported employers' social responsibility concerning workers' accidents, vocational training, and collective rights. It seems to be French tradition to adopt this legislative measure approach to extend necessary protection to independent workers, instead of expanding the notion of employees.[48]

This approach tends to be piecemeal measures. However, if the necessary protection of those individuals located in a grey zone is not universal but dependent on respective circumstances, such an approach might be one possible way to deal with new forms of work. The difference between this approach and the introduction of an

47. Eri Kasagi, 'Uber-gata Rodo to Rodo-ho Kaisei (Uber style work and labor law reform)', Nihon Roro Kenkyu Zasshi, No. 687, 89 (2017).
48. Takashi Araki, Ryuichi Yamakawa and JILPT (ed.), *Shogaikoku no Rodo Keiyaku Hosei (Labour Contract Laws in Foreign Countries)*, 213 [by Kaoko Okuda] (JILPT, Tokyo, 2005).

intermediate category of workers is whether or not the needed protection can be uniformly categorized by the intermediate notion of workers and applicable laws can be listed up categorically. If such uniform categorization is difficult, specific legislative measures responding to the specific needs should be taken.

[4] Legal Protection Outside the Scope of Labour Law and Non-legal Measures

Even if it is difficult to regard platform workers or other nonemployee workers as employees and they are not subject to labour law protection, it would be worthwhile utilizing other legal and non-legal measures to protect them from vulnerability and unfair practices.

[a] Legal Protection Provided by Other Laws than Labour Law

When work providers are not employees and thus not protected by labour laws, other laws, such as civil law, economic law or competition law, may provide certain protections.

For instance, in Germany,[49] general clauses in the Civil Code, according to which illegal and immoral agreements are void (sections 134 and 138 of the Civil Code), may provide certain protection. Furthermore, according to the Civil Code, provisions in general terms and conditions (adhesion contract or standard form contract) are void 'if, contrary to the requirement of good faith, they unreasonably disadvantage the other party to the contract with the user' (section 307(1), sentence 1, the Civil Code). Such an 'unreasonable disadvantage' must be presumed to exist in case of doubt when a provision's 'fundamental notion deviates from and is incompatible with legal regulations' or when it 'limits essential rights or duties inherent in the nature of the contract to such an extent that attainment of the purpose of the contract is jeopardised' (section 307(2), the Civil Code). Based on these civil law provisions, the German courts can review the content of the contract, which could provide protection to the weaker party to the contract.

In Japan, where the employee/self-employed dichotomy is adopted, when workers or service providers are not regarded as employees, they are independent contractors and their contracts to provide service are subject to economic law or antimonopoly law. The Japanese economic law prohibits abuse of a superior bargaining position in the market as a type of unfair trade practice (Article 2, paragraph 9 item 5, Antimonopoly Act). For instance, unfair refusal to accept goods, delay in payment, or reduction in the amount of payment, can be deemed unfair trade practice and illegal. Similarly, the Subcontract Proceeding Act applied to subcontractors also bans the unfair trade practices of companies that order the work. The regulation includes the orderer's obligation to issue written contracts to subcontractors, to specify the date of

49. *See* Bernd Waas et al., *Crowdwork – A Comparative Law Perspective*. HSI-Schriftenreihe Band 22, 171, 266 (Bund Verlag, 2017).

payment for subcontractors, prohibition of the orderer's refusal to receive goods, delay in payment, reduction in payment, and so forth. Some of these regulations are similar to the labour law protection concerning employment contracts and wage payment.[50]

In the EU, on 26 April 2018, the 'Regulation of the European Parliament and of the Council on promoting fairness and transparency for business users of online intermediation services (COM(2018) 238 final) was proposed. Although this was proposed from the competition law policy and treats platform workers as 'business users',[51] the proposal pays attention to potentially harmful trading practices[52] and a lack of effective redress mechanisms. Thus, it proposes provisions that establish a range of requirements for: (1) the clarity, accessibility and modifications of predefined, standard terms and conditions used by providers of online intermediation services (Article 3); (2) a statement of reasons from a provider of online intermediation services if it suspends or terminates the use by a business user of its intermediation services (Article 4); (3) a description of the main parameters determining ranking of business users (Article 5); (4) a description of any differentiated treatment given to goods and services offered by the provider of online intermediation services itself, or by business users (Article 6); and so forth.

In short, regulations in contract law or fair competition law supporting weaker parties to a contract can provide protection for individuals who are not employees. However, whether or not such regulations are sufficiently effective to protect workers should be further examined.

[b] Eliminating Possible Conflict Between Collective Labour Law and Economic Law

When economic law (competition law, antitrust law, or antimonopoly law) applies not only to independent contractors but also to workers who might be subject to labour law, a fundamental question arises. Labour law envisages legally concluding collective bargaining agreements for establishing minimum working conditions, but economic law prohibits such collective agreements as hard-core cartels. Labour unions' collective actions might be deemed illegal actions distorting free and fair competition in the market under economic law.

---

50. Takashi Araki, '*Worker in the Labour Union Act and enterprise in the Antimonopoly Act: A study of the collision and interplay between labour law and economic law*' in Kazuo Sugeno et al (eds), Rodo-ho ga mezasubeki mono (What Labour Law should seek for)', 185 (Shinzan-sha, Tokyo, 2011).
51. Article 2 of the proposed Regulation defines 'business user' as 'any natural or legal person which through online intermediation services offers goods or services to consumers for purposes relating to its trade, business, craft or profession'.
52. The Proposal lists the following trading practices: unexplained changes in terms and conditions without prior notice; the delisting of goods or services and the suspension of accounts without a clear statement of reasons; lack of transparency related to the ranking of goods and services and of the undertakings offering them; unclear conditions for access to, and use of, data collected by providers; and a lack of transparency regarding favouring of providers' own competing services and so-called most-favoured nation (MFN) clauses, which restrict undertakings' ability to offer more attractive conditions through other channels than the online intermediation services.

In the US, from the birth of labour law, conflict between labour law and anti-trust law was recognized. From the 1890 Sherman Act, the 1914 Clayton Act, and the 1932 Norris-LaGuardia Act to the 1935 National Labor Relations Act, developments in American labour law were a history of establishing labour exemption from antitrust law.[53]

In the EU, since the so-called Laval quartet cases[54] in the Court of Justice of the European Union in the late 2000s, the conflict between employees' fundamental right to collective action and collective bargaining and the rights to free movement and freedom of economic activities in the EU attracted much attention.

In Japan, the recent Supreme Court decisions of 2010 and 2011 held that the Labour Union Act applied to those workers who were not regarded as employees under the Labour Standards Act but organized labour unions and requested collective bargaining to the purported employers. These decisions triggered legal discussion on how to demarcate the applicable scope between collective labour law and antimonopoly law in Japan. On this issue, the Fair Trade Commission's Study Committee published 'the Study Group Report on Human Resources and Competition Policy' in February 2018. It clarifies the principle that where labour law regulations are applicable, antimonopoly law prioritizes labour law regulations and refrains from intervening except for exceptional cases where the labour law purpose is transgressed.[55]

Therefore, as many scholars have pointed out,[56] it is necessary to clarify how collective labour law and economic law apply to the intermediate category workers.

[c] Utilization of Soft-Law and Market Reputation

Concerning crowdwork, some advocate a soft-law approach such as the corporate social responsibility of platform corporations or the ethics of crowdwork.[57] In

53. Robert Gorman and Mathew Finkin, Basic Text on Labor Law, 886 ff. (2nd ed., 2004); Michael LeRoy, 'The Narcotic Effect of Antitrust Law in Professional Sports: How the Sherman Act Subverts Collective Bargaining' 89 Tulane L. Rev. 859 (2012).
54. C-438/05 The International Transport Workers' Federation and The Finnish Seamen's Union [2007] ECR I-10779; C-341/05 Laval un Partneri [2007] ECR I-11767 C-346/06 Rüffert [2008] ECR I-1989; C-319/06 Commission *v.* Luxembourg [2008] ECR I-4323.
55. *See* Takashi Araki, 'Hataraki-kata no tayoka to rodo-ho to dokusen-kinsi-ho no Kosaku (Diversified work style and the collision and interplay between labor law and antimonopoly law)', Kosei Torihiki No. 811, 21 (2018).
56. Valerio De Stefano, 'The Rise of the "Just-in-Time Workforce": On-Demand Work, crowdwork, and labour protection in the "Gig-Economy"', Condition of Work and Employment Series No.71, 23 (ILO, 2016); Bernd Waas et al., *Crowdwork – A Comparative Law Perspective*. HSI-Schriftenreihe Band 22, 269 (Bund Verlag, 2017); Seth Harris and Alan Kruger, *A Proposal for Modernizing Labor Laws for Twenty-First-Century Work: The 'Independent Worker'*, The Hamilton Project, Discussion Paper 2015-10, 15 (December 2015); Takashi Araki, 'Hataraki-kata no tayoka to rodo-ho to dokusen-kinsi-ho no Kosaku (Diversified work style and collision and interplay between labour law and antimonopoly law)', Kosei Torihiki No. 811, 21 (2018).
57. For instance, Miriam Cherry and Winifred Poster, 'Crowdwork, corporate social responsibility, and fair labor practices' Saint Louis University School of Law, Legal Studies Research Paper Series, No. 2016-8, 299ff (2016) advocate fair wages, transparency and disclosure as well as due

Germany, 'Code of Conduct, Paid Crowdsourcing for the Better, Guideline for a prosperous and fair cooperation between companies, clients and crowdworkers' was adopted and has currently been signed by nine companies or organizations.[58] The principles declared in the Code of Conduct include such matters as clarification on legal situations, fair payment, clear tasks and reasonable timing, freedom and flexibility, constructive feedback and open communication, regulated approval process and rework, data protection and privacy.

In the UK, the Taylor Review advocates non-legal measures by stating: '[t]he best way to achieve better work is not national regulation but responsible corporate governance, good management and strong employment relations within the organization, which is why it is important that companies are seen to take good work seriously and are open about their practices and that all workers are able to be engaged and heard.'[59]

As for the workers' side, if a proper website is established through which workers can share the reputation of requesters (clients), they can choose good requesters' offers and avoid bad ones.[60] In 2008, a website and browser extension called 'Turkopticon' was designed by Silberman and Irani for workers of AMT (Amazon Mechanical Turk) to review requesters, mainly along the criteria of pay, pay speed, fairness of evaluation, and communication. A group of economists found that effective wages among requesters with 'good' reputations on Turkopticon were about 40% higher than effective wages among requesters with 'neutral' or 'bad' reputations, and that requesters with good reputations attracted workers to their tasks at nearly twice the rate as requesters with bad reputations.[61] Thus, thanks to the shared reputation, the market has seemingly functioned to protect workers.[62]

Labour unions are also expected to play a significant role in providing effective mechanisms to monitor the fair functioning of new forms of work. Kezuka proposes that labour unions should administer platforms and monitor transparent and fair operation of platform work arrangements.[63]

There is no reason not to encourage these non-legal measures. However, it should be carefully examined whether these measures are sufficiently effective, and whether adoption of these measures results in the abandonment of other more effective

process as an agenda for ethical crowdwork. *See also* Alek Felstiner, 'Working the Crowd: Employment and Labor Law in the Crowdsourcing Industry', 32 Berkeley J. Emp. & Lab. L, 143, 201ff (2011).

58. http://crowdsourcing-code.com.
59. The Taylor Review of Modern Working Practices (2017), Good Work, 9.
60. *See also* Sangreet Paul Choudary, 'The architecture of digital labour platforms: Policy recommendations on platform design for worker well-being' ILO Future or work Research Paper Series 3 (2018).
61. M. Six Silberman and Lily Irani, 'Operating and employer reputation system: Lessons from Turkopticon, 2008–2015', 37 Comp. Lab. L. & Pol'y J. 505, 507 (2016).
62. However, Silberman and Irani, who established Turkopticon, confess that the website has serious problems and occasionally becomes a site of harassment, insults, sexism, racism, profanity, baseless accusations, and occasional threats that trouble other online communities. *Ibid.*
63. Katsutoshi Kezuka, 'Crowdwork no rodohogaku jo no kento kadai (Labor law issues on Crowdwork)' Kikan Rodo-ho No. 259, 53, 65 (2017).

measures that can strike a better balance. Of course, the decision depends on each country's circumstances.

[C] The Role of State, Law, Social Partners and Policy Choice

It was sensationally alleged that almost all human work could be automated and replaced by robots, but it turned out that these claims did not count new jobs created by the new economy. Therefore, the scale of job loss due to automation is estimated to be much more limited than is alleged. However, this depends on how effectively the state can implement appropriate and well-coordinated policies to deal with the digital economy. In particular, lifelong education and support for changing jobs are essential to cope with the rapid technological developments.

Even if proper policies could mitigate the impact, it is still certain that technological developments would, to a certain extent, cause job displacement and changes to occupational structure. More workers would be forced to change jobs or to adapt to changed working environments. The work format under the digital economy would be quite different from the traditional one. According to various research studies, new forms of work bring about flexibility and this is evaluated positively not only by employers but also by workers as it enables them to achieve a better work–life balance and to increase their level of autonomy, responsibilities and the content of tasks. However, flexibility may entail job insecurity, higher stress levels and work intensity, as well as social/professional isolation including the lack of workers' representation.

Most of the social problems stem from the fact that workers on platform work as well as other new forms of work are not considered as employees and not covered by labour law protection. To protect these nonemployee workers, four approaches were examined: (1) to expand the notion of employee; (2) to introduce an intermediate category between employee and self-employed; (3) to extend protection to nonemployee workers by legislation; and (4) to utilize other laws, soft-law and non-legal tools.

These four approaches are not exclusive to each other. Expanding the notion of employee (1) and, on top of that, introducing an intermediate category between employee and self-employed (2), or adding special protection by legislation (3), would be possible. Whether to take approach (2) or (3) depends on whether workers' protection can be properly categorized by the intermediate notion of workers or not. As for approach (4), the application of law other than labour law, especially the application of economic law, which might conflict with the guarantee of workers' collective rights, it is important to clarify which law applies to whom. Soft-law measures and non-legal tools such as market reputation are of course compatible with other approaches.

The choice – whether to take one approach or multiple approaches – depends on each country's circumstances, including the law system,[64] feasibility of legislation,[65] employment system,[66] industrial relations,[67] dispute resolution mechanism, etc.

The approaches discussed above presuppose that when an individual's legal category is decided (employees, intermediary workers or self-employed), the applicable law and norms will be specified. However, looking at current labour law for employees, the regulations become more and more diversified in accordance with the diversification of employees. On the one hand, labour law itself introduces flexible regulations (e.g., the flexible arrangement of working hours, such as the flex-time scheme) and derogation mechanisms, which allow unfavourable deviation from minimum labour standards on the condition that social partners or the parties to collective agreements agree with it. On the other, labour law has also introduced exceptions and exemptions when the universal application of the minimum standards is not appropriate (managerial personnel exception or white-collar exemption). Introducing exemption for white-collar employees overlaps with the discussion of intermediary workers. In both cases, the workers in question have broader discretion on how to perform their work and wider freedom from employers' direction compared to ordinary employees.

Therefore, discussions on the notion of employee, which determine the scope of the application of labour law, should be conducted hand-in-hand with discussions on how to make labour law regulations adaptable and effective for the diversified workforce. The content of contemporary labour law is not entirely decided by the legislature, but delegated to the social partners at the sector level, or sometimes to the labour and management at the company or establishment level, in order to adapt to diversified realities in respective industries and worksites. This leads us to the second topic: decentralization of collective bargaining.

§12.03 DECENTRALIZATION OF COLLECTIVE BARGAINING

Decentralization of collective bargaining and decentralized collective bargaining are different things. On the one hand, in Europe where centralized (national- or sector-level) bargaining system has long been rooted in society, decentralization, which means a shift from the centralized bargaining to the decentralized bargaining, is a

64. In a country where each respective labour law has its own different definition of employee, the choice regarding each labour legislation would need to be further discussed taking into account the purpose of the legislation.
65. If the legislative feasibility of adding special protection to nonemployee workers is low, such countries cannot help but pursue the interpretative measure (approach (1)) to expand the notion of employee.
66. A country where lateral mobility is very high may support workers' mobility by lessening their cost of mobility and providing retraining rather than expanding employee protection.
67. In countries where sector-level labour unions exist, collective bargaining coverage is wide (*see* s. 2 of this General Report). By appropriate coordination with economic or competition law (approach (4)), sector-or national-level collective bargaining agreements may provide suitable protection to all workers. By contrast, for countries with decentralized collective bargaining systems, such measures will not work well.

significant change. After the financial crises in the late-2000s, decentralization has been vigorously encouraged by states. However, such drastic change may have a serious impact on each nations' industrial relations.

On the other, there are many countries that have never experienced centralized bargaining and where collective bargaining has, from the beginning, taken place at the decentralized (company) level. What these countries is experiencing is not decentralization but declining union density and diminishing collective bargaining coverage.

Certainly, decentralized bargaining becomes prevalent because it brings about several merits for both employers and employees and meets workplace needs. However, as discussed below, the common risk of 'de-collectivization' of industrial relations surfaces in both countries with a centralized system and those with a decentralized system.

[A] Decentralization of Collective Bargaining in Europe

Many western European countries have been characterized by a centralized system of collective bargaining and a prevalence of bargaining at the sectoral level. This common feature does not mean a uniformity among those countries which can experiment a wide variety of systems of industrial relations, of articulation of levels of collective agreements or of coverage of collective bargaining. However, analysis of European developments in labour law since 2008 highlights a common trend: the decentralization of industrial relations systems.[68] What can we then learn from this European experience if you compare it to the American ones?

The decentralization of collective bargaining in Europe is a marked trend that is noted by observers of this period across the board.

> 'Once this rapid reaction stage was over, the situation in the various countries began to diverge, and developed very differently depending on the scale or perception of the crisis. Some practices or projects were nevertheless fairly widespread. There were frequent examples of civil service pay freezes or pay cuts, sometimes accompanied by job losses. Various methods were used to reduce the level or duration of certain social benefits, and VAT was sometimes increased. The crisis has sometimes had an accelerating effect, being used to justify reforms which had already been announced. Pension reform is the key example of this. In terms of labour law reform, three types of measure are very common and could have a major impact on national social rights (although not all countries are affected by these changes). The first of these are the sweeping reforms to the civil service, which call into question the specific nature of the rules applying to this type of employment. Secondly, at a time when it has become clear that the employment situation in EU countries is not dependent on job protection legislation, this very legislation is being challenged in various ways. Some measures have already been adopted, while others are in the pipeline. These include redundancy avoidance measures, avoiding recourse to the courts in the event of disputes, increasing the length of service required before redundancy rules apply, reducing the level of compensatory sanctions, calling into question the principle of reinstatement as a

68. *See* S. Laulom (ed.), *Collective Bargaining in Time of Crisis*, Bulletin of Comparative Labour Relations, 99, 2018, from which this part is mainly based.

penalty for unfair dismissals, increasing the thresholds used to define specific obligations in the area of redundancy, etc. Finally, in some countries the crisis resulted in the adoption of new relationships between labour law rules, amounting to a decentralisation of collective bargaining. Company level collective bargaining has gained ground and the normative function of branch level collective agreements has become less important'.[69]

This finding has been made by several other authors. For example, I. Schömann and S. Clauwaert state that '*a clear policy and/or ambition can be identified in many countries to decentralize collective bargaining, shifting from national/sectoral level to company level. The professed aim is to give businesses more flexibility and help them adjust to labour market conditions*'.[70]

This trend towards decentralization is not new and predated the 2008 crisis. After World War II, the professional sectoral level was confirmed in many European countries as the favoured level for regulating labour relations and a space structuring labour relations;[71] the first trends towards decentralization of collective bargaining, in particular in terms of regulating working time, appeared in the 1980s and the movement has since intensified, from 2008 onwards in particular.

From this point of view, while widely disseminated rhetoric has highlighted the need for labour market reforms to tackle the crisis, in reality this is essentially a device permitting the legitimization of processes already broadly underway prior to 2008. Another aspect of this decentralization is apparent throughout this period: the emphasis placed hereafter on uncontrolled decentralization of industrial relations systems at the expense of controlled decentralization. New articulations of labour law standards have been implemented, granting precedence above all others to standards negotiated at company level.[72] The French law, known as El Khomri, is particularly revealing of this trend which has been further exacerbated in France by the adoption of the 'Macron' ordinances.[73]

These national developments have been broadly encouraged by the European Union particularly in the context of the 'European Semester'. The next step, therefore, is to consider the reality behind this decentralization of collective bargaining. Comparative study reveals very varied forms of decentralization of collective bargaining systems with very different consequences. However, it can be observed that the term decentralization often masks a situation which is more one of de-collectivization of labour relationships, namely the absence or rarity of collective regulation of labour relationships at a company level.

69. S. Laulom, E. Mazuyer, Ch. Teissier, C.-E. Triomphe, P. Vielle, *How has the Crisis Affected Social Legislation in Europe?*, ETUI Policy Brief (2/2012).

70. S. Clauwaert, I. Schömann, *The Crisis and National Labour Law Reforms: A Mapping Exercise*, ETUI Working paper 04 (2012). *See also* N. Brunn, K. Lörcher, I. Schömann, *The Economic and Financial Crisis and Collective Labour Law in Europe* (Oxford: Hart Publishing 2014).

71. A. Jacobs, *Collective Labour Relations*, in B. Hepple and B. Veneziani (eds), *The Transformation of Labour Law in Europe*, 201–231 (Oxford: Hart Publishing 2009).

72. A. Jacobs, *Decentralisation of Labour Law Standard Setting and Financial crisis*, in B. Hepple and B. Veneziani (eds), *supra*.

73. Law no. 2016-1088 of 8 August 2016 on work, the modernization of labour relationships and securing of career paths. *See* Ordinances of 22 September 2017, ratified by the ratification Law No. 2018-217 of 29 March 2018.

[1] *The European Context: The Aim of Decentralizing Collective Bargaining*

National developments have been taking place within a European context that strongly supports this decentralization of collective bargaining.[74] Traditionally, and particularly since the 1980s under the leadership of Jacques Delors, the European Union has supported action by social partners, in particular European social partners. Article 154 of the TFEU which institutionalizes the participation of European management and labour in the European decision-making process particularly attests to this support. However, the economic means of governance[75] have been implemented on the whole without any consultation with European social partners, to the extent that in 2013 the European Commission published a communication calling in particular for the strengthening of social dialogue.[76] Above all, these very governance mechanisms have revealed themselves to be formidable instruments of convergence between national policies. One of the consequences of the new economic governance is a massive intrusion into collective bargaining systems, encouraging their decentralization. To put it simply, national policies in the euro area have not been able to use traditional monetary mechanisms to support national economies and European institutions have put the emphasis on wage restraint or decreasing labour costs to ensure that companies are competitive. The aim of decentralization of collective bargaining is precisely that: to impact on salary negotiations and decrease the cost of labour.

It is within the framework of the European semester, an annual cycle of coordination of economic policies and the main pillar of this new governance that the

74. Also *see* in this volume, P. Loi, *Decentralisation of Wage Setting Mechanisms and Statutory Minimum Wage: Towards the End of Sectoral Collective Bargaining?*, in S. Laulom (ed.), *Collective Bargaining in Time of Crisis*, *supra*.
75. The terms of the new European economic governance refer to a set of rules and procedures that have been developed since 2008, but particularly since 2010, aimed at implementing more restrictive coordination of national economic policies. These new rules were adopted in the framework of the 'six pack' (Directive 2011/85/EU, of 8 November 2011, on the requirements for budgetary frameworks of the Member States, JOUE, L 306 of 23/11/2011, p. 41), the 'two pack' (Regulation (EU) no. 473/2013, of 21 May 2013, on common provisions for monitoring and assessing draft budgetary plans and ensuring the correction of excessive deficit of the Member States in the euro area, JOUE, L 140 of 27/05/2013, p. 11) and the Treaty on Stability, Coordination and Governance (the TSCG is an intergovernmental agreement, signed by 25 Member States excluding the United Kingdom, the Czech Republic and Croatia). The six-pack strengthened the Growth Pact and introduced a new macroeconomic surveillance tool: the procedure on structural imbalances. The two-pack requires Member States in the euro area to submit their draft budget plans in mid-October for the following year, so an examination of budgetary policies can take place at an early stage and the European Commission's guidance can be taken into account prior to the adoption of national budgets.
76. COM(2013) 690 final, *Strengthening the social dimension of the economic and monetary union*, Brussels 2.10.2013: '*the EU-level social dialogue plays an essential role in advancing our social market economy, producing benefits for employers, workers, and for the economy and society as a whole. When strengthening economic governance, it is critical to involve the social partners in policy debates and decision-making processes. This is not only to increase the ownership of policies and to ensure meaningful implementation but also to enhance the effectiveness of policy coordination at euro area level. It is therefore vital that we invest in strengthening social dialogue at both European and national levels.*'

European Commission explicitly provides an incentive to Member States to contribute to the decentralization of collective bargaining.

Each year, the European Commission analyses in detail the plans for Member States' macroeconomic and structural budgetary reforms, providing them with recommendations for the following twelve to eighteen months. In this framework, euro area countries are subject to specific obligations and, in particular, a sanctions mechanism has been defined for States that do not respect the recommendations issued as part of the alert mechanism. There are even greater restrictions for countries where European financial aid is deemed to be indispensable. In exchange for financial loans, these countries have been obliged to bring in major reforms, set out either in 'Memoranda of Understanding', with the troika composed of the EU, the ECB and the IMF (this is the case for Greece, Ireland and Portugal) or 'Stand-by Arrangements' with the IMF (in the case of Hungary, Lithuania and Romania).[77] Spain, which likewise benefited from aid to support its financial sector, was obliged to commit itself to the implementation of specific national recommendations in the context of the European semester.

All the Member States have therefore been subject to injunctions from the European Union, and while the degree of restriction may vary, it is no longer a matter of entirely voluntary recommendations. Analysis of the subject of these recommendations[78] reveals a high number of them fall into the category of social policies. So while the TFEU Treaty explicitly places salaries outside the competence of the European Union,[79] salary policy is one of the ongoing concerns of the European semester as salaries are the main adjustment variable for tackling economic imbalances and boosting competitiveness.[80] Taking salary-related action is basically taking action on collective bargaining, and decentralization of collective bargaining is a central component of the structural reforms to labour markets that Member States are called upon to perform. Company-level collective bargaining, which must be separated from that at a sectoral level, must be encouraged.

Using just a few examples of the pressure brought to bear by the European Union on the restructuring of collective bargaining, it is possible to cite the specific recommendations made to the Member States by the European Commission in the context of the European semester.[81] Thus for France in 2016, the Commission's diagnosis was that: '*the reforms carried out recently only gave employers a few options to derogate from*

77. D. Natali, B. Vanhercke (eds), *Bilan social de l'Union européenne 2012, 14th Annual Report*, 190 (Brussels: ETUI, 2013).
78. S. Clauwaert, *The Country-Specific Recommendations (CSRs) in the Social Field. An Overview and Comparison Update Including the CSRs 2014–2015* (Brussels: ETUI, 2014).
79. We should revisit here the terms of Art. 153.5 TFEU under which, 'the provisions of this Article shall not apply to pay, the right of association, the right to strike or the right to impose lock-outs.' Introduced by the Social Protocol of the Maastricht Treaty, this article excludes salary policies from European policies, at the precise moment when the Economic and Monetary Union is being put into place.
80. D. Natali, B. Vanhercke (eds), *Bilan social de l'Union européenne 2012, 14th Annual Report*, 192 (Brussels: ETUI, 2013).
81. All these documents can be accessed on the European Commission Site, Europe 2020. https://ec.europa.eu/info/publications/2017-european-semester-country-specific-recommendations-commission-recommendations_en, accessed 5 June 2017.

sectoral agreements'.[82] In Italy's case, the Commission found that '*second-level collective bargaining is not sufficiently widespread in Italy, which hinders the adoption, at a company level, of innovative solutions that could improve productivity and make salaries more reactive to labour market conditions*'.[83] As some countries have never had or no longer have collective bargaining at a sectoral level and some countries have already reformed their system, the Commission does not provide, or no longer provides, them with any incentive to carry out reforms in this area. Thus in 2014, the Commission found that the Spanish 2012 reform of the labour market had contributed to '*granting companies greater internal flexibility and limiting job losses, while giving priority to collective agreements at a company level and providing more opportunities for companies to derogate from a collective agreement*'.[84]

While it is difficult to establish direct causality between European recommendations, or more generally the objectives defined by the European Union in the context of the European semester, and national legislative policies, it should be noted that the majority of States will sign up for this European scheme and propose reforms that are intended to be structural in terms of labour relations systems, where the aim is their decentralization.[85]

[2] Towards Decentralization of Collective Negotiations

Comparison of national experiences (some of which are in quasi-permanent evolution) does not challenge the widely apparent trend towards decentralization of collective bargaining. Indeed it highlights very varied forms of decentralization of collective bargaining systems with very different consequences. In this regard, it is possible to distinguish three different groups of countries: those where it is not possible to talk of the decentralization of a system because it is no longer or has never been centralized, systems where the sectoral level is still strong and finally systems where the State has been heavily involved in helping to drive the decentralization of collective bargaining with varying results. The aspect that sometimes distinguishes the second group from the third is the State's role, because a country may maintain a strong role at sectoral level, while at the same time the State may implement reforms aimed at decentralization. This comparison highlights another trend which often masks the use of the term

82. COM(2016) 330 final, Brussels, 15.05.2016, *Recommendation on the 2016 national reform programme of France and delivering a Council opinion on the 2016 stability programme of France*.
83. COM(2016) 332 final, Brussels, 18.05.2016.
84. COM (2014) 410 final, Brussels, 2.06. 2014.
85. M.-C. Escande-Varniol, S. Laulom, E. Mazuyer, P. Vielle (eds), *Quel droit social dans une Europe en crise?* (Brussels: Larcier, 2012). S. Clauwaert and I. Schömann, *supra*; A. Koukiadaki, I. Tavora, M. Martinez Lucio, *The transformation of joint regulation and labour market policy in Europe during the crisis, Comparative project report* (University of Manchester, 2014). http://www.research.mbs.ac.uk/ewerc/Portals/0/Documents/Social%20Dialogue%20and%20Collective%20Bargaining%202015%20Comparative%20report%20-%20final%20version.pdf, accessed 10 January 2019. *See also*, Conseil d'orientation pour l'emploi, *Les réformes des marchés du travail en Europe* (5 November 2015), http://www.coe.gouv.fr/Detail-Nouveaute.html%3Fid_article=1275.html, accessed 20 July 2017.

decentralization: that of the de-collectivization of industrial relations systems where in reality the absence of actors capable of negotiating at company level should be observed.

[a] Absence of Decentralization

The term decentralization, frequently used to describe national systems of labour relationships, may refer to two distinguishable situations. On one hand, the term evokes the idea of evolution of a system where collective negotiation is relocated to company level; on the other, the term likewise evokes a state where collective bargaining is to be situated mainly at a company level. Obviously this is a very simplistic depiction, the degree of evolution, the articulation of the levels and the definition of the negotiation unit may appear in a wide range of configurations from State to State. For various reasons Turkey, the United Kingdom (UK), Hungary and Poland may not be used as examples of systems where collective bargaining is decentralized. First, collective bargaining at a branch or sectoral level is kept to a minimum and sometimes even non-existent nowadays; consequently there is no decentralization of these systems. Second, collective regulation of labour conditions at a company level remains low.

Thus in the UK, the challenge to the more centralized system of collective bargaining which took place in the 1980s did not really lead to the development of collective bargaining in private-sector companies where the rate of unionization was decreasing. Labour conditions there are, therefore, increasingly defined by the employer unilaterally, and it is even possible to ask whether collective laissez-faire, the famous expression used by O. Kahn Freund to describe the British system of industrial relations,[86] has given way to laissez-faire or to a law of the labour market.[87]

In Turkey, the collective bargaining system has been broadly structured and developed by the State, and since 1982, collective bargaining has only taken place at company level (the establishment, company or group of establishments). The last reforms took place in 2012 and were basically justified by the need to integrate international labour standards, namely ILO Conventions Nos. 87 and 98 and Articles 5 and 6 of the European Social Charter revised in 1996. Unlike the majority of Member States of the European Union, the economic situation was not invoked to justify the reforms: '*During the last 30 years, collective agreements have not been considered either among the reasons for, or the solutions to economic crisis. This result is also related to the narrow coverage of collective agreements*'.[88] With some rare exceptions, the collective agreement does not appear as a labour conditions flexibility instrument. It may also be governed fairly strictly as when, for example, legislation prohibits

86. O Kahn-Freund, *Labour Law* in M Ginsberg (ed.), *Law and Opinion in England in the 20th Century* (Stevens 1959).
87. R. Dukes, *The Labour Constitution: The Enduring Idea of Labour Law (chapter: From Collective Laissez-Faire to the Law of the Labour Market)* (OUP, 2014).
88. Dogan Yenisey and B. Ceylan Ataman, *Decentralized collective bargaining: a solution to economic crisis? The case of Turkey*, in S. Laulom (ed.), *Collective Bargaining in Time of Crisis*, *supra*.

collective agreements from improving on legal provisions. As a result, since a 2003 law came into effect, the amount of unfair dismissal compensation, defined in legislation, may not be increased under a collective agreement. The implicit aim of the legislation here is to protect the public budget in public companies where union membership is still high. In a similar vein, a provision of Law no. 6356 of 2012 prohibits collective agreements from increasing the legal compensation set out for cases of trade union discrimination. The growing number of these provisions is such that they represent a major curb on the collective autonomy of social partners.

Poland and Hungary demonstrate many common features. In these two countries, as elsewhere in the ten Member States of Central and Eastern Europe, [89] industrial relations systems are characterized by the decentralization of collective bargaining, low coverage of collective agreements and a low rate of unionization. Can these systems really be described as decentralized collective bargaining systems? On one hand, they were never really centralized and collective sectoral bargaining is very rare and, on the other, collective bargaining at a company level remains low. Again, in these two countries, legislation has intervened with the aim of developing collective bargaining particularly with a view to introducing more flexibility, notably in matters of working time. However, these new collective bargaining spaces are struggling for implementation. At the same time, legislation has authorized negotiation of these agreements with non-trade union actors, a situation which offers fewer guarantees, and which is likely to weaken trade union representation. However, until now, collective bargaining has likewise failed to gain ground with these new staff representatives.

Thus in Poland, only a small proportion of employees is covered by the provisions of collective agreements. Consequently, the Polish system is characterized by the important role of the law and collective agreements hold a rather more marginal place in the regulation of labour conditions. Thus, as L. Pisarcszyk observes, the economic crisis which, for Poland, began in the early 2000s when unemployment reached 20%, exists alongside a profound crisis in collective bargaining.

The legislator was able to adopt certain provisions aimed at favouring the signature of 'anti-crisis' collective agreements. These might allow new flexibilities to be introduced in areas such as working time along with the temporary erosion of labour conditions or even the introduction of partial unemployment mechanisms. Thus, when so justified by the company's economic situation, social partners may sign collective agreements where labour and salary conditions are at stake. Under these agreements, it is possible to suspend the applicable provisions of collective agreements and take a new look at the labour conditions defined in employment contracts. Agreements may not be for a duration of more than 3 years. No obligation to safeguard jobs has been acknowledged and the employer may undertake a collective redundancy procedure even when it has signed such an agreement. Thus, according to L. Pisarczyk, '*the agreement modifying individual employment standards refers directly to the conditions*

89. *See* T. Gyulavári, *Chasing the holy grail? Stumbling collective bargaining in Eastern Europe and the Hungarian Experiment*, and L. Pisarczyk, *The Impact of the Economic Crisis on Collective agreements in Poland, Ibid.*

arising from employment contracts concluded with individual employees. It can therefore be criticized as a far-reaching interference in the autonomy of the will of the parties to the employment relationship'.

The articulation of different levels of collective bargaining has also undergone changes. Development of derogatory negotiation has nevertheless remained limited: '*Polish law leaves very limited space for deviation from statutory standards. The list of legislative provisions that can be modified is closed and concerns only selected matters. During the economic crisis, the list was extended mainly when it came to working time regulations (e.g. longer reference periods). With regard to the structure of collective bargaining, the legislation allows the suspension of multi-establishment collective agreements concluded at a company level. This possibility does not play a particularly important role due to the very limited practical importance of sectoral negotiations*'.

These new fields of bargaining are open not only to trade union actors but also atypical agreements can be adopted in the absence of trade unions. In such cases it is down to 'ad hoc' representatives to negotiate these agreements. Works councils themselves cannot enter into negotiations, even though legislation does not grant these 'ad hoc' representatives sufficient guarantees to allow for balanced negotiation.

The situation in Hungary is relatively similar. Labour law was the subject of major reform in 2012 with the adoption of a new Labour Code, the aim of which was to achieve the most flexible employment market in the world.[90] One of the mechanisms for rendering employment conditions more flexible has been promotion of the role of collective agreements in labour regulations and making it very broadly possible for company collective agreements to derogate from the law, even where this is unfavourable. Therefore, the aim has been to develop company collective bargaining in a country where, like Poland, the collective agreement norm is rare, even at a company level. The incentive consists of derogation authorized by law: '*The legislator expected that the wide possibility of in pejus derogations (...) would increase collective agreement coverage, because employers would be motivated to conclude such agreements*'.[91]

The new labour code also reforms the relations between collective agreements at different levels, relationships that were previously regulated by the favourability principle. Now, a company agreement may derogate from the sectoral agreement, if this sectoral agreement so authorizes it. Nevertheless, sectoral agreements are rare so this mechanism should not be used.

According to Tamás Gyulavári, it is possible that the new labour code could eventually strengthen the role of unions if they are in a position to negotiate quid pro quo. Nevertheless, union organizations risk not reaching the level of 10% membership which is now required in order to sign an agreement and at the same time, reforms might have contributed to weakening trade union organizations. Finally, the fact that works councils are given the possibility of signing such agreements represents a real

90. Tamás Gyulavári, Gábor Kártyás, *The Hungarian Flexicurity Pathway? New Labour Code after Twenty Years in the Market Economy* (Budapest: Pázmány Press, 2015).
91. T. Gyulavári, *Chasing the holy grail? Stumbling Collective Bargaining in Eastern Europe and the Hungarian Experiment*, in S. Laulom (ed.), *Collective Bargaining in Time of Crisis*, *supra*.

danger because this can also lead to the weakening of trade union presence in companies.

[b] Maintaining a Centralized System of Collective Bargaining

Developments in national systems of labour relations and the major incentives that exist with regard to the decentralization of collective bargaining must not mask the fact that some countries have not undergone such developments, or only to a very limited degree.

Within the range of countries studied, Austria, Germany, Belgium, Sweden and the Netherlands are in this situation, although their systems may be subject to a greater or lesser degree of pressure. These countries are all characterized by the fact that they have maintained a high level of unionization (even if here once again, this rate might come down) and persistent abstentionism on the part of the State. Above all, the processes of decentralization that exist remain controlled by high levels of collective bargaining and sectoral salary negotiations are still essential.

Austria is certainly the country where the labour relations system appears the most stable. Sectoral agreements still represent the main level of collective bargaining; it is at this level that minimum salaries are fixed and 95% of employees are covered by agreements at this level. Works councils agreements may only be entered into on matters defined under the law or if the sectoral agreement so authorizes and they may not contravene the provisions of sectoral agreements. This is confirmed by Elisabeth Brameshuber, '*the Austrian system of sectoral collective bargaining has proved to be quite successful. It leads to a cartelisation of wages, with hardly any sector of industry currently offering a minimum wage of less than EUR 1,500/month for a full-time position. The regulatory function of the cartelised wages should not be underestimated either, leading to a de facto perishing of low-performing companies in the long run. By bargaining the wages and working conditions for one sector rather than just a single employer, the employer's position especially is reinforced, thus leading to relatively low strike rates. In this way, the Austrian system provides for a very distinct peace function. Another important feature is its innovation function, which was particularly visible during the crisis of the past few years where important decisions to stabilise the labour market were taken at the level of sectoral collective bargaining. Although current political developments are threatening the system's stability, it seems highly unlikely that it is going to change in the near future*'.[92] Tensions may appear, but so far it has been possible to find solutions and they do not threaten the system's stability.

The Swedish system has also traditionally been depicted as a centralized system and this description is still valid, even though nowadays collective bargaining, particularly in relation to salaries, may take place at a decentralized level. '*In Sweden, collective bargaining has traditionally been described as highly decentralized. This description is still valid. Nevertheless, the collective bargaining structure also contains*

92. E. Brameshuber, *The Importance of Sectoral Collective Bargaining in Austria*, in S. Laulom, *Collective Bargaining in Time of Crisis*, *supra*.

significantly decentralized elements – particularly regarding bargaining on wages. The decisive steps towards this partial decentralization of collective bargaining in Sweden was not taken during the crisis years, but mainly in the early 1990s. Furthermore, this partial transition of the collective bargaining system is not a product of political decisions that have been implemented through legislation. Instead the development has taken place in the area of industrial relations, and its outcome has been operationalized in collective agreements'.[93]

Finally in Germany, the sectoral level is still important. However, the development of opt-out clauses and the decrease in extension procedures has led to the weakening of this level. Opt-out clauses set out in sectoral agreements related to establishments, namely employers and works councils, have progressively changed the structure of collective agreements by moving the centre of gravity closer to the company. In practice and under existing law, trade unions have accepted the need to sign opt-out clauses more frequently in sectoral agreements. These opt-out clauses appeared in the 1980s and authorized amendments made by agreements entered into between the employee and works councils on the subject of pay and working time. By the end of the 1990s, these opt-out clauses were spreading to companies experiencing major financial difficulties, which could lead to redundancies. Such agreements were basically related to salaries and working time and were able to derogate unfavourably from the sectoral agreement standard. But while in the 1980s and 90s these opt-out clauses on the whole concerned companies in difficulty, nowadays they can be found in companies who are not yet experiencing problems. Another development is that nowadays sectoral agreements may no longer contain clauses on salaries and working time which thus leads to a reduction in the scope of bargaining. The introduction of a minimum salary bears witness in part to this decline in the sectoral agreement.

[c] Legislative Intervention to Help Drive Decentralization of Labour Relations Systems

The 3rd group of countries (Italy, Spain, Portugal, Greece, Romania, Slovenia)[94] is characterized by legislative intervention, to a greater or lesser degree, aimed at decentralizing industrial relations systems. The movement towards the decentralization of collective bargaining, in itself, is not a recent phenomenon. What is new is the desire on the part of different regulators to prioritize the company level over the sectoral level.

The notable common thread among these companies is the intervention, in some case massive and in others repeated, by the State. Some reforms have been at the demand of the European institutions, in particular in the context of Memoranda of Understanding. For example this is the case with Portugal and Greece. Social partners

93. J. Julén Votinius, internal report on Sweden, INLACRIS VS/2014/0532.

94. *See* A. Koukiadaki, I. Tavora, M. Martinez Lucio, *Continuity and change in joint regulation in Europe: structural reforms and collective bargaining in manufacturing*, 22 European Journal of Industrial Relations, 1 (2016).

have sometimes been associated with reforms; however in the majority of countries studied the main trade union organizations have been opposed to them.

The measures adopted in order to develop company collective bargaining are varied and more often than not a set of measures is adopted and combined. Despite certain specific national characteristics, there are some common traits.

A country's legislation may revise the conditions for signing collective agreements at a sectoral level. This is the case for example in Portugal and Romania, where new conditions of representativeness have led to a reduction in the number of agreements entered into at this level. Procedures aimed at extending sectoral agreements may also be reviewed and the options of extension reduced. A limit on the term of the duration of agreements made at a higher level may also be allowed. The favourability principle may be called into question or see its field of application reduced and the regulator may review the articulation of bargaining levels by granting company level the possibility of derogating from higher level agreements in a way that is unfavourable to employees. The desire to develop collective bargaining at a company level also involves the acknowledgement of new actors in collective bargaining. In this way, elected or ad hoc representatives are sometimes granted the option of negotiating company agreements.

Thus the State has intervened in the regulations governing articulations between collective agreements and employment contracts to prioritize company agreements.

This State intervention is of a kind to call into question the very collective autonomy of social partners. This is the case particularly when the regulator seeks to impose a certain type of articulation between collective agreement standards themselves, granting precedence to company agreements over sectoral collective agreements. This type of intervention has sometimes even been acknowledged as being contrary notably to basic ILO standards. In 2012, when discussing the reforms made in Greece at the request of several Greek trade union organizations, the ILO Committee on Freedom of Association found '*numerous, significant interventions against the principle of the inviolability of freely concluded collective agreements*' and an extensive deficit of social dialogue. '*The elaboration of procedures systematically favouring decentralized bargaining of exclusionary provisions that are less favourable than the provisions at a higher level can lead to a global destabilization of the collective bargaining machinery and of workers' and employers' organizations and constitutes in this regard a weakening of freedom of association and collective bargaining contrary to the principles of Conventions Nos. 87 and 98*'.[95]

The effects of reforms on these collective bargaining systems are very diverse. Examination of the results of the research carried out by Aristea Koukiadaki brings to light three groups of countries: countries where the collective bargaining system has collapsed (Greece, Romania), countries where the system is being eroded (Portugal, Spain, Ireland, Slovenia) and countries where the system demonstrates continuity or resilience, such as Italy or up until now France.

95. 365th report of the committee on freedom of association, GB316-INS_9-1_[2012-11-0030-01]-Web-Fr.docx. http://www.ilo.org/wcmsp5/groups/public/---ed_norm/---relconf/documents/meetingdocument/wcms_193264.pdf, pp. 286 et seq, accessed 20 July 2017.

One of the major consequences of these reforms has been the sometimes drastic reduction of a sectoral level due both to the contraction of the field of application of sectoral agreements and the contraction of the subjects of negotiation. Thus in Portugal, '*the number of employees covered by collective agreements fell from almost 1.9 million in 2008 to some 246,643 in 2014*'.[96] The conclusion for Portugal is '*the changes in the collective bargaining legal framework during the period of financial assistance did not promote organized decentralisation but a dramatic erosion of sector bargaining and coverage by collective agreements*'. The conclusion for Romania is still more pessimistic: '*The legislative intervention was brutal, without involving the social partners, and has ruined the social dialogue and the system the social partners had managed to build over the two decades, following the fall of communism. Decentralisation of collective bargaining to the lowest level has weakened the social acquis achieved so far by the trade unions at national and local level and affected sectoral collective bargaining. It has also lowered the standard of rights recognised so far, anchored in higher-level collective agreements*'.[97]

Another general and widespread consequence is that there has not been a parallel and intended development of company-level collective bargaining. We might take Spain as an example. Post 2012, the law granted priority to company agreements. However, the option of negotiating at company level has not been exercised. One of the reasons for this is related to the specific characteristics of the Spanish industrial base, which is comprised basically of small- and medium-sized companies. The size of the companies means that it is difficult for negotiation to take place at this level. The disappearance or weakening of negotiation space at a sectoral level results in an extension of the employer's unilateral decision-making power.[98] This same observation has been made in Portugal.

It can also be seen that in countries where this erosion has taken place, recent developments have demonstrated that the sectoral level can stand its ground. In Portugal, since 2015 the government has been seeking to strengthen sectoral bargaining and the country has seen an increase in the number of agreements signed at this level, which has not been the case since 2012. In France, until the adoption of the Labour Law of 8 August 2016, the development of collective bargaining at a company level had basically not called into question the coordinated articulation of standards negotiated at company and sectoral level. This is the finding of the Combrexelle report: '*the effects of the law of 4 May 2004 allowing derogation by company agreement from a higher level, including outside of the favourability principle, appear to have been limited. A review of the law made in 2008 demonstrated that social partners in fact had a tendency to 'lock' the companies' power to derogate in sectoral agreements, as they were authorised to do by law. Over the following years, there was no monitoring, either by the social partners or the State, that would make it possible to provide an assessment*

96. T. Coelho Moreira, *The Revival of Sectoral Collective Bargaining: the Portuguese Experience*, in S. Laulom, *Collective Bargaining in Time of Crisis, supra*.
97. F. Rosioru, *Collective Bargaining in Romania: the Aftermath of an Earthquake*, in S. Laulom, *Collective Bargaining in Time of Crisis, supra*.
98. Y. Maneiro Vázquez, J. María Miranda Boto, *The Spanish Example*, in S. Laulom, *Collective Bargaining in Time of Crisis, supra*.

of the importance of 'derogatory' company agreements'.[99] The Labour Law of 8 August 2016 aims to go well beyond this and sets out a new labour law architecture where company agreements must prevail over sectoral agreements and the law. This law only targeted the field of working time, and the aim of the Macron rulings and the reform that should be implemented in summer 2017 is to go beyond this.[100]

[B] Decentralized Collective Bargaining System in the US and Asia

[1] US

Collective bargaining system in the US is decentralized and lacks national- or sector-level bargaining practice. In accordance with the declining union density, the US seems to exemplify a typical case of de-collectivization.

Although most labour unions are national and international organizations, the great majority of collective agreements are negotiated at the individual plant unit level by locals of the national or international unions. Multi-employer bargaining is possible, but it is lawful only if the union has majority support from each employer's employees and if each employer and the union agree to be bound on a multi-employer basis.[101]

The majority rule, or the exclusive representation system, is a peculiar feature of American collective labour relations. In order to acquire an enforceable right to bargain collectively, a labour union must be elected by the majority of employees in the bargaining unit as an exclusive representative or recognized by the employer based on card check. Once chosen as the exclusive representative, the union represents all employees in the unit irrespective of union membership.

Exclusivity applies both to other unions and individuals. Therefore, the employer is forbidden from not only negotiating terms and conditions of employment with any other labour organization but also making an agreement with an individual employee that differs from the collective bargaining agreement. Thus, an employee covered by the agreement cannot individually negotiate an improved employment package because the employer is bound to negotiate only with the exclusive representative.

As a result, in the US, there is no discussion of the favorability principle (*Günstigkeitsprinzip*) between a collective bargaining agreement and an individual agreement. When an employer and labour union agree to conclude collective bargaining agreements, they can uniformly and swiftly modify the terms and conditions of employment without obtaining individual employee's consent.

However, such an exclusive representation system based on the majority principle is declining. In 2016, only 12% of employees (6.4% in the private sector) were

99. J.-D. Combrexelle, *La négociation collective, le travail et l'emploi, Rapport au Premier ministre* (France Stratégie 2015) http://www.gouvernement.fr/sites/default/files/document/document/2015/09/rapport_combrexelle.pdf, accessed 20 July 2017.
100. Ch. Vigneau, *Negotiating Working Time in Time of Crisis: The 'El Khomri Law'*, in S. Laulom, *Collective Bargaining in Time of Crisis, supra*.
101. Douglas E. Ray, 'The Role of Collective Bargaining in Labor Law Regimes: United States National Report', submitted paper for the XXth Congress of the International Academy of Comparative Law in Fukuoka, July 2018.

represented by unions. Recent enlargement of the 'Right to work states', which prohibit labour unions from collecting union dues or an equivalent amount from non-union members who are represented by the union, also spurs this trend.[102]

When employees are not represented by unions, the terms and conditions of employment are entrusted to individual negotiation. The US is a rare country that still maintains the employment-at-will doctrine as a default rule,[103] so employees are generally situated in a weaker position in negotiating working conditions. As national or sector-level bargaining is alien in the US, declining union density results literally in de-collectivization.

[2] East Asia

In East Asia, especially in Japan, Korea[104] and Taiwan,[105] decentralized collective bargaining has been predominant. Japan represents the most typical model of a decentralized system.[106] As of 2015, 93.5% of all labour unions in Japan were enterprise-based unions, and they comprised 88.7% of all organized workers. Consequently, Japanese collective agreements are concluded at the company level. However, enterprise unionism and decentralized system are neither required nor encouraged by law. Therefore, not only enterprise unions but also industrial unions, craft unions and local unions that organize workers across companies in a certain region, are all legitimate unions under the Labour Union Act.

Apart from some historical reasons,[107] the main reason for the enterprise unionism that has continued to predominate to date is its functional excellence (flexibility, adaptability and responsiveness to the grass-root needs of workers) in the Japanese employment system.

---

102. On 27 June 2018, in Janus *v.* American Federation of State, County, and Municipal Employees, Council 31, No. 16-1466, *585 U.S.* (2018), the *United States Supreme Court* ruled that taking collective union fees from non-union members in the public sector violates the First Amendment (freedom of speech), overturning the 1977 decision in *Abood v. Detroit Board of Education* that had previously allowed such fees.
103. Of course, the classic at-will doctrine has been modified in various ways by case law developments. However, American Law Institute, *Restatement of the Law (Third), Employment Law* (2015) confirms that at-will employment is still the default rule in the US.
104. Kiu Sik Bae, 'Collective Bargaining in Korea', ILO-Japan Multi –Lateral Project (2006).
105. Chin-Chin Cheng, 'The Role of Collective Bargaining in Labor Law Regimes in Taiwan' submitted paper for the XXth Congress of the International Academy of Comparative Law in Fukuoka, July 2018.
106. *See* Takashi Araki, 'Japan's Decentralized Industrial Relations, Internal Flexicurity, and Challenges Japan Faces' in Adalberto Perulli & Tiziano Treu (eds), *Enterprise and Social Rights*, 173 (Wolters Kluwer, 2017); Tadashi Hanami, Fumito Komiya and Ryuichi Yamakawa, *Labour Law in Japan (2nd.)*, 177ff (Wolters Kluwer, 2015).
107. Historically Japan had little experience of industry-wide unionism before World War II. The experience of the wartime regime, which mobilized all workers into units at the enterprise level, may have had an influence. After the war, when GHQ (General Headquarters of the Allied Powers) encouraged labor unions as vehicles to democratize Japanese society and employers could no longer suppress union activities, workers freely used the enterprise-level workplace facilities as the most convenient place and unit of organization. Tadashi Hanami, Fumito Komiya and Ryuichi Yamakawa, *Labour Law in Japan (2nd.)*, 45 (Wolters Kluwer, 2015).

Under the long-term employment system, employment security of regular workers has been highly respected. In turn, regular workers are subject to the flexible adjustment of working conditions. These workers are transferred within a company and receive in-house education and on-the-job training. The promotion and wages of each regular worker are determined mainly by that individual's length of service and ability to perform work. In such a highly developed internal labour market within a particular company, industry or national-level negotiations have made little sense. So, enterprise-based unions and enterprise-level collective bargaining have been the most efficient mechanisms for responding properly, swiftly and flexibly to the needs of both employers and regular workers. Thus, even though labour unionists in the 1950s endeavored to transform enterprise unions into industry-level unions, enterprise unionism has continued to be predominant and the hallmark of Japanese industrial relations.

However, the system built on enterprise unionism has several defects, such as weak bargaining power, a lack of universal impact across the industry or nation, and a lack of social and political influence on national labour policy. To compensate for weakness in bargaining power and the absence of any industry or nation-wide impact of collective bargaining, since 1955 Japanese labour unions have developed a unique wage determination system called *Shunto* (Spring Offensive). Under the *Shunto* system, every Spring, industrial federations of company unions set the aim for wage increases and co-ordinate the schedule of company-level negotiations and strikes across companies and industries. According to the schedule, strong company unions in a prosperous industry chosen as a pattern-setter begin negotiations first, setting the market price for that year. Other unions then follow suit. The market prices established in *Shunto* have also been reflected in the public sector and regional minimum wages.

Another important compensatory mechanism is the tripartite Labour Policy Council and its subcommittees established in the Ministry of Health, Labour and Welfare. These bodies consist of representatives of public interest (academics), labour unions and management organizations. It is established practice that the content of a government's labour law bill is deliberated and decided in these tripartite bodies. In a sense, deliberation in these bodies is quasi-collective bargaining at the national level involving government and academics as mediators and conciliators.

One of the debated problems in the Japanese decentralized system is the derogation system. Unlike the European derogation system, Japanese law gives the right to conclude derogatory agreements to decentralized parties in the establishment: namely a labour union that organizes the majority of employees in the establishment, or if such a union does not exist, an employee elected as the majority representative in the establishment. Where there is no majority union, as is often the case with small and medium-sized enterprises, it is reported that employers abusively conclude derogation agreements with a majority representative who has little power to resist employers' pressure. Thus, improvements in the derogation system, such as strengthening the procedures for the election of majority representatives and introducing a works council system, is under discussion.

[C] From Decentralization of Collective Bargaining to De-collectivization of Industrial Relations Systems?

In many EU Member States, the crisis provided grounds for a rarely equalled level of state intervention in the regulation of labour relations with an explicit aim: the decentralization of collective bargaining. This movement began long before the crisis, but without a doubt intensified from 2008 onwards. This evolution calls into question the role that the State can or must play in the field of labour relations. In that perspective, the situation we described for the UK, Hungary, Poland and Turkey is very similar to the one in Chile, Mexico, Canada and the United States where bargaining predominantly takes place at firm or enterprise level.[108] In these European and American countries, collective bargaining coverage remains low whereas this coverage is high only in countries which have at least some forms of sector-level bargaining. When there is none, coverage tends to go hand in hand with trade union membership since having a Trade Union or worker representation at the workplace is a necessary condition to be able to negotiate an agreement.[109]

Other American countries have witnessed important reforms of Labour Law which present some similarities with some of the European experiences especially as regard the intervention of the State to favour a decentralization of collective bargaining. This is the case for example in Brazil, where traditionally collective bargaining agreements take place at industry level. In 2017, an important reform of Labour Law was adopted[110] introducing several amendments popularly referred to collectively as the 'labour law reform.' Here again, the rhetoric of crises has been largely used to justify a drastic reform of Labour Law. The official purpose of the reform is to modernize the Brazilian labour code. The reform should lead to the creation of new jobs and reduce unemployment rates, through the implementation of more flexible rules.[111] The decentralization of collective bargaining is one of the tool used and with the 2017 Act, for certain matters, collective bargaining agreements and union agreements will predominate over the law. These include for example: (i) working hours (observing the constitutional limitation); (ii) annual bank hours; (iii) company regulation impacting payroll charges; (iv) incentive rewards in goods or services, eventually given in incentive programs; (v) profit sharing plans, etc. It is too early to evaluate the effect of this law on industrial relations.

What the comparison highlights is a changing role of the State in collective relations. Traditionally, the State has intervened by various measures to support collective autonomy and favour an environment conductive to the development of collective bargaining. State interventionism which, as we have seen, could be particularly intense, nowadays takes new forms. It is not so much a matter of supporting

108. OECD (2017), *Collective bargaining in a changing world of work*, in OECD Employment Outlook 2017, Editions OECD, Paris, https://doi.org/10.1787/empl_outlook-2017-8-en.
109. *Ibid*, p. 167.
110. 14 July 2017, Brazil's Law 13.467/2017.
111. L. Correia Da Silva, L'instrumentalisation de la négociation collective vers la flexibilisation du droit du travail en France et au Brésil: une analyse comparative à l'aune des réformes mises en place en 2017, Mémoire de Master 2, Université Lumière Lyon 2, July 2018.

actors and helping to drive collective agreement-making activity, as allowing businesses to conclude a certain type of agreement and take action with regard to the structures and indeed content of collective bargaining. There have been no (or very few) measures adopted to promote collective bargaining at the company level and to strike a better balance between the parties in terms of their negotiation power. Generally, reforms have been only interested in allowing collective bargaining at the company level without introducing specific measures to improve the abilities of the actors to bargain. The sole measures taken regarding the actors have been allowing employee representatives to negotiate in lieu of trade unions.

The consequences of these policies are not uniform. The decline in coverage by collective agreement can be dramatic, as has been the case in Greece, Portugal and Romania. The main lesson is that the decline in regulation of working conditions by professional sector has not been twinned with the development of collective bargaining at a company level and that decentralization that is not sector-led generally leads to the absence of a collective agreement, namely a de-collectivization of labour relations. Today this is the situation in which Poland and Hungary find themselves.

In this context, comparative analysis indicates that another path could be taken by national policies which would consist in engaging in reflection on how best to develop and support the sector level. Changes in productive organizations that are currently taking place, which see the development of small and very small businesses, networked businesses and work via digital platforms likewise suggest this is the right approach. The Hungarian and Polish situation show the need to rebuild a collective bargaining system. There can be no doubt that this (re)construction would require complex measures and that it is anything but a certainty. As a result, the question is necessarily raised as to the evolution of labour rights in the absence of collective regulation of labour conditions. The process of decentralization has more often than not led to an extension of the employer's unilateral power where salaries and labour conditions are ever more frequently determined by direct negotiations between employer and employees, with the State becoming the sole guarantor of employee protection. Paradoxically, there is no certainty that the flexibilities sought by companies are necessarily achieved, except in terms of extending the employer's unilateral powers still further.

§12.04 CONCLUSION

This general report has dealt with the two independent themes: new forms of work and decentralization of collective bargaining. These two different themes are, however, raised by a common driver: the introduction of flexibility in employment relations.

New forms of employment have been emerging due to an increased demand from employers and/or employees for enhanced flexibility.[112] New forms of work enable employers to use just-in-time workforce efficiently. They also give workers more

112. Eurofound, Overview of new forms of employment-2018 update, 18 (Publishing Office of the European Union, 2018).

opportunities to earn and an autonomous way of working to achieve a better work–life balance. However, such flexibility entails job insecurity, social/professional isolation, higher stress levels and work intensity, lack of collective representation and dispute resolution mechanism, etc.

Decentralization, especially that in Europe after 2008, has been promoted to cope with the financial crises by prioritizing company-level negotiation, which enables more flexible adjustment of working conditions responding to both companies' economic situations and workers' grass-root needs. For instance, in the case that unfavourable adjustment of working conditions helps avoid economic dismissals and securing employment, such concession bargaining can serve both parties' needs. However, as mentioned in the previous section, in countries with no national or sector-level bargaining practice, decentralization often results in de-collectivization of industrial relations.[113] In this case, flexibility might simply result in an increase in employers' unilateral control of employment relations.

Therefore, the introduction of flexibility itself is not necessarily the problem.[114] The problem is what kind of flexibility should be introduced, and how the flexibility should be balanced with security or protection of workers. Deciding the mode of flexibility and striking a balance between flexibility and security have traditionally been the roles of the state and law. However, because employees and work patterns are diversified, and demarcation between employee and self-employed is blurred, uniform regulations or one-size-fits-all standards will not work properly anymore.

This report discussed four approaches to deal with new forms of work (2.2, *see* Figure 12.3). In a sense, they are an attempt to cope with diversified workforce. For instance, discussion to introduce an intermediate category of employees, such as employee-like persons, is an attempt to provide three sets of regulations responding to the diversified workforce: one for employees, another for employee-like persons, and no labour law protections for the self-employed. However, this approach does not reflect diversification *within* the group of employees or that of employee-like persons. When we look at current labour laws applied to employees, they have already incorporated various measures to accommodate diversified employees and the need for flexibility, such as flexible work hour regulations, exemptions for employees with autonomy or discretion, and *inter alia* derogation scheme (Figure 12.4).

113. As for the similar observation, *see* Ulla Liukkunen, 'The role of collective bargaining in labour law regimes' General Report submitted for the XXth Congress of the International Academy of Comparative Law in Fukuoka, July 2018.

114. According to the Proposal for a Directive on transparent and predictable working conditions in the EU (COM(2017) 797 final), the flexibility coming with new forms of employment has been a major driver of job creation and labour market growth. Since 2014, more than five million jobs have been created.

Figure 12.3 Four Approaches to Deal with New Forms of Work

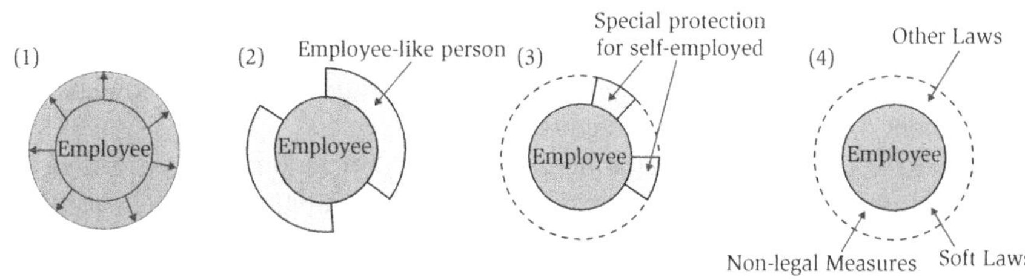

Figure 12.4 Current Labour Law

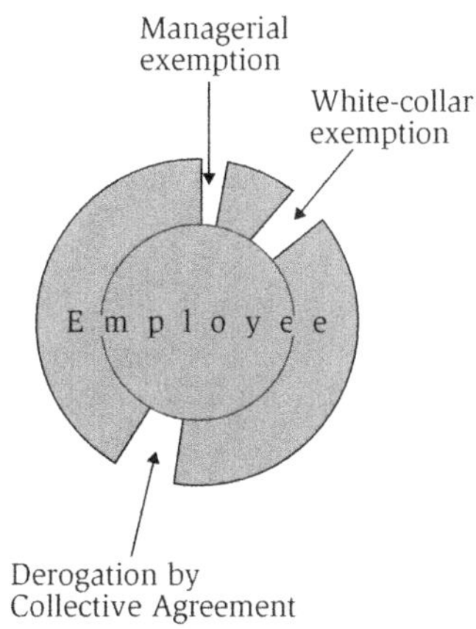

Derogation scheme allows parties to collective agreement to agree to deviate unfavourably from the statutory minimum standards.[115] A typical example often adopted in many countries is working hour regulations. Deviation of the maximum work hour regulation is allowed on the condition that collective agreements are concluded for that purpose. Germany has a long tradition of derogation known as 'law open to the disposition by a collective bargaining agreement (*Tarifdispositives Gesetzrecht*)'. Since the 1980s, as part of the trend of decentralization, it has been opened to works council agreements under the control of the parties to the collective bargaining agreement. Recently, France witnessed remarkable developments in derogation scheme, especially with the 'Loi Travail' of 8 August 2016.[116] Open clauses, which allow unfavourable derogation from sector-level collective bargaining agreement by

115. Both in Germany and France, it is understood that legislature has discretion over whether to introduce derogation scheme in labour protective laws except for matters that are not allowed by the Constitution or EU Law. *See* Yumiko Kuwamura, *Rodo-sha Hogo-ho no Kiso to Kozo (Toward a New Framework for Labour Protection Laws)*, 319ff (Yuhikaku, Tokyo, 2017).

116. According to Emmanuelle Mazuyer, derogation 'in pejus' to the Law will not be the exception, but the principle in France. France is moving from a system that had to explicitly authorize derogations to make it possible, to a system where it has to be explicitly forbidden for it not to

way of company-level or establishment-level collective agreements, are also spreading in Germany in order to introduce flexibility.[117]

The derogation scheme denotes the decentralization of norm setting from the national level (law) to the sector level (sector-level collective bargaining agreement) and further to the company or establishment level (company-level collective bargaining agreement or works council agreement).

There are two legal problems here. First, the derogation scheme reverses the traditional norm order established by the so-called 'favourability principle'. Traditionally it was only possible for lower level agreements to deviate from higher level norms favourably to workers (norm strength order: Law > CBA > WCA [Works Council Agreement] > individual contract) (*see* Figure 12.5). However, the derogation scheme allows unfavourable deviation based on the collective agreement concluded at the lower, decentralized level. Therefore, on what subject and to what extent, derogation should be allowed is the first key question.

Second, in accordance with decentralization, the worker-side party becomes weaker in negotiation power compared to the centralized party. Thus, to whom derogation power should be given is the other important question.

happen. Emmanuelle Mazuyer, 'The Role of Collective Bargaining in Labour Law, French Report.' submitted paper for the XXth Congress of the International Academy of Comparative Law in Fukuoka, July 2018.

117. Bernd Waas describes the spread of derogatory agreement at the company level as follows: 'the parties to collective agreements have increasingly been making use of so-called opening clauses that permit derogatory agreements and, by doing so, allow for more flexibility... Nowadays, collective agreements often follow the example of the Pforzheim accord [that established the rule of derogation] by providing, for instance that special payments can be postponed, reduced or canceled altogether in economically difficult times if both parties to the collective agreement agree.' *See* Bernd Waas, 'The Role of Collective Bargaining Agreement in Germany' submitted paper for the XXth Congress of the International Academy of Comparative Law in Fukuoka, July 2018.

Figure 12.5 Norm Order and Decentralization

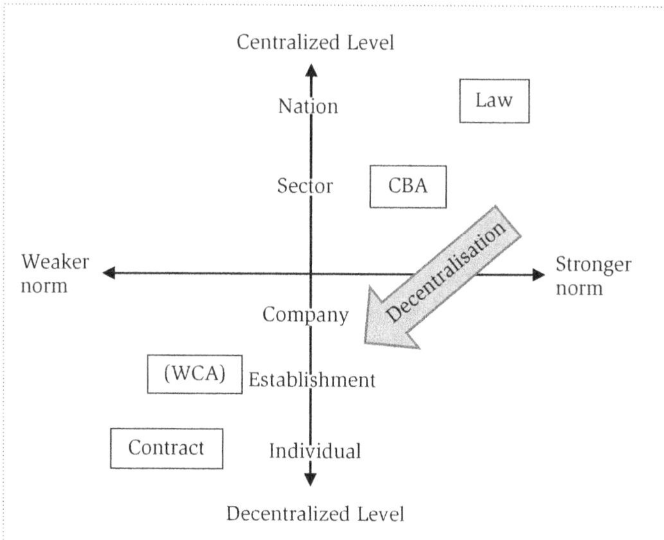

Therefore, on what subject, to what extent, and to whom, derogatory power should be entrusted is the key question here. In Japan, where derogation can be entrusted not only to the majority unions at the establishment level but also to the majority representative of workers in the establishment, a number of abusive derogations have been reported. In this regard, Germany allows derogation only when sector-level labour unions agree as a principle. Such a controlled derogation (controlled flexibility) might be one device to strike a good balance between flexibility and protection. However, such measures are only available in countries where sector-level industrial relations have existed. For countries where collective bargaining has always been decentralized, other options should be explored, such as the introduction of a works council system to strengthen the party to a derogation agreement.

As discussed in the last section, de-collectivization is feared not only in countries with a centralized system but even more so in countries with a decentralized system. This is because union density is universally declining, and in countries with a decentralized system declining union density is directly linked to shrinking collective bargaining coverage. If such de-collectivization is left as it is and no countermeasures are taken, it is impossible to protect employees and guarantee well-being at work in such an era of drastic technological changes.

Then, what can the possible countermeasures be to protect diversified employees and workers? First, restructure labour legislation to be more adaptable to the diversified workforce, such as appropriate derogation scheme consisting of the combination of substantive and procedural regulations. However, it is indispensable to establish a legitimate mechanism that can fairly represent diversified workers' interests and that is strong enough to resist control and intervention by employers. Second, given the universal tendency of declining union density, it is therefore worth considering the introduction of new collective bodies to represent diversified workers in the workplace, such as a works council, which represents all workers irrespective of union membership or standard/non-standard status. Third, when workplaces are de-collectivized and employers' unilateral actions prevail, court reviews of employment contracts from the viewpoint of social reasonableness would be an option. For instance, in Japan, courts review the reasonableness of work rules unilaterally modified by the employer and such work rules become binding only when the court regards the modification as reasonable (Article 10, Labour Contract Act).[118] Fourth, soft law is another option, working together with giving incentives and utilizing market reputation. For example, soft law can set a certain social goal, such as work-life balance or diversified workforce, and the government can give awards to good corporations that have attained socially desired goals or allow them to use certified labels for their business; conversely, it can publicize bad corporations that neither comply with labour laws nor respect social goals. These are just a few examples that are in no way mutually exclusive; in fact, they are compatible with each other.

The challenge we face is seeking a better balance between flexibility and security or protection of workers who are increasingly diversified. Although we face common and similar challenges in the globalized economy, policy choice will be different depending on the respective country's situation. In envisaging best policy choice, what we as labour lawyers should bear in mind is that labour law policy can only work effectively if it is well coordinated with other associated policies such as social security law,[119] tax law, competition law, consumer law, education and vocational training policy, and market functioning policy.[120]

At the same time, however, we should examine and clarify the peculiar role that labour law should play in relation to the other associated policies by considering the effectiveness of implementing the intended social goal. For instance, as we discussed in section two, competition law may provide similar protection as labour law, but associations of the self-employed or independent contractors may not engage in strikes or other collective actions. Effective and accessible dispute resolution mechanisms such as labour inspection or a labour court system are not available in the competition law regime. Therefore, the task of coordination with other legal policies requires us to identify and confirm the role and function of labour law that should not be transferred and delegated to other law systems. We believe that many social issues raised remain in the sphere that labour law should deal with, by developing and further enhancing its effectiveness.

118. *See* Takashi Araki, 'Japan's Decentralized Industrial Relations, Internal Flexicurity, and Challenges Japan Faces' Adalberto Perulli & Tiziano Treu (eds), *Enterprise and Social Rights*, 173, 187ff. (2017).

119. *See* Christina Behrendt and Quynh Anh Nguyen, 'Innovative approaches for ensuring universal social protection for the future of work' ILO Future of Work Research Paper series research paper 1 (2018).

120. *See* the 'European Pillar of Social Rights', jointly proclaimed by the European Parliament, the Council and the Commission at the Social Summit for Fair Jobs and Growth in Gothenburg on 17 November 2017.

BCLR - BULLETIN OF COMPARATIVE LABOUR RELATIONS

Vol. Author/Title/Year/ISBN

1. Roger Blanpain, *Individual Employment Contracts: Collective Agreements,* 1970.
2. Roger Blanpain, *Social Planning,* 1971 (ISBN 90-312-0018-2).
3. Roger Blanpain, *Guaranteed Income Funds,* 1972 (ISBN 90-312-0019-0).
4. Roger Blanpain, *Employee Participation at the Level of the Enterprise,* 1973 (ISBN 90-312-0020-4).
5. Roger Blanpain, *Vastheid van Betrekking: Staking en Bezetting,* 1974.
6. Roger Blanpain, *Labour Law and Industrial Relations (International Bibliography),* 1975 (ISBN 90-312-0023-9).
7. Roger Blanpain, *Multinational Enterprises,* 1976 (ISBN 90-312-0024-7).
8. Roger Blanpain, *Worker's Participation in the European Company,* 1977 (ISBN 90-312-0044-1).
9. Roger Blanpain, *Women and Labour,* 1978 (ISBN 90-312-0077-8).
10. Roger Blanpain, *European Conference on Labour Law and Industrial Relations: Multinational Enterprises,* 1979 (ISBN 90-312-0091-3).
11. Roger Blanpain, *Job Security and Industrial Relations,* 1980 (ISBN 90-312-0147-2).
12. Roger Blanpain, Greg Bamber & Russell Lansbury, *Technological Change and Industrial Relations: An International Symposium,* 1983 (ISBN 90-312-0205-3).
13. Roger Blanpain, James Janssen van Raay & A. Moulty, *Worker's Participation in the European Community: The Fifth Directive,* 1984 (ISBN 90-654-4187-5).
14. Roger Blanpain, *Equality and Prohibition of Discrimination in Employment,* 1985 (ISBN 90-654-4215-4).
15. Roger Blanpain, *Restructuring Labour in the Enterprise: Law and Practice in France, F.R. of Germany, Italy, Sweden and the United Kingdom,* 1986 (ISBN 90-654-4283-9).
16. Roger Blanpain & E. Kassalow, *Unions and Industrial Relations: Recent Trends and Prospect: A Comparative Treatment,* 1987 (ISBN 90-654-4294-4).
17. Roger Blanpain & Marco Biagi, *Trade Union Democracy and Industrial Relations,* 1988 (ISBN 90-654-4394-0).
18. Roger Blanpain & Jelle Visser, *In Search of Inclusive Unionism,* 1990 (ISBN 90-654-4439-4).
19. Roger Blanpain, *Flexibility and Wages: A Comparative Treatment,* 1990 (ISBN 90-654-4461-0).

20. Roger Blanpain, Stephen Frenkel & Oliver Clarke, *Economic Restructuring and Industrial Relations in Industrialised Countries*, 1990 (ISBN 90-654-4488-2).
21. Roger Blanpain & Friedrich Fürstenberg, *Structure and Strategy in Industrial Relations*, 1991 (ISBN 90-654-4559-5).
22. Roger Blanpain, Amira Galin & Ozer Carmi, *Flexible Work Patterns and Their Impact on Industrial Relations*, 1991 (ISBN 90-654-4572-2).
23. Roger Blanpain, *Workers' Participation: Influence on Management Decision-Making by Labour in the Private Sector*, 1992 (ISBN 90-654-4600-1).
24. Roger Blanpain, Brian Brooks & Chris Engels, *Employed or Self-Employed*, 1992 (ISBN 90-654-4613-3).
25. Roger Blanpain & Tiziano Treu, *Industrial Relations Developments in the Telecommunications Industry*, 1993 (ISBN 90-654-4642-7).
26. Roger Blanpain & Marco Biagi, *Industrial Relations in Small and Medium Sized Enterprises*, 1993 (ISBN 90-654-4696-6).
27. Roger Blanpain & Marco Biagi, *Participative Management and Industrial Relations in a Worldwide Perspective*, 1993 (ISBN 90-654-4769-5).
28. Roger Blanpain, Jacques Rojot & Hoyt N. Wheeler, *Employee Rights and Industrial Justice*, 1994 (ISBN 90-654-4804-7).
29. Roger Blanpain & Ruth Ben-Israel, *Strikes and Lock-Outs in Industrialized Market Economies*, 1994 (ISBN 90-654-4841-1).
30. Roger Blanpain, Kazuo Sugeno & Yasuo Suwa, *The Harmonization of Working Life and Family Life*, 1995 (ISBN 90-411-0064-4).
31. Roger Blanpain & Laszio Nagy, *Labour Law and Industrial Relations in Central and Eastern Europe*, 1996 (ISBN 90-411-0298-1).
32. Roger Blanpain, *Labour Law and Industrial Relations in the European Union*, 1997 (ISBN 90-411-0527-1).
33. Taco Van Peijpe, *Employment Protection under Strain*, 1998 (ISBN 90-411-0528-8).
34. Roger Blanpain, Takashi Araki & Ryuichi Yamakawa, *The Process of Industrialization and the Role of Labour Law in Asia*, 1999 (ISBN 9-041-1104-7-X).
35. Roger Blanpain & Marco Biagi, *Non-standard Work and Industrial Relations*, 1999 (ISBN 90-411-1117-4).
36. Roger Blanpain, *Private Employment Agencies: The Impact of ILO Convention 181 (1997) and the Judgment of the European Court of Justice of 11 December 1997*, 1999 (ISBN 90-411-1118-2).
37. Roger Blanpain, *Multinational Enterprises and the Social Challenges of the XXIst Century: The ILO Declaration on Fundamental* Principles *at Work, Public and Private Corporate Codes of Conduct*, 2000 (ISBN 90-411-1280-4).
38. Roger Blanpain, Ryuichi Yamakawa & Takashi Araki, *Deregulation and Labour Law: In Search of a Labour Concept for the 21st Century*, 2000 (ISBN 90-411-1370-3).
39. Roger Blanpain, *The Council of Europe and the Social Challenges of the XXIst Century*, 2001 (ISBN 90-411-1543-9).

40. Roger Blanpain, *On-Line Rights for Employees in the Information Society, Use & Monitoring of E-Mail & Internet at Work*, 2002 (ISBN 90-411-1626-5).
41. Roger Blanpain, *The Evolving Employment Relationship and the New Economy: The Role of Labour Law & Industrial Relations*, 2001 (ISBN 90-411-1691-5).
42. Roger Blanpain, *Involvement of Employees in the European Union, Works Councils, Company Statute, Information and Consultation Rights*, 2002 (ISBN 90-411-1760-1).
43. Michele Colucci, *The Impact of the Internet and New Technologies on the Workplace: A Legal Analysis from a Comparative Point of View*, 2002 (ISBN 90-411-1824-1).
44. Roger Blanpain, *White Paper on the Labour Market in Italy: The Quality of European Industrial Relations and Changing Industrial Relations*, 2002 (ISBN 90-411-1841-1).
45. Roger Blanpain, Russell D. Lansbury & Young-Bum Park, *Impact of Globalisation on Employment Relations: A Comparison of the Automobile and Banking Industries in Australia and Korea*, 2002 (ISBN 90-411-1850-0).
46. Roger Blanpain & Antoine Jacobs, *Employee Rights in Bankruptcy: A Comparative-Law Assessment*, 2002 (ISBN 90-411-1942-6).
47. Roger Blanpain, Takashi Araki & Shinya Ouchi, *Corporate Restructuring and the Role of Labour Law*, 2003 (ISBN 90-411-1949-3).
48. Roger Blanpain, *Collective Bargaining, Discrimination, Social Security and European Integration*, 2003 (ISBN 90-411-2010-6).
49. Roger Blanpain & Luis Aparicio-Valdez, *Labour Relations in the Asia- Pacific Countries*, 2004 (ISBN 90-411-2239-7).
50. Roger Blanpain & Ronnie Graham, *Temporary Agency Work and the Information Society*, 2004 (ISBN 90-411-2252-4).
51. Roger Blanpain, *The Actors of Collective Bargaining: A World Report*, 2004 (ISBN 90-411-2253-2).
52. Roger Blanpain & Michele Colucci, *The Globalisation of Labour Standards: The Soft Law Track*, 2004 (ISBN 90-411-2303-2).
53. Roger Blanpain, Takashi Araki & Shinya Ouchi, *Labour Law in Motion: Diversification of the Labour Force & Terms and Conditions of Employment*, 2005 (ISBN 90-411-2315-6).
54. Roger Blanpain, *Smoking and the Workplace*, 2005 (ISBN 90-411-2325-3).
55. Roger Blanpain, *Confronting Globalization: The Quest for a Social Agenda*, 2005 (ISBN 90-411-2381-4).
56. Roger Blanpain, Thomas Blanke & Edgar Rose, *Collective Bargaining Wages in Comparative Perspective: Germany, France, the Netherlands, Sweden and the United Kingdom*, 2005 (ISBN 90-411-2388-1).
57. Roger Blanpain & Anne Numhauser-Henning, *Women in Academia & Equality Law: Aiming High - Falling Short?*, 2006 (ISBN 978-90-411-2427-6).
58. Roger Blanpain, *Freedom of Services in the European Union: Labour and Social Security Law: The Bolkestein Initiative*, 2006 (ISBN 978-90-411-2453-5).
59. Roger Blanpain, Frans Pennings & Nurhan Sural, *Flexibilisation and Modernisation of the Turkish Labour Market*, 2006 (ISBN 978-90-411-2490-X).

60. Roger Blanpain & Boel Flodgren, *Corporate and Employment Perspectives in a Global Business Environment*, 2006 (ISBN 978-90-411-2537-X).
61. Roger Blanpain, Shinya Ouchi & Takashi Araki, *Decentralizing Industrial Relations and The Role of Labor Unions and Employee Representatives*, 2007 (ISBN 978-90-411-2583-3).
62. Roger Blanpain, *European Framework Agreements and Telework: Law and Practice: A European and Comparative Study*, 2007 (ISBN 978-90-411-2560-4).
63. Roger Blanpain, Jim Kitay, Leanne Cutcher & Nick Wailes, *Globalization and Employment Relations in Retail Banking*, 2007 (ISBN 978-90-411-2620-1).
64. Roger Blanpain, Russell Lansbury, Jim Kitay, Nick Wailes & Anja Kirsch, *Globalization and Employment Relations in the Auto Assembly Industry: A Study of Seven Countries*, 2008 (ISBN 978-90-411-2698-6).
65. Roger Blanpain & Michele Tiraboschi, *The Global Labour Market: From Globalization to Flexicurity*, 2008 (ISBN 978-90-411-2722-8).
66. Roger Blanpain, Michele Colucci & Frank Hendrickx, *The Future of Sport in the European Union: Beyond the EU Reform Treaty and the White Paper*, 2008 (ISBN 978-90-411-2761-7).
67. Roger Blanpain, Linda Dickens, *Challenges in European Employment Relations: Employment Regulation, Trade Union Organization, Equality, Flexicurity, Training and New Approaches to Pay*, 2008 (ISBN 978-90-411-2771-6).
68. Roger Blanpain, Hiroya Nakakubo & Takashi Araki, *New Developments in Employment Discrimination Law, 2008* (ISBN 978-90-411-2782-2).
69. Roger Blanpain, Andrzej Marian wiątkowski, *The Laval and Viking Cases: Freedom of Services and Establishment v. Industrial Conflict in the European Economic Area and Russia*, 2009 (ISBN 978-90-411-2850-8).
70. Roger Blanpain, William Bromwich, Olga Rymkevich, Silvia Spattini, *The Modernization of Labour Law and Industrial Relations in a Comparative Perspective*, 2009 (ISBN 978-90-411-2865-2).
71. Roger Blanpain, Juan Pablo Landa & Brian Langille, *Employment Policies and Multilevel Governance*, 2009 (ISBN 978-90-411-2866-9).
72. Roger Blanpain, European Works Councils; *The European Directive 2009/ 38/EC of 6 May 2009, 2009* (ISBN 978-90-411-3208-6).
73. Roger Blanpain, William Bromwich, Olga Rymkevich & Silvia Spattini, *Labour Productivity, Investment in Human Capital and Youth Employment: Comparative Developments and Global Responses*, 2010 (ISBN 978-90-411-3249-9).
74. Greg J. Bamber & Philippe Pochet, *Regulating Employment Relations, Work and Labour Laws: International Comparisons between Key Countries*, 2010 (ISBN 978-90-411-3199-7). General Editor: Roger Blanpain.
75. Roger Blanpain, Desislava Nikolaeva Dimitrova, *Seafarers' Rights in the Globalized Maritime Industry*, 2010 (ISBN 978-90-411-3349-6).
76. Roger Blanpain, Hiroya Nakakubo & Takashi Araki, *Regulation of Fixed- Term Employment Contracts*, 2010 (ISBN 978-90-411-3356-4).

77. Roger Blanpain, William Bromwich, Olga Rymkevich & Iacopo Senatori, *Rethinking Corporate Governance*, 2011 (ISBN 978-90-411-3450-9).
78. Roger Blanpain & Frank Hendrickx, *Labour Law between Change and Tradition: Liber Amicorum Antoine Jacobs*, 2011 (ISBN 978-90-411-3424-0).
79. Roger Blanpain, Thomas Klebe, Marlene Schmidt & Bernd Waas, *Trade Union Rights at the Workplace*, 2012 (ISBN 978-90-411-3460-8).
80. Roger Blanpain, William Bromwich, Olga Rymkevich & Iacopo Senatori, *Labour Markets, Industrial Relations and Human Resources Management: From Recession to Recovery*, 2012 (ISBN 978-90-411-4004-3).
81. Roger Blanpain, Hiroya Nakakubo & Takashi Araki, *Systems of Employee Representation at the Enterprise: A Comparative Study*, 2012 (ISBN 978-90-411-4080-7).
82. Roger Blanpain & Frank Hendrickx, *Temporary Agency Work in the European Union and the United States*, 2013 (ISBN 978-90-411-4769-1).
83. Roger Blanpain, Toker Dereli, Y. Pınar Soykut-Sarıca & Aslı en-Tabaı, *Emerging Patterns of Work and Turkish Labour Market Challenges under Globalization: Readings on Labour and Employment Relations*, 2014 (ISBN 978-90-411-4983-1).
84. Roger Blanpain, Pablo Arellano Ortiz, Marius Olivier & Gijsbert Vonk, *Social Security and Migrant Workers: Selected Studies of Cross-border Social Security Mechanisms*, 2014 (ISBN 978-90-411-4770-7).
85. Roger Blanpain & Nikita Lyutov, *Workers' Representation in Central and Eastern Europe: Challenges and Opportunities for the Works Councils' System*, 2014 (ISBN 978-90-411-4746-2).
86. Roger Blanpain, Ulla Liukkunen & Chen Yifeng, *China and ILO Fundamental Principles and Rights at Works*, 2014 (ISBN 978-90-411-4984-8).
87. Roger Blanpain, *The Use of Languages and Employment Relations*, 2014 (ISBN 978-90-411-5606-8).
88. Roger Blanpain, Hiroya Nakakubo & Takashi Araki, *Protection of Employees' Personal Information and Privacy*, 2014 (ISBN 978-90-411-5608-2).
89. Roger Blanpain, Jan Wouters, Glenn Rayp, Laura Beke & Axel Marx, *Protecting Labour Rights in a Multi-polar Supply Chain and Mobile Global Economy*, 2015 (ISBN 978-90-411-5662-4).
90. Roger Blanpain & Stefania Marassi, *Globalization and Transnational Collective Labour Relations: International and European Framework Agreements at Company Level*, 2015 (ISBN 978-90-411-4748-6).
91. Roger Blanpain, Frank Hendrickx & Petra Herzfeld Olsson, *National Effects of the Implementation of EU Directives on Labour Migration from Third Countries*, 2016 (ISBN 978-90-411-6257-1).
92. Roger Blanpain, Frank Hendrickx & D'Arcy du Toit, *Labour Law and Social Progress: Holding the Line or Shifting the Boundaries?* 2016 (ISBN 978-90-411-6747-7).

93. Roger Blanpain & Frank Hendrickx, *Reasonable Accommodation in the Modern Workplace: Potential and Limits of the Integrative Logics of Labour Law*, 2016 (ISBN 978-90-411-6258-8).
94. Roger Blanpain, Frank Hendrickx & Bernd Waas, *New Forms of Employment in Europe*, 2016 (ISBN 978-90-411-6239-7).
95. Roger Blanpain, Frank Hendrickx, Hiroya Nakakubo & Takashi Araki, *The Notion of Employer in the Era of the Fissured Workplace: Should Labour Law Responsibilities Exceed the Boundary of the Legal Entity?*, 2017 (ISBN 978-90-411-8470-2).
96. Elena Sychenko, *Individual Labour Rights as Human Rights: The Contributions of the European Court of Human Rights to Worker's Rights Protection*, 2017 (ISBN 978-90-411-8629-4).
97. William Bromwich & Olga Rymkevich, *Improving Workplace Quality: New Perspectives and Challenges for Worker Well-Being*, 2017 (ISBN 978-90-411-8628-7).
98. Sarah De Groof, *Work-Life Balance in the Modern Workplace: Interdisciplinary Perspectives from Work-Family Research, Law and Policy*, 2017 (ISBN 978-90-411-8630-0).
99. Sylvaine Laulom, *Collective Bargaining Developments in Times of Crisis*, 2018 (ISBN 978-90-411-8999-8).
100. Frank Hendrickx & Valerio De Stefano, *Game Changers in Labour Law: Shaping the Future of Work*, 2018 (ISBN 978-90-411-9953-9).
101. Ivana Palinkaš, *The Legal and Institutional Framing of Collective Bargaining in CEE Countries: Between Europeanisation and Decentralisation*, 2018 (ISBN 978-90-411-9199-1).
102. Jeremy Waddington, *European Board-Level Employee Representation: National Variations in Influence and Power*, 2018 (ISBN 978-90-411-9202-8).
103. Jan Pichrt & Kristina Koldinská, *Labour Law and Social Protection in a Globalized World: Changing Realities in Selected Areas of Law and Policy*, 2018 (ISBN 978-94-035-0093-5).
104. Matthew W. Finkin, *American Labor and the Law: Dormant, Resurgent, and Emergent Problems*, 2019 (ISBN 978-94-035-0654-8).
105. Giuseppe Casale & Tiziano Treu, *Transformations of Work: Challenges for the Institutions and Social Actors*, 2019 (ISBN 978-94-035-0891-7).

Made in the USA
Monee, IL
18 October 2026

66041376R10214